UNMARRIAGES

THE MIDDLE AGES SERIES

Ruth Mazo Karras, Series Editor
Edward Peters, Founding Editor

A complete list of books in the series
is available from the publisher.

UNMARRIAGES

Women, Men, and Sexual Unions
in the Middle Ages

RUTH MAZO KARRAS

PENN

UNIVERSITY OF PENNSYLVANIA PRESS

PHILADELPHIA

Published by
University of Pennsylvania Press
Philadelphia, Pennsylvania 19104-4112
www.upenn.edu/pennpress

Printed in the United States of America on acid-free paper

10 9 8 7 6 5 4 3 2 1

Library of Congress Cataloging-in-Publication Data
Karras, Ruth Mazo, 1957–
   Unmarriages : women, men, and sexual unions
in the Middle Ages / Ruth Mazo Karras.—1st ed.
      p. cm.—(The Middle Ages series)
   Includes bibliographical references and index.
   ISBN 978-0-8122-4420-5 (alk. paper)
      1. Marriage—Europe—History—To 1500. 2. Marriage
(Canon law)—History—To 1500. 3. Unmarried couples—
Europe—History—To 1500. 4. Unmarried couples (Canon
law)—History—To 1500. 5. Man-woman relationships—
Europe—History—To 1500. 6. Mate selection—Europe—
History—To 1500. I. Title. II. Series: Middle Ages series.
HQ513.K37 2012
306.84'1—dc23   2011043923

For Nicola Karras Wilson and Will Wilson

Contents

Introduction

Marriage and Other Unions

Histories of marriage are inevitably teleological: they put "marriage" as we know it at the center, and they evaluate all other forms of union in terms of that model. It is understandable, of course, that people want to know how an institution that is so important in contemporary society came to be the way it is. Given the contested nature of marriage today—between groups who think that it is primarily a bond between two people who love each other and should therefore be available to all such couples, and groups who think that it is primarily a way of creating a family environment in which to bear and rear children and should be limited to opposite-sex couples—tracing the history to see how we got to where we are can be very useful. Of course, history may be more relevant to those who base their claims on "tradition" than to those who argue that cultural change necessitates changes in marriage as well. However, even people who do not wish to see a return to "traditional marriage" can benefit from understanding the history of the institution and alternatives to it, if only to be able to identify where claims from historical truth are distorted or tendentious. Only by historicizing marriage can we see the inherent illogic of claims that there is only one "real" form.

Stephanie Coontz's *Marriage, a History* is a good example of a book that looks at marriage in the past with an eye not to the unchanging elements of "tradition" but of what changed and why over the centuries.[1] But it is still concerned with the present, using the past to make clear what is distinctive about today's marriages. Other work, on medieval marriage specifically, has regarded marriage largely as a legal contract or as a sacrament. It remains both these things for many people, and since many of both the theological and contractual elements of marriage can be traced to the medieval period, it makes sense to study them, especially for those who find the medieval views important and binding as precedent.[2]

But if the history of marriage is the history of how we got to where we are today and focuses on those elements that are seen as important today in constituting marriage—the exchange of a binding vow, the blessing by a clergyman, the sexual union—we lose sight of the elements that fell by the wayside. History's blind alleys—the customs and practices that did not continue, or that continued but were not deemed important or mainstream—were a part of the medieval experience as much as those aspects that became the roots of contemporary institutions. If we consider marriage a legal contract, we will follow one trajectory in tracing its history; if we consider it a sacrament, another trajectory; if we consider it a personal commitment, a third; and if we consider it an avenue for channeling sexual activity, yet a fourth. But even if we could agree on what marriage is today, looking for the roots of that institution would exclude relationships that were of central importance in their own societies but look very different from modern Western marriage.

The question "What is marriage?" is being asked today in a way that it never has before. Biblical texts that are normative in Christian and Jewish traditions take marriage as a given and do not explicitly define it. There are some contexts in which medieval people discussed the question of what made a marriage, but for the most part, the line between what was marriage and what was not was not sharply drawn. I do not propose to sharpen it, to impose categories on medieval society that it did not impose itself, but to demonstrate its fuzziness and the different ways in which various sexual unions were understood by different groups of people and defined in different discourses. But we need to remember that even though medieval people did not always define the line sharply between what was marriage and what was not, they persisted in the belief that such a line did exist. There was indeed a variety of statuses. Cordelia Beattie suggests that we should envision a variety of statuses approaching marriage as a continuum of singleness.[3] It could also be seen as a continuum of types of pairings. However, either way, a continuum implies that there are endpoints—in this case, marriage and singleness—and that other types of arrangement are in a straight line, closer to one end than the other. A more accurate mathematical image would be a multidimensional graph that would include axes of formality, sexual exclusivity, sharing of resources, emotional involvement, dissolubility, and so forth. Yet while people may have been quite content to leave vague where a particular union fell among the options, both the law and cultural expectations were constructed such that firm judgments sometimes had to be made.

Some scholars working on the history and anthropology of marriage define it in a broad way so as to make the definition valid cross-culturally. This means going well beyond contemporary definitions. In the modern United States, it is clear what is a marriage and what is not: each state defines which individuals are authorized to perform a valid marriage and what they are required to do to make it valid. Even so, of course, there is room for disagreement: a marriage recognized as valid by one state may not be recognized by another, and a marriage deemed valid by all fifty states may not be deemed valid by particular religious institutions (as, for example, between a Jewish man and a Catholic woman). None of the state laws creates a cross-culturally valid definition, and even to say that one must have gone through some particular ritual or satisfied some state- or church-established requirement is not true across all cultures. On the other hand, if we make the definition so broad as to encompass multiple cultural traditions, as with anthropologist Kathleen Gough's classic definition, "a relationship established between a woman and one or more other persons, which provides that a child born to the woman under circumstances not prohibited by the rules of the relationship, is accorded full birth-status rights common to normal members of his society or social stratum," it may be so broad as to not be very useful.[4] Many societies do not distinguish among children according to the status of their parents: does that mean that any fertile sexual relationship is a marriage, under Gough's definition?

In other ways, a definition based on the status of the children may be too restrictive: it privileges reproduction in a way that may not reflect all societies and may also obscure a situation in which a woman has fewer rights than another woman who enters another kind of union, even though their children may have the same rights. A more useful approach to a cross-culturally valid definition might be that whatever pair relationship is most privileged in a given society is ipso facto what that society considers marriage. But there might be several different types of unions in a given culture that scholars might choose to call "marriage." Most of these would likely be sexual unions, but that does not necessarily have to be the case: a marriage in the Middle Ages, at least under canon law that emerged in the twelfth century, did not have to be consummated in order to be valid.[5] Nevertheless, medieval Europe shared with other societies a close association among sexual activity, fertility, and long-term unions. The absence of contraception meant that the onset of sexual activity was often closely followed by the onset of childbearing, and the decision of a couple about whether to recognize a permanent bond often was prompted by the arrival of offspring. Even spiritual marriages that were metaphorical unions with Christ were described as fertile in their production of spiritual fruit. In practical terms, the presence of offspring is useful to the historian in determining whether a sexual relationship can be considered a long-term union rather than a casual liaison: while pregnancy can result from the latter, for the man to acknowledge the child as his implies a confidence in his paternity that suggests a meaningful bond between the partners.

The problem of studying pair bonds in medieval Europe is both less and more complex than in cultures more distant from our own. We can identify particular terms that may quite comfortably be translated as "marriage" because the system of laws regulating marriage in medieval Europe is ancestral to our own and there is so much that seems familiar in it. But this is precisely where the danger of teleology enters in: we focus on the aspects that led to contemporary arrangements, and we risk falling into a history of what we today call marriage rather than the full variety of pair bonds.

This book focuses on sexual unions between women and men, thus omitting two categories of relationship on which there has been considerable recent scholarship. There were undoubtedly many cases, if not of the ritualized same-sex partnerships suggested by John Boswell and doubted by other scholars, then of same-sex couples living together. There were also women who chose to preserve their chastity and enter a spiritual union with another person or with Christ.[6] An unknown but considerable number of medieval people engaged in one of these two types of union instead of, or alongside of, marriage. Here, however, we consider the majority of people who lived as couples, those involving a man and a woman in a sexual relationship. To get a full picture of the history of male-female unions—the dead ends as well as the characteristics that continued to the present day—we need to look at a variety of unions, some of them considered marriage, some of them not, and some of them very much in question. There is excellent scholarship available on various aspects of medieval marriage—James Brundage on legal aspects; Dyan Elliott, David d'Avray, and Christopher Brooke on theology; Georges Duby on contested definitions of marriage in one particular geographical and chronological setting—but most of it does not look at the context of a variety of pair bonds.[7] This book begins from the assumption that sexual pair bonds between women and men were a dominant social form in medieval Europe. They were undoubtedly more common in lived experience—and arguably more important in the cultural imaginary—than same-sex unions or lifelong celibacy. Even while avoiding privileging only those types of unions that led to modern marriage, a history of medieval pair bonds inevitably comes circling back to medieval marriage. The important question to ask is not "What unions should modern scholars and social analysts consider to have been marriages?" but "Where, and why, did medieval people draw the line between what was, and what was not, marriage?" The line was often important because it determined the transmission of property between and within families. My goal is to analyze pair bonds without privileging marriage, while still recognizing that medieval people did, in fact, privilege marriage.

Here we look at a range of sexual unions in the European Middle Ages, some of which people at the time considered formal marriage, some that they clearly did not, and still others that were at the margins. Those whose official nature was disputed or denied, or never proposed in the first place, are nevertheless part of the history of pair bonds. The book will consider, in the later sections of this introductory chapter, models that medieval Europe received from its biblical, classical, and "Germanic" heritage. It will then turn in Chapter 1 to the process by which the church effectively imposed its control over marriage: the variety of types of unions in the earlier Middle Ages, including disputes (both at the time and among modern scholars) as to whether they qualified as marriage or not, the elaboration of the consent theory, and the triumph of a centralized regulation of marriage by the papacy. Chapter 2, dealing with the period after the church managed to articulate and enforce a fairly consistent set of definitions of types of heterosexual union, looks at groups who could not legally marry each other, such as Christians and Jews, or free and enslaved people, or could not make their sexual relationship socially acceptable as marriage because their status was so different, as well as at individuals whose formal marriages were determined by political considerations and who formed supplementary unions. One particular group who was unable to marry from the central Middle Ages onward, the higher clergy, forms the subject of Chapter 3. Chapter 4 looks at the everyday life of the people of fifteenth-century Paris, providing insight into various reasons that couples could not marry—including those trapped in unhappy marriages but to whom divorce was not available—and also examining couples who could have married but chose not to. The book examines a series of moments in medieval history rather than providing a chronologically and geographically complete account.

Throughout the variety of different cases from different times and places across the western European Middle Ages that this work considers, we find a number of common threads. One is that the legal and social status accorded a union—including whether it was considered a marriage—was determined in the first instance not by what legal or contractual arrangements were made but what the status (social or legal) of the partners was. This is a bit jarring to someone working with a twenty-first-century model of marriage, in which as long as the partners are of age and mentally capable and not already married to others, they may marry in a civil marriage (various religions, of course, have their own rules). But we still have vestiges of a system for which the legal status of a union depends on who the parties are: for example, in most U.S. and European jurisdictions as of this writing, the parties to a valid marriage must be a woman and a man. In the Middle Ages, not only the sex of the parties but also their religion, clerical status, freedom or unfreedom, family prominence, and previous sexual behavior were relevant. Because clandestine marriages, performed by the partners themselves rather than by a priest at church, were valid, and parish records were not kept, it is not possible now and was not possible at the time to say that a particular union was not a marriage because of the lack of a formal ritual. Nor was a union legally not a marriage if there was no dowry or other transfer of wealth. Of course, most unions that were intended to be taken as marriages were publicly performed and did involve a transfer of wealth, such that any relationship that did not involve these elements was likely to be considered a different type of union. What led parties to choose to do without public ceremony and dowry, though, was their social standing. If both were poor, there might be no dowry available; if the woman were of lower social status than the man, the dowry would likely not be sufficient (although a large dowry could make it possible for a merchant's daughter to marry into the landed nobility or gentry). If the parties were of different religions, or one had taken religious vows, there could be no ceremony, since the only ceremonies available were religious. And, of course, if one partner was married already, even with a ceremony and a dowry it was not considered a marriage.

Tying the status of the union to the relative social status of the partners had an especially harsh effect on women. In partnerships between two people of different status, it was usually the woman who was of lower status, although this was less so in the case of formal unions, in which an elite daughter could be married to a promising young man. But being involved in a sexual relationship that was not considered a marriage could be deleterious to a woman's reputation (more than to a man's), thus creating a vicious cycle. It is a commonplace that a man's honor in the Middle Ages could depend on a wide variety of things—his reputation for honesty, his physical and military prowess, his control over his household—but a woman's depended only or mainly on her sexual reputation. Yet because the status of a union depended on the relative social status of the parties, a woman of lower social status was likely to be considered a concubine or prostitute rather than a wife. Social dishonor thus was intimately tied to sexual dishonor. The status of concubine, in other words, was less than honorable, not only because it was sexually suspect but also because it implied that the woman was of low rank. This was true at any level of society: from the workingman who had a sexual relationship with his slave to the great lord who had a mistress from the lower gentry, a woman of lower rank was not respectable enough to marry. The two types of dishonor fed on each other, and it is not possible to say which came first, the sexual suspicion or the social disadvantage. Even though nonmarital unions were seen as routine and normal in many segments of society, this attitude was compatible with one that saw the women involved as dishonorable. (Unmarried men tended to get a pass on the honor issue.) Since women of higher status rarely married men of lower status, the result was that the only honorable status for a woman was a relationship with a social equal.

The pattern of higher-status men in sexual partnerships of various kinds, but mainly not marriage, with women of lower status is hardly limited to medieval Europe. Many of the unions described in this book will look very familiar to students of other historical periods; indeed, there may be as much similarity between patterns in one part of the Middle Ages and those in the nineteenth century than between different periods or places in the Middle Ages. The importance of the medieval moments I describe is that they came during an era that saw the emergence and elaboration of Christian marriage; thus the relationships were in negotiation and counterpoint with marriage rather than simply outside it. The range and variation of unions comes as a surprise to those who regard the church as having been dominant (and unified) in the Middle Ages. At each particular moment, local context mattered greatly. Men in many societies have had sexual relations with the women who worked for them, but only in some were the women treated as property with no volition; unmarried couples have had ongoing sexual relations in many societies, but only in some could those unions be adjudged to create a lifetime bond without any formal ceremony.[8]

Medieval people would have recognized the sexual unions discussed in this book as resembling marriage because they were exclusive, or long-lasting, or involved the formation of a joint household. Given the nature of the sources, it is not always possible to tell just how casual or committed a given union was, but there was a rich variety of arrangements that were assimilated or analogized to marriage or contrasted with it to various degrees. It is difficult to find appropriate language to refer to the broad range of unions I talk about here. "Quasi-marital union" was my first attempt, but it assumes marriage as the model that other unions only approached, an assumption I do not wish to make. "Domestic partnerships" would leave out people who were in long-term relationships but did not live together. "Concubinage" had very specific meanings at various points in the Middle Ages, so cannot be used as a general term. "Heterosexual unions" works if one takes "heterosexual" as a synonym for "opposite-sex" or "involving a man and a woman" but not if one thinks of "heterosexual" as describing the people involved; the concept of "heterosexuality," like that of "homosexuality," is anachronistic for the Middle Ages.[9] "Opposite-sex unions" describes what I want to talk about, as a parallel to John Boswell's "same-sex unions," though I have tried to minimize its use because of its awkwardness.

Many couples in the Middle Ages could not marry or chose not to marry when they could have. "Many" is a vague word, but as with so much of medieval demography, the sources just do not exist to provide accurate numbers. Scholars have assumed that the formally married were the majority, and there is no evidence to prove otherwise. But marriage could be a social expectation without being the only alternative, or even an option, for many people; celibacy and virginity were held up as social goods and high goals without any realistic hope that they would be widely adopted, and formal marriage may have functioned in a similar way. We often do not know how formal the unions of the poorer strata of society were, when they were not accompanied by the property exchanges that created new households among the more affluent. This book is in part an exploration of that question, but it cannot answer it quantitatively.

The book also demonstrates that different types of pair bonds as alternatives to marriage did not emerge full-blown from the social revolution of the 1960s and 1970s. I do not suggest that the variety of unions into which medieval people entered were in a direct line of development with contemporary ones, but rather that the process of pair bonding in the Middle Ages was more complicated than a history of marriage alone would suggest. The Latin Middle Ages are often viewed as the time when the teachings of early Christianity were codified and institutionalized—to good or to bad effect, depending on one's religious views. When people speak of "traditional marriage," they do not mean a world where plural marriage was common, as in the Hebrew Bible, or where divorce was easy, as in ancient Rome, or where marriage was suitable only for those who could not be continent and unnecessary for believers since the kingdom of God was soon to come, as in the New Testament. They mean a world in which marriage is monogamous, indissoluble, and nearly universal, a world that they imagine to have existed in the Middle Ages. This book will demonstrate that, while those were indeed the norms and expectations of marriage, the lived experience was considerably messier.

Because the contemporary movement for marriage equality for same-sex couples first started me thinking about the history of marriage and other pair bonds and the ways that they have been reinvented over the centuries, it is ironic that the book does not have much to say about unions between two men or two women. There are plenty of cases we can point to of two men or two women sharing living quarters. We do not know what their physical relationship was, but we do not demand proof of sexual relations to assume that two people of opposite sex living together were, in fact, a couple, so why should we demand it for two people of the same sex? Nevertheless, we do not find much evidence about the domestic lives of these same-sex couples. For all the medieval texts that have been "queered" by modern literary critics, for all the tales of cross-dressing, and for all the claims of a type of same-sex ritual that has some resemblances to marriage, medieval writers rarely raised the possibility that two men or two women could marry, even to reject it. When they did mention it, it was only for the sake of a very medieval systematic completeness, not because they were really considering it. Jean Gerson, the fifteenth-century Paris theologian, wrote that the argument that there could be a marriage between two men or two women was merely a frivolous objection to the (by his time universally accepted) theory that marriage was created by the consent of the parties.[10] Same-sex couples were not on the boundaries in the same kind of way as opposite-sex couples: there was no confusion between their unions and legal marriage. They were rarely hauled into church courts and fined for their relationships; indeed, they are rarely mentioned anywhere. But this book's limitation to opposite-sex unions should not be taken as in any way a denial that same-sex couples entered into many of the same kinds of domestic partnerships, and no one will be more delighted than I if another scholar can demonstrate that I was too pessimistic about the evidence for this.

The sources are nearly silent on same-sex unions, but they are not much better on the women involved in opposite-sex unions. It is much easier to know what these unions meant for the men and their families than for their female partners. Throughout this book are scattered portraits that explore individual cases of women involved in various kinds of domestic partnerships, some well-known historical figures, some fictional, some real but no more than a name to us. These portraits, while based, like the rest of the book, on available sources, are set apart because they are slightly more speculative: determining what women may have been thinking or feeling in different situations can be a chancy task, given the level of information we have. Through the portraits, I hope to balance somewhat the masculine-inflected provenance of the sources. Nevertheless, some aspects are simply unrecoverable. Of the twelve women represented in the ten portraits, Heloise is the only one who expresses what we would recognize as love. That does not mean that it was absent in most medieval unions, but we must remember that, like marriage, love is not a human constant; expectations and experiences of different kinds of love were shaped by the societies in which people lived, and the contemporary notion that love is the main reason for couples to choose to form a domestic union does not necessarily apply.

The medieval women about whose feelings of love we have the most evidence are those whose love was for the divine. A great deal of the scholarship on medieval women over the last several decades has been on women who rejected marriage for spiritual reasons and focused their lives on a union with Christ or a relationship with a holy man. Either of these types of union could be, and was, discussed in marital language.[11] These women underscore how important marriage was as a structuring image or metaphor for women's lives, even women who chose not to enter it. This book, however, focuses on unions that were sexually active and that filled the social and economic and not just the spiritual and emotional space that might otherwise be occupied by marriage. Women often chose spiritual bonds as resistance to marriage; the women discussed in this book were, for the most part, not resisting but existing in parallel with marriage.

Biblical Sources for Medieval Understandings of Unions between Women and Men

Religious as well as secular traditions shaped medieval attitudes toward sexual unions. The church had jurisdiction over Christian marriage at least since the twelfth century, and had attempted to claim it earlier. Jewish and Muslim courts had jurisdiction over marriage in their own communities. The Bible was considered by the church fathers and by medieval ecclesiastical authorities as authoritative. The Hebrew Bible, which medieval Christians called the Old Testament, however, had surprisingly little to say about marriage and other unions. It simply assumed the existence of what we can translate as "marriage" but did not define it, nor in the midst of detailed lawmaking did it give guidance on how it should be formed. Its narratives depict alliances being formed through one man giving his daughter to another, but these unions were not religious in nature, nor was it divine consecration that made a marriage.[12] Medieval writers took as a precedent the scene in the Book of Ruth (4:11) where all the people bless the marriage of Ruth and Boaz.[13] But the Bible never required this, remaining remarkably unconcerned about what rituals created a valid union. Marriage was mentioned a good deal less in the law-code portions of the Bible than in contracts of the same era or in Mesopotamian law codes, and medieval people took their information mainly from the narrative portions of the Bible, which discussed unions only when they were important to the story, not in a theoretical or prescriptive way.

St. Jerome, the fourth-century translator of the Latin Vulgate version of the Bible widely used during the Middle Ages, rendered *ishah*, the word for a woman given to a man as the prospective mother of his children, as *uxor*. Like the modern German *Frau* or the Old English *wif*, *ishah* had a semantic field that included "woman" as well as "married woman." In translating *ishah* as *uxor* ("wife") instead of *mulier* ("woman") in certain contexts, Jerome was making a choice, interpreting a term that had some possible ambivalence as one whose denotation was more specific. It was "Adam and his wife," not "the man and his woman" (another possible translation of the Hebrew *ha-adam v'ishto*) who were not ashamed of their nakedness (Gen. 2:25). Jerome's choice was likely correct in the context of the way the word was understood in his era, both by churchmen and rabbis, and a broader meaning in ancient Hebrew does not matter here. The Septuagint, the Koine Greek translation of the Hebrew Bible, has *gyne*, which also can mean either woman or wife.

Medieval people found guidance for the conduct of their own unions in the stories of the patriarchs and matriarchs. Old Testament stories in which the relationship could not easily be assimilated into a Christian idea about what a sexual union between a man and a woman should be are key places to look for medieval interpretations and understandings of marriage and its alternatives. For people in the Middle Ages, the larger-than-life stories of revered patriarchs were true as literal history, as prescriptive sources delineating appropriate behavior and as pointers to a deeper metaphorical or moral meaning. These patriarchs had more than one *ishah*. Scholars may doubt now whether polygamy was as common as it was depicted in the Hebrew Bible, but in the Christian Middle Ages, the Bible was the historical source par excellence as well as providing normative guidance and spiritual meaning.

Abraham was often understood in the Middle Ages as having been a polygamist, that is, having more than one wife, not just more than one sexual partner. Genesis 16 described the barrenness of Abram's wife (*uxor*) Sarai. She gave her *ancilla* (servant or slave; Hebrew, *shifḥah*) Hagar to her husband as an *uxor* to bear him a child. The two women were clearly not of the same status: Sarai could dictate that Hagar would be Abram's sexual partner, and after Hagar became pregnant and behaved with a lack of respect toward Sarai, Sarai had the ability to mistreat her so that she ran away. However, though Hagar belonged to Abram's wife as a slave, she also belonged to him as a wife in much the same way that Sarai did, and her child was his child. In fact, after Sarah (the renamed Sarai) bore a child herself, she asked Abraham not to allow Hagar's son Ishmael to inherit along with Sarah's son Isaac. The implication is that otherwise he would have inherited alongside him, although not first as an eldest son. Even though under most medieval legal systems, the son of a married man and his slave could not inherit, the story assumed that he might have. In both the Jewish and later in the Muslim tradition, Hagar's son Ishmael became the ancestor of the Arabs. His descent from Ibrahim (Abraham) became very important to the Muslims (Qur'an 2:127). In Muslim tradition, Hagar was not just a slave: though not named in the Qur'an, she appeared in the post-Qur'anic tradition as an enslaved princess, or a free and royal woman given to Ibrahim as a wife.[14]

The stories of plural marriage among the ancient Israelites, particularly that of Abraham, Sarah, and Hagar, posed a conundrum for early and medieval Christians. Modern scholars long explained the Near Eastern background to the Abraham/Sarah/Hagar story in terms of the Babylonian Hammurabi Code, in which a man with an infertile wife could marry a second wife only if his wife did not give him a slave instead. A slave who bore her master's child could not be sold, but she did not assume equality as a wife either. Her sons, however, if acknowledged by the father, had equal inheritance rights with the sons of the first wife.[15] The distinction between the two women was in their social circumstance, not on a particular form of ritual that they entered into. But medieval interpreters, although they distinguished between the status of the two women, considered them both wives. Unwilling to take plural marriage as a prescription for behavior, they had to explain why the Bible depicted patriarchs behaving in ways that went against God's wishes. A modern historian might simply say that they were living at a time with different customs and standards. Indeed, the *Glossa Ordinaria*, the biblical commentary that was widely known and used throughout Europe from the twelfth century on and provided the closest thing to a standard line in medieval theology, said something very close to that. "Abraham was not an adulterer if he was joined to a slave while his wife was alive, because the law of the Gospel about one wife was not yet promulgated."[16] St. Augustine had written something similar in his *On Christian Doctrine*: "On account of the necessity for a numerous offspring, the custom of one man having several wives was at that time blameless," and the patriarchs fathered these multiple children without lust.[17]

But the *Glossa* also treated the passage allegorically, following in a long tradition that began with Paul of Tarsus, who wrote in his letter to the Galatians (4:21–31) that Hagar's son was born according to the flesh but Sarah's son according to the promise. Hagar represented the earthly Jerusalem and Sarah the heavenly Jerusalem. By the third century, Christian writers were following Paul's lead and explaining Hagar as the fleshly synagogue and Sarah as the spiritual church, among other meanings of the story.[18] The *Glossa*'s interpretation here, attributed, like the previous passage, to the ninth-century theologian Hrabanus Maurus, held that Ishmael, expelled from his father's household in favor of the second-born child, represented the Jewish religion that was displaced by its more favored sibling Christianity.[19] Nevertheless, the allegorical meaning did not drive out the literal one: the idea that the patriarchs had plural marriage was not forgotten through the Middle Ages.

Indeed, although Sarah and Hagar were not of equivalent status, Abraham's grandson Jacob was described in Genesis as being in unions with two women who were of the same status—sisters, in fact. Again, Jerome introduced terminology not found in his Hebrew original: Jacob wished to marry the younger sister, Rachel, but her father said that "it is not our custom to give the younger in marriage [*nuptias*] first" (Gen. 29:26), where the Hebrew says "to give the younger before the elder," with no word specifically denoting marriage. Jacob's twelve sons, the founders of the twelve tribes of the Israelites, were born to four different women. Besides Rachel and Leah, the others were Zilpah and Bilhah, whom Jerome called *ancilla* and *famula*, both translating *shifḥah*. This Hebrew term was used elsewhere as the female counterpart to *eved*, "slave," but scholars have suggested that it was used especially of a woman in a sexual relationship with her owner, or her owner's husband.[20] Jerome chose two different terms to render it into Latin, the former denoting (in Jerome's time, anyway) unfree status and the latter servant status but not necessarily unfree. Neither had a particularly sexual connotation beyond the fact that serving women were always vulnerable to sexual advances from their owners or employers. The Hebrew says that the two women, slaves of Rachel and Leah, respectively, were given to Jacob as *nashim* (plural of *ishah*) (Gen. 30:4 and 30:9), but Jerome translated the first as *dedit in coniugium* ("gave in marriage") and the second merely as "gave to her husband."[21] Jerome thus associated *coniugium* with the *famula* and did not name the union with the *ancilla*. We should not make too much of his different vocabulary choices here; he chose different terms to translate identical language, but it is difficult to tell whether he was really trying to make a distinction because of the ambiguity of *nashim*.

Jerome also had another key term to translate: "Reuben went and lay with Bilhah his father's *pilegesh*" (Gen. 35:22). He rendered this term as *concubina*. Millennia of scholarship, ancient, medieval, and modern, have taken every word in the Hebrew Bible as having a very deliberate and specific meaning, and modern scholars have exercised great ingenuity creating elaborate typologies of marriage based on this and similar stories: a slave-wife was of lower status than a concubine, but because Bilhah was Rachel's slave and Rachel had died, Bilhah was automatically freed and therefore promoted to the status of concubine.[22] Medieval exegesis, however, did not seem to be disturbed that the same woman could be called both a *concubina* and a *famula*.[23] As we will see, even though in Roman law, concubines had to be free women, the term had very strong implications of low status. When Jerome translated the passage about King Solomon's partners (1 Kings 11:3), the seven hundred princesses (*nashim sarot*) became *uxores quasi reginae* (wives like queens), but the *pilagshim* were *concubinae*. Jerome clearly saw Solomon, like Jacob, as practicing plural marriage, not just polygyny, but not all his partners were considered wives. While Near Eastern societies had a range of kinds of unions that might or might not be considered marriage, Jerome as translator had fewer categories to work with.

Jerome and later writers would likely have known that the Jews did not leave plural marriage behind in the biblical era. In the Second Temple period in Palestine, plural marriage seems to have become less common than earlier, although it was not formally outlawed and was more common in Babylonia. It still appeared in the Talmud and was practiced occasionally in early medieval Europe. Gershom Me'or ha-Golah (the Light of the Exile), an eleventh-century German rabbi, possibly under Christian influence, eventually forbade it.[24] Concubinage became a good deal less common than in patriarchal times as well, as far as one can tell: there are few references to it in later books of the Hebrew Bible or in the sparse documents of practice that survive. Talmudic references to the status of the *pilegesh* reflected the societies in which the authors lived, but these references were few.[25] It may be that the infrequency of mention, at least in the Palestinian Talmud, reflected the fact that concubines had little legal status or recourse, and therefore there was little need for legal comment; but given the elaborate commentary that the rabbis provided on many other topics, the paucity of comment indicates that it was likely not a major concern (see further discussion of medieval Jewish concubinage in Chapter 2). The detailed and sometimes confusing rules about different stages of the marriage process—betrothal, the transfer of the bride, and consummation—that developed in Jewish society were largely rabbinic rather than biblical.[26] Medieval Christians got their biblical precedents from stories in which ritual and legal procedures played a smaller role.

One aspect of legal procedure that was absent from biblical accounts of unions between women and men—conspicuously so, since so many scholars have taken it as a key element of both biblical and medieval marriage—is the payment of bridewealth of any sort. Scholars who have written about ancient Hebrew marriage have generally explained that a valid marriage was accompanied by the payment of a bride price (*mohar*) to the bride's father by the groom. The term, however, appears only three times in the Hebrew Bible (Gen. 34:12, Exod. 22:16, 1 Sam. 18:25), and in two of these, it refers to a situation in which the man is paying a penalty for having previously raped or seduced the woman.[27] It appears to have been interpreted as a bride price based on cognates in other Semitic languages (Arabic *mahr*) and on analogy with a payment in the Old Babylonian Hammurabi Code (early second century BCE) and other payments in ancient Near Eastern sources.[28] In later Jewish usage—for example, in Aramaic documents from the Jewish military colony at Elephantine—it was a payment to the bride's representative which became part of her dowry.[29] Jerome translated *mohar* twice as *dos* (the Roman word that originally meant a dowry paid by the woman's family) and once as *sponsalia*, betrothal gifts, so he clearly understood it as something that happened on the occasion of a marriage, but not as a bride price.[30] The most famous biblical case involved not bride price but bride service: Jacob worked seven years for his uncle Laban, only to be given the elder sister he had not asked for, and had to work another seven years for the younger sister (Gen. 29:15–28). Indeed, the customary role that property transfers came to play in the formation of medieval unions came not from biblical or Germanic precedents, as many have argued, but from Roman law and custom.

Roman Legal Traditions

Medieval western European ideas about marriage absorbed much from ancient Rome as well as from the Bible. Like the Greek culture that influenced it, Roman society was characterized by a resource polygyny (wealthy men had sexual access to many women) in which only one of these women had the official title of wife. Other women could be attached to a wealthy man's household, especially as slaves.[31] Formal marriage was expected of leading families, for reasons of alliance, but it was not expected—in fact, not available—at the lowest social levels. Roman marriage was a private matter between the families involved and did not require any action by a state or religious official to make it valid.[32] Nor in the early period did it require, in theory, any particular property exchanges, although property exchanges were very common and came to have an evidentiary quality and eventually to be required. Although it was not publicly created, however, marriage was legally recognized and had very specific and detailed legal consequences, with regard to the legitimacy of the children and to the parties' control of property.[33] Although the state did not validate individual marriages, it had a concern with marriage and the procreation of citizens, and from the time of Augustus (27 BCE–14 CE) took an important legislative role in the regulation of matrimony.

Rome recognized *matrimonium*, which we may translate as "marriage," only between citizens, who had *conubium* (the right to marry) with each other (or with citizens of other Latin cities, depending on the time period). If there could be no *matrimonium* because one of the partners was not a citizen or not freeborn, concubinage was an acceptable alternative.[34] Unions without *conubium* were not legally recognized: the husband had no right to the wife's dowry, she had no right to its return if he did have control over it, and the wife could not be prosecuted for infidelity. The jurists, however, still spoke of such unions—which, up until 197 CE, included those of soldiers—using the language of marriage, although without officially recognizing them (*matrimonia iniusta*). Slaves could enter only into a union called *contubernium*, and a slave woman's children were the slaves of her owner, no matter who the father was, because the union granted the father or his owner no rights. The difference among types of union lay not in their permanence—the dissolution of even a formal marriage through divorce was not very difficult in pre-Christian Rome—but in the legal rights they conveyed, particularly with regard to the offspring.

Medieval legal systems generally did not follow the Old Testament pattern in which all a man's sons could inherit, but rather a Roman custom where whether the union was a formal marriage made a great deal of difference to the inheritance prospects of the child. The sons of concubines could not be their fathers' heirs. The other fundamental difference between Roman and other concubinage was that in Rome, concubinage was not a secondary union alongside marriage: it was available only to unmarried men. A woman with whom a married man had a relationship, even an ongoing one in which he supported her, was not technically his concubine.[35] Concubinage was typical for a young man of high status before he had a wife, or for an older man who was widowed and did not want further legitimate children who might compete with his heirs. But as the writings of St. Augustine show, the slave of a married man could also be referred to as his concubine; concubinage in this situation was condemned, but the concubinage of an unmarried man was not.[36]

In Roman law, marital intent—particularly the man's intent—legally distinguished the formation of concubinage from marriage. The Roman law called it *maritalis affectio*, "marital affection," but this did not mean "affection" in the contemporary sense; rather, it meant the disposition of the male partner toward the union. Concubines were generally of lower social status than their male partners, and that status was presumed, to some extent, to determine marital intent. Indeed, Roman law suggested that a freeborn woman should be considered a wife unless the evidence proved otherwise, while a freedwoman was prima facie a concubine. This remained the case up through the time of the Christian emperors until Justinian (r. 527–65), who allowed marriage between men of high and women of low status even where it would earlier have been prohibited, but required written documents indicating that marriage rather than concubinage was intended.[37] These documents did not create the marriage; they proved the *affectio*. As the old social barriers of Roman culture broke down, there must have been an increasing number of cases for which intent was in question because it was no longer unthinkable or staggeringly inappropriate to consider a union with a woman of low status a marriage. In most cases, marital intent would be clear from the way the parties treated each other, but when it came into question because of a matter of inheritance, evidence of property arrangements or of a formal ceremony could confirm intent.

Although Roman law theoretically applied across the empire, particularly after Roman citizenship was extended to all free residents of the empire in 212 CE, there was still local variation in the kinds of unions available to women and men. Roman laws on unions between relatives were stricter than those in many parts of the empire, for example, and Roman ideas about fidelity were not universally accepted, although they fit well into the rising Christian moral framework. After the Roman empire split, the laws issued by the Eastern emperors were more favorable to inheritance by children born from less formal unions (those without property exchanges, or records thereof) than those in the West, for example.[38] In Egypt, where a relatively large amount of documentation has survived, both "written" and "unwritten" unions were recognized as marriages.[39] As Brent Shaw notes, however, "differences in the development of the ritual and form accompanying marriage from the early to the later empire are very difficult to measure, given the fact that so little is known of marriage ceremonial in the earlier period."[40] He suggests that we know little about marriage among the lower orders, and I would add that one thing that we do not know is how many of them chose to go through formal ceremony at all or cared whether their union was considered a marriage.

Was There a "Germanic" Law of Marriage?

As Roman practices and prescriptive law spread through western Europe, they encountered another group of legal systems that are often thought to have contributed much to the medieval understanding of forms of union: the traditions of the pre-Christian, Germanic-speaking groups that came to inhabit much of northwestern Europe and the Mediterranean region as well. As with the ancient Hebrews and the Romans, among these groups it was not uncommon for a wealthy or powerful man to have several women in his household or in separate households with whom he had ongoing sexual relationships. But because of the nature of the sources available to us—sources almost entirely filtered through Romanized and Christianized culture—it is extraordinarily difficult to discover the statuses of different women, whether it made any difference to have gone through a ceremony, or whether property transfers were necessary to form a recognized union. The problem, once again, is that documentation survives only from social levels at which property transmission was an issue. Nevertheless, scholars have made major claims for what constituted Germanic marriage in the pre-Christian era. Scholars "know" what marriage "is," so they look at the early Middle Ages and find it there, as well as other relationships that they decide are not marriage or are distinct types of marriage. The scanty evidence, however, points once again to a distinction not between the nature of the rituals and contracts that created different types of union, but a distinction between partners (mainly women) of different statuses.

Modern scholars since the nineteenth century have recognized that most of the sources for the early Middle Ages are ecclesiastical sources with a particular point of view. Their authors may have wished to label as concubines women who considered themselves, and were considered by their families and partners, as wives. Scholars tried to get around this source problem by constructing a story about what they thought to have been primitive Germanic marriage customs before church influence. For this, they turned to the so-called barbarian law codes, which were thought to codify pre-Christian and pre-Roman practice that could be traced back to an ancient common Germanic culture. They also used Scandinavian sources (sagas and law codes) that, while chronologically later than the continental laws, were thought to encode an earlier stage of Germanic development. Neither of these assumptions holds any longer, as both the continental and Scandinavian legal material has been shown to be heavily influenced by Roman or canon law.

The received wisdom went something like this: the early Germanic peoples had two distinct types of marriage, *Muntehe* and *Friedelehe*. The former involved the transfer of the guardianship over a woman from the woman's kin group to her husband. This guardianship was called *Munt*, from a word meaning "hand," Latinized as *mundium*. The transfer had at some original point in the past taken place in exchange for a bride price, which gradually was replaced by a payment known as *dos*, which went to the woman herself rather than to her relatives. *Dos* can translate as "dowry," but in this situation was a "reverse dowry," from the man to the woman. The second form of marriage, *Friedelehe*, did not involve the transfer of the *Munt*, which remained with the woman's natal family. A woman married in a *Friedelehe* was recognized as a wife, and she received the *Morgengabe*, or morning gift, a payment directly from the groom after the consummation of the marriage (and sometimes interpreted as an acknowledgment of her virginity), which was also paid in *Muntehe*. *Friedelehe* did not, however, involve a bride price and was more easily dissolved. According to this story, when the church began to claim control over marriage, it did not approve of *Friedelehe*, wanting to recognize only those marriages contracted with a formal ceremony and a *dos*. By the Carolingian era, the *Friedelfrau* had been relegated under church influence to the status of a concubine. Thus the imposition of church regulation of marriage put women in a devalued position.

The strange thing about this story is that neither term, *Muntehe* or *Friedelehe*, appears in any extant source. The attempt to reconstruct a common pre-Christian Germanic culture and set of institutions by tracing backward—from a term in a seventh-century Lombard law, an incident in a thirteenth-century Icelandic saga, a story in a sixth-century Frankish ecclesiastic's chronicle, an ethnographic description by a first-century Roman who never visited Germany and wrote about it in order to critique his own Roman culture—has come under serious question. Many scholars today reject the idea that a common "Germanic" past can be reconstructed from its cultural descendants. Yet while they do not accept the method that gave rise to the theory of Germanic marriage forms, and while they question the Nazi-era scholarship that presented these marriage forms as evidence of German superiority, allowing it to posit a prehistoric institution that allowed for matches based on love, too few have questioned the existence of the forms *Friedelehe* and *Muntehe*. A reexamination of the evidence suggests that they should.[41] Suzanne Wemple, in her pathbreaking *Women in Frankish Society*, called *Friedelehe* "quasi-marriage" rather than considering it a different form of marriage, and pointed out that the evidence often adduced for its existence "actually provides a corrective to the romantic picture German historians usually present of *Friedelehe*" because it shows that women who arranged their own unions without family involvement and bride price had greatly reduced legal rights vis-à-vis their partners.[42] Yet other recent and careful work that has abandoned the idea of finding common Germanic marriage practices, and has focused, for example, on *Friedelehe* as a phenomenon of Merovingian and Carolingian society, still accepts its existence as an institution.[43]

The 1986 article on *Eherecht* (marriage law) in the *Reallexikon der Germanischen Altertumskunde* may be taken to represent the late twentieth-century scholarly state of play. Already at that point, Rainer Schulze recognized that the modern term *Friedelehe* was used to cover many different things and could not be considered a single institution of great antiquity: "Very differently formed marital relations are attributed to *Friedelehe* (in the narrower sense). Usually it is a matter of cases in which account must be taken of social inequality between the parties. Whether the multiple legal forms that developed in this context go back to a common Germanic origin seems doubtful."[44] Nevertheless, Schulze was able to catalog several different circumstances under which *Friedelehe* took place (or, otherwise put, several circumstances that he found convenient to call *Friedelehe*): 1) the bride's family was socially or economically superior to the groom, and he therefore did not receive the rights over her and her property that usually adhered to a husband with marriage; 2) a woman married down but was able to keep her legal status; 3) a widow remarried but kept control over the property and status she gained from her first marriage; 4) the bride had no kin group or was unfree, and the husband therefore gained full marital rights over her without paying a bride price; and 5) a man of a ruling or aristocratic family wished to marry more than one wife but could only marry one with the bride price. For Schulze, *Friedelehe* was a term of convenience covering a wide variety of situations; but it still had a certain reality to it, since what tied these cases together was that the marriage took place without the exchanges of property that accompanied early medieval marriage, and without the transfer of rights over the wife to the husband—features that Schulze considered defined "standard" marriage. It is doubtful whether contemporaries would have considered these five sets of circumstances part of the same institution. Nevertheless, historians lumped them together, romanticizing *Friedelehe*. Because no payment to the woman's family was required, neither was their consent, and the couple themselves made the choice to enter into the relationship. Because the tutelage over the wife did not pass to the husband (remaining with her father or brother, or whoever held it previously), she had a more independent status than a woman who underwent *Muntehe*. Because the husband did not have legal control over the wife, she could leave the marriage if she were mistreated, or wished to for any other reason. This understanding of *Friedelehe* as empowering the woman sat well with scholars who wished to present "the Germans" as enlightened and morally superior to decadent Romans.[45] Some feminists also found appealing the idea of a past age when things were more fluid and therefore better for women (before the iron hand of patriarchy, clad in the velvet glove of the church, took away their freedoms and status).

As a modern term of convenience, *Friedelehe* is inconvenient. It brings with it too much baggage: assumptions about a primitive common Germanic culture, erroneous ideas about the status of women, and the implication of the existence of a formally recognized institution where none existed. To use it as an omnibus term for unsanctioned, nonmonogamous or otherwise "different" long-term relationships risks losing sight of the variety of arrangements that medieval people made and obscures distinctions that some drew between an honorable and a dishonorable or unfree union. Just as the fact that lords in the high Middle Ages occasionally or even frequently had sex with their serfs does not mean that a *droit de cuissage* existed, so too the fact that some unions in the early Middle Ages took place without financial exchange and the consent of the relatives does not mean that a distinct form of marriage existed.

But to say that *Friedelehe* was not a distinct form of marriage is to beg the question: Not distinct from what? The point of comparison, *Muntehe*, although less questioned by scholars, is also problematic. The term is based largely on the Lombard laws, which used the term *mundium* both for guardianship over a woman and the payment for that guardianship. On this basis, it has been assumed that all Germanic peoples transferred such a guardianship at marriage and that the transfer of a bride price to the bride's family and eventually of a *dos* to the bride herself was a payment for this guardianship.[46] Neither assumption, however, is tenable. If we exclude the automatic assumption that everything in any "Germanic" law code must derive from a primitive, common Germanic culture, it is not at all clear why the Lombard laws provide evidence for Frankish, Visigothic, Anglo-Saxon, or Norse social arrangements.[47]

Since *Muntehe*—a particular form of union that transferred a particular bundle of rights from the father or kin to the husband—is not a common Germanic concept any more than *Friedelehe*, it is especially unsafe to leap from there to the conclusion that a bride price, or any other particular transfer of property, denoted this particular form, although such a leap is very common. For example, Hans-Werner Goetz, in making the point that *dos* and *Morgengabe* were required for legitimate marriage in the Germanic kingdoms generally, cited Benedictus Levita, an early collector of a forged group of capitularies, to buttress his statement that "marriage with guardianship (*Muntehe*) was a marriage with a *dos*." But what Benedictus Levita actually said was drawn from the Visigothic law: *Nullum sine dote fiat coniugium; nec sine publicis nuptiis quisquam nubere audeant,* "let there be no marriage without a *dos*; nor let anyone dare to marry without public nuptials."[48] This did not say anything about *Muntehe* or guardianship. I cannot prove by an argument from silence that there was no *mundium* transferred in "Germanic" marriage other than among the Lombards; but one certainly would not be warranted in arguing from silence that there was.[49]

Where did the *mundium* of Lombard law come from if not from an earlier, pan-Germanic legal system? Republican Roman law featured the concept of *manus*, also meaning "hand," which denoted the tutelage over a woman transferred from her father to her husband at marriage. *Manus* marriage was in disuse by the age of Augustus.[50] Its most prominent articulation appears in Gaius's *Institutes*, a Roman legal textbook.[51] The shortened version of the *Institutes* found in the Breviary of Alaric (a Roman law compilation, dating from 506, for the Roman subjects of the Visigothic kingdom) omits this section, as do Justinian's *Institutes*, which are based on those of Gaius.[52] However, the full version of Gaius's *Institutes* circulated in Ostrogothic Italy and could have been known to the Lombards, since the surviving manuscript comes from fifth- or early sixth-century Verona.[53] *Munt* may well have had a Roman rather than a Germanic origin, and we should think twice about extrapolating from the Lombard law to all the Germanic groups.

Lombard law is not the only problematic witness: all the barbarian or Germanic law codes were textualized under the influence of the church and placed within a framework of Roman law.[54] A number of traits of Roman marriage resembled those found in the law codes, and undoubtedly influenced them. One is the absence of a required, formal ceremony. Germanic marriage, as scholars commonly understand it, included the stages of betrothal; the handing over of the woman, or *traditio puellae*; and the bedding of the couple. However, none of these were specified as requirements consistently across the various codes. Barbarian laws, for the most part, followed Roman laws in keeping marriage a private matter. When they did prescribe the payment of a *dos*, they did not stipulate that the marriage was invalid without it (this issue will be discussed further in Chapter 1).

What, then, do the sources tell us about pre-Christian Germanic forms of union? This question is based on a false assumption that there was one system underlying the practices of all the barbarian kingdoms in the early medieval era. The surviving sources cannot properly be made to fit an evolutionary schema, and all have been influenced by Roman or Christian culture in different ways. The one text that certainly was not influenced by the church, the *Germania* of Tacitus (first century CE), which has often been taken to epitomize primitive Germanic culture, is not highly reliable. Tacitus lumped all the Germans together as one group and attributed to them characteristics intended to contrast with Roman decadence.[55] Nevertheless, it is worth noting what Tacitus did say: "Alone among the barbarians, they are content with one wife, except for a few who, not because of lust but because of their nobility, enter into several marriages. The wife does not bring the dowry to the husband, but the husband to the wife."[56] This would seem to indicate that the bride gift was a customary part of marriage, but it may be something that Tacitus's informants particularly noticed among one group of Germans because it contrasted with Roman practice, rather than being a universal custom. Tacitus does not say that it was required, and his statement that the *dos* was paid to the woman contradicts the theory that the law codes represent a late mutation of a primitive bride price that went to the male guardian in return for the *Munt*.[57] It is also notable that he made no reference to any other form of union; but this was not a legal treatise—it was an ethnographic and moral one, and he was concerned with contrasting German marriage with Roman marriage.

If there was no *Friedelfrau* who occupied a status between that of fully recognized wife and that of concubine, and a wife's status did not depend on the transfer of guardianship to her husband, and if there was a whole range of social statuses that could be held by a female partner with no clear vocabulary to distinguish between them, does it make any sense to look for a sharp line between what was "marriage" and what was not? On what basis did people assign status to different kinds of pairings? The criterion most often suggested by scholars is that of the payment of a *dos* from the groom to the bride's family or, somewhat later, to the bride herself. As we will see in the next chapter, the church attempted to enforce such a line.

We have seen here, however, that although various rituals and property exchanges may have been typical in marriage formation, none of the traditions that Western medieval culture inherited—Hebrew, Roman, or "Germanic"—used them to distinguish formally between marriage and other forms of union. The concept of marriage itself was rarely defined. Unions between two members of the elite that appear in the sources accompanied by property exchanges were only the tip of the iceberg; because no particular process was technically required, we do not know how people of lower status formed long-term partnerships. We risk mistaking a usual process for a necessary one.

Across several different traditions that contributed to medieval understandings of sexual unions, this Introduction has shown that a woman who was important enough relative to her partner might have certain legal rights recognized, and otherwise not. The status of a particular union was intertwined with the status of the woman in a very complicated way. The nature of the union depended on who she was; at the same time, her reputation—and her well-being, which could be contingent on whether her children inherited from their father—might depend on how the union was perceived by others. A man's position in life generally depended a great deal less on who his partner was than did a woman's. As subsequent chapters will show, while definitions tightened up considerably during the Middle Ages, various categories of union still remained blurred, and attribution of a union to one type or another was still often based on the status of the woman rather than on particular processes of formation.

Chapter 1

The Church and the Regulation of Unions between Women and Men

The traditions discussed in the Introduction took on new configurations as the Western church claimed control over marriage. The Hebrew Bible allowed one man to have several permanent partners, either several women with full wifely status or one woman as primary and the rest secondary but with all the children having inheritance rights. Ancient Roman law, however, did not: Roman marriage was monogamous, and only the children of a wife could inherit. Prehistoric Germanic forms of union are, as we have seen, very difficult to document, but the evidence points to a pattern more like that of Rome, where one woman and her children were privileged; the idea that there once existed a separate form of full marriage that allowed for the free choice of the parties, not their families, and that was later devalued by the church, is largely a myth.

The standard story that scholars tell about the effects of the church on the formation of legitimate sexual unions is true to this extent: in trying to assert the exclusive legitimacy of marriage, and in doing so claim control over it, the nascent church legal system attempted to assert its authority to draw a sharp line, declaring certain unions to be valid marriages and all others to be invalid, and lumping together all other types of unions. The church did not speak with a unified voice, and in every dispute over the validity of marriage, there were churchmen and laymen on both sides. Whatever side they took in individual cases, however, churchmen tended to devalue any sort of sexual union outside of marriage, both for men and for women, although the weight of tradition and enforcement made this weigh much more heavily on women. This process began in the Christian Roman empire, but the motives behind it were not the same across the medieval millennium, nor were the types of unions that appeared as alternatives. Because a number of other scholars have written in eloquent detail about the history of Christian marriage, this chapter does not attempt a full narrative overview but focuses on those unions that were not considered marriage and the church's attempts to draw a line.

Late Antique Christianity

Christian views on approved and unapproved sorts of unions as they developed in the late antique period drew heavily on both biblical and Roman law and traditions, but they also brought several innovations. Perhaps surprisingly to us, in light of the relative ease of Roman and Jewish divorce compared with later Christian law, the idea that marriage differed from other unions in its permanence was not the major change. Christian emperors did make it harder for a man to divorce his wife without cause, but although Augustine of Hippo (whose later views on marriage may or may not have been influenced by his earlier experience with the mother of his child, discussed below) argued strongly that even in the case of divorce for cause the parties could not remarry, this did not become entirely accepted in the church until the Carolingian period.[1] Rather, the important Christian innovations were the expectation of fidelity on the part of men as well as of women (which is not to say that all Christian men or women lived up to this expectation) and the idea that marriage was now a religious institution, even if it was not yet formally a sacrament. Both these factors worked toward the valorization of marriage as opposed to other types of union. Marriage was no longer mainly an institution for the allying of families and the procreation of heirs, although that remained part of it; it was also the only legitimate outlet for sexual desire and a way for the spouses to participate together in devotion to God.

The ascetic impulse toward the restriction of desire was not unique to Christianity; it was also found in a number of pagan Roman thinkers.[2] What was particularly Christian was the idea that the kind of relationship that two laypeople had with each other defined their relationship to God, and that only one form was acceptable. The adoption of a nuptial blessing or other specifically Christian rituals that went along with marriage was part of the new understanding of marriage, although such blessings were not required for a valid marriage.[3] Marriage retained an important secular aspect in terms of inheritance rights for the children, however, often involving formal written documentation, and there continued to be tension about whether this was a necessary constitutive element. Probus (r. 276–78) had held that lack of documentation did not invalidate a marriage if the couple were generally held to be married. The emperors Valentinian III (419–55) and Majorian (r. ca. 457–61) legislated that a marriage would not be valid and the children not legitimate without solemnities of marriage or the provision of a dowry, although Theodosius II (401–50) rejected this view for the Eastern empire, sticking with the classical position.[4]

This spate of marriage legislation spurred by Christian custom had the effect of sharpening the line between marriage and other types of union. With the condemnation of sexual activity in all forms except marriage for men as well as for women in late Roman pagan as well as Christian circles, the difference between marriage and concubinage became not just one of social class but also one of morality, as Augustine's account quoted below indicates.[5] But Christians in late antiquity did not completely condemn concubinage. The Council of Toledo in 400 ruled that a man who had a concubine and not a wife could still take communion within the church, as long as he was faithful to her. Ambrose of Milan (ca. 340–97) condemned married men with concubines and unmarried men who took concubines intending to leave them upon marriage, but not men who kept concubines in lieu of marriage.[6] In other words, concubinage, as an exclusive union between a man of higher and a woman of lower status, was recognized as a legal institution by late antique Christian leaders. Yet it was clearly accorded lower status than marriage. In the fifth century, Pope Leo I (440–61) could express the clear view that marriage should be contracted between freeborn people and equals, and a priest could marry his daughter to a man with a concubine without worrying that the bridegroom would be considered already married, unless the concubine was "made freeborn, legitimately endowed, and publicly married."[7] This was, as Judith Evans-Grubbs points out, a view based on "Roman ideas about status and social honor" rather than on Christian views.[8]

What Christian Europe inherited from the Romans, then, was the idea that an individual could be involved in only one sexual union at a time that could create legitimate heirs, and that that union had to be between partners of equivalent social status. The idea that marriage was the only valid form of union was not part of that legacy (at least not for a man; a woman who entered into a relationship other than marriage, unless with a man of higher status than she, might lose respect and status). As we shall see, some Christians struggled a bit with these ideas, wishing to make of marriage a spiritual joining instead of a property relationship and therefore trying to assimilate other forms of union to it. We turn now to what this might have meant for one particular woman in the later Roman empire, a woman whose name we do not know but who has been immortalized by the writings of her partner. Augustine of Hippo was the church father whose writings most influenced those of medieval authors about marriage and sexuality, particularly important for his emphasis that marriage is a good thing (although not as good as virginity), rather than a lesser evil for people who would otherwise fornicate. Augustine's account in his *Confessions* indicates that in his youth, marriage was not expected to be the only union into which an elite man would enter. It also shows us how, in his maturity, he attempted to assimilate a loving and faithful partner to a wife and therefore lend her a respectability that he did not otherwise think she would have.

"With Whom I Was Accustomed to Sleep": The Anonymous Mother of Adeodatus

Sometime between 370 and 372, when he was between sixteen and eighteen years old and studying in Carthage, Augustine, the future bishop of Hippo, formed a sexual relationship with a woman whom he never named in his *Confessions*.[9] Most translators have inserted the word "mistress" or "concubine" into Augustine's first mention of her, but in fact he said simply *unam habebam*, "I had a woman": "not known in that which is called legitimate marriage, but whom my roaming passion, lacking prudence, had sought out; yet only one, keeping faith to her bed."[10] He later referred to her as "the woman with whom I was accustomed to sleep."[11] They had a son, Adeodatus, and remained together until 385, when Augustine's mother, Monnica, chose a girl for him to marry. The mother of Adeodatus returned from Milan, where they had been living, to North Africa, where Augustine reported that she took a vow of chastity.[12] Augustine never made the marriage; the fiancée whom Monnica chose for him was underage, and before she was old enough to marry, Augustine underwent his conversion and chose celibacy.

We know about the unnamed woman who was Augustine's long-term partner only from his writing and only in later life, when she was long gone and he had undergone conversion. Scholars have not thought much of her or the relationship. She must, they have assumed, have been a prostitute or an actress, two professions whose practitioners' sexual reputations might make it difficult for them to marry at all, or of a lower social class such that someone of Augustine's rank could not legally marry her.[13] Augustine described the relationship as being based on lust, both in the passage quoted above and in his description of his actions after the woman returned to Africa, where he described himself as a "slave to lust" who took another concubine. Philip L. Reynolds, taking this description at face value, says: "In Augustine's eyes, she was not so much a person as an object of carnal desire."[14] But there is no reason why she could not have been both. In Augustine's view, as he explained in his *Confessions*, marriage was a treaty (*foederatum*) for the sake of offspring, whereas the other relationship, while still a *pactum*, or agreement, was for the sake of lust. Children were unwanted in the latter, although the parents learned to love them once they were born.[15] A man who (at the time he wrote) thought all carnal love was sinful lust, excusable only for the sake of creating a legitimate family, was going to have negative things to say about any union with which he was involved that was not marriage, but they did not mean that he did not care about the woman. Augustine wrote, in fact, that his heart was "cut and wounded and bled" when she was "torn from his side," and that he never got over the pain of the separation, although some recent scholarship has doubted whether all the blame for the tearing belongs to Monnica.[16] The tone in which he said that he was unable to emulate his partner's chastity after their breakup indicates his respect for her.[17]

In fact, Danuta Shanzer suggests that Augustine may have viewed her as a wife, spiritually if not legally, and that he drew a clear distinction between the long-term concubinage that involved fidelity, and his later, more casual partnership.[18] He later wrote in his treatise *On the Good of Marriage* that if two people were faithful to each other, even if having children was not the purpose of their union, "doubtless without absurdity it can indeed be labeled a marriage." He went on to suggest that a man who takes such a woman until he finds another "worthy of his status or his wealth whom he can marry as his equal" is an adulterer in his heart—committing adultery with the concubine, not with the potential future wife—but the woman, "should she maintain sexual fidelity with him, and after he takes a wife she gives no thought to marriage herself and steels herself to refrain utterly from such sexual intercourse, I should not perhaps readily presume to call her an adulterer." Even though she sinned in having sex with him without being married, if she had done so because she wanted children, "she is to be ranked higher than many matrons." The hypothetical situation he described here seems very similar to the one in which he and his unnamed partner had found themselves.[19]

Augustine's unnamed lover cannot have been happy to have been forced to leave her partner of many years and her adolescent son, who remained with his father. The fact that she took a vow (to the God to whom Augustine addresses the *Confessions*) never to know another man indicates that she was a Christian. Shanzer suggests that she had been one all along, even when Augustine went through his Manichaean phase; the Christian name given to their son might suggest this. It would not be surprising for a Christian woman to have entered into a union of this nature, and she need not have been a slave or prostitute. Shanzer suggests that Augustine's partner may have been his social equal, someone whom he could conceivably have married, but lower than his mother's ambition hoped for him. Monnica wanted to wait until he could marry a wife who could help him rise above the provincial petty nobility into which he had been born.[20] It is possible that Monnica as a Christian was troubled by the fact that her son had a concubine, but this was so typical of the time for not-yet-married men that scruples about the lack of formalities are not likely to have been the entire reason for her disapproval.[21] Shanzer may be right that Augustine could legally, and even socially, have married her. But if Augustine had trouble getting his mother's permission to marry his partner, surely a woman from his own social class would have equal, if not more, trouble getting her parents' permission to live with a man outside of "that which is called legitimate marriage," with no inheritance rights accorded to her children, all the more so if her family were Christian. Most likely, she came from somewhere between the level of the slave or prostitute and the level of Augustine's family: respectable but not so prosperous. Her family likely calculated that their daughter would be better off as the concubine of this rich young man than as the wife of someone with a less promising future.

Of course, the more respectable her family, the less choice she is likely to have had. If Augustine was as young as sixteen, she would likely have been of a similar age. It may be that they met and fell in love, but she is unlikely to have moved in with him without some familial involvement. The relationship seems, on the slender evidence, to have been affectionate on his side and, we may hope, on hers as well—at least he wished to present it as affectionate, which tells us something about expectations. But as much as Augustine spoke of the "pleasures of my way of life" in contrast to a friend's promiscuous habits, he still recognized that his relationship lacked "the respectable name of matrimony," and that was a great deal to lack. The fact that after fifteen or so years there was only one surviving child may indicate the use of birth control, which, in turn, indicates the lack of marital intent.[22] The couple may well have esteemed each other, but the fact that she could be "torn from his side" underscores her lack of options in the situation, and the way that Augustine discussed the union suggests that people were aware all along that it was not just different from, but less than, a marriage. A marriage in all but name, if the community was aware that the name was absent, might have been companionable, even loving, but it allowed the woman to be discarded.

The Frankish Church

The church's effort to control sexual partnerships—and lay magnates' attempt to use the church to control the partnerships of others—can be clearly seen in the relatively well-documented Frankish realms, approximately the areas that later became France and Germany. "The church" is a nebulous concept, and, of course, not all churchmen agreed; in relation to patterns of marriage in Francia, "the church" largely means the Frankish bishops. These bishops made an effort to define which unions were legitimate and which were not by emphasizing the public nature of marriage, basing their views upon the authority of tradition, although, as we shall see, not even all Frankish bishops were in agreement. One important text they quoted widely was not Frankish in origin: a letter of Pope Leo I in 458–59 to Rusticus, bishop of Narbonne, which is often taken by modern scholars to indicate that the payment of *dos* distinguished marriage from concubinage.[23] The passage was often quoted by medieval authors without its context. Rusticus had asked Leo what should be done in the case of a priest or deacon who wished to give his daughter in marriage to a man with a concubine who had borne him children. Leo responded:

> Not every woman joined to a man is the wife [*uxor*] of the man,
> just as not every son is the heir of his father. Marriage is a legitimate
> agreement between freeborn and equal persons. . . . A wife is one
> thing, a concubine another; just as a female slave is one thing and a
> free woman another. Because of which the Apostle brings forward
> a witness as to the clear distinction between these persons, where it
> is said to Abraham: "Drive out your slave woman and her son; for
> the son of the slave-woman shall not inherit with my son Isaac.". . .
> Therefore, the cleric of whatever place, if he gives his daughter in
> marriage to a man having a concubine, is not to be taken as though
> he gave her to a married man; unless perhaps that woman has been

made freeborn, and legitimately endowed [*dotata*], and is seen to be made honest by public nuptials.[24]

There are several problems with taking this passage as a deliberate effort to declare all unions without a dowry less than marriage. First, Leo wrote in the context of slavery. He assumed that the concubine was unfree (which, as we shall see, is how Gregory of Tours, writing in the later sixth century, used the term), although Rusticus's query did not specify this. He did not say anything about free concubines and, indeed, did not recognize the possibility. Nor did he consider that a slave can be an *uxor*, suggesting that he was still continuing in a Roman tradition about the invalidity of slave marriage, a position that the church came to reject. Second, Leo returned Paul's metaphorical use of the Sarah/Hagar story in Gal. 4:30 to a literal reading of the narrative in Gen. 21:10. Paul was making a point about Christians inheriting the kingdom of God, but Leo considered him to be making a point about slave inheritance rights. Third, his statement of what would need to take place for the man in question to be considered married to his concubine did not indicate that these are requirements for all marriages. It is not clear what he meant by the woman being "made freeborn [*ingenua facta*]"; a slave could be freed but was generally not afterward referred to as freeborn. He may have meant "recognized" rather than "made freeborn." In any case, he said that free status, a *dos*, and a public ceremony would raise the previous union to the status of an impediment to the new one; he did not discuss the possibility of a public union with a free woman without a *dos*.

The laws of the successor states to the Roman empire, redacted under Roman and church influence, as discussed in the Introduction, cannot be taken as evidence for prehistoric Germanic culture. We return to them here as evidence of the role of *dos* in defining the status of a union at the time of their writing. The term for the payment of bridewealth varied among the laws. The Salic law of the Franks, often regarded as the most "primitive" of the *Leges*, in part because it preserved so many Germanic legal terms (the "Malberg glosses"), used the Latin term *dos* rather than a Germanic term for the payment to the bride or her family.[25] Though the Salic law assumed property transfers in marriages, it did not systematically set out requirements for a legal marriage, either in terms of property exchange or of consent. In the case of inheritance, both it and the Frankish *Lex Ripuaria* spoke of sons and daughters without raising the question of the legal status of their parents' relationship. The *Lex Ripuaria* assumed that a *dos* was usual but also considered the situation in which there was none: if nothing was given to a wife by means of charters (*per series scripturorum*), she should receive fifty solidi if she outlived her husband.[26] This did not suggest that such a woman was not a wife or provide any means of determining who was and who was not a wife; it merely provided for a situation in which the support of a widow had been neglected. The lack of emphasis on parental consent in the Frankish codes may indicate that secular authorities were not as concerned with it as was the church; but it may also be that these laws just did not address the issue of what constituted a valid marriage. Legal formulas dating from the late seventh or eighth century, and demonstrating how the Salic laws may have been put into practice in a period after the full establishment of Christianity, show that a *dos* was an expected part of the marriage ceremony but do not prove that marriage was valid without it.[27]

The *Lex Saxonum*—codified well after the Christianization of much of western Europe, but supposedly containing the laws of a group of people converted only in the ninth century—also did not distinguish among children in terms of inheritance according to the status of the parents' relationship, but did require a *dos*. If a man did not pay a *dos* of three hundred solidi to the bride's parents, he was liable for a fine to them in the same amount.[28] Neither this law nor the Salic or Ripuarian connected the payment to the family with the transfer of rights over the woman or indicated that *dos* was ever constitutive of marriage (rather than customary and probative of it) or made the difference between types of union.[29]

The relation of the law codes to practice at any given time is problematic. Narrative sources from the Frankish kingdoms may help fill the gaps as to how unions were formed on the ground. Already in the Merovingian period, Latin (ecclesiastical) sources classified female partners into *uxores* and *concubinae*, but a man could have more than one *uxor*, and *concubinae* were women of lower status (including slaves). Merovingian rulers, if not the entire ruling class, practiced polygyny, and the church sometimes recognized more than one woman as a wife.[30] The same language was used for unions in which the woman made a choice for herself and ones in which her father gave her to her partner. The Frankish narrative sources contain no examples of situations in which a woman, no matter what her status, is not under the control of her male partner; we cannot distinguish among types of union based on the rights that he held.[31] Gregory of Tours, the most famous Frankish author of the Merovingian period, may tell us only about the highest level of the aristocracy, and only about the Touraine, but much of what we know about the unions of

Merovingian kings comes from him.[32] The way that Gregory used terminology indicates that he did not distinguish among different types of unions, calling them all "marriage," as long as they involved free women and even using the same vocabulary sometimes for the unfree.

According to Gregory, Basina, wife of the king of Thuringia, left her husband and followed Childeric (r. 457–81) on his return from exile; he married her (*eam in coniugio copulavit*). When Clovis (r. 481–511) married Clotild, he asked her father for her *in matrimonio* and "associated her with himself in marriage [*coniugio*]."[33] Even though one of these two unions was made with the consent of the woman's family and the other not, Gregory used *coniugio* for both. Radegund (ca. 520–86), too, although she was captured rather than given in marriage by her father, was described in the same terms as Clotild (*in matrimonio sociavit*).[34]

Theudebert (r. 533–48), as Gregory told the story, was also involved in a less formal union made by choice as well as a formal marriage arranged for diplomatic reasons. After a woman named Deuteria arranged for him to capture the city of Béziers peacefully, he married her (*eamque sibi in matrimonio sociavit*). However, he was also betrothed to a king's daughter, Visigard, and the Frankish assembly insisted that he leave Deuteria, here referred to as his *sponsa*, and marry (*uxorem ducere*) Visigard.[35] It is tempting to suggest that *uxorem ducere* meant a formal wedding and *in matrimonio sociare* was more informal, but this does not seem to be true in other cases (for example, Clovis and Clotild). The chronicler Fredegar, who reported the same events, used *uxorem ducere* for both Deuteria and Visigard.[36] Indeed, according to Gregory, Chilperic (r. 561–84) asked to marry Galswinth because she was of social rank worthy of him, and offered to leave his other wives to do this, but the wives to be repudiated were called *uxores*.[37] Galswinth's family was more powerful and therefore she was less vulnerable than the other women, but there is no indication that their unions were considered of lesser status until she came on the scene, or whether any sort of ceremony was involved. Other women called *uxores* could also be repudiated at will, as with Clothar's (r. 511–61) wife Vuldetrada and Charibert's (r. 561–67) wife Ingoberg.[38] Sigibert (r. 561–75) was upset that his brothers "took unworthy wives [*uxores aciperent*] and by their own vileness even married slaves [*ancillas in matrimonio sociarent*]."[39] It is not clear whether this was simply a matter of elegant variation meaning that "they took unworthy wives, even slaves" or whether Gregory was making a distinction and saying that "they took unworthy wives and even entered into unions with slave women," but *matrimonium* in Gregory's usage probably did mean the same thing as *uxorem accipere*, and both could be used of free or slave partners.

In Gregory's depiction, then, some unions were more important politically than others, but those by women's choice do not seem, as a rule, to have been weaker than those arranged by fathers, except insofar as those arranged by fathers tend to involve more powerful families and were therefore more dangerous to attempt to dissolve. All aristocratic women, even where a man was in a union with more than one of them, were *uxores*, and "concubines" were slaves. Fredegar referred to Bilichild, the former slave who married Theudebert, as *uxor* and *regina* (queen).[40] In the later Frankish period, some church legislation continued to question the marriageability of slaves (see discussion in Chapter 2), but in the Polyptyque of St.-Germain des Près, an inventory from a monastery near Paris in the early ninth century, people of slave status (*servi*, which, by this time, some people would want to translate as "serfs") could be, or have, *uxores*, although there is no indication of the payment of a *dos*.[41]

The Frankish church was very concerned about the sexual behavior of the laity both within and outside sanctioned unions, but Merovingian and Carolingian councils focused particularly on issues of marital incest (marrying within prohibited degrees of relationship), the abduction of betrothed women or those under a religious vow, and the permissibility of divorce.[42] The councils paid remarkably little attention to the question of what made a valid marriage, except when considering particular cases, such as that of Lothar II, Theutberga, and Waldrada (discussed below). Merovingian church councils punished marriage without the consent of the woman's family with excommunication rather than making it invalid.[43] A council held in Bavaria between 740 and 750 was explicit about the question of impediments: no one should marry without notifying the local priest, relatives, and neighbors, "who can investigate their degree of relationship, and with their advice and agreement."[44] Publicity was key to identifying and avoiding impediments to the marriage. The Council of Ver in 755 issued a one-sentence decree: "Let all laypeople make public marriages, both noble and non-noble."[45] Yet the absence of publicity did not form a boundary between marriage and non-marriage: neither council invalidated marriages that were not conducted publicly, or not accompanied by a *dos*. The Council of Mainz in 852 declared that unions without formal betrothal were dissoluble at the man's will: "If anyone has a concubine who was not legitimately betrothed, and afterward marries a girl betrothed according to the rite, having put aside the concubine, let him have her whom he legitimately betrothed."[46] But it did not prohibit such unions for unmarried men or specify what was required for a legitimate betrothal.

Nor do other Carolingian-era writings indicate that a *dos* was widely considered to constitute the difference between a valid marriage and other forms of union. A decree attributed to the second-century pope Evaristus and included in the "pseudo-Isidorian decretals," composed in the mid-ninth century by a Frankish author, suggested that marriage was not valid unless the man had requested the woman's hand from whomever had guardianship over her, and there had been an official betrothal and a priestly blessing of the marriage (along with a payment to the priest).[47] But this was wishful thinking, not a reflection of practice. No canonical collection, in fact, required a priestly benediction, although by the Carolingian period, such benedictions were commonly used in marriage among the nobility.[48] The forged collection of Benedictus Levita included a canon drawn from the Visigothic law saying that no one should marry without the blessing of a priest. The forger changed it to apply to all Christians; but in the original context, it applied only to converted Jews.[49]

Jonas of Orleans, who wrote in Aquitaine in the first half of the ninth century and was closely associated with the emperor Louis the Pious, indicated that the status of a union depended not on ritual but on social status. When he composed *De institutione laicali* for the lay nobility he did not aspire for all their unions to be performed with a priestly benediction—or indeed, with any other sort of formality. Rather, he counseled his (male) audience to be continent before marriage on the grounds that if they wanted chaste and incorrupt wives, they should be chaste and incorrupt themselves. Citing Ambrose, he told them that they could not engender heirs with women of lower status, and heirs were the purpose of matrimony, simply assuming that a union with a woman of lower status would be concubinage rather than marriage.[50] His main concern, however, was to combat other unions not before or instead of marriage, but alongside marriage. He spent much more effort discouraging married men from having a concubine than he did unmarried men, citing mainly passages from Augustine, but also Ambrose and Lactantius. A man should not expect his wife to accept his sleeping with his slave, any more than he would accept her sleeping with hers.[51] Halitgar of Cambrai's penitential (early ninth century) similarly attempted to restrict a man to one partner: "Let a man be content with a union with one woman, either a wife or a concubine, as it pleases him."[52] The espousal of a single standard of fidelity for men and women underscores how common practice was to the contrary, but it is also notable that this fidelity did not have to be within a marriage.

If the Frankish church did not unanimously attempt to make a *dos* and publicity requirements for a validly recognized union that it would call marriage, even less did the Roman church do so.[53] Pope Nicholas I wrote in 866 in response to a legation from the Bulgars, answering some questions that they had about Roman Christianity. He made clear that the consent of the parties was all that was required for marriage: not the consent of the parents, not a blessing. The formalities, including a betrothal with the consent of the families, an exchange of rings, and a *dos* transferred from the man to the woman with a written document, and then the marriage ceremony with the blessing of a priest and a ceremonial veil, ought to be included. However, it was not a sin to marry without them, especially for poor people: "These are the laws of marriage, these, in addition to other things that do not come to mind, are the solemn pacts of nuptials; however, we do not consider it a sin if all these things do not happen in a marriage agreement . . . especially because such great lack of means oppresses some people, that they have no assistance in preparing these things."[54] When Charles the Bald's daughter Judith married Baldwin of Flanders in 862 without her father's permission, Charles had Baldwin excommunicated by the Frankish church; but Pope Nicholas ruled that the excommunication was invalid, and the couple were given a wedding benediction. The Roman church was attempting to assimilate to marriage unions that the Frankish church might have considered something less.

Unlike Gregory of Tours, Carolingian writers used the term "concubine" for women who clearly were not slaves.[55] The labeling of a free woman as a concubine might not depend on what rituals did or did not take place. Silvia Konecny points out that often, it was the success of a woman's sons that determined whether Frankish writers—and modern historians—considered her a wife or a concubine. The mother of a king or other magnate was likely to be classified retrospectively in the more respectable category. If her son inherited, the mother would be treated as belonging to a category of woman whose son could inherit.[56] Himiltrud, mother of Charlemagne's son Pippin the Hunchback, is usually taken as a concubine, although from a noble family; but the fact that her son bore a name from his paternal lineage indicates that he may have been thought of at the time of his birth as a potential heir. Charlemagne did eventually formally marry Himiltrud, and a less formal union may have been a prelude to marriage.[57]

Charlemagne's daughters also provide examples of unions of indeterminate status. Sources tell us that these daughters did not marry, nor did they become nuns, and that their father did not object to their having lovers; according to Charlemagne's biographer Einhard, he pretended not to pay attention to the rumors swirling about them.[58] The unions seem to have been of long duration. Scholars have claimed that Charlemagne's son and successor Louis the Pious dissolved the unions, not considering them marriages since there was no *dos*, but the sources do not say so. Nithard reports only that Louis "immediately ordered them to leave the palace for their monasteries," and the *Vita Hludowici Imperatoris* tells us that "he conceded to each of his sisters the land that she had received from her father; those who had not received any were endowed by the emperor."[59] Whatever relationships the daughters were involved in, they were not purely love matches based on the couples' choices; these were politically arranged unions.[60] It may be that Charlemagne did not want his daughters to enter into formal alliances with *dos* because he did not want to create that sort of obligation to other families, or because he wanted them to retain the flexibility that the church was beginning to deny to marriage. These unions can be taken as evidence of a gray area in marriage in the early ninth century, but the daughters of Charlemagne were hardly typical of society as a whole.

A famous case from the later Carolingian period has been taken to indicate that the church was attempting to assimilate to concubinage any woman whose marriage was not formal and based on rough equality of status. The case is a complex one, and the woman involved risks being lost in the complexity.

"She-Wolf": Waldrada

Waldrada, probably born in the mid- to late 830s, was a Frankish aristocrat.[61] Sometime before 855, she entered a union with Lothar, son of Lothar I, ruler of Lotharingia, the central one of the three Frankish kingdoms established after the death of Louis the Pious. There is no information about how the union between Waldrada and Lothar was formed. It may have been by the initiative of the couple, though we may guess that her family was involved.[62] It would be a coup for them to have their daughter partnered in some way with the heir to the throne, even if it was not a marriage according to the procedures that were beginning to be recognized in church law.[63] Waldrada's family was lower in the social hierarchy than those of many royal spouses. Later court proceedings indicate that Lothar had a strong affection for Waldrada, but that does not mean that it was a love match; in a system in which families make the arrangements, love between the partners can often emerge as a result of the union, rather than as a cause. The name of the couple's son, Hugo, was not one typically given within the Carolingian royal family, which some scholars have taken as an indication that he was never considered legitimate.[64] There were also three daughters of the union.[65]

Upon his father's death in 855, Lothar II became king of Lotharingia. His rule, however, was threatened by his powerful uncles who ruled the other two Frankish kingdoms. He needed support, and one way of acquiring it was to marry the daughter of a powerful Lotharingian noble family, which he did that same year.[66] Theutberga's family members were sufficiently more important than Waldrada's that the latter were not able to complain effectively when she was ousted. She may not have been completely abandoned, as Lothar and Waldrada may have continued their sexual relationship although not their living arrangements. By 857, Lothar was unhappy with Theutberga and wanted Waldrada back, perhaps on personal grounds, perhaps because Waldrada had proved her fertility and Theutberga had not (although if fertility were the only concern, he could undoubtedly have found another high-status woman to marry). His attempt to divorce Theutberga had become a cause célèbre by 858. The writings of Bishop Hincmar of Reims about the case became very influential in the church's evolving doctrines on the indissolubility of marriage and in later arguments about whether the church or the secular power controlled marriage.[67] Most of what scholars have written about the case has focused on Lothar and, to a lesser extent, Theutberga.

If we want to understand Waldrada's position, we need to know whether she would have expected the union to be permanent or whether she always knew that she could be supplanted. Régine Le Jan notes that from the second half of the ninth century, the age at marriage of men of the Carolingian dynasty rose dramatically, but their fathers often assigned them what she calls an *épouse de jeunesse*, an aristocratic woman who could be dismissed when they came to make a formal, dynastic marriage. Waldrada, she suggests, was one of these women, whom she calls *Friedelfrauen*.[68] Wemple suggests that unions like that of Waldrada and Lothar were "trial marriages," arranged by the women's families in the hopes that the relationship would last and turn into a real, recognized marriage. She rejects the term *Friedelehe* for them and stresses that the women involved had little choice.[69] For reasons discussed in the Introduction, I agree with Wemple that we should reject the term *Friedelehe*, but both Wemple and Le Jan may be right: from the man's point of view, the union may have been temporary, but the woman's family likely hoped that it would not be. Most recently, Karl Heidecker, also rejecting *Friedelehe*, simply calls Waldrada Lothar's "boyhood mistress," although he also acknowledges the possibility that their union was more formal.[70] Andrea Esmyol claims that the case shows that there was a clear line between the wife and the concubine and that *Friedelehe* played no role; again, the latter part of the statement is correct, but the line was perhaps not as sharp in the ninth century as she wishes to make it.[71]

Perhaps the fact that Lothar saw the union with Waldrada as temporary did not mark it as low-status. He thought that his union with Theutberga was also temporary, in that he could dismiss her in order to take Waldrada back. Indeed, he might have been able to do so if not for the political situation.[72] In other words, the nonbinding nature of the union with Waldrada may not have distinguished it in her or Lothar's eyes from a marriage. Whether the church was unwilling to accept the dissolution of Theutberga's marriage because it had been done in a formal, ecclesiastically approved manner or whether it was acceding to the (rapidly dwindling) power of Theutberga's family and the ambitions of Lothar's uncle Charles the Bald, who may have preferred to see Lothar remain with an apparently infertile woman, is an open question.

Many ecclesiastical writers—not just Hincmar but others as well—referred to Waldrada as a concubine.[73] It is likely that among her peers, she had a good deal more status than that word implied; she was a woman whom Lothar could potentially have married and was clearly not unfree—indeed, she was an aristocrat.[74] Janet Nelson suggests that "[p]erhaps the pair were married according to custom: in Carolingian Francia, canon lawyers were still in the process of clarifying just what procedures they would accept as constituting a valid marriage."[75] Certainly, Lothar did treat Waldrada as his wife after his repudiation of Theutberga.[76] But both sides, at least the churchmen on both sides, agreed that Lothar could have only one wife, and according to the winning side, Theutberga was she. Churchmen—whether those who rejected the union with Waldrada, or Bishop Adventius of Metz, who supported it—by the second half of the ninth century had asserted the church's role in the validity of marriage, and drew a distinction between marriage made with a *dos* and concubinage.[77] The *Annals of St. Bertin*, also written by Hincmar, would in 869 call Charles the Bald's second wife Richildis a concubine until he held a betrothal ceremony and paid a *dos*.[78] There is little evidence for how the laity felt because churchmen on both sides made the written case.

Lothar's supporters, including Adventius, argued that the union with Waldrada was a valid marriage, publicly celebrated and involving property exchanges. But it is also significant that they apparently did not make the argument until 863.[79] At the beginning of the controversy, it was not obvious that that was a crucial piece of the puzzle, and Waldrada and Lothar's backers realized only belatedly that her case would be greatly strengthened by claiming not only Theutberga's ineligibility to marry but also a *dos* for Waldrada. This belated argument was probably specious. At the time of the union, Lothar may have been reluctant to commit with the publicity that the church now required or at least urged. But Lothar and Waldrada may still have considered themselves married. There is no question that his marriage to Theutberga followed all the formalities; Lothar's claim against her was based on charges of interfemoral incest with her brother (followed by an abortion), not on the circumstances of her wedding. Indeed, Stuart Airlie suggests that Lothar himself was not a victim of the church's emerging law of marriage as much as he was attempting to take advantage of it himself, using incest rules to justify his repudiation of Theutberga.[80] It may also be, as Rachel Stone suggests, that an accusation of incest was particularly useful for Lothar, because if Theutberga were guilty she could be put to death, thus freeing Lothar to remarry regardless of whether his marriage to Theutberga had been valid.[81]

Waldrada's initial repudiation probably took neither her nor her family by surprise. They would have been aware that with the social gap between her status and his, if he had to change his sexual allegiance for political reasons, as was certainly not unknown for monarchs, she would have little protection. Her family likely saw a tremendous opportunity to make a match for their daughter, even at a high risk. As with the mother of Adeodatus, we do not know how much and what kind of affection she felt for her man. Lothar must have thought her a good partner, since when he attempted to repudiate Theutberga, it was to return to Waldrada rather than seek a new wife. Although it is only a guess that Lothar and Waldrada were fond of each other, we cannot conclude from the silence of the sources about her views that she was no more than a pawn in a political game, with no agency (nor indeed can we conclude that about Theutberga). Waldrada may have wished to stay in the union for reasons of personal honor, or because of her children, or because she loved Lothar. The woman's intention and wishes did not matter a great deal at this point as to the legal validity of the marriage. But Hincmar's suggestion that she had used witchcraft to draw Lothar away from Theutberga must have stung, and could have put her in real physical danger. In the *Annals of St. Bertin*, Hincmar claimed that "it was said" that in dismissing Theutberga and taking Waldrada back, Lothar had been "demented by witchcraft."[82] The life of St. Deicolus, written in the tenth century, indicates that this rumor had some traction. The author of this work, hostile because Lothar had given his

monastery to the "whore" Waldrada, recorded that Lothar put away his wife
in order to marry a "she-wolf" who "enchanted the soul of the king with various kinds of witchcraft."[83] Waldrada was eventually excommunicated, but the
union continued even without her living at court; she retained political influence. When Lothar died in 869, he was on his way home from Rome, where
he had met with the new pope, who had lifted Waldrada's excommunication
and who Lothar hoped would declare her his wife.[84]

While wondering about Waldrada's personal role and feelings in this situation, we may also wonder about Theutberga. She kept her royal husband,
but one who had made shocking and no doubt painful accusations about her
sexual activity with her brother. After he had been forced to take her back but
still retained Waldrada on the side, she attempted to leave to enter a monastery. There was no happy ending for her. In the Louvre sits a large piece of rock
crystal engraved with images of the story of Susannah and the elders (Daniel
13), the "Lothar crystal." Some scholars have suggested that it was made on the
occasion of the reconciliation of Lothar and Theutberga, an admission on his
part that he had falsely accused her. But when Carolingian authors (including
Hincmar) used the Susannah story, Genevra Kornbluth suggests, it was usually not to illustrate Susannah's chastity but to illustrate the importance of just
judgment. The crystal was meant to emphasize the royal virtue of Lothar, not
as an apology to Theutberga.[85] Lothar's early death probably did not come as
a huge disappointment to her.

This case, and particularly Hincmar's writings in response to it, marked
a turning point in the church's position on which unions were and were not
valid; among the different views represented in this case, it was Hincmar's
that became influential. By the tenth century, the church's attempts to assert the exclusive legitimacy of Christian marriage had resulted in the dif-
ferentiation of the latter from other forms of union, such as marriage *more
Danico*, "in the Danish manner," as some chronicles put it, in tenth- and
eleventh-century Normandy. Herleve, mother of William the Conqueror, for
example, was something less than a fully accepted wife to the duke, but, as
the daughter of a court official, she is not likely to have entered the union
without her father's knowledge and permission.[86] Probably, her family sought
to gain from her relationship with a powerful man. Marriage *more Danico* was
not necessarily a survival of some older Germanic custom, nor can we assume
that the "Danish" and Christian modes were in fundamental opposition. The
most oft-cited case is Gunnor, wife of Richard I of Normandy (942–96). The

eleventh-century writer William of Jumièges reported that Richard married her *Christiano more*, "in a Christian manner," and she bore him five sons and three daughters. Robert of Torigni in the twelfth century, however, reported that she was only married to him *more Christiano* later in life, when the duke wanted to make one of his sons archbishop.[87] Neither text implies anything different about the two types of marriage except the ceremony. Richard did not make a new payment to Gunnor's family or acquire new rights over her when he married her *more Christiano*. The distinction is likely to be that the second, Christian marriage was blessed by a bishop.[88] It is not clear, however, that chroniclers considered the other form looser or more voluntary. It seems that the laity did not change their sexual attachments at the pace that the church hoped they would.

Early medieval sources reveal a fluidity in the way that people understood unions between men and women. The status of a union depended more on the status of the participants than on the process used to enter it (although the former influenced the latter). The lower the woman's status in relation to the man's, the less likely it was that property exchanges and a benediction would take place, the less likely that the church and others would regard it as marriage, and the easier it would be to call the union into question. Bernadette Filotas makes the intriguing suggestion that strictures found in penitentials against the use of love magic by a woman against her husband may have aimed at just such precarious and vulnerable unions: "[T]he temptation must have been very strong for a woman in this position to use all means to strengthen her hold on her partner's affections."[89]

Fluidity in types of unions would have been all the more present among the classes of society that did not make their way into the narrative sources. Indeed, one may wonder whether property exchange was usual at all at a lower level of society. A story of a miracle of St. Emmeram (d. 652) illustrates the expectations of marriage among the lower orders in Germany in the eighth century, when the story of his life was written by Arbeo of Freising. The events had to have taken place after 739, when Emmeram's relics were moved to Regensburg. A traveler captured in Bavaria was sold into slavery in Thuringia, in central Germany, near the lands of the pagan Saxons. His new owner wanted him to marry a widow on his estate, presumably so that he could work the land that her late husband had worked. The man protested that he already had a wife and therefore, as a Christian, could not marry again; the owner threatened to sell him to the Saxons if he refused. He went through a marriage ceremony with the woman. When they were alone together, he refused to consummate the marriage, and persuaded her to undergo three nights of continence (as Christians were recommended to do, the so-called Tobias nights). During these nights, the groom prayed to St. Emmeram, who facilitated his escape and return to his own land.[90]

The language used for the marriage of the slave to the widow (who may or may not also have been a slave but was clearly an agrarian laborer) was fully that of early medieval marriage: *in matrimonio sociare* clearly meant "to marry"; she was a *coniunx*, or spouse; the owner *tradidit*, or gave her in marriage. Their right hands were joined and a cloth wrapped around them "as the custom of weddings dictates." They then got into bed to take a meal "according to the custom of weddings." As Carl Hammer points out, what is important in this story is what is missing. The owner must be understood as Christian in order for his threat to sell the slave to the pagans to make sense. Yet despite the detail of the story, there was no mention of a nuptial blessing.[91] Nor was there any reference to an exchange of property; the idea that the slave might take over his wife's late husband's landholding is logical but not stated or even clearly implied. The man for whom the saint performed the miracle, according to the author, thought that what he was being asked to commit was bigamy rather than adultery; there is no doubt that the union was intended as a marriage. Clearly, a ritual was connected with it, though the fact that the author twice pointed out that what they did corresponded to what was usual at weddings indicates that there may have been some doubt about the union's conformity to law or custom. Perhaps the doubt arose from precisely the fact that the formal marriage of slaves was unusual.

No *dos* was involved in this wedding. The *dos* and the ceremonies that made a union public were only important if there was wealth to be transferred and a public that took an interest. Formal marriage, indeed, may have been a luxury. I am not suggesting that the lower orders benefited from informal unions based on love whereas elites were limited by dynastic considerations, but I am suggesting that the wish to determine what was a real marriage was primarily important to the laity in cases where property and inheritance were at stake. Even among magnates, before the twelfth century there was no accepted and codified body of marriage law. In early medieval Europe, as in ancient societies, the status of the parties and particularly the woman, rather than the procedure, often determined the status of the union. Throughout the early medieval period, the church claimed the ability to legislate about appropriate sexual unions, though neither exclusively nor consistently; by the ninth century, it was beginning to claim that church-sponsored rituals were necessary. Eventually, the claims would begin to stick. By the twelfth century, this would develop into the idea of marriage as a sacrament, but the idea that it was status and not ritual that made a wife was strangely persistent.

The Consent Theory

As we saw with the earlier Middle Ages, so in the high and later Middle Ages, we need to understand how the church came to decide among conflicting opinions on the formation of marriage in order to understand the range of unions into which people entered and what distinguished them. A turning point in the church's treatment of what made a union legitimate—indeed, what might be taken as the origin of modern ideas of marriage—came in the twelfth century. The elaboration of the church's rules, the treatment of marriage as a sacrament, and the focus on the consent of the parties, none of which was entirely new but all of which received new emphasis, were not due to a fundamental concern with the state of pair bonds. The church was not operating on an abstract principle of, to put it negatively, surveillance and control of the lives of the laity, or, to put it positively, the holiness of matrimony. Rather, the development of the church's position on marriage grew out of the reform movement of the eleventh and early twelfth centuries. This movement was concerned with church reform in a very broad sense: not only improving the behavior of the clergy (discussed in more detail in Chapter 3) but also correcting the general relationship of the church to the secular world. A series of popes successfully staked out their claim to choose bishops and otherwise govern the church without the interference of secular lords. Part of the church's claim to independence rested on the elaboration of an ecclesiastical legal system, and part of that legal system was a claim to jurisdiction over marriage. This claim had been made or implied before, as we have seen, but not so clearly and directly. Georges Duby argued, especially with reference to northwestern France, that "two conceptions of marriage clashed in Latin Christendom about the year 1100. It was the climax of a conflict resulting in the introduction of customs that have lasted almost up to our own day."[92] Rather than two different conceptions of marriage, what was going on was a fight over authority: who got to decide which particular unions were valid and which were not. This led to the privileging of something that the church labeled "marriage" over other forms of union described in similar terms but lacking some characteristic, often church sanction. Of course, getting one set of churchmen to approve a particular union did not mean that "the church" as a unit supported it, but once the principle of church authority over marriage had been established, it became easier for the popes and a universalizing system of canon law to enforce particular rules.

Ivo of Chartres (d. 1115) provides a good picture of the canon law of marriage just before the great age of the elaboration of the canon law. Ivo placed great emphasis on the consent of the two partners to the marriage, rather than their families; in this, he drew both on Roman law and on the letter of Nicholas to the Bulgars, discussed above. He included in his compilations several Carolingian texts and forgeries requiring marriage to be public, but he himself did not hold that the presence of a priest or a blessing was necessary for the marriage to be valid. He also argued that informal unions such as concubinage could be legitimated as marriage, although only if the parties were unmarried.[93] Ivo was particularly interested in the indissolubility of marriage. Indeed, the individual cases about which Ivo and others were most concerned were disputes between a powerful layman and the church over whether he remained bound to a particular woman—for example, Philip I's repudiation of his wife Bertha of Holland and his attempt to marry Bertrada de Montfort, which Ivo opposed.[94]

Few voices, in the twelfth century or earlier, spoke out on principle against the sacralization of marriage, and certainly not against marriage as an institution, unless they proposed chastity instead. That is why the story of Heloise and Abelard is so fascinating and unusual: a twelfth-century woman who explicitly preferred a type of sexual union to marriage. Their union fit into neither of Duby's two models: it was neither arranged by the families for the sake of property, nor was it divinely consecrated. Heloise, in fact, argued forcefully that marriage was not the type of union that she wished to have.

"The Sweeter Name Will Always Be 'Friend'": Heloise

In 1115, Heloise was a young woman in her mid-twenties living in Paris with her uncle Fulbert, a cathedral canon.[95] She was highly educated and had a strong intellectual reputation. We know a bit about Heloise's interior life from her letters, but about the events of her life mainly from Peter Abelard's autobiographical work, *The Calamities*. Abelard does not tell us how Heloise came to be living with her uncle. It was not unusual in the period for children to be sent to live with a relative who was wealthier and could give them a better

start in life than their parents, and Heloise may have chosen to remain with
Fulbert when she reached adulthood. She had been educated at an abbey in
Argenteuil, an indication that her family was fairly well-off, and she may have
wanted to live in Paris with her uncle because of the intellectual life there. Because later, when she was abbess at the Paraclete, she recorded only her mother's and not her father's name in the abbey's necrology, scholars have suggested
that she may have been of illegitimate birth, which might also explain why she
was being supported by her uncle (who could actually have been her father).[96]

Peter Abelard, the younger son of a knightly family, sought a career in
theology. This required him to become a cleric, although not a priest. He
described his scholarly career in terms that indicate he may have seen it as a
substitute for knightly success: "[M]y primary interest lay in the weapons of
dialectical reasoning, so I traded all my arms for these and gave up the trophies
of war for the noisy clash of argument."[97] In 1115, Abelard was in Paris, lectur-
ing at the university, and had heard of the unusually learned woman Heloise:
"Now, having carefully considered all the things that usually serve to attract
a lover, I concluded that she was the best one to bring to my bed. I was sure
it would be easy: I was famous myself at the time, young, and exceptionally
good-looking, and could not imagine that any woman I thought worthy of
my love would turn me down. But I thought that this particular girl would
be even more likely to give in because of her knowledge and love of letters."[98]

He asked to lodge in her uncle's home, and Fulbert asked him to tutor
Heloise. Writing in retrospect fifteen years later, Abelard may have taken on
himself more responsibility for premeditation than he had actually exercised
at the time. He may have gone to live with Fulbert for practical reasons, and
there is a possibility that Heloise had some initiative in the sexual relationship.

Heloise and Abelard became lovers. Abelard describes the initiative as
being on his side and indicates that winning Heloise's consent was not the
primary issue: "When [Fulbert] put her in my hands not only to teach but to
discipline as well, what else was he doing but giving me complete freedom,
even if I never took advantage of it, to convince her by force if more gentle
inducements did not prevail?"[99] This force, however, was not necessary, as
Abelard described it, although he did beat Heloise as any tutor would be expected to do his student:

> First we were joined in one house, and then in one heart. Under
> the pretext of study, we had all our time free for love, and in our
> classroom all the seclusion love could ever want. With our books

open before us, we exchanged more words of love than of lessons, more kisses than concepts. My hands wandered more to her breasts than our books, and love turned our eyes to each other more than reading kept them on the page. To avert suspicion, there were some beatings, yes, but the hand that struck the blows belonged to love, not anger, to pleasure, not rage—and they surpassed the sweetness of any perfume. We left no stage of love untried in our passion, and if love could find something novel or strange, we tried that too.[100]

The couple also exchanged letters during this time. Some scholars, led prominently by Constant J. Mews, believe that these letters have survived in an anonymous fifteenth-century manuscript known as the *Epistolae Duorum Amantium*, or *Letters of Two Lovers*.[101] For present purposes, we do not need to judge the authenticity of these letters as belonging to the couple. The letters spoke passionately of love but did not refer to a long-term domestic partnership of any sort, which could be consistent with the idea that the couple did not make long-term plans until they knew of her pregnancy. Yet even if the attribution were certain, the letters would not be definitive evidence of their intentions. The love that the *Epistolae* expressed was different from Abelard's autobiographical account, which made the relationship mainly about carnal lust, but the latter was written in retrospect, after he had been castrated and become a monk. The letters did express a fear of discovery, which Heloise and Abelard would have felt, but so would many other lovers, fictional or real.

After a few months, Fulbert discovered the liaison and threw Abelard out of the house. Within several months, Heloise discovered that she was pregnant, and Abelard sneaked her out of the house in disguise and sent her to stay with his sister in Brittany. He confessed to her uncle, using as his excuse "the great power of love and what women had done from the beginning of the human race to bring even the greatest men to ruin," and made what he thought was a generous proposal, "offering him a satisfaction he never could have hoped: I undertook to marry the girl I had wronged, as long as it was all done in secret in order to keep my standing intact."[102] Scholars have taken the idea that Fulbert never could have expected such a marriage, and the need for secrecy, as due to Abelard's clerical standing, but it may also have to do with disparate social status.

According to Abelard's later account, Heloise did not want to marry him. He recounted that she did not want to be remembered "as the woman who brought my name to ruin and shamed us both,"[103] and she cited the great loss to the church and to philosophy. She told him that it would be more honorable to be called his "friend" (*amica*) rather than "wife," so that "I would be hers through a love freely offered, not forced and constrained by some marital tie, and the time we spent apart could only increase the sweetness of our reunion, our joys together as precious as they were rare."[104] Scholars have often translated *amica* here as "mistress" (Levitan's translation, which I have been using, has "lover"); indeed, the term carries something of that meaning in this context. But (assuming that Heloise did actually say this) she may have meant that being an intellectual companion was more important to her than marriage. It does not mean that the friendship was not sexual, but that it was not only sexual.[105] The passage also envisioned a relationship in which the couple did not live together. Abelard claimed that she wanted him to love her freely rather than because of a bond. Later, in a letter that survives (the authenticity of these later monastic letters, as opposed to the letters possibly exchanged before their marriage, is not in much doubt today), Heloise claimed that she would rather be Abelard's whore (*meretrix*) than the wife and imperial consort (*imperatrix*) of a Roman emperor. She said that "the name of wife may have the advantages of sanctity and safety, but to me the sweeter name will always be friend [*amica*] or, if your dignity can bear it, concubine [*concubina*] or whore [*scorta*]."[106]

Abelard's *Calamities* also quoted Heloise as making a detailed argument against marriage based on the writings of St. Jerome. She wrote both of the dangers of sexual indulgence to a scholar or philosopher, and of the distractions of family life. "Scholars and nursemaids, writing desks and cradles, a book and a distaff, a pen and a spindle—what harmony can there be in *that?* What husband could ever concentrate on philosophy or scripture and still put up with babies howling, nurses mumbling their lullabies, and a riotous gang of servants trampling all throughout the house?"[107]

If Abelard were the only witness, one might wonder whether he put words into her mouth, but she referred to them in her letters. In any case, these arguments are not exactly the same as saying that she would rather be his friend or mistress. They are directed against sexual involvement and domestic partnership, not against marriage in particular. But it was marriage that would give her a legal claim on him, a claim that she wished to renounce so as to allow him to remain a philosopher.

Heloise and Abelard did marry. Their marriage would have been considered clandestine, at least at a later date when the canon law of marriage was more thoroughly worked out, not because her family did not consent (they

were present, according to Abelard) but because it was not performed publicly
in the parish of the parties' residence with a calling of the banns. Nevertheless,
it was a valid marriage. Abelard was a cleric in minor orders, if any at all (even
if he had been a priest, the marriages of priests were forbidden but had not yet
been declared invalid by the church, as discussed in Chapter 3). It is not clear
that in Abelard's time, a cleric would have lost his position in the university
by marrying. He might have lost a benefice if he had had one; but he does not
seem to have had one. He may, however, have thought that marriage would
undermine his moral authority if it were known.[108] After the wedding, Heloise
stayed with Fulbert, but the latter, "looking for some way to restore his public
honor, began to spread word of the marriage," at which point Heloise denied
its validity, "cursing him and swearing it was a bare-faced lie, and he exploded
with fury and fits of abuse."[109] Heloise went to stay at Argenteuil, although
she did not make profession as a nun. Fulbert, according to Abelard, believed
that the latter had repudiated the marriage by making Heloise a nun, and
bribed a servant to let some of his kinsmen or followers into Abelard's lodgings
at night, where they caught him asleep and castrated him. Fulbert may have
been angry at Abelard for (as he thought) repudiating the marriage and for letting people believe that Heloise continued to live in sin, but he may also have
been angry at Abelard for getting her pregnant in the first place. Her family
may have wished for her to become a nun and eventually an abbess and been
furious with Abelard for preventing this. Heloise later wrote indicating clearly
that she did not consider the marriage disparaging: she referred to Abelard's
having humbled himself and "elevated me and all my family alike."[110] But it
is not entirely clear what the relative social statuses of the families were. It
has been suggested that Heloise's father was Gilbert de Garlande, a member
of a leading family in the Île-de-France, which would have given her important connections even if she were of illegitimate birth.[111] Fulbert might have
thought that Heloise could have done better than Abelard, either in religion
or in marriage.[112] Almost certainly, he thought that she could have done better
than to enter into concubinage with Abelard.

    Heloise's attitude toward her union with Abelard was very complex.
Even after his castration, she was not eager to become a nun. Abelard says
that she did so "freely at my command,"[113] but she claimed that the entrance
into religious life was something that "you alone decided, you alone": "It was
not any commitment to the religious life that forced me to the rigors of the
convent when I was the young woman I once was: it was your command
alone," although she followed that command voluntarily.[114] Some scholars

have concluded that she would have been happy to continue living as a couple with Abelard without being married. There is a difference, however, between saying this in retrospect, after she had taken the veil, and having sufficient disregard for propriety to be willing actually to do it. In another of her letters, she indicated that she accepted a moral distinction between unions outside of marriage and those that were licit:

When we were still pursuing the joys of love
and—to use an ugly but a more expressive phrase—
abandoning ourselves to fornication,
God spared us his hard judgment.
But when we took steps to correct what we had done,
to cover the illicit with the licit
and repair our fornication with the proper rites of marriage [*honore coniugii*],
the Lord raised up an angry hand against us. . . .
It was for no adultery that you suffered,
but for a proper marriage [*coniugium*] with which you thought
you had made good any wrong you might have done.[115]

Heloise stands as an example of several important ideas, including the lack of regard with which families in the twelfth century might hold clandestine marriages, and the possibility that a woman who spoke for herself could regard marriage as not the most desirable form of union.[116] She listed traditional antifeminist propaganda points about women corrupting men, but added that she herself had no guilt about having tempted Abelard into marriage, which had been his idea.[117] Yet, although both parties agreed that Heloise did not seek marriage, it made a positive difference for her, providing, in her words, "sanctity and safety." When Heloise wrote to Abelard as a nun, after reading his *Calamities*, written in 1132 or 1133, she claimed that she had never wanted a dowry and suggested that a woman who would rather marry a rich man than a poor man "is after property alone and is prepared to prostitute herself to an even richer man given the chance." Yet she referred to his still being "obliged to me by the sacrament of marriage [*nuptialis foedere sacramenti*]" as well as the fact that "I have always held you in my heart with a love that has no measure."[118] Abelard wrote about his care for the community of nuns who had been expelled from Argenteuil by the abbot of St.-Denis, justifying it on the grounds of the obligation of men to care for their wives' material needs even if they have entered religion and no longer have carnal relations with them. Marriage gave women, even chaste women, a claim on their partners that unmarried ones did not have. The position on marriage expressed by Heloise was actually taken by important twentieth-century scholars as evidence that she could not actually have written the monastic letters, though people as early as the thirteenth century believed that she did: How could an educated woman ever have espoused such a ludicrous position?[119] If we do not discard the evidence because it disturbs modern assumptions about what pair bonds were appropriate, we can see that Heloise was staking out a principled but, in her world, highly impractical position. Her views, like Abelard's, were expressed retroactively, at a time when she was a professed nun and in no danger of being asked to make good on her words, but she still shows us that in the early twelfth century, people could envision an alternative kind of partnered life.

Heloise's story is unique in depicting a woman's preference for a sexual union other than marriage. It is atypical also in that no attempt by the church to control the formation of the union appears, although such attempts were prominent enough in her era. These attempts were not, however, as the great anthropologist Jack Goody argued, a deliberate effort to decrease the availability of legitimate heirs so that church institutions would inherit more property: "For the Church to grow and survive it had to accumulate property, which meant acquiring control over the way it was passed from one generation to the next. Since the distribution of property between generations is related to patterns of marriage and the legitimization of children, the Church had to gain authority over these so that it could influence the strategies of heirship."[120] As the church's law developed, it included a presumption in favor of matrimony in cases of doubt, especially when there were children involved, which would not have happened if the church's purpose was to diminish the number of possible heirs.[121] What the church was really attempting to do (if such a large, diffuse, and diverse institution can be said to have coherent goals) was not to discourage the laity from marrying or declare lay unions illicit but to claim the authority to determine the validity of those unions, which, in the case of powerful families, could transfer a fair amount of their power to the church. In Heloise's case, intervention to determine the validity of the marriage was not necessary: both parties acknowledged that it had once existed, but it was quite in accord with canon law for married people to agree to stop living together and to take up the religious life.

Not everyone was in such agreement about the conclusion of their sexual

unions as Heloise and Abelard. In the central Middle Ages, as in the early
Middle Ages, a main area in which the church came into conflict with the
laity was over the termination of marriage. Anyone who owned property was
concerned about having children who could inherit it. In most places, children had to be born within marriage to inherit fully, so if a marriage resulted
in no children or no sons, a wealthy landholder might be very eager to replace
his wife. Women might have been eager to replace their husbands, too, but
we know less about this, as it was not generally for reasons of inheritance of
land. Although medical theory was fairly evenhanded in placing responsibility
for infertility on women and men, even medical texts, as Joan Cadden notes,
"tended in the aggregate to place the burden upon the woman," whether because of the frequency of medical conditions that could lead to female infertility, the existence of the genre of gynecological treatise, which had no male
counterpart, or the importance of childbearing as women's work.[122] In addition, elite men had more opportunity than their wives to demonstrate their
fertility with another partner, and this made it easier to blame their wives for
"barrenness." The church's view of marriage as indissoluble (except with papal
dispensation, which underscored papal authority), which we have seen already
in the Carolingian period, interfered greatly with the ability of magnate families to assure their scions' reproduction.

We are concerned here particularly with the church's rules about the ending of unions insofar as they depended a great deal upon the rules about their
formation and required reclassifying them as something other than marriage.
The church did not recognize what we today call divorce, the dissolution of
a marriage leaving the parties free to remarry while recognizing that the marriage had once been valid. The rules that it came to adopt provided in cases
of adultery or cruelty for a legal separation that looks much like what we call
divorce today—there might be a property settlement, child support, and visitation rights—but the parties, even if one of them was deemed innocent, were
not free to remarry, and if they formed later unions, they would be of some
other sort. The only way of dissolving a marriage that allowed remarriage was
what we today would call an annulment, a declaration that the marriage had
never been valid in the first place. This could be done on a number of grounds,
generally the existence of an impediment (the couple were related, or one of
them had been previously married to someone else). The lack of a proper ritual
was rarely in itself a reason for declaring a marriage invalid, according to the
rules under which the church operated from the twelfth century on.

These rules took some time to develop and elaborate. By the eleventh century, the consent of the two parties was being taken as an important criterion for marriage, even the definitional criterion. If marriage was to be a sacrament—and sacramental theology was beginning to argue that it was—it could hardly be defined by something as impure as coitus. Although theologians assumed that women would usually marry according to their fathers' choices, their fathers could not compel them if they objected.[123] A union could be deemed other than marriage if one party successfully claimed not to have consented to a marriage.

The great codifier of the canon law, Gratian, made his first collection of the church's legal pronouncements around 1140. It was later much expanded either by Gratian himself or his followers.[124] He drew upon earlier canon law collections, including those of Burchard of Worms and Ivo of Chartres, but Gratian's work had the larger impact. The collection took the form of questions, with arguments on both sides of each answer, supported by quotations from the Bible, the church fathers, papal decrees, and other normative texts. Gratian argued for a two-stage model of marriage, which was first undertaken by an agreement, *matrimonium initiatum*, but was not complete until the marriage had been consummated, *matrimonium ratum*.[125] While Gratian was the preeminent canon lawyer of his time, canon law as a field of scholarship was not yet separate from theology (nor, indeed, did the overlap ever entirely disappear), and the question of the formation of marriage was also addressed by the author of the most important theology textbook, Peter Lombard's four books of *Sentences*.[126] Like Gratian's work—and like numerous other works of the period, in which disputation was a major genre—the *Sentences* included arguments pro and con on each point, along with supporting quotations, and presented what the author deemed the correct conclusion.[127] For Peter Lombard, it was consent alone that made a marriage: "What is marriage? Wedding or matrimony is the marital joining of a man and a woman, between legitimate persons, maintaining an undivided way of life. The undivided life means that neither can maintain continence without the consent of the other. . . . [A]nd while they live, the conjugal bond between them shall remain, so that it will not be permitted to them to marry elsewhere. . . . The efficient cause of matrimony is consent, not of any sort, but expressed in words, not in the future tense, but in the present."[128]

The parties had to consent to entering into marriage, not just to sexual intercourse or to a domestic partnership.[129] And it was the parties themselves, not their families, who had to consent. Once that had taken place, the marriage was complete and indissoluble, regardless of whether sexual intercourse took place, or whether their parents agreed or provided a dowry. Peter Lombard also forcefully articulated the idea that marriage was a sacrament and stood for the union of Christ and the church. For that reason, he made the physical union an important part of it, although not a requirement: "Since therefore marriage is a sacrament, it is also a sacred sign of a sacred thing, that is to say, the conjunction of Christ and the Church. . . . As, therefore, between spouses there is a conjunction according to the consent of souls and according to the mixing of bodies, thus the church is coupled to Christ by will and by nature."[130]

A huge amount of commentary, direct and indirect, upon the works of Gratian and of Peter Lombard flowed over the course of the twelfth century. The position synthesized and codified in decretals of Alexander III (r. 1159–81) and in legal textbooks in the early thirteenth century became the accepted law of the church.[131] The effects in practice of this synthesis, however, remained attenuated. As Charles Donahue, Jr., explains, Alexander's rules were not a statement of contemporary practice but rather a vision of what marriage could and ought to be; over subsequent centuries, it was largely, but not entirely, put into effect:

> This is not to say that the victory of the consent position, with the
> particular emphasis Peter [Lombard] gives to it, was able to come
> to grips with the many ways in which it fails to square with mar-
> riage as practiced in medieval societies and as regulated by medieval
> codes of secular law in and after Peter's time. Parents continued to
> force children into unwanted marriages; dowries remained essential
> requirements for marriage. . . . [T]he high and mighty continued
> to ignore or to manipulate the principle of marital indissolubility,
> when it suited their convenience; and the dependent, the poor, and
> the semi-free found that their status and circumstances stood in the
> way of making their own free choice of marriage partners.[132]

Writing from the perspective of the later Middle Ages, Christiane Klapisch-Zuber notes that local custom continued within the context of the church's law: "A couple's consent thus became the foundation of Christian marriage, and this choice tended to force into the background other criteria of 'just marriage,' such as the validation of the union by recognition of conjugal cohabitation alone, or the conclusion of an alliance founded in law and guaranteed by written acts, gifts, and donations. . . . [T]he absence of the *iura nuptiarum*—

for example, if the couple were too poor—did not stigmatize as illegitimate any marriage to which the parties had freely consented."[133]

Marriage by consent alone led to interesting consequences. If a couple could enter into it anywhere, without an officiant or a nuptial blessing, it remained difficult to draw a line between marriage and other types of union. By the later Middle Ages, when we start to get surviving church court records, such as those that we will examine in Chapter 4, the courts upheld the validity of marriages that were entered into informally by the consent of the parties alone. It did so even when the parents were powerful patrons who opposed the match. In a 1469 case that is well known because the family's letters have survived, Margery Paston of Norfolk in England married the family's bailiff, Richard Calle, by simply exchanging vows with him without her parents' permission. Her parents, who knew the local bishop well, complained to him. He examined Margery and Richard separately and found that they were in agreement about the form of words that they had exchanged and that it was a valid form for marriage. Although the bishop delayed in the hopes of being able to fulfill the family's wishes and invalidate the union, he did not find grounds to do so. This case shows to what extent the theological and canonistic views of the twelfth century had become ingrained by the end of the Middle Ages.

> The Bishop said to her right plainly and put her in remembrance how she was born, what kin and friends she had, and should have more if she were ruled and guided by them; and if she did not, what rebuke and shame, and loss it should be to her, if she were not guided by them, and cause of forsaking of her for any good, or help, or comfort that she should have of them; and said that he had heard say that she loved such one that her friends were not pleased with what she should have, and therefore she should be right well advised how she did, and said that he wished to understand the words that she had said to him, whether they made matrimony or not. And she repeated what she had said, and said, if those words made it not sure, she said boldly that she would make that surer before she went thence, for she said she thought in her conscience she was bound, whatsoever the words were. . . . And then Calle was examined apart by himself, that her words and his accorded, and the time, and where it should have been done. And then the Bishop said that he supposed that there should be found other things against him that might cause the letting thereof; and therefore he said he would not

be too hasty to give sentence thereon, and said that he would give over until the Wednesday or Thursday after Michaelmas, and so it is delayed. They would have had their will performed in haste, but the Bishop said he would have it no other wise than he had said.[134]

Essentially, the church was finding, if it wanted to control people's sexual unions, it had to assimilate and declare legitimate the ones that they made informally and by their own choice. The church was not entirely happy with this state of affairs, and although it insisted that consent lay with the couple involved, it did not insist on their independence from their parents. At the aristocratic level and that of the urban bourgeoisie, for which we have the richest sources, families continued to be very closely involved indeed, because property exchanges formed an important part of the process (when they were excluded, they were very upset, as with the Pastons). Property exchanges were still not a legal requirement for marriage under canon law, although Gratian did quote the earlier statement about no marriage without a *dos*. However, they were normal and expected, and their presence or absence continued to be important from an evidentiary point of view in determining whether a sexual union constituted marriage.[135]

The church also attempted to require the formation of a marriage to be carried out in a public manner. The intent to marry was to be announced publicly in the parties' own parish church, with the banns proclaimed on three consecutive Sundays to give anyone with information about any impediment an opportunity to speak up. A betrothal or spousals ceremony often preceded the calling of the banns, but this was a private arrangement between the families and not carried out at church; the ritual varied in different parts of Europe.[136] The final vows were supposed to be exchanged publicly, in front of the church, and could be accompanied by a nuptial mass and a benediction.

Any marriage that was not concluded publicly at church was considered clandestine, but not all unions that were claimed to be clandestine marriages were what we would consider secret. A wedding could be conducted with guests, gifts, and feasting, but still be clandestine in the sense that it was not carried out before the church (or was carried out at the wrong church—for example, an exempt jurisdiction rather than the parish church of the parties). Clandestine marriages could be punished with fines, but they were still valid.[137] As long as both parties agreed that they had exchanged marriage vows (either in the present tense, or in the future tense followed by sexual intercourse), the union was indissoluble. Margery Paston and Richard Calle's marriage is an example of this.

The real problems surfaced when the two parties did not agree as to whether a marriage had taken place. The parties' intention and consent were very difficult to prove without dowry, banns, witnesses, or a benediction. Late medieval court records are full of cases in which one party (most often the woman) claimed that vows had been exchanged, and the other party (most often the man) admitted to sexual intercourse but denied that there were any promises of marriage involved. As will be discussed in Chapter 4, no doubt sometimes the man was telling the truth and the woman lying to try to trap him into a marriage; sometimes the woman was telling the truth and the man was lying after the fact, as he had lied to her before the fact in order to get her into bed; and sometimes they both thought that they were telling the truth because the nature of the union had been deliberately left vague.

Besides simply denying the promises, parties who wanted to get out of a marriage had the option of suddenly discovering impediments. Medieval writers noted that aristocrats were so interrelated that it was fairly easy for anyone who wanted to escape from a marriage to discover a relationship within the prohibited degrees. Peter the Chanter, a Paris theologian at the end of the twelfth century, reported that he had heard a knight speak of the woman he was about to marry: "She is related to me in the third kind of affinity. If she doesn't please me, I can procure a separation."[138] That Peter related this anecdote disapprovingly indicates that those who thought about such things considered the loophole created by affinity (relationship by marriage) a serious problem, somewhat less so after the Fourth Lateran Council in 1215 decreased the number of prohibited degrees of relationship from seven to four. Court records from the later Middle Ages, especially from England, reveal that consanguinity and affinity were much less frequently claimed as impediments than precontract, previous vows of marriage by one of the parties with another person. Because such previous vows, if in the present tense, were binding and indissoluble, consummation did not have to be demonstrated, nor did the presence of a priest, and if the parties to a supposed earlier union wanted to claim that it was marriage and therefore the later one was not, it was difficult to contradict them.[139]

This set of rules could lead to confusing situations in which individuals did not know whether or not they were married. This could be true at lower levels of society, as we will see in Chapter 4 from fifteenth-century evidence, but it could also be the case at the highest levels of elite society, for which we have evidence from the central Middle Ages. The story of the wives of Philip II Augustus, king of France from 1180 to 1223, indicates the way that canon law became tied up with politics, to the detriment and unhappiness of all parties involved. The question of whether Philip II's second marriage was valid was a matter of international politics; it also reveals what kinds of unions aristocratic men and women wished to enter at a time when the church was defining and enforcing an international system of canon law and claiming the authority to decide the status of unions. In this case, as in many others, the vision of canon law that won out was one that steadfastly protected the rights of the woman in the relationship.

"Bad France! Rome, Rome!" Ingeborg of Denmark

Philip Augustus had married for the first time in 1180, to Isabelle (also known as Elizabeth) of Hainaut. Her father was count of Hainaut and her uncle count of Flanders, both extremely strategically important provinces of the Low Countries. She was only ten years old at the time of their betrothal. In 1184, he tried to repudiate the marriage on grounds of consanguinity, apparently as a repudiation of Flemish influence, but also perhaps because of the lack of an heir, although it is not at all clear that the marriage had been consummated by then. Isabelle conducted a penitential procession through the streets of Senlis, which stirred up public support and seems to have had its desired effect: the marriage continued.[140] Isabelle died in childbirth at the age of nineteen, leaving Philip with a surviving three-year-old son. One young son, especially one whose health was in question, was not enough for a king in this era of high child mortality, and Philip needed more legitimate heirs. A marriage contract was drawn up with the Princess Ingeborg, sister of King Knud VI of Denmark. John Baldwin, author of the authoritative book on Philip, doubts the political value of this marriage to Philip because any claims that he could have thereby acquired to England would have been impossible to make good; Ingeborg's dowry was cash rather than strategic territory.[141] The eighteen-year-old Ingeborg came to Amiens for the wedding, on 14 August 1193, and chroniclers commented on how beautiful and virtuous she was. It was not unusual for chroniclers to comment favorably upon princesses, but it is notable that prior to the wedding, no one claimed to take issue with her, and that a historian writing about and for Philip even afterward did not describe her otherwise than "beautiful, holy and of good morals."[142]

The next day, after the couple's coronation, Philip announced that he had thought better of the wedding and no longer wished to be married to Ingeborg: he "began violently to abhor, tremble, and pale at her sight."[143] Scholars have speculated for years about what transpired on their wedding night. Baldwin calls it "acute sexual trauma."[144] According to the thirteenth-century biographer of Innocent III, writing in retrospect, the king attempted to consummate the marriage after the coronation ceremony, but "when he had entered the marriage bed, he quickly left her, conceiving such hatred for her that he could scarcely bear the mention of her in his presence. But the Queen asserted that the King had consummated the marriage. The King, however, maintained that he was unable to consummate the marriage."[145] Rigord, the French monk who completed the first version of his chronicle around 1196, suggested that it was witchcraft that had turned Philip against his wife, although he does not say that Philip made that claim: "That same day, by the instigation of the devil, the king, it is said impeded by witches with certain sorceries, began to detest the wife so long desired."[146] Jim Bradbury interprets Rigord here as alleging that Agnes of Meran was a witch and impeded the marriage to Ingeborg, although the passage does not need to be read that way, and it is not clear that Philip and Agnes were acquainted at the time of his marriage to Ingeborg.[147]

We do not know why Philip took such a strong dislike to Ingeborg, or what he could have discovered on that wedding night that would make him want to go through public difficulty and humiliation. They may not have communicated very well, although she likely spoke some Latin. Something could have happened to offend or repulse him, such as bad breath, but given all the accounts of her beauty, and given standards of hygiene at the time, it is hard to understand why this would have put Philip off so permanently and severely.[148] If she was too pure and virginal and he preferred an "earthier" partner, he seems still to have managed all right with Isabelle, whom he married when she was ten.[149] Jane Sayers, in her biography of Innocent III, suggests that Philip was disappointed at the lack of support that the Danes were willing to provide against England.[150] Nothing in this regard changed on the wedding night, however. Surely Philip at thirty was enough of a statesman to know that once he had gone through with the marriage, he would lose any bargaining position that he had, and that his future options would be much greater if he and Ingeborg had not married.

Philip got a French church council at Compiègne led by his uncle, the archbishop of Reims, to declare the marriage invalid on the grounds that

Ingeborg was related to his first wife, which created the impediment of affinity. This claim was spurious, but the council was likely to do whatever Philip wanted. Innocent's biographer described the scene: "The queen was totally ignorant of the proceedings. Abandoned after her compatriots had left, she was totally ignorant of the French language. . . . When [the sentence of divorce] was explained to the queen through an interpreter, she, more astonished than she could express, wept and lamented and cried out: 'Bad France! Bad France!' and she added 'Rome! Rome!' For she did not know how otherwise to protest in French or to appeal the sentence to the Apostolic See."[151] This passage is often taken to indicate that Ingeborg's Latin was not very good, but in the context of the decision's being interpreted from French for her, this may be the author's translation into Latin of her poor French response. Certainly, Ingeborg sent eloquent Latin letters, although she, like many other secular aristocrats of the time, did not likely compose them herself.

Pope Celestine III, persuaded by the Danes, sent legates to France to investigate the matter. Philip ignored him and proceeded to form another union in 1196, this time choosing a German noblewoman, Agnes of Meran. Although her father's family was originally from Bavaria, he had been made duke of Meranien in Dalmatia by the Hohenstaufen emperor, so (unlike the Danish royal house) the family was on the same side of imperial politics as Philip. Philip went through a marriage ceremony with Agnes, and they had two children, a boy and a girl. Ingeborg did not take this situation lying down. Although the pope had inclined to take her part, he had not done much about it when Philip ignored him.[152] Ingeborg continued to be in contact with her brother and Danish churchmen who lobbied on her behalf, and with the pope, writing to Celestine in 1195, for example, that she had been "thrown on the earth as a dry, useless stick, desolate of comfort and advice."[153]

In 1198, a new pope was elected: Lothar di Segni, who took the name Innocent III. Innocent would turn out to be one of the most powerful popes of the Middle Ages, calling the Fourth Lateran Council, which reformed and clarified church doctrine and discipline, combating heresy, assenting to the establishment of important new religious orders, and exercising a great deal of political authority and influence across Europe. Innocent took up Ingeborg's case during the first year of his pontificate.[154] He may have wanted, on principle, to help a woman who had right on her side, but he also was eager to demonstrate that even a very important monarch could not encroach on papal power by deciding for himself whether his marriage was valid. When he ordered Philip directly to send Agnes out of France and take Ingeborg back, he said that "you cannot set yourself against, we do not say ourselves, but God, whose authority we, however unworthy, exercise on earth" and that if he did not obey, "your enemies will prevail against you and the kingdom of France, nor will your small temporal power be able to oppose the omnipotence of eternal divine majesty."[155] Yet he did not immediately excommunicate Philip and Agnes personally, as he could have done, and he called Agnes a *superinducta*, a "woman additionally taken," a term that clearly implied that there was something wrong with the relationship but that was not as demeaning as "concubine" or "whore." The fact that he did not use derogatory language for her is undoubtedly related to her noble birth.[156] When Philip refused to comply with Innocent's order, Innocent had his legate put all of France under interdict, meaning that no sacraments could be performed. This pressure led Philip finally to agree in 1200 to be separated from Agnes. She remained in France and died in 1201. Clearly, not everyone in France approved of the union: Rigord commented on her death, "For five years, he had and kept her against the law and the decree of God."[157]

After Agnes's death, Philip asked Innocent to legitimize the two children he had had with her. Philip could thus achieve the goal of acquiring an heir while allowing Innocent to maintain his authority to define the nature of the union. As he could use Philip's backing in his policy toward the empire, Innocent agreed and legitimated the children. He and Philip were allies, at least some of the time, up until Innocent's death in 1216. These alliances were a matter of geopolitics. The fact that Philip had sought the pope's legitimation of his children was, in itself, a kind of submission, but it is likely that this legitimation was far more important to him than the marital validity of his union with Agnes.

Very little is known about Agnes's life—not even the year of her birth. Indeed, Rigord gave her name as Marie rather than Agnes. The union was arranged rather than being a love match, and Agnes's family, if not she herself, must have known when it was arranged how precarious political marriages could be, especially if it was dubious as to whether they were marriages in the first place. Agnes was not the first choice for Philip's third wife. He first sought to marry the daughter of Conrad, Count Palatine, but according to the English historian William of Newburgh (a source quite hostile to Philip), she refused: "I have heard from many how the king sullied and rejected a most noble girl, that is the sister of the king of Denmark, and the example frightens me."[158] William also recounted that Philip sought to marry Joanna, the widowed sister of Richard I of England, but that "many noble women, fearing the recent example of the Danish girl to whom, after one night of marriage, he gave a writing of repudiation, shamefully rejecting her with great scandal, spurned marriage with him."[159] He did arrange a contract with another German noblewoman, but she never made it to Paris: on her way, she passed through the territory of a nobleman who had previously sought to marry her, and she married him instead.[160] Only after this did he turn to Agnes.

The reaction that William described to Philip's overtures indicates how widely known were his travails, and Agnes's parents would have been well aware. To send one's daughter off to marry a very powerful man, but one whom the pope was being urged to recognize as already married, was likely a calculated risk. William claimed that her parents sent her to be a concubine. Even if that was not the intention, they knew that it was a possibility. Philip and she got on well: Innocent's biographer mentions not only that Philip did not want to take back Ingeborg because he hated her so vehemently but also that he was reluctant to lose Agnes.[161] It is not clear how far he would have gone to support her rights if she had not died; in order to get the interdict lifted, he did banish her from court, but he managed to convince the papal legate that she should not be driven from the kingdom because she was pregnant. (This pregnancy may have caused her death: "But the Lord himself gave judgment in the case, because after she gave birth, she became seriously ill and died").[162] No doubt having her marriage declared invalid and her children bastards would have been very upsetting if only for the shame and the loss of status, even if she did not have feelings for Philip. Philip may well have come to love her, but he was also concerned with the legitimacy of his children. He did found a monastic house where she was buried, and memorialized her dead parents and sister as well.[163]

Philip was still most reluctant to take Ingeborg back. He wished to marry yet again, and continued in negotiations with the pope, now claiming not affinity with Ingeborg but lack of consummation.[164] Consummation was not, according to accepted canon law, required for a valid marriage, but the ability to consummate was. Impotence caused by witchcraft did not warrant immediate nullification but, according to theologians and canon lawyers, required a five-year period of penance and repeated attempts to consummate. There was disagreement on whether a marriage dissolved on this basis allowed remarriage for the impotent party or whether the recovery of sexual ability would require a return to the earlier marriage; to the extent that it was a juridical incapacity that prevented the contracting of a marriage, it applied to all marriages of the affected party.[165] Perhaps Philip had not pushed non-consummation earlier because his advisers knew that it did not automatically lead to nullity. It might, too, have derogated somewhat from his own virility, although he had already demonstrated the latter by fathering a son. But perhaps the marriage actually had been consummated, as Ingeborg steadfastly claimed—"as the natural order required, he paid the marriage debt"—and he was merely grasping at straws.[166] Jean Gaudemet suggests that the focus on consummation during the pontificate of Innocent III represents a shift in the direction of canon law, but it seems more likely a case of desperation, since the affinity argument did not work.[167] Philip's lawyers tried to make a distinction between intercourse (the commingling of sexes) and the commingling of seed; in other words, there had been penetration but not ejaculation. The church did not, however, recognize this distinction, which was not a good enough ground to declare the marriage null, and Innocent continued to insist that Ingeborg be treated with full wifely rights: "that he should attempt to treat the queen, admitted to the fullness of royal grace, with marital affection."[168]

Philip had other sexual relationships; his known illegitimate child, Pierre de Charlot, was born between 1205 and 1209 to "a certain lady of Arras." Pierre became bishop of Noyon and held many other high positions. Philip was still seeking to be free of Ingeborg so that he could remarry, but he did not claim that his union with this lady was a marriage: she may not have been of high enough status, or the experience with Innocent over Agnes may have warned him off making such a claim. Yet he did not acknowledge Ingeborg as queen until 1213, having attempted to marry again in the meantime. As Duby suggests, the fact that his son Louis now had a son and the succession looked more secure may have had something to do with his newfound willingness to be married to Ingeborg, although Davidsohn suggests that having Denmark on his side at a time of worsening relations with England may have mattered more. He probably never had sexual intercourse with her again. Ingeborg undertook many religious good works, and we do not know much about her life beyond this. Philip died in 1223 and left her a modest legacy. His son Louis VIII (the son of his first wife, Isabelle) seems to have treated her well in terms of her dower lands, and she made numerous donations for Philip's soul.[169]

We know a bit more about Ingeborg's feelings than Agnes's because some of her letters survive. They reveal shame and loss of status, accompanied by sadness, loneliness, and anger. At least, this is what she wanted to present: presumably, she had someone to write letters for her, and they are highly literary productions. Having met Philip only briefly, she cannot have loved him, but she clearly had a strong sense of her rights and a determination to claim her position as queen, which she had acquired through the exchange of vows. She also claimed to have been treated very harshly after Agnes's death. The situation may not have been as bad as her hyperbolic claims, although it had apparently worsened between the time that the papal legate wrote to the king of Denmark in 1199 and her move to Étampes in 1201, when the pope wrote to Philip, likening her situation to "a hut in a cucumber patch."[170] A letter survives that Ingeborg wrote to Innocent in 1203, cataloging the harsh treatment that she had undergone:

> My lord and husband Philip, the illustrious king of the Franks, persecutes me, since he not only does not treat me as a wife, but seeking to make my youth loathsome with the solitude of prison, he does not cease to annoy me with the insults and calumnies of his followers, that I should consent to him against the laws of marriage and the laws of Christ. . . . Know, holy father, that in my prison there is no solace and I suffer innumerable and unbearable troubles, nor does anyone dare to visit me nor any religious person come to comfort me, nor can I hear the word of God from anyone's mouth to nourish my soul, nor do I have the opportunity to make my confession to a priest. I can rarely hear mass, and never the other hours. Furthermore, no person or messenger from the land of my birth is permitted to come to me or speak with me, with or without letters. My food is often restricted, but I daily eat the bread of tribulation and the drink of want. I can have no medicine that is useful to human frailty, nor anyone to take care of the health of my body or do what will be good for me. I am not allowed to bathe. If I want to be bled, I cannot, and therefore I fear for my vision and lest serious illness come upon me. I have insufficient clothing and it is not such that a queen should have. To complete my misery, low people, who speak with me by the will of the king, never say good words to me, but afflict me with insulting and injurious words.[171]

Étienne of Tournai wrote, probably in 1210 when Philip still had other marital plans in mind, that "because she is destitute of sustenance she has to sell little by little her mean clothing and few dishes."[172] If any of these claims were true, she certainly had other reasons than pride to be unhappy; but whether or not they were true, she succeeded in presenting herself as a wronged woman who patiently and piously bore her mistreatment. She was aware of Agnes, but her tone, in a letter written before the latter's death, speaks not of personal jealousy but of jealousy of her prerogatives: "[B]y diabolical instigation and seduced by the persuasion of some malicious princes, he took additionally [*superinduxit*] the daughter of Duke S. and kept her as his wife."[173]

The legitimation of Philip's children by Agnes cannot have been pleasant for Ingeborg, either, as she considered the bearing of Philip's royal children part of her prerogatives. Bradbury finds Ingeborg's actions as difficult to explain as Philip's: Why did she just not give up and go home when it became clear that she was not wanted?[174] Or why did she not accept Philip's offer of an annual income to join a convent?[175] But if the marriage had, in fact, been consummated, as she claimed, she would have doubts about her future marriage-ability; she might have been concerned that she would not be welcome home in Denmark and her pride would have been severely hurt. And she could not take the veil in a way that would allow Philip to remarry without agreeing that her marriage had not been consummated. Whether through stubbornness and an unwillingness to be forced into a religious life that she had not chosen, through spite, or a sense that Philip was her husband before God, she refused to do so. Indeed, she feared that she might be pressured to join a monastery. When she wrote to Innocent in 1203, she added that if she should later agree to anything that denied the validity of her marriage, he should realize that she did so under duress: "[I]f, compelled by threats and terrors, in feminine fragility I should propose anything against the rights of my marriage, let it not prejudice that marriage, and let it not be received by you, who are the investigator of forced confessions."[176] The reference to ensuring that confessions are not coerced indicates that someone with some knowledge of canon law was helping her write the letter.[177] It is notable that her opposition made a difference in this case. If both parties wanted the divorce, the church would likely have been willing to grant it, but there was considerable backing for a woman who stood her ground.

This case treated the lack of consummation as though it could be a ground for annulment, if only both parties agreed about it. It was, if not a sine qua non, then at least a factor that made the annulment much easier in practice. Philip's case came at the end of the twelfth century, before marriage law in practice had developed as far as it later would, but it was quite clear to Philip that he could not reject one wife and take another, nor could he declare the children of the latter to be in the line of succession, without the church's approval, and that the church as a whole was not prepared simply to accept the opinion of churchmen who were in Philip's pocket. Philip's side had cited a decretal of Alexander III that an unconsummated marriage could be dissolved if one party wanted to enter religion; on this basis, they might have pushed Ingeborg into monastic life and freed Philip to marry.[178] Although "a respectable body of canonical and theological opinion maintained that the pope had the power to dissolve any unconsummated marriage," however, Innocent did not do so (nor, indeed, did other popes until the fifteenth century).[179] It is quite clear that canon law did not hold such a marriage as automatically null.

The case of Philip's marriage to Ingeborg was not the only marital cause célèbre of the period. Philip, in fact, cited to the pope his own father's marriage to Eleanor of Aquitaine, which had been dissolved on the basis of consanguinity (even though they had had a papal dispensation for that consanguinity at the time of their marriage, and the real reasons had to do with personal incompatibility and the lack of sons).[180] Other magnates unhappy with their wives also claimed Philip's situation as a precedent, perhaps one reason that Innocent was so keen on maintaining papal authority in the case.[181] But after Philip, it was largely accepted, at least until the era of Henry VIII of England, that the pope's decision was final.

It was less important that the law governing unions between women and men was now fixed (although it was) than that the question of who had the authority to fix it was now resolved. The ideas that consent made a marriage, that marriages were valid or invalid depending on how they were entered into, and that it was ultimately the pope who was to be the arbiter had taken hold. The way in which a union was formed, and whether the church recognized it as having been validly formed, were taking their place as the basis for evaluating the status of the union. Yet the relative status of the partners, as we shall see in the next chapter, did not lose its importance.

Chapter 2

Unequal Unions

Many unions noted in the previous chapters were between partners of different social levels. Often an elite man formed a union other than marriage with a woman of lower status, either before marrying or while married to a woman who was selected for him for family, political, or economic reasons. This was especially true of monarchs and the highest aristocracy, among whom the practice continued well past the Middle Ages (and is not unheard of today). Considered from the standpoint of marriage as a central institution for the transfer of wealth, these unions were side affairs of little permanent consequence; but they were so common as to become a main avenue for social mobility. At the same time, they let class and gender difference reinforce each other so that relatively wealthy and powerful men could dominate those they felt to be their social inferiors through control of the group's women. These women entered these sexual relationships for many of the same reasons that they might enter a marriage: economic or social advantage or personal desire. Long-term unions involved more than just sexual attraction: they often involved forming a household unit (even if the male partner did not live in it all the time). The partner, usually the man, who contributed more resources had more say over the terms of the liaison. In medieval Europe, men lost less in terms of public reputation by being involved in a union that was not considered marriage, and since their chastity was usually not as highly valued as that of women, they had less incentive to make a permanent bond such as marriage if the resources that the partner brought were not adequate. Social circumstances often dictated that the unions remain in the gray area on the margins of marriage. Perhaps such women would not always have married their partners had they had the opportunity, but the question is moot: the opportunity was not there.

That such a pattern was pervasive does not mean that it was always the same. The relatively free access of men to women of lower status (but not of women to men of lower status) assumed different configurations under different cultural circumstances. This chapter will focus specifically on those unions that were not considered marriage because of the social or cultural distance between the partners, but it will consider widely disparate cases that have only a few features in common. In some such unions, the parties were not legally capable of marrying each other: for example, a slave and a free person, or a Jew and a Christian.[1] In others—for example, a free servant and her master—marriage would have been legally possible but socially impossible (indeed, before the twelfth century, not all canonists agreed that it was legally possible).[2]

In the broadest sense, we can say that the pattern of higher-status men with lower-status women is a result of male dominance or patriarchy: men have generally had more sexual freedom and more economic options than women. This statement does not, however, explain very much. A somewhat more useful model in some societies is "resource polygyny." Where it is an advantage for a man to have more children—especially sons—regardless of who their mother is, because they are potential heirs, because they can be valuable and unthreatening supporters for their legitimate siblings, or simply because it enhances their father's masculine reputation, wealthy men can use their resources to support more than one woman in long-term unions.[3] They can attract more women for short-term liaisons as well, but to the extent that offspring are intended, ongoing relationships are often involved. The church, of course, frowned upon these unions, and both ecclesiastical and secular law generally came to limit inheritance by children of women other than those born of a legally recognized marriage.[4]

Even when conceiving children was a consequence, welcome or unwelcome, rather than a goal, resources still had a great deal to do with the formation of status-imbalanced unions. Both free men and free women chose their partners under various constraints of economic need, parental pressure, and community attitudes. Men were much more likely to have control over resources than women, whether in the form of aristocratic ownership of land or a worker's wages. Where women did have land or other resources, a male relative often exercised some sort of control over them and might be less willing to let them enter a union that did not provide legal protections, as marriage did. Families, status groups, and religious communities could be reluctant to give up women who were seen as belonging collectively to the group.

Enslaved people, the majority of whom were women, had even less

opportunity to choose their partners. We cannot know what went through
the minds of the many slave women who were sexual partners of and had children with their masters. The fact that they were vulnerable to coercion does
not mean that they did not exercise agency. No doubt some women fought
back against coerced sex either physically or by passive noncooperation; no
doubt others acquiesced gladly or even initiated a relationship, in order to
avoid punishment or to secure better living conditions for themselves or their
children. In a situation of domestic intimacy, affection and understanding
could have grown between masters and slaves. Studies of slaves in the Atlan-
tic world indicate this whole range of possibilities, and there is no reason to
think that the range did not apply in the Middle Ages as well. Coercion did
not mean that the woman had no choices, and a woman's making choices did
not mean that she was not coerced. To some extent, the coercion that enslaved
women underwent was different only in degree from that of servants or other
wage workers: any woman who relied on a man for her livelihood, whether she
was that man's wife, employee, or slave, was under some sort of pressure. (Far
fewer men relied on women for their livelihoods.) Slaves had an added layer
of complication in that they were often deracinated: servants might be apart
from their families but were more likely to have communities or resources to
fall back on than slaves who were kidnapped and taken overseas.[5]

Slaveholding societies tolerated married men's long-term extramarital liaisons with their own slaves more readily than most societies did other extramarital unions. This may also be true of serfdom. It is not always possible to
draw a sharp line, legally speaking, between slaves and serfs; the same Latin
term, *servus*, and the same Roman or Roman-influenced legal provisions applied to them. The distinction was largely economic: unfree people who lived
in their own households and supported themselves from the land they worked
for their lord were serfs, those who depended more directly on the owner for
their maintenance were slaves, and there was a market in the latter.[6] Known
across Europe in the early Middle Ages, slavery tended to be a Mediterranean
phenomenon after the first millennium, although it could still be found in
other parts of Europe. The kinds of sexual contact discussed here arose particularly between elite men and women in their household workforce, which
usually meant that the women were slaves or free servants rather than serfs.

Because so many medieval enterprises—whether mercantile, artisanal, or
agricultural—were organized on a household basis, it is not easy to draw a
sharp line between domestic service and other forms of labor. Workers hired
for their masters' enterprises could be made to do domestic chores for their

employers, and domestic workers could be assigned commercial tasks if necessary. Apprentices might have the protection of a contract that stated what kinds of work they could do; slaves, of course, had no choice. As a general rule, however, women slaves' and servants' tasks tended to be more on the domestic side—feeding and clothing the household, rather than producing for the market. This fit in with prevailing gender ideologies about women's responsibility for the maintenance of the family. It also meant that, although they were by no means restricted to the home, much of their work was performed there, and they would come into frequent contact with the men of the household and were perhaps more vulnerable to sexual coercion from within their own household than outside it.

Slaves also formed long-term unions with each other. By the twelfth century, the church officially recognized marriage between two slaves, but owners still exercised a good deal of control, whether the slave was marrying a slave of the same owner or another.[7] Since slaves formally owned nothing that could be inherited and the child was generally the property of the mother's owner, marriage did not have as great a legal impact on slaves as on those higher up in society; however, to two people who could not make many choices about their lives, the ceremony of marriage may have been more meaningful than to people who could take it for granted. But despite the formal recognition of some slave marriages, as this chapter will discuss, many unions between slaves, like those between slaves and free people, took other forms.

It is fair to call the status of partners in cross-religious unions not just different but unequal: each religious community considered the others lesser in truth, if not in power, and each tried to prevent their women from forming relationships with the men of the others. Marriage was a religious phenomenon, so Christians and Jews could not technically marry each other unless one of them converted; a mixed marriage was an oxymoron.[8] (Islam recognized marriages between Muslim men and Christian or Jewish women, but not between Muslim women and Christian or Jewish men.) Someone who did convert in order to marry was likely to be shunned by his or her community of origin and was not likely to bring much to the marriage in the way of material support. Nevertheless, the sources provide evidence for long-term unions other than marriage between people of different religions. Again, it was usually the man who belonged to the dominant group and the woman to a subordinate group.[9]

The argument that women of lower status entered into unions other than marriage because they did not have the bargaining power to make them marriages assumes that marriage was the better situation for a woman. That was not always the case, as we saw with Heloise. Women may have chosen not to marry because they did not want to be under the legal control of a husband, and there were a surprising number who remained single both in religion and in the secular world.[10] Married women had legal protection but also often lost control over whatever resources they had, and they had less recourse than the single in situations of domestic violence.[11] The question of whether women (or men) were better off in a long-term domestic partnership than outside of one is not really answerable, nor is the question of whether any individual woman of lower status in a domestic partnership was better off married or not married. Medieval society fairly clearly assumed that it was an advantage for such women to be married, which could mean that it was a disadvantage to their husbands.

Aristocrats and Other Elites

A considerable number, perhaps most, of the medieval unions about which we have information, whether they were marital or not, involved aristocrats, who left the most records. Many aristocratic men formed unions either before or during their marriages with women whom they had no intention of marrying, usually lower in rank. Often we have very little information about the women, not even their names, and the only reason we know about the unions at all is that chronicles tell us about noblemen's illegitimate children. Before a marriage had been arranged for them for political or economic reasons, aristocratic young men had the option to enter relationships with women who were not potential marriage partners (as happened with Waldrada in Chapter 1). This pattern continued throughout the Middle Ages, with considerable chronological and regional variation that cannot be discussed in detail here. Georges Duby makes a major point of Lambert of Ardres's invocation of the sexual double standard in late twelfth-century France/Flanders: men were expected to have a number of affairs while women were expected to be faithful.[12] Close examination of this source and others from the period shows that this was considered acceptable and normal for a bachelor, but once he was married, fidelity was the church's expectation for him, too.[13] But plenty of aristocratic men throughout the Middle Ages continued to have relationships with other women after they married. It is clear enough why they might wish to, if their marriages were arranged with little thought to compatibility. It is also clear enough why, despite being equally or more unhappy in marriage, most aristocratic women did not form similar unions with lower-status men: their social position and the legitimacy of their children was at risk. But what of the women of lower status who entered into unions with aristocratic men? Why did women who were not starving or in need of a means to keep body and soul together choose to do so? Once again, we have very little information about their motivations, but sometimes there is material from which to infer.

This section only scratches the surface of unions of this sort because the focus of this chapter is on clear-cut status differences (slave/free, Jew/Christian). I present only one case involving two aristocrats—hardly a typical one, but perhaps the one from the Middle Ages for which the most information is available. Unlike slaves, who had no choice, women from minor noble or gentry families were not generally coerced into the sexual unions they entered with the high nobility. Like Waldrada in Chapter 1, they or their families made a decision. An example from later fourteenth-century England suggests some reasons why such a woman, of relatively high status in relation to the society as a whole, would agree to or even seek out a relationship that did not bring her the privileges of marriage. This case is a rarity because the woman did end up marrying her partner, and the reasons that it was possible in this instance, the couple's motivations, and the reaction of their contemporaries to the reclassification of the union as a marriage tell us something about the parameters of cross-rank unions in the period.

"A Lady Who Knew Much of Honor": Katherine Swynford

Born in 1350, Katherine de Roet was the daughter of a knight from Hainault associated with the court of Philippa, wife of Edward III of England. Katherine made an expected sort of marriage—to an approximate social equal—in her teens with an English knight, Hugh Swynford.[14] They had at least two children. Her sister Philippa married an up-and-coming man of bourgeois origin, Geoffrey Chaucer, who held various posts in the royal administration of Edward III and wrote poetry on the side.

Katherine had served as a lady-in-waiting to Blanche of Lancaster, first wife of John of Gaunt, son of Edward III (the title Duke of Lancaster was given to Gaunt after Blanche's father died without a son). She remained a part of Blanche's household after her marriage to Hugh Swynford.[15] This sort of court position was open to women of middling rank like Katherine: not a servant, but still far from an equal of the ducal household in which she lived.

Her daughter Blanche Swynford, named after the duchess, was raised in the household, and John of Gaunt was her godfather. After Blanche's death in 1368, Katherine helped care for John and Blanche's children. In 1371, two or three years after Blanche's death, Lancaster made another political marriage, to Constance of Castile, and they had a daughter. Katherine became part of Constance's household.

Sometime after the death of Blanche, either before or shortly after John's marriage to Constance, he and Katherine began a sexual relationship. It is not clear whether the beginning of this union preceded the death of Hugh Swynford in 1371–72.[16] By 1380, Katherine and John had had four children, and Katherine had become governess to John's two daughters by Blanche. Constance died in 1394, and John and Katherine married in 1396, twenty to twenty-five years after they had begun their relationship. They remained together until his death, in 1403. The relationship was public knowledge even during Constance's lifetime: in addition to the grants of land and other valuables that Katherine received from Gaunt for herself and for the care of his and Blanche's daughters, she also received gifts from those who wanted her influence with him.[17] For example, the account books of the mayor of Leicester for 1375–76 list sixteen shillings for wine for "Lady Katherine of the Duke of Lancaster" and for 1377–79 money for a horse for "Lady Katherine of Swinford" and a pan of iron, "given to the said Katherine for expediting the business touching the tenement in Stretton, and for other business for which a certain lord besought the aforesaid Katherine . . . so successfully that the aforesaid town was pardoned the lending of silver to the King in that year."[18]

For a member of the royal family to maintain a relationship with a woman for a long period of time was not unheard of. Alice Perrers was openly the mistress of Edward III even before his queen's death in 1369 and remained with him until his death, in 1377. But Perrers, wildly unpopular for her corruption, was hardly a good model; although Edward enriched her greatly, he certainly did not marry her after his wife's death. For a duke to marry the daughter and widow of mere knights, the mother of illegitimate children (even his own!) was very unusual. It was possible with Katherine, while it would not have been with a servant, because Katherine's birth and upbringing were not all that low: she was the daughter of a knight in royal service, and she herself had served at court, so she knew courtly manners.

The reasons for Katherine's and John's turning their union into a marriage may have involved romantic love. But even the novelist Anya Seton, who made of Katherine Swynford's life a great love story, suggested that the affair had cooled off significantly by the time of the marriage and that the main reason for the marriage was to benefit the children.[19] The children bore the surname Beaufort; after their parents' marriage, John became earl of Somerset, Henry bishop of Lincoln, Thomas duke of Exeter, and Joan countess of Westmorland (by marriage). Once again, titles for the illegitimate children of royalty were not uncommon, and John of Gaunt, as the most powerful man in his nephew Richard II's kingdom, could do as he liked. The fact that he chose not merely to provide adequately for his children but also to place them among the highest nobility probably indicates not only a sense of responsibility but also real paternal care for them. He may also have thought that they could help support his and Blanche's son, Henry Bolingbroke (who became Henry IV in 1399), as indeed they did.

Legitimacy for children born in this kind of relationship was not easy. English common law did not allow for the legitimation of children by subsequent marriage of their parents, as canon law did, but Gaunt got Parliament to legitimize them in 1397.[20] Perhaps he would have had a harder time doing this had he not married their mother. This particular marriage did not automatically legitimize the children under canon law, either, because they were conceived in adultery, but once Constance was dead, Gaunt and Katherine had little problem getting a dispensation from the pope to marry despite the adultery and the further impediment that Gaunt had been godfather to Blanche Swynford.[21] In 1407, Henry IV confirmed the legitimation of his half-siblings but took them out of the succession to the throne. This did not stop Henry Tudor in 1485 from successfully claiming it through his mother, Margaret Beaufort, granddaughter of Katherine's son John.

Although the marriage to Gaunt made Katherine a duchess, it did not make her an equal in the eyes of the other duchesses, her sisters-in-law, as the chronicler Jean Froissart reported:

> For love of these three [*sic*] children, the duke of Lancaster married their mother, to the great astonishment of France and England, for she was of low lineage compared to the two other ladies, the duchesses Blanche and Constance, whom Duke John had previously had in marriage. The high ladies of England, such as the duchess of York, the duchess of Gloucester, the countess of Derby, the countess of Arundel, and the other ladies descended of the royal blood of England, were very astonished and greatly blamed this deed, and said that the duke of Lancaster had greatly lowered and disgraced

himself when he had married his concubine, and because things
had come to where [Katherine] would be the second lady in the
kingdom, "the queen will now be received with recriminations."
They said further: "We will let her do the honors all alone. We will
not go any place where she might be; because we would be greatly
criticized if such a duchess, who comes from a base lineage and who
has been the concubine of the duke for a very long time during his
marriages, even if she is now married, should come before us." And
those who spoke the most of this, the duke of Gloucester and the
duchess his wife, thought the duke of Lancaster was mad and out
of his mind when he had married his concubine, and said that they
would not do him honor for this marriage, and call her neither lady
nor sister. . . . She was a lady who knew much of honor, because she
had been since her youth and her whole life brought up at court,
and the Duke of Lancaster greatly loved the children that he had
with this lady, as he well showed them in death and in life.[22]

Froissart was no fan of John of Gaunt and also had a strong tendency to
embroider his stories. He may well have exaggerated the reaction of other aristocratic women, but given the unusual nature of the marriage, it is plausible.
Other chroniclers similarly directed their vehemence not against Katherine
alone but upon Gaunt as well. He was criticized for his adultery and for his
general lechery, not only in relation to Katherine. Thomas Gascoigne (1404–
58) wrote that he died of a putrefaction of his genitals "caused by his frequenting of women. For he was a great fornicator."[23] The monastic chronicler of
St. Albans wrote that the people in the late 1370s were upset with Gaunt because of his troops' pillaging and, in addition, "disregarding shame before men
and the fear of God, he was seen riding about the country with an infamous
whore, a certain Katherine called de Swynford, even holding her reins publicly
not only in the presence of his wife but with all his countrymen seeing."[24] This
chronicler as well as others report that after the Peasants' Revolt of 1381, when
his palace was burned down, he repented his past life and did not continue the
relationship with Katherine. As one chronicler put it, "as he supposed, God
wanted to chastise him for his misdeeds and the evil life which he had lived
for a long time, namely in the sin of lechery, of which he had special shame
with lady Katherine of Swinford, a devil and enchantress, and many others
around his wife, against the will of God and the law of holy church."[25] Henry
Knighton reports that "he turned over in his mind how, and how often, he

had heard both from churchmen and from his servants how much his reputation in almost all parts of the kingdom had been denigrated for a long time,
and how he had not considered how it would be said that he was blinded by
concupiscence, neither fearing God nor blushing before men," specifically because of Katherine, and therefore "vowed to God that as soon as he could, he
would remove this lady from his household."[26] Thomas Walsingham reported
that because of his repentance, "he abhorred the company of this Katherine Swynford, or rather abjured it."[27] These contemporaries suggested that
aristocratic men, although it was not surprising if they had mistresses, could
come under considerable criticism for flaunting them. The chroniclers, loyal
churchmen, had reasons for enmity toward Gaunt—notably, his patronage of
John Wycliffe and his general hostility toward the institutional church—but
they framed the enmity in terms of his sexual morality. Alison Weir suggests
that Katherine's great fertility before 1381 and the lack of it afterward, although
she was still only in her early thirties, indicate that the chroniclers may be right
about the separation, but that Gaunt hardly abhorred her, continuing his gen-
erosity; she also lent him money. They were back together in the early 1390s.[28]

Katherine may have loved Gaunt, as Seton suggests. She may have seen
an opportunity to improve her life and achieve wealth and power, as indeed
she did, holding many lands and wardships; but her position also suffered for
years because of the unofficial status of their union. Even after they married,
she may have been hurt that Gaunt left instructions that he be buried next to
his first wife, Blanche, although he did leave Katherine substantial legacies.[29]
Henry of Bolingbroke, after he seized the throne in 1399, confirmed Katherine
in the sizable income from Lancaster lands that his father had given her.[30] And
Katherine perhaps got the last word. During the reign of Henry VII (1485–
1509), a new tombstone was made for John of Gaunt, listing his three wives:
"And third he married Catharine, from a knightly family, and a woman of the
highest beauty, from whom he had numerous children, from whom Henry
VII, the most prudent King of England, traces his maternal line."[31]

Today, unlike John of Gaunt's more aristocratic but less colorful first and
second wives, Katherine has multiple blogs and a Facebook group devoted
to her, as well as at least one novel and a scholarly biography. The fascination comes largely from her anomalous position: very few women made the
crossover from mistress to wife. In the later Middle Ages, if a woman was
of low enough status relative to her partner to enter into a union that was
not considered a marriage, she was generally not of high enough status for
him to marry later. By the time Constance died, however, Gaunt could please

himself. As the uncle of Richard II, he was one of the most important men in the kingdom, and possibly the wealthiest. He had little need to shore up his social position. He had a son to succeed to his lands and titles (indeed, Richard's reluctance to let his cousin do so led to Henry's rebellion and seizure of the throne). He was of high enough rank to be able to marry a princess, but he had already been there and done that: his marriage to Constance had brought him a claim to the throne of Castile on which he had spent years trying to make good. Richard might well not have been eager to let him remarry a woman who would bring him even more wealth and claims to power, and, at this point, he would have had little incentive to do so. Although his relationship with Katherine may have begun before his marriage to Constance, however, there was no question of his marrying her at that time. Marriage, among people of his rank, was usually for dynastic purposes, and other purposes called for other kinds of union.

Men like Gaunt could simply have picked out a woman and made her an offer that she could not refuse. But one could tell an equally plausible story about a woman in Katherine's situation seeking the relationship, whether out of desire for the man or for the material support that he could offer. In England, the status of "concubine" was not formally recognized, even though the chroniclers used the term and described contemporaries using it as an insult. But aristocratic men with mistresses of slightly lower status were common enough. Marriage to a concubine was possible occasionally in the Italian urban context, as it was among the English nobility. Carol Lansing documents a Bologna case in which one Zannos was accused by a woman named Divitia of raping her after promising her marriage; he said that he had promised, rather, to take her as an *amica* (girlfriend or concubine) until they had children. "When I have children from you I will have just cause to ask my father's permission to take you as my wife without a dowry and then I'll take you as my wife." The prospect of a man getting his father's permission to marry his concubine in order to legitimate his children was apparently plausible enough that Zannos won his case, even though it was not very common.[32]

As Emlyn Eisenach notes in her work on sixteenth-century Verona, in an argument that could be made about aristocrats as well as urban elites, relations between elite men and their concubines may be more complex than scholars have assumed. It is true, she notes, that "concubinage gave elite men the opportunity to establish one or more emotionally satisfying relationships; these could be either in addition to a legitimate wife, before settling down to legitimate marriage, or when aristocratic family strategy required that a man remain single in order to limit the number of legitimate heirs and thus demands on family patrimony."[33] However, Eisenach points out, concubinage could also challenge the aristocratic marriage system, as women of lower status became absorbed into elite families and created links between social levels. Indeed, she suggests that "one can imagine elite men themselves seeing the practice from two perspectives: as men who kept concubines and as the fathers of daughters married to men who kept concubines."[34] A concubine could threaten the authority and honor of the wife; at the same time, she could arrogate some of that authority and power to herself. The same principle could work in circumstances lower down the social scale. Lansing presents another case from Bologna from 1285, in which a concubine whose partner had married was accused of returning to his house and ejecting his wife. Henricho had a child with his *amaxia* Adelasia. She left his home when he married. A witness claimed that when the wife's dowry was not paid as promised, Henricho had dismissed her and taken Adelasia back. Whether or not that testimony was true, it is clear that a bond existed between the man and his earlier partner, and plausible that the initiative in the situation was not all with Henricho. As Lansing points out, since the case was brought by the new wife's family seeking to restore her position in Henricho's household, there was a reason for them to attribute the agency to Adelasia rather than Henricho.[35]

Not all wealthy men wanted to marry the mothers of their children and legitimate the children, even if they could. If a man already had children from a previous marriage and did not have resources like those of the duchy of Lancaster, he might not want to break up the inheritance by making more offspring eligible for it. Sending a concubine into the marriage pool generously endowed when her partner married elsewhere, a not uncommon practice, not only encouraged the circulation of dowry wealth (a significant factor in late medieval Italian towns) among the lower classes as well as the elites but also gave such a woman options in the choice of a husband of her own status that she might not otherwise have had, especially if it was a lack of dowry that compelled her to enter a union other than marriage in the first place.[36]

These few examples stand in for a quite common practice of elite men before, or even during, their marriages. The pattern in which the woman was economically dependent on the man such that the union may have been coercive—a pattern that was found also in marriage—permeated all social levels. Slavery and other forms of service were common especially in the Mediterranean region and provided an institutionalized, if not entirely legal, means

for men to establish long-term unions with women they could not and would not marry.

Masters, Slaves, and Servants

Roman law was particularly influential in the law of slavery in the Middle Ages; under it, slaves could not marry. The legal consequences of their unions were minimal. The personal status of any children followed that of their mother; they were slaves, as she was, and the property of her owner, a situation that the Romans attributed to the law of nations (*ius gentium*) and not merely their own statute.[37] The Romans generally presumed that the partners would both be slaves or that the male partner would be of higher status: a freedman or a free man who had a child with a slave. If the woman were of higher status—in particular, if she were free and of good family—a union with a slave, even a legal marriage with a freed slave, was looked on with horror. If a free woman had a child with someone else's slave, furthermore, the child could be considered a slave even if the mother were free, and the woman herself could be enslaved.[38]

The early church pushed for the recognition of slaves' unions as marriage, although not unanimously. In Christ, there was "neither slave nor free" (Gal. 3:28), but the New Testament did not demand the abolition of slavery in this life. The church, like the secular world, still recognized the existence of social hierarchy.[39] Changing social conditions in late antiquity, however, made marriage between slaves less problematic for owners. Slaves were increasingly "hutted" (*casati*), meaning that they had their own houses and plots of land and were responsible for supporting themselves rather than living in barracks and being fed, however skimpily, by their owners. In this situation, the owner may have had an interest in the slaves having families so that they could work as households. Promoting permanent unions was one way of achieving this. By the later Roman period, mixed unions between free people and slaves became more common, and Judith Evans-Grubbs suggests that legislation of Constantine in 320 indicated that young free women of low social status might be all too easily fooled into entering unions with slave men without parental permission. Women in unions with their own slaves were punished severely, and this was expanded in the fifth century to unions in which the woman had freed the man and married him.[40] The successor kingdoms adopted similar laws.[41]

Slave owners who preferred their slaves to live in family groups may also

have had a religious interest in making these unions legal marriages. As noted
in Chapter 1, in the story from the life of St. Emmeram, masters might compel
their slaves to go through a formal marriage because they thought that it would
tie them to their locale and provide reliable workers. Polyptychs of the ninth
century indicate that slaves were considered married, using the term *uxor* for
wives.[42] The Council of Verberie in 756 dealt with slave marriage extensively: a
free man or woman who unknowingly married a slave was allowed to remarry,
and if a slave had his own slave as a concubine, he could dismiss her to marry
the slave of his master.[43] No reference was made there to a *dos* or any other formal elements of a marriage. The Council of Tribur, legislating for the eastern
Frankish kingdom in 895, actually used Leo's letter to Rusticus to support the
claim, not that a marriage with a slave woman was invalid, but that a marriage with a freed woman was valid: "If a free man takes a freed woman, that
is, a slave woman made free by manumission and royal liberality, in legitimate
marriage, he must keep her thenceforward as with a woman born of a noble
family, except in case of fornication; and as long as she lives, he shall not take
another. She is, according to the aforementioned decree of Pope Leo, made
freeborn and legitimately endowed and made honest by public marriage, and
because of this she is now not a concubine, but a legitimately acquired wife.
Let the law be the same, according to sex, with a woman and a freed man."[44]
This canon required only the step of freeing the slave, not a *dos* or even public
marriage. Like many church rulings, it reflects more evenhandedness between
the genders than was probably observed in practice.

The Council of Chalons in 813 held that slaves' marriages were valid even
if they belonged to different owners, although this statement was qualified
with the statement "where there was a legal union by the will of their lords."[45]
In the Byzantine empire, the emperor Alexius Comnenus in 1095 ruled that
slaves who were married in Christian ceremonies were not automatically free,
implying that such marriages were valid and encouraging masters to allow
them. Despite such proclamations, slaves continued to live in other kinds of
unions, partly because owners had an easier time selling them separately than
as a couple.[46] Gratian's twelfth-century legal compilation makes clear that in
his view, unlike in Roman law, slaves could legally marry; Gratian took a passage from Justinian's code out of context to make a blanket statement about
the indissolubility of slave marriage.[47] He did not mention the need for the
master's consent to a marriage between two slaves, which other sources agreed
upon, just as he did not deem parents' consent necessary to the marriage of
their children.[48]

By the time of Gratian, canon law was even recognizing the possibility of marriage between a slave and a free person. As Anders Winroth points out, Gratian was very concerned with the question of "error of condition," that is, when a free person (particularly a woman) married an unfree person (particularly a man) without knowing it. Such a marriage was not valid because there was no real consent, since the free partner thought that the consent was given to a different person. Gratian made the analogy to a purchaser who received an alloy instead of gold, and termed the situation one of fraud.[49] He seemed to think, however, that such a marriage would be valid if the free partner were aware of the slave's status, a position that was not universally accepted. Of course, this awareness would be required in order for the free partner first to purchase the slave (if necessary), then free him or her, which would have been the usual practice for a formal marriage.

Most unions between free persons and slaves about which the sources tell us were not formal marriages. Elite men's sexual access to subordinate women was not uncommon in agricultural populations—it is precisely this phenomenon that gave rise to the myth of the *ius primae noctis*, or *droit de cuissage*.[50] But most agricultural slaves and other workers, at least on larger estates, did not live with their masters. Although some scholars have assumed that the weaving workshops (*gynecaea*) of the early Middle Ages were the equivalent of harems, there is little evidence for this. Slave women in such workshops may have been sexually available to their owners but were not acquired primarily for sexual purposes, and their living arrangements could hardly be called a domestic partnership.[51] Where masters and subordinates lived under the same roof, however, especially in towns, such unions would become more common.

Whether one was a slave or a servant made a great deal of difference in some ways, but not so much in others. Servants in later medieval towns were generally hired on one-year or multiyear contracts, and if they left a position before the end of the contract, the employer's only likely remedy would be withholding wages due at the end of the contract, or preventing someone else from hiring them.[52] If they did not want to work for a particular employer, they did not have to take that position. Slaves did not have a choice and could be bought and sold against their will, far from home. Economic circumstances, however, could erode the autonomy of servants; they could not, in practice, leave a job if they had no prospect of finding another and no family nearby to turn to, as was often the case. (Although servants were not drawn from the ranks of foreigners, as slaves often were, they often came from outside the town in which they worked.) Some girls were put into service by their families quite young, for long periods of time, so their freedom was, in practice, very circumscribed.[53] In addition, some workers of intermediate status, particularly in Italy, were contracted to work as servants and compensated only with their food and clothing and a dowry to be given at the end of the contractual period.[54] Legally, they were not unfree, but they had no freedom of movement. They were placed under contract by their parents in situations quite similar to those in which girls might be sold into slavery. While slaves were generally foreign, these girls, called *anime* in Venice, could come from the nearby countryside: Venetian legislation in 1388 decreed that children from nearer than Corfu could not be enslaved but would be under contract as *anime*, whereas anyone from farther away would be considered enslaved.[55]

By the later Middle Ages, slaves were most likely to be found along the edges of Christian western Europe, especially the Mediterranean. Technically, Christians were not supposed to enslave other Christians; that often did not stop Latin Christians from enslaving Orthodox Christians, but Muslim slaves were most common. In northern Europe, the conversion of Scandinavia meant that new recruitment into slavery had ceased by the eleventh century; slavery was officially abolished only in one province of Sweden, in 1335, but it was probably not a significant social force after the twelfth century.[56] In the Baltic region, pagan Prussians and Lithuanians captured by the Teutonic Knights and their allies could be enslaved—especially women and children—but there is little hard evidence on numbers or on where they ended up.[57] Large numbers of people conquered in the course of the German push into the Baltic regions became unfree peasants but were not enslaved.

It was in the Mediterranean region, which was more heavily urbanized and where there was a greater degree of contact with non-Christians, that slavery was most prevalent in the central to later Middle Ages. In Spain, Muslims who had been captured in the course of the wars of reconquest could be enslaved, but by the later Middle Ages, most slaves there were Muslims from North Africa, acquired through trade as well as war and piracy, as well as local Muslims in penal servitude.[58] Throughout the Mediterranean, slaves worked in agriculture but increasingly in the household, whether assisting with domestic production in the crafts or with reproduction, that is, feeding and clothing the family. Large households might have as many slaves as they did family members, but even more modest artisan households owned slaves.[59]

The preponderance of women in the slave population seems to have been a function of both supply and demand. Slaves were valued particularly in domestic service, which was a feminine occupation. Women might also be thought less likely to flee.[60] Bensch suggests that many slave owners were women, and the preponderance of women slaves, which emerged in the thirteenth century, had to do with the articulation of a separate sphere for women.[61] But enslaved women were also more available on the market overall. Mark Meyerson has shown that of 583 Muslim slaves sold on the slave market at Valencia between 1479 and 1503, only 42 percent were women, and he suggests that the continued raiding in this region brought in male as well as female captives.[62] But where slaves entered western Europe through trade rather than raids, they did tend to be female. Girls were more likely than boys to be sold or bartered into slavery by needy families.[63]

The sexual use of female slaves was undoubtedly also a factor in the gender imbalance in slavery. While it was generally known and even accepted in western Europe that some men had sexual relations with female slaves, or paid attention to physical attractiveness when they purchased slaves for general domestic work, it was not openly acknowledged the way it was, for example, in Muslim culture, where it was allowed by the Qur'an (Sura 23:6), or, as Sally McKee points out, in Italian overseas colonies.[64] Christian men who purchased slaves explicitly for sexual purposes were probably relatively rare; it was more likely, from their point of view, a serendipitous arrangement. For married men, it was usually the wife who supervised the household workers, and while she might not be able to do anything about the husband's sexual relations with his female slaves or servants, she might be able to prevent the acquisition of one just for that reason. In one example that stands for many more, a baptized former Muslim named Maria, a slave in a household in Alicante in 1503, was sent to Valencia to be sold because the wife of her owner was jealous.[65] It was not unusual, on the other hand, for a free woman to marry a man who had had previous sexual relations with slaves or servants, and to raise the children of those relationships in her home. Margheretta Datini, wife of Francesco Datini of Prato, had no children but raised Ginevra, her husband's daughter by a slave. She wrote to him when Ginevra was ill: "Be assured that I look after her as if she were my own, as indeed I consider her."[66]

Unmarried men may have bought female slaves to fulfill the various functions that a wife would otherwise perform—not only sex but a whole range of domestic labor, including the preparation of food and general management of the household. While some men lived in their parents' households until they married, others, including merchants, needed to establish a temporary household in an unfamiliar city. As Stuard writes of Ragusa, "Slaves provided this bachelor population with domestic services, which promoted civil tranquility.

An urban, largely male, unmarried population could be as detrimental to the keeping of the peace as roving bands of male servants. Female slaves provided some a domestic establishment, and, in all likelihood, companionship and a sexual outlet."[67]

Scholars know as much as they do about slaves in Mediterranean cities because of the large number of acts of sale and purchase recorded in notarial registers, which have been studied by Charles Verlinden, Jacques Heers, and, more recently, Debra Blumenthal, Steven Epstein, and Sally McKee. These acts specify the price paid for a slave, and usually the name, national origin, sometimes a physical description, and age. It is impossible to determine from this information whether the slave was considered a potential sexual partner. However, from series of data, it is possible to determine numbers of slaves, who owned them, and which ages and ethnic groups were valued most highly.

In Italy, slaves were found particularly in the major port cities of Genoa and Venice but in Sicily and throughout the rest of the peninsula as well. They included southern Slavs from Dalmatia, Russians, Circassians, Greeks, North Africans, and, especially after 1450, sub-Saharan Africans. Patterns of purchase varied over time and space. For Sicily, for example, Charles Verlinden found that in the thirteenth century, slaves came primarily from Spain and North Africa and were 97 percent Muslim. In the fourteenth century, Greeks, Tartars, Albanians, and Russians became more numerous, and men became more numerous among most ethnic groups (although women remained more expensive). By the second half of the fifteenth century, there were many more "black" slaves.[68] Similar patterns prevailed in Genoa, and elsewhere in Italy: slaves from the western Mediterranean in the thirteenth century, a shift to slaves from the Black Sea region from the late thirteenth century to the mid-fifteenth, and the western Mediterranean again in the second half of the fifteenth century, when Italians no longer had access to Black Sea ports.[69] Among "Saracen" slaves in Italy, men tended to be the majority throughout, perhaps because they were the most likely to have been captured in pirate raids.[70]

Jacques Heers estimated that in towns like Barcelona and Genoa, slaves probably constituted 10 percent of the female population between twenty-five and thirty years of age.[71] Stephen Bensch found that of 263 laypeople who made wills in Barcelona from 1100 to 1290, 21 percent owned at least one slave.[72] A detailed census of one section of Palermo (Sicily) in 1480 indicated that slaves constituted 12 percent of the overall population: of 513 slaves, 166 are known to have been males and 255 females.[73] Debra Blumenthal found that between 1460 and 1480 in Valencia, while the Muslim captives of corsairs and penal slaves were the majority of slaves, perhaps a quarter of slaves came through trade from the eastern Mediterranean, and they were overwhelmingly female; toward the end of the century, slaves were increasingly black Africans and Canary Islanders acquired through trade.[74] Sally McKee's database of more than 2,000 contracts of sale for slaves around the Mediterranean, mostly from Venice and Genoa, between 1360 and 1499 found an overall percentage of 80 percent women.[75]

Women in their late teens through early thirties commanded the highest prices, presumably because they were the most capable of work. Verlinden found in a study of Venice notarial registers that the prime age for women in terms of price was eighteen to twenty-two, and prices dropped sharply for women older than thirty.[76] Younger girls or older women would not be expected to have the same strength and skill. Eighteen to twenty-two are also among the years in which women would be most valued as sexual partners, but there is no way to know how much of the price difference, if any, is for this reason. McKee argues compellingly, however, that "[t]he price of slaves grew so high over the course of the fourteenth and fifteenth centuries that the purchase of a slave woman for domestic work could in no way be considered economically efficient. If, however, sexual service is factored into explanations for increased demand, then the rise in the cost for female slaves in this period becomes more understandable."[77]

It is unlikely that the potential of these slaves for childbearing was the reason for the high price. Pregnancy in a slave woman at the time she was sold was considered a defect, thought to make her work less efficient and to put her life (and therefore a valuable piece of property) at risk. The cost of rearing a child to the point where it would be valued as a worker was apparently so high as not to make it worthwhile, and the children of slaves seem frequently to have been abandoned. A slave who had given birth could be of value to her master by being hired out as a wet nurse, but this required giving up her own child, which owners were apparently quite happy to do. Indeed, renting out the slaves as wet nurses may have been an excuse for preying sexually on slave women.[78] In Florence, of 7,584 children placed in the orphanage of the Innocenti from 1385 to 1485, at least 1,096 were the children of slave women and unacknowledged fathers.[79] In one instance, a woman who had a child by her master and sent it to the Innocenti later kidnapped the child back.[80] A *catasto* (tax assessment) from 1458 from Florence listed 557 illegitimate children. Of these, the name of the mother was given for 407. At least 141 of the mothers were slaves; another 84 were servants. Of the remainder, it is entirely likely that some of the mothers were slaves or servants and merely not listed as such.[81] Sometimes slave children (not necessarily only those fathered by their masters) were raised within the household, playing with the legitimate children as they grew up.[82] But pregnancy in slaves was still not generally considered an advantage.

The records show a consistent pattern of lower prices for "Moorish" or "black" slaves than for Greeks or Slavs. Scholars disagree on the applicability of "race" as a category in the medieval period, since some see the category itself as coming into existence only with the invention of scientific racism in the nineteenth century. However, already in the later Middle Ages, if not earlier, people were making distinctions on the basis of skin color, more often for identification purposes than to determine how the slaves would be treated.[83] Perhaps it would be best to see this process as belonging to the prehistory, rather than the history, of "race." It is not clear how much of the difference in the desirability of various national groups as slaves had to do with physical attractiveness. Guy Romestan found in Rousillon and Perpignan that in the early fifteenth century, the women sold as slaves were mostly white, while the men were called black or Saracen, and that when people placed orders with merchants, there was a strong preference for white slaves.[84] Blumenthal found in Valencia in the late fifteenth century that black women brought a much lower price than white ones; the effect was not as strong for black men until the end of the century.[85] Beliefs about the reliability, hard work, susceptibility to illness, or moral laxity of different groups, as well as about their sexual desirability, no doubt affected price. As McKee points out, we cannot assume that "sexual acts were motived [sic] chiefly by desire inspired by beauty."[86]

Whether or not enslaved women were purchased for their sexual attractiveness, the law did little to protect them from the sexual attentions of their masters. Slaves were not treated entirely the same as other sorts of property— the law did protect them from some violent punishments—but forced sex with the master was not prosecuted as rape.[87] A black woman in Valencia, Leonor, described her arrival into the household of Luis Almenara: "Seeing himself as her lord and seeing that she could not contradict him, he took 'love' from her whenever he willed, knowing her carnally one and many times." The sex was coerced, but when Leonor gave birth to a daughter, Luis threw a large baptismal feast and celebrated the occasion "as if she were the daughter of his wife."[88] Because she had no legal personality, the slave could not bring a paternity claim and demand that her master recognize her child as his; however, the example of Leonor and similar cases indicate that masters did frequently do so.

Even if the owner did acknowledge his paternity, in Christian jurisdictions this did not automatically bring the mother legal rights, as it did under Islamic law. In the kingdom of Valencia in 1283, however, Pedro III legislated that if a man has a child with his slave, the woman and child must both be baptized and freed.[89] The example of the Russian slave Anna, who brought a claim in 1457 for freedom on the grounds that she had given birth to her master's child, shows how precarious the enforcement might be: she was returned to her master's custody for the duration of the trial, savagely beaten, and shipped off to another town, where she was a total stranger.[90] Fernando II of Aragon in 1488 ruled that if the man swore that the child was not his, he, not the woman, was to be believed.[91] Blumenthal notes that it was expected that a man would have sexual relations with his slave women, in contrast with free servants, who routinely had contracts requiring that they be asked to do only "honorable" service; these contracts might not have been entirely enforceable, but they reminded owners that these women had relatives who were concerned for their honor.[92] Iris Origo cited a letter about a pregnant slave who arrived in Genoa from Majorca: she claimed that her previous owner had gotten her pregnant. The matter was investigated, but as the correspondent reported back, "He says you may throw her into the sea, with what she has in her belly, for it is no creature of his. And we believe he is speaking the truth, for if she had been pregnant by him, he would not have sent her."[93] The assumption that a master would not send away his own child may not always have been justified. Typically, however, if a man believed that a child was his, he was expected to provide some sort of care.

Blumenthal, in noting the numerous archival references in Valencia to slave women whose masters treated them as concubines or "as if she was his wife," finds that where those women sought their freedom through the legal system, both owners and enslaved women used the rhetoric of love and intimacy. Women who wished to prove that their children had been acknowledged by their father depicted themselves as domestic partners rather than chattel, thus challenging their masters to behave honorably. The use of a sophisticated legal strategy does not prove that the women really loved the men to whom they were bound by both legal and co-parental ties, but it does show that they were empowered enough to stake out a case for their own rights and knew that they could strengthen their cases by arguing that their masters treated them like family members. Masters responded not by denying sexual relations with the slaves, which would not have been plausible, but by suggesting that the slaves had been promiscuous. If accepted, this allegation not only let the master off the hook for the freedom of the slave and her child, but also allowed him to paint her as rebellious because of her sexual appetite. Men were at pains to deny paternity because not only would it cause them to lose possession of the slave, it also might damage their marriages.[94]

As Blumenthal points out, even if some of these enslaved women were able to "turn their master's sexual desire to their own advantage," the imbalance of power meant that any agency that the slaves exercised through the use of their own sexuality to obtain freedom for themselves or their children was within a very limited range of unpleasant choices.[95] Scholars of New World slavery have also noted that some enslaved women (at least in the sources written by white men) were able to "transcend the horrors of slavery through their skillful manipulation of privileges gained as a result of close involvement with whites."[96] Even if these sources accurately reflect the actions and motives of the women involved, and even if the process was similar in medieval slavery—which it seems to have been—those women gave up a great deal for those privileges, and they were the exceptions. Being the sexual partners of their owners offered women opportunities, but within a situation far from their own making.

Court cases indicate that free men who fathered children with slave women were often not the owners but other men, either friends who had visited the home or strangers who had met the women outside the home. A woman who managed her conjugal household and supervised the domestic help would not be happy to see her husband involved with the slave women (she might be less bothered about her sons), and he might seek out slave women in other households. Such instances are also likely to be more visible in the legal record than a man's sexual activity with his own slaves. Venice in 1287 and again in 1452 prohibited men from sexual relations with other men's slaves (and in 1287 servants also). Servant women could be branded, whipped, and banished for bringing a sexual partner into their master's house.[97] The punishment of the women indicates that the offense committed by the male partner was not against the slave or servant herself but against her owner; a man who got her pregnant, or risked doing so, would be damaging her value.

The birth of a child to a slave woman could lead to various sorts of litigation about restitution to the owner for loss of the woman's labor, the status of the child, and eventual manumissions.[98] Heers, discussing Genoa, identifies fines paid by men for making other men's slaves pregnant, and then, from 1417 on, a sort of life-insurance system, where a man would acknowledge his paternity, agree to pay the costs of the childbirth, and insure against the woman's death.[99] In Florence, the father of a slave's child was responsible for paying for her childbirth; the woman was to be believed as to the identity of the father, if she had two witnesses.[100] The enslaved woman's consent did not necessarily make a difference as to how sexual relations with her were punished. For example, in Florence in 1453, one Francesco was punished for breaking into the house of Andrea della Stufa and raping his slave Caterina. His punishment was based on the amount of work that she missed, that is, on the damages to her master, not to herself.[101] In Valencia, having a sexual relation with another man's slave was considered harmful to the owner not only economically but also in terms of his honor, and seducing a slave was a way of covertly attacking her master.[102]

The records show some men making provisions for the children they had had with other men's slaves. In Venetian Crete, where the children of a man and his own slave were free, this was not true of his children with the slave of another.[103] Sometimes the father of another owner's slave took steps to make his offspring free, rather than the mother's owner prosecuting the father for damages. A Palermo document of 1430 shows Conta de Claromonte agreeing with Nicolaus de Cataldo that she would free her slave Gracia, fathered by Nicolaus with Conta's slave Helena. Conta was to keep Gracia as a servant, but Nicolaus was to provide her clothing.[104] While masters or fathers had success in initiating such litigation, mothers sometimes made the attempt as well. In Pisa in 1400, a former slave, now free and married, attempted to get the father of her two-year-old child (who was not her former owner) to pay maintenance.

The appeal of a servant, and especially a slave, to a man of the master class is not hard to find. He could exercise power over those women who were his employees or his property. Even women who were not directly under his domination were in a vulnerable position, as they were isolated from their family members, may not have spoken the language well, and had no economic resources. A man could offer, as he chose, threats or promises, and the woman might have little choice but to accept them. For a man who was unable to marry because of his age or status as a younger son, or even for economic reasons, a relationship with a woman from his household or that of a friend might be more appealing than relatively impersonal visits to prostitutes.

The appeal of such a relationship to the woman involved is more problematic. To the extent that any choice on her part was involved, as opposed to coercion, the possibility of improving her economic circumstances would have been important. Epstein raises the question of whether the strategy of becoming pregnant by her owner or another man was ever in the interests of an enslaved woman. He notes that many slaves were Muslim and therefore used to a body of religious law in which the slave who bore her master's child acquired rights. A slave who was in a Christian jurisdiction for any period of time would soon discover that this was not the case, but "[e]ven if Christian law or religion did not give any benefits, a child conceived in affectionate circumstances may have cemented the bonds between the free man and the slave woman."[105] But, of course, this was up to the benevolence of the owner, who did not have to treat his own children or those of other free men any better than he treated any of his other slaves. Sometimes men did explicitly free the mothers of their children, but they were not required by law or social pressure to do so.[106]

These slave pregnancies in which the father was not the owner were not merely the result of casual encounters, coerced or consensual; sometimes the union was a long-term one, with marriage as a possibility. In Genoa, free men and enslaved women wanting to marry were perceived as enough of a problem in the fifteenth century for the authorities to be concerned. If the slave belonged to the male partner, he could simply manumit her, and if she belonged to someone else but her owner consented, there was also no problem: the owner's consent was considered the equivalent of manumission. There remained, however, the situation in which the owner did not want his slave to marry. In 1459, a statute made the man who married someone else's slave responsible for paying her value (not her original purchase price, but her market value at the time of the marriage) to her owner.[107] This could result in some unions whose status was up for grabs. In 1490, for example, Bernardino de Scarpa married Anna, the slave of Francesco Pamoleo, without her master's knowledge. The couple then asked him to consent to the marriage retroactively. An agreement was reached that Anna could live with Bernardino *in figura matrimonii,* "in the form of marriage," in return for a payment of seventy lire. Bernardino was unable to pay the whole sum at once and agreed to pay eight lire a year. However, until the full amount was paid, Anna was legally still Francesco's slave, and he had the right to sell her.[108] Canon law would have considered the couple indissolubly married, but *in figura matrimonii* suggests that the Genoese law did not consider it to be complete marriage.

In other ways, too, legal practice in Italian towns and colonies did not correspond to the prescriptions of the learned law. The precept of the Roman

law of slavery, that a female slave's child automatically followed the status of
the mother and remained a slave, does not seem to have been followed in
medieval Italy. Sally McKee has shown that in Venetian Crete, where many
Greeks were enslaved but to be a Latin was by definition to be free, children
were accorded the national identity of their father; many children of slave
women were free on this basis, even if the father did not wish it.[109] McKee
traces this development toward children following the status of the father to
the beginning of the fourteenth century, and has also demonstrated that in the
Italian peninsula itself by the later Middle Ages, a child born of a slave woman
and a free man, if acknowledged by the father, was considered free. This was
not statute law but was assumed, rather than explicitly stated, by jurists. As
McKee demonstrates, Florentine and Genoese notarial registers reveal a number of acts of legitimation of slave children without manumission. It would be
a contradiction in terms for an unfree child to be a legitimate heir, and therefore the step of emancipation must have been understood as unnecessary. She
cites an opinion by Bartolomeo de Bosco in a Genoese case from the colony
of Caffa from the early fifteenth century, which discusses in detail whether a
child born to a slave can be legitimated, without any mention of the necessity
for freeing the slave.[110]

The automatic emancipation of acknowledged children noted by McKee
is evidence for several important social patterns in late medieval Italian urban
society. First, it confirms that free men's fathering children with slaves was
reasonably common, so that a significant number of men had a stake in the
position of those children. Law on this point is not likely to have changed
all by itself; social custom must have exerted pressure and created a general
expectation that such children would be emancipated. In Venetian Crete, illegitimate children of Latin men and Greek slave women seem to have been well
accepted, more so than the illegitimate children of free Latin women. Slave
women could not legally be concubines because the latter implied free status,
but courts tended to treat them as such, and their children accordingly.[111]

Second, the acknowledgment of such children implies certainty about
paternity and thus likely an ongoing relationship between the parents. A man
who has casual encounters with his friends' slave women but does not form
a relationship with any of them is unlikely to believe one of them when she
claims him as the child's father, and her master might not accept her word as to
the identity of the father, either, if it were not an ongoing and generally known
union. To acknowledge a child, a man must have had a degree of trust in the
mother as well as affection and a sense of responsibility. Sometimes there was

no such trust and affection. The Valencian money changer Gabriel Torregrossa refused to acknowledge the paternity of the eleven-year-old son of his former slave Marta, despite the fact that he had had sex with her: "Considering the fact that he is a rich man with no sons, it is not at all plausible . . . that the said Torregrossa, if he knew or believed that the slave woman was pregnant with his child, that he would have sold the said slave woman."[112] Acceptance by the society and by individuals of the principle of responsibility for one's children did not mean that a man automatically accepted any child of one of his slave sex partners as his child. Of course, if a relationship produced more than one child, as occasionally appears in the records, we may assume that it was a serious long-term liaison. If the children of slave women by their masters were raised within the household (perhaps along with other "natural" children of male family members), they were not always freed; even so, we may take this as evidence of some affection and a long-term relationship.[113]

McKee provides several examples from Venetian Crete of close ties of affection between masters and their subordinates. She notes one priest who made his servant (not a slave) his executor and her and her children his heirs. The children may or may not have been his, but he certainly accorded her a great deal of respect. Another wealthy man left a great deal of his estate to his servant who was pregnant with his child; yet another ordered in his will that his wife take his concubine into her household, or else pay her a dowry.[114] Some slave owners' wills collected by McKee made clear the relationship: "I grant freedom to Maria Vercia, my slave. I grant Franco, my natural son whom I had with the said Maria, ten hyperpera." Others made grants to slaves as well as to natural children, but we can only guess at the exact nature of the relationship based on juxtapositions: "I grant freedom to Little Maria, my slave. And if she wants to be married let her be given two hundred hyperpera of my property for her dowry. Also I grant Galaceo, my bastard, two hundred hyperpera to be given him when he reaches the age of eighteen years."[115]

For the most part, however, women in Crete did not receive much in the wills of their Latin partners or their families, even when the children of the union did. In a particularly poignant case cited by McKee, Marchesina Habramo in 1348 left goods in her will to her illegitimate grandchildren, including Hemanuel, the child of Marchesina's son and her slave Herini, but nothing to the slave herself.[116] The Florentine Antonio Guinizzi de' Rizzi legitimized the son he had by the slave Caterina (since he and his wife had no children) but did not free Caterina herself.[117]

Many records hint at masters' fathering children with their slaves without indicating it definitely. Alfonso Franco Silva notes that the Sevillan archives in the fifteenth and sixteenth centuries include many examples of the children of slaves being freed, with the owner citing the service of the parent or the love they felt for a child they had known since birth, but not acknowledging paternity.[118] Cases also exist in which a man purchased a woman and her child only to free them, in which the purchaser was probably the father. If the father already owned the mother, or even if he did not and purchased her in order to free her, he might provide for her future by arranging a marriage for her. In Florence, Francesco Datini arranged for the enfranchisement of his slave Lucia and her marriage to another of his servants before he adopted and left a sizable legacy to her daughter. A large enough dowry could make attractive a marriage even to a former slave who had borne a child out of wedlock—indeed, such a marriage could create an important tie of patronage as well. The men whom freed slaves eventually married were usually not of high social standing; rather, they were often men from the rural hinterlands who had come to towns to look for work.[119] The dowry was not a ticket to wealth but did provide some respectability. In Crete, unfree Greek peasant women often married men of their own social status after bearing a child to a Latin father.

Free servants might be in very similar situations—in a long-term relationship either with the master or one of his peers, giving birth to a child who might be acknowledged and legitimated, eventually married off to another man. This pattern can be seen in towns across Europe, both those where slavery was practiced and those where it was not. In the case of servants as well as of slaves, there is a serious problem of evidence in trying to determine the relationship between the partners, and where there were no children, there is no evidence at all. It was quite common for a servant (or even a slave) to receive a bequest in a master's will, or even the will of another man; both men and women received such bequests, and we cannot assume a sexual relationship on that basis. Even in cases in which one woman received a bequest much larger than those of the other servants, she could be the testator's old nurse, for example, rather than his sexual partner. When a testator left money to the child of one of his servants, this could simply be a child living in the household for whom he had some affection.[120] Sometimes in a will, a man specified a bequest to a child and his or her mother; occasionally, it was noted that the mother was the testator's servant, but sometimes she was merely called the wife of someone else, and it is not clear what their earlier relationship was. When a man left property to several children by the same woman, it was likely an ongoing relationship, and the woman in this situation often received property as well, but not always. And when a man left property to natural children born of several different women, it is impossible to tell what the relationships were. Except for rare cases in which a woman sued for paternity, as in a case from the region of Pisa around 1400 in which a freed woman testified that her son was fathered by her former master rather than her husband,[121] or where the law allowed or required her to name a father and bring witnesses, it was generally a man's prerogative to decide whether to leave something to his children, and the status of the mother was not always mentioned.

Legal documents can inform us about sexual relationships only when the relationships had some sort of legal existence. Slaves stood in a property relationship to the master, and servants a contractual one, but the sexual relationship was not legally recognized except where concubinage was a formal category. Some jurisdictions recognized the Roman law category of concubine, but others did not. In Florence, the status of concubine was defined as a woman kept in one's home; a woman who was kept by a man in a long-term relationship, but did not live with him, was not legally a concubine. However, a servant, even if she did live in the home and had a sexual relationship with the master, might also not be considered a concubine.[122] Francesco Accolti, a fifteenth-century jurist, wrote that a slave or servant (*ancilla sive serva*) can be considered a concubine, which implied that her children would be considered natural and could inherit. Generally, he said, one sign of concubine status is that the man and woman live together in the same house; as this is always the case with a man and his slaves, however, a slave or servant has to be called a concubine in order to be treated as one.[123]

Legal opinions like Accolti's help us see how jurists thought about these nonmarital unions and how they reconciled the rules inherited from Roman law with the changed circumstances of a gender system constructed quite differently under Christian influence. *Consilia* written by eminent civil lawyers, which included references to Roman law, other jurists, and occasionally canon law, provide a way into elite, theoretical understandings of the position of slave and free women who had unions of concubinage or other sorts with their masters. Some of the *consilia* were written for hypothetical cases (often marked by stereotypical names; Titius was their equivalent of John Doe). Some were on abstract points of the law, but many seem to have been written in response to actual cases. Jurists were asked to consult, usually by a judge, sometimes by one of the parties to a case; a *consilium* does not normally state who retained the author.

The *consilia* were consultative opinions; even if definitive in a particular case, they did not become binding precedent for future cases, though they might be cited as authorities.[124] The *ius comune*, that set of legal traditions common to much of Europe that included both canon and civil law, did not rely on precedent as English common law did; rather, the opinions of legal authors gave a certain weight of consistency and historical tradition. Each medieval jurisdiction had its own law (*ius proprium*), but (Roman) civil law and its traditions were crucially important to the legal system throughout much of southern Europe and the German-speaking regions, and very influential elsewhere.[125] Marriage was, from the twelfth century, solidly within the realm of the canon law, but many aspects of inheritance were in the realm of civil law, and most cases discussed here had to do with issues of inheritance. Civilians were not reticent, though, about commenting on issues of canon law when they came up in the course of a case. They often did come up, because property transmission through inheritance was a main reason for choosing legal marriage over another form of union and also for questioning the legality of marriage.

The civil law made a place for children born outside of wedlock. Illegitimate children could be either "natural" or "spurious" under Roman law as it developed during the Middle Ages. Natural children were those born outside of marriage to a couple who could have been married. Those children a single man or a widower had with his servant (or someone else's) would fall into this category. Natural children could be legitimated, in a procedure that varied by region. Spurious children were those whose parents could not have been married: children born from adultery, incest, or (in the view of some commentators) a relationship between a slave and a free person, since the couple would not have been allowed to marry.[126] Legitimating spurious children was more difficult, but it could be done, especially when a man had no legitimate children (although the more distant relatives who were his legal heirs might oppose it).[127] However, not everyone thought that this was possible with children borne by servants or slaves. Luis de la Puente (Ludovicus Pontanus Romanus), commenting in the early fifteenth century about a case in which a count had granted a father's request to legitimate his children without knowing that their mother was a slave, responded to the views of earlier jurists who seemed to place barriers in the way. He argued that the children of a free man and a slave (though not of a free woman and a slave, or two slaves) should be considered natural rather than spurious because it was possible that the parents could marry, if the father freed the mother. That possibility, even without the actual marriage, allowed the children to be legitimated.[128]

The jurist Angelo degli Ubaldi (1323–1400) wrote that the children of servants should not be considered blood relatives of their fathers "because they are vulgarly conceived, either from those serving maids who daily traverse through cities and villages, or from those vile women whom we call domestics, to both of whom very much so, although not publicly and openly, access may be had easily and in secret, as we see them daily and touch them. Therefore those born of such women . . . cannot point to a certain father because of the variety of men who had the capacity of mingling with these women."[129] Bartolo de Sassoferrato (1314–57), a law professor at Perugia and one of the most important jurists of the period, made an exception to his rule that anyone acknowledged as a son should be considered legitimate unless the father specifically calls him "natural": the child of a servant. "[F]or example, if some honorable and noble citizen should have children by some servant who served him or another, then by those words he cannot say he is legitimate because marriage cannot happen with that women, at least honorably."[130] Similarly, Benedictus de Benedictis considered a case in which a certain Renodellus wished to name as his heir his concubine Jacobutia, "who was such that Renodellus could not worthily [*digne*] contract marriage with her."[131] Giovanni Morelli of Florence seemed to put this idea into practice when he refused to name his uncle's wife in his *ricordanze* because she had been a slave and he considered such a marriage "not an honest thing."[132] The jurist Franciscus Curtius the Younger (d. 1533) explained that in order to legitimize the offspring of a "low-born single woman" whom a man kept in his household and later married, the woman had to be one "with whom there could be a marriage according to the good custom of the city, such that in contracting such a marriage he would not contract with a woman of shameful, infamous and vile condition." Children were not legitimated by subsequent marriage "unless it was with a woman who could be conveniently married."[133] Thus it was a question not of slave women being legally unable to contract any legal marriage, but of too great a disparity between a servant and her employer to make a marriage socially possible.

That members of the elites in the late medieval Italian towns, where honor was central to the life of the status-conscious bourgeoisie, found servants unsuitable as marriage partners is not surprising. For a woman, honor was sexual, and she preserved her honor by engaging in sexual relationships only within marriage. However, honor also inhered in rank. A woman engaged in a sexual relationship with a man of the same or lower social class would be dishonored, but a woman with a man of a higher class might not; she might still be able to marry someone from her own social level. For the man of higher social class to marry a woman servant would be disparaging, not in the legal sense but in the way society would view him, as Bartolo de Sassoferrato indicated. He would have a wife whose honor was questionable to members of his own group, if not to her own. This was even more true of slaves. Indeed, it has been suggested that the essence of slavery was the lack of honor, or the exclusion from an economy of honor. A female slave had no sexual honor to lose, although, as Blumenthal points out for Valencia, her sexual behavior might reflect on her owner's honor.[134] A free man of the lower classes who married a former slave, especially if she had been provided with a dowry, might not lose much honor, but a man of the upper classes would not even consider it. This does not mean, however, that he would not live in a long-term union with such a woman and treat her in everyday life as he would treat a wife, except that she would be excluded from the formal rituals of social life.

Further down on the social scale, men's honor was likely to play out in different ways. In the Florentine *catasto* of 1480, Thomas Kuehn has identified sixty-nine bastards in households with less than 400 florins in wealth. Of those, forty-six had fathers with no wife listed, and sixteen were born to fathers who were married but had no legitimate children.[135] It is likely that, while elite men fathered illegitimate children during marriage (or whenever they felt like it), poorer men did so instead of marrying. This implies, of course, that there was a degree of choice in fathering a child. This is, to some extent, true even though the only known form of male contraception was coitus interruptus. Other more or less effective methods were available to women, and we may assume that at least some of the slave and servant women who bore children chose to do so, perhaps because they thought that it would lead to a better economic situation. Furthermore, men often had a choice about whether to acknowledge paternity; it took a very persistent woman to make a charge stick in the face of denial and calumny.

Wives' adultery, unsurprisingly, was considered more serious than husbands' in the Italian towns (men were punished for adultery, too, and often more harshly than women, but they were mainly men who had slept with married women, not unfaithful married men).[136] A wife's adultery with a slave or other person of low status was considered especially serious. Such dishonor damaged not only her but also her entire family. Even when it took the form of legal marriage, such a union was less likely than one that went the other way around. Angelo Gambiglioni (d. 1461) discussed a case in which Philomena, daughter of a well-to-do man, married a man of low birth. He noted that under civil law, a daughter who was under her father's *patria potestas* did not have the right to marry without his permission, but under canon law, she did have that right: no parental consent was required. However, if she married without her father's permission, she had no right to a dowry, even though her sisters got one. When Philomena tried to claim a dowry's share in her father's estate after his death, she was denied it because of her husband's low and illegitimate birth: "Because of such a vile marriage, contracted with a low person, she can be disinherited, and deprived of the gift of a dowry. . . . [T]he said Philomena joined herself with a man of low condition, and, what is worse, of illegitimate birth, so that he could not aspire to the dignity or honors of the Republic, therefore the same Philomena brings shame and ignominy and disgrace not only on herself, but on the memory of her illustrious father and her family."[137] The marriage was not invalid because of the lack of dowry or family consent, but the language used in this *consilium* emphasizes how shocking such a case was.

Philomena was in a recognized, if not socially accepted, marriage. Most of the slave and servant women involved with elite men were not, and we know little about the internal workings of the partnerships or how the women understood their choices. In these cases, they had chosen—or the man had chosen—a relationship of unequal power, in which his dominance over his partner extended beyond that accorded to husbands over wives. In some cases, the woman may have fulfilled the other functions of a wife besides the sexual— notably, running his household. In some, she may have been a companion for him, but the evidence rarely speaks to this one way or the other. There were undoubtedly couples where the man used the women for sex as well as domestic work, and pensioned or married her off when he was no longer interested or when he married. There were undoubtedly also couples for whom a real affection grew. Franciscus Curtius, when he was explaining which children could be legitimated, also drew the distinction between children born of "a concubine kept with matrimonial affection" and one kept "for shameful reasons."[138] For a man who did not need to marry—for example, a widower who already had children and who did not need the dowry that a new wife would bring—a relationship with a member of his household for whom he already had some affection might be the best solution to the problem of household management as well as of companionship. Merchants who traveled regularly to the same town and wished to have a domestic establishment there also found liaisons with servants convenient.

What the sources do not tell us, but what we cannot overlook, is what these relationships offered the women involved. Some had little or no choice, either because the man had legal rights over them or because they had no viable economic alternatives. However, it would not be right to envision exclusively a situation in which women minding their own business are harassed and exploited by men. Some women no doubt actively attempted to arouse the interest of elite men, with the hope of improving their station in life through easier work or an eventual dowry, gifts, or other support. As with most medieval women of the lower ranks of society, we do not have these women's voices to determine how they themselves experienced their lives.

"He Never Gave Her Anything but Words": Beneventa

Sometimes a woman's actions allow us to guess how she may have felt. The jurist Bartolomeo Cipolla of Verona (d. 1477) was consulted on a case in which a woman named Beneventa, wife of Zacharius of Cremona, was accused of stealing forty-one ducats from Francesco de Mazolis.[139] According to Bartolomeo, it was proven at her trial that Beneventa had been for twelve years the servant of Francesco, and he owed her a wage. Bartolomeo used two different Latin terms for Beneventa's status: *famula* (servant) and *pedisequa* (also a servant, but in the late Middle Ages used especially of women in sexual relationships with their masters). Francesco had gotten Beneventa pregnant, "but he never gave her anything but words."[140] Beneventa had repeatedly asked him for what he owed her because her husband could not bear the sight of her, as she had brought him no dowry.

Under the circumstances, Bartolomeo suggested, Beneventa thought that she could take the money from Francesco without it being considered theft. Beneventa's lawyer, he said, cited the Israelites leaving Egypt with Pharaoh's valuables to indicate that theologians did not consider such behavior to be a sin, but only fair wages for labor. The definition of theft was Bartolomeo's main concern. He also considered whether the statute in question applied only to men or to women, too, considering grammatical as well as social issues, and eventually decided that Beneventa could be punished. Bartolomeo did not discuss the rights of a servant in this situation, in which she has been not only the employee but also the sexual partner of her master. Indeed, the case does not tell us whether Beneventa's child was born while she was still living in Francesco's house, or whether the child was living with her or even still alive at the time of the case.

Beneventa had managed to find a husband despite the fact that she was

older than the typical Italian bride (even if she had started working in Francesco's household as a young child, she would have been in her late teens, at
least). When girls came to work as servants, they would typically be promised
wages in a lump sum at the end of their term. Her husband certainly seems to
have married her in expectation of a dowry. Bartolomeo's account does not tell
us whether she had been promised a specific amount. Since forty-one ducats
is not a round number, it may well be accurate as to the amount stolen but
not necessarily the amount that she thought she was owed. Forty-one ducats
would not be the highest or the lowest dowry for a former servant.[141] Either
her husband was wealthy enough to hire a lawyer for her or there was considerable sympathy for her position as having been cheated by her employer.
Beneventa's taking law into her own hands indicates what she thought she was
entitled to; apparently, many in her community agreed.

Marriage and Servitude in the North

Although slavery was most common in the Mediterranean region, it was also
known elsewhere in Europe. We can turn northward for a different type of
slave system that still followed the basic pattern of servile women in unions
with free men. Iceland produced a literature that depicts a number of women
slaves in coerced unions. These representations are imaginative; the sagas were
written centuries after the events that they described, and at least a century
after the latest evidence of slavery in Iceland. However, they may tell us something about how Icelanders in the thirteenth century regarded unions between
partners of widely differing status, and they displayed at least some concern
about the impact of these unions on slave women.

Iceland was settled by people of Norwegian ancestry starting in the ninth
century. Many of the settlers did not come directly from Norway but rather
from Norse settlements elsewhere in the North Sea region, including the
Faeroes and the Scottish Isles. Many of these settlers had participated in Viking raids, particularly in Ireland and Scotland, in which they had captured
slaves. Norsemen also intermarried with local women in the Celtic regions
and brought their wives with them to Iceland.

We know about unions between people of Norse and Celtic ancestry not
only from literary sources but also from DNA studies. Because Iceland is a
fairly small country that did not see much immigration between the tenth
and twentieth centuries, it has a fairly homogenous and stable gene pool

that, when combined with the Icelandic fascination for genealogy and good record-keeping, has made it a good choice for DNA studies.[142] Mitochondrial DNA (found in all human cells and inherited through the maternal line) and y-chromosome DNA (found only in the cells of genetic males and inherited through the paternal line) in the Icelandic gene pool have been compared with the same from the west of Norway, from where historical sources tell us the settlers came, and from Ireland. The mitochondrial DNA in the Icelandic gene pool more resembles that from Ireland than the y-chromosome DNA resembles its Irish equivalent; the situation is the reverse for the west of Norway. In other words, the male ancestors of the current Icelandic population are more likely to have come from Norway than the female, and the female more likely to have come from Celtic regions than the male.[143] The DNA evidence, of course, cannot tell us what proportion of these Celtic female ancestors were legal wives, but Icelandic literature indicates that at least some were slaves.

Silence: Melkorka

The title of each of these portraits has included a quotation from the woman, if possible, or a quotation from her partner or another man if her own words do not survive. The fictionalized Melkorka's most notable statement was her silence. Melkorka, like other saga figures, is based on a real historical character, though the saga that discusses her cannot be taken as an accurate retelling of events; it contradicts other sources on some points and contains obvious exaggerations and literary topoi.

Hoskuld Dala-Kolsson was the son of a major Icelandic family in the tenth century; several sagas trace his descent from some of the earliest settlers of Iceland. *Laxdæla saga* ("the story of the people of Laxardal") focuses mainly on his descendants. Hoskuld married Jorunn Bjarnardottir, also from an important family, and they had children together. *Laxdæla saga* tells us that when Hoskuld went with a Norwegian royal expedition to Brännö, off the cost of Sweden, he asked a merchant called Gilli the Russian if he had a female slave for purchase. Gilli had twelve for sale, and offered to sell him any of them for one mark of silver, except the one Hoskuld preferred, whom Gilli valued more highly than the others, at three marks. Gilli told him, however, that "the woman has a major flaw and I wish you to know of it. . . . The woman cannot speak. I have tried to speak with her in many ways, but never got so much as a word from her."[144] Hoskuld purchased her anyway, for the three marks of silver, and shared a bed with her that night.

When Hoskuld returned to Iceland, he brought the slave with him. His wife asked him who she was, and he replied that he did not know her name. Jorunn's response was sarcastic: "Unless the stories I've heard are lies, you must have spoken to her enough to have at least asked her name." Hoskuld told his wife the whole story and "asked her to show the woman respect and said that he wanted her to live there at home with them."[145] Jorunn was reluctant, and the saga tells us that Hoskuld slept with her rather than with the slave. The winter after arriving in Iceland, the slave gave birth to a son, Olaf, later nicknamed Peacock because of his expensive clothing.[146] By the next summer, according to the saga, Jorunn was annoyed with Hoskuld's obvious affection for Olaf and insisted that the slave do her share of the farmwork or leave; Hoskuld assigned her to wait on him and Jorunn.

One day when Olaf was about two years old, Hoskuld heard voices near a stream and came upon the slave—who, up to this point, had still not displayed the ability to speak—chatting with her son. He insisted that she tell him her name, saying that "there was no point in pretending any longer."[147] She told him her story. Her name was Melkorka, and her father was a king of Ireland named Myrkjartan (the Irish form was Muirchertach). She had been kidnapped by slave raiders when she was fifteen. Jorunn doubted this story when Hoskuld repeated it to her. Hoskuld began to treat Melkorka better, but Jorunn struck her one day, resulting in a fight in which Melkorka came out the better. Hoskuld moved Melkorka and Olaf to another farmstead and later arranged for Olaf to be fostered by a wealthy, childless man who could leave him land, although Melkorka did not think the man was of good enough family. Hoskuld later tricked his and Jorunn's sons into allowing him to leave more money to Olaf than he could legally do without their permission.

By the time Olaf was grown, Hoskuld "became more and more reluctant to look after Melkorka's affairs, saying he felt it was just as much Olaf's responsibility as his." Melkorka felt humiliated by this. She suggested that Olaf go abroad in search of his maternal family. Hoskuld would not provide funds for this, and Olaf's foster-father's property was in land rather than goods. In order to finance the trip, Melkorka accepted a marriage proposal from a local farmer named Thorbjorn Pock-Marked, telling Olaf, "I've had my fill of people calling you the son of a slave-woman."[148] She gave Olaf a gold arm ring, knife, and belt that her family would recognize—clearly, a literary embroidery, as it is entirely unlikely that she would have been kept these items with her through her kidnapping and sale. Hoskuld was not happy about the situation but apparently could do nothing about it. The saga never explicitly said that Hoskuld had freed Melkorka, but the audience would no doubt have understood that he had, or she would not be marrying a free man (or marrying at all, especially without Hoskuld's permission).

Olaf sailed off and became a great favorite at the Norwegian court (as did many Icelandic saga heroes), and the king's mother financed a trip to Ireland for him to seek his relatives. When Olaf identified himself, speaking the Irish that his mother had taught him, both King Myrkjartan and Melkorka's old nurse were able to recognize the tokens he had brought with him. The king offered to make Olaf his heir, but Olaf was concerned about disinheriting Myrkjartan's sons, so he returned to Norway and then to Iceland with even more wealth. He married Thorgerd, daughter of the great warrior-poet Egill Skallagrimsson (this marriage is well attested elsewhere). The later part of the saga told the story of a love triangle involving Olaf's son Kjartan, his nephew Bolli Bollason (son of Bolli, son of Hoskuld and Jorunn), and Gudrun Osvif-sdottir, known as the most beautiful woman in Iceland.

There are obvious fairy-tale elements to the story: the kidnapped princess's son returning to his grandfather's kingdom with the tokens to make himself recognized, the slave who turns out to be a princess. The saga author may have given Melkorka the royal ancestry because her descendants were his patrons. It was likely fairly widely known in the thirteenth century that the famous Olaf had been the child of a slave, or at least of a woman who was not formally married to his father. The saga author had Thorgerd initially refuse to consider Olaf as a husband for this reason.[149] By making Melkorka an enslaved princess, however, the author removed a good deal of the stigma of slavery. The author of *Landnámabók*, which records (not entirely accurately) the earliest settlers of Iceland, where they settled, and their genealogies, said explicitly that the point of the work was to make it clear to foreigners that the Icelanders were not "descended from slaves,"[150] but in cases where they actually were, their descendants had to make the best of it.

The way Melkorka reacted to her enslavement, however, was not a common topos and may reflect either a kernel of historical truth or the way that people in mid-thirteenth-century Iceland imagined a woman might react to being enslaved and forced into a sexual relationship. Melkorka, as depicted in the story, was hardly a typical slave; she was a princess and thus more likely to resent and resist her enslavement. But the story would also have reminded people that enslaved people did have a past before their capture. The saga does not say that Melkorka was unhappy with Hoskuld; indeed, it implies that they got on well together, but the fact that over years together, she did not reveal that she was capable of speech indicates that she had chosen to resist a coercive union. Women born into slavery, with a different horizon of expectations, might have been less likely to resist.

Iceland, where we have both medieval law codes and literary sources—and, to some extent, the other Scandinavian countries, for which we have law codes but not sagas—has been treated by some scholars as though it harbored some pre-Christian, proto-Germanic type of marriage; in fact, the term *Friedelehe* was extrapolated in part from the Icelandic term *frilla* or *friðla* (see Chapter 1). However, close examination of the Scandinavian sources reveals that concubinage was closely related to slavery. In Iceland—and perhaps also in other slaveholding cultures, as in Italy—the availability of slave women for informal unions had an effect on the status of free women in similar unions.

The term *frilla* was still in common use in Iceland in the thirteenth century, when slavery was no longer a factor. Else Ebel provides a list of forty-seven women who appear in the "Contemporary Sagas" (the Sturlunga saga compilation and Bishops' sagas) as *frillur*.[151] These sagas were written in the thirteenth century, as were the family sagas, but describe events roughly contemporary to the writing. They were certainly subject to political influence from (or authorship by) churchmen and members of major magnate families, but we can expect that the sociological details that they included were not too far off from the actual arrangements of the time. The women who appeared in these sagas as *frillur* were of lower social status than the men with whom they were in unions, and the unions were socially devalued compared to marriage. However, the women were not necessarily servants or in other ways abjected; some came from major families. Giving one's daughter as a *frilla* to a patron, in a public relationship, could boost a family's status. These unions also tended to be serially monogamous: a man would have a *frilla* before or instead of marriage.[152]

By the time the contemporary sagas were written, the church had been able to influence social customs in Iceland, which formally converted to Christianity in the year 1000. The better-known family sagas, which purport to describe the events of the Viking Age, were also written around the same time and under the same influences; yet the *frillur* there were quite different. Given the pride of the Icelanders of the thirteenth century in their ancestry, it is not likely that a saga describing the ancestors of a leading Icelandic family—even a saga written under church influence—would take an ancestor who was a wife or a free concubine and turn her into a slave, even an enslaved princess. It is far more likely that an unknown slave would be turned into the daughter of a king and a young man whom the author knew to have a future as an outstanding chieftain ahead of him be given an inheritance through a subterfuge than that a woman of high status would be turned into a concubine and a co-heir into an illegitimate son. The slave *frilla* seems to have been an authentic feature of saga-age Iceland.[153]

In several sagas, long-term unions appear between free men and free women who are not called *frilla*. These include Hrodny Hoskuldsdottir, mother of Njal's son Hoskuld, in *Brennu-Njáls saga* (the *Saga of Burnt Njal*).[154] This Hoskuld was considered enough of a member of Njal's family to be caught up as a victim in blood feud and to be avenged by Njal's legitimate sons. Hrodny lived in a separate household, but referred to Bergthora, Njal's wife, as *elja*, which meant roughly "co-wife."[155] Hrodny's brother Ingjald spoke of his bonds of affinity (*tengda sakir*) with Njal and his sons. But when Hrodny later urged her brother not to participate in an action against Njal, she did so at first not on the grounds of the relationship but rather on the grounds of services that Njal had done him in the past.[156] In *Vopnfirðinga saga*, Helgi's wife was ill and could not manage the household; he betrothed himself to a widow and brought her into the household.[157] His first wife returned to her family, but there was no mention of divorce, and Helgi hoped that she would come back. In these cases, where the woman was closer to the same status as the man, the term *frilla* was not used. Njal's union with Hrodny was not full marriage in that it did not give inheritance rights to her son, but both she and Helgi's partner enjoyed a certain social recognition.

When *frilla* was used in the family sagas, it was associated with slavery. In *Egils saga Skallagrímssonar*, Egil entered into a lawsuit on behalf of his wife, Asgerd; Berg-Onund, husband of her half-sister Gunnhild, had taken control of the property of their father, and Egil wanted his share. Berg-Onund claimed that only Gunnhild was the rightful heiress because her mother was "the woman whom Bjorn had legally married," whereas Asgerd's mother had been "abducted, and afterward taken as a *frilla*, and without the consent of her kin."[158] Significantly, Berg-Onund claimed that this "abduction," when a woman left home with a man without the consent of her relatives, meant that she was a slave: he called Egil's wife an *ambátt* (female slave), and Egil equated this with calling her *þýborna* (born of a slave woman). Absence of the consent of the kin, and absence of formal ceremonies and payments, did not legally make a woman a slave, but Berg-Onund's insinuation that it did hints at a fundamental connection between the status of *frilla* and slavery. It is unlikely that the situation depicted in *Egils saga* is a projection backward into time of conditions in the thirteenth century, since slavery no longer existed in the thirteenth century when it was written.[159] Neither is it a reflection of conditions at the time of the saga's writing; what it tells us is how people in the thirteenth century imagined social relations in the tenth.

Asgerd's mother is the only woman called a *frilla* in the Icelandic family sagas who (at least in the story) entered into the relationship on her own, and her adversary alleged that the union reduced her to the status of a slave. All the other *frillur* in the family sagas were either slaves or came from relatively powerless families so that they could be coerced into the relationships. In the kings' sagas, too, another thirteenth-century genre that told stories of an earlier period, being involved in a nonmarital union was also considered the equivalent of being a slave. Snorri Sturluson's thirteenth-century history of the Norwegian kings, the *Heimskringla*, referred to both Thora Morstrstong, mother of the Norwegian king Harald Fairhair's son Hakon the Good, and Alfhild, mother of St. Olaf's son Magnus, as slaves even though they came from magnate families.[160] A highborn woman who entered into a low-status relationship with a king could be called a slave in a derogatory way. Again, it is not likely that this is a later Christian interpretation. These sorts of unions, too, could be coercive in various ways, but at the same time could provide significant advantages to the women.

The earliest extant Icelandic law code, the *Grágás*, did not mention the *frilla* at all, indicating that in the twelfth century, this was not a formal legal status. *Grágás* did allow free children born out of wedlock to inherit from their father if there were no heirs born in wedlock.[161] However, it also equated all children born out of wedlock with those born of slaves.[162] The Norwegian law of the Gulathing, dating from the twelfth century, gave special names to the children of different types of union: the son of a free woman for whom no *mundr* had been paid but where the relationship was public, the son of a free woman in a secret relationship, and the son of a slave.[163] Publicity, of course, was one factor that the church emphasized for a marriage; but in these Norwegian laws, none of these unions was considered a marriage, even if publicity was key in distinguishing between types of union.[164] The so-called "King Sverre's Christian law," probably from between 1269 and 1273, said that if a man had a *frilla* whom he treated as his *eigin kona* ("own woman," or wife), eating and sleeping with her, he had the right to compensation for her if

another abducted her.[165] This law envisioned that *frillur* were in domestic partnerships, like the *frillur* in the Icelandic contemporary sagas of about the same
time. Some *frillur* in the twelfth century, too, were domestic partners. Another
passage in the Gulathing law provided that if a man lived with his *frilla* openly
for twenty years, their children acquired inheritance rights and the law recognized their community of property.[166] These legal rights were presumably not
accorded to the *frilla* or her children otherwise. A 1305 addition to *Jónsbók*, the
late thirteenth-century Icelandic law book, stated that if a couple had lived
together for ten years and the woman was not publicly known as a *friðla* or
horkona (adulteress or loose woman), their children could inherit; *friðla* here
was a low-status category.[167]

I argued in a previous article that concubinage in Viking Age Scandinavia had its roots in slavery, rather than in a pre-Christian polygamy that was
relabeled by the church.[168] I would not now insist on "roots" but would call it
an association. Certainly, there were plural unions, at least among the royalty
and highest aristocracy, in pre-Christian times. Some women involved in these
unions were equated with slaves, even when they were formally of free status.
Just because the language of slavery was occasionally used in the thirteenth
century to describe concubines in earlier centuries does not mean that concubines continued to have the legal disabilities of slaves. But the equation with
slaves is not likely to have been church-inspired or to represent the demotion
of plural marriage to concubinage under church influence. It is very difficult
to discover here which came first—the low status of the woman or the low
status of the union. When a free woman was referred to in the language of
slavery because of the nonmarital union she had entered, it was the status
of the union that is decisive; but it is likely that it was the frequency of the
practice of men entering such unions with slaves that led to the use of slave
language in regard to them.

Unequal Religions

Unions between people of two different religions did not necessarily imply
different economic status, but any given community was most likely to enslave people of other religions, and religious minorities had distinct legal status. The laws of various Christian polities were full of prohibitions on the
enslavement of other Christians; although these were not always crystal-clear
(did Eastern Christians count? what if a slave were baptized?), they helped

promote a situation in which Muslim women (especially) were open to slavery and sexual exploitation by Christian men.[169] In all three religious communities in medieval Europe, men's sexual relations with their slaves were considered quite usual, if frowned upon, but also complicated by the religious aspects.[170] Even when servitude was not involved, mixed-religion partnerships still followed the general trend that the status of the parties dictated the status of a given union.

In many parts of Europe, Christians and Jews lived in close proximity. Christians worked as servants in Jewish homes, although Christian law frowned upon this.[171] Rabbinic texts acknowledged, albeit with disapproval, that it was common for Jewish men to have sexual relations with their servants, including Christian ones. Documents from the Cairo Geniza, a repository of discarded documents from the Jewish community there, demonstrate that some men in Mediterranean communities did marry their servants as second wives during the lifetime of the first; in marriage contracts from the twelfth century on, the husband promised not to take a second wife or to take a maidservant not approved by his wife. If he violated this provision, his wife could demand a divorce and the return of her dowry.[172] Solomon ibn Adret of Barcelona (Rashba, 1235–1310) considered a case in which a servant became pregnant by her master and ended up being taken as a second wife.[173] Polygamy was in disuse in Ashkenaz (Germany/northwestern Europe), but the tradition still meant that Jewish law often treated men's sexual relations with their servants (even married men's) as something that could be tolerated, as long as those servants were Jewish.[174] Although the Mishnah forbade a man from marrying his non-Jewish servant after freeing her, Maimonides (d. 1204) suggested that it was permissible for him to marry her even though it went against established law because this was less harmful than continuing to have nonmarital relations with her.[175]

Jewish law recognized informal unions as well as plural marriage. Rabbi Chaim ben Isaac Or Zarua, who wrote in thirteenth-century Germany, considered a case where a man who had a son left his wife for another woman, but did not remarry. The son married and then died. The question was whether his widow was obligated to either contract levirate marriage with her father-in-law's son from the later union, her husband's out-of-wedlock half-brother, or be released from it. Or Zarua noted that because the mother of the surviving half-brother had fornicated with the father-in-law, she may have had other partners as well; he implied that a loose woman was a loose woman. However, he concluded that the father-in-law, although not her husband, was her main partner, although he did not come to a firm decision in the case.[176] Rabbi Asher ben Yehiel (1250–1327), who moved from Germany to Spain in 1303, also considered the question of concubinage among Jews. The laws of incest prohibited a man from marrying a woman who had been his uncle's wife: What about a woman who had been his uncle's concubine (*pilegesh*)? He concluded that concubinage was not considered marriage for these purposes.[177] Rabbi Nissim Gerondi of Barcelona (d. ca. 1375) referred to concubinage as an accepted relationship. He considered a servant who had become pregnant by her master's son and was set up in a separate house as a *pilegesh*; as with a divorcée, if she later wished to marry someone else, she had to wait three months to ensure that she was not at that time pregnant from the union.[178] The ruling was not occasioned by concerns over the permissibility of concubinage but by her wish to marry. In these cases, the woman in the union was not necessarily a servant.

These sexual unions were of greater concern when they involved partners of another religion, and all three major religious communities were especially concerned about women of their own group. The Fourth Lateran Council in 1215, when it ordered that Jews be forced to wear a distinguishing badge, gave the specific reason that it would prevent Christian women from having sexual relations with Jewish men unknowingly.[179] Some Jewish responsa (answers by rabbis to questions of law) held that if a Jewish woman were alone in a house with a non-Jewish man, her husband was permitted, though not required, to divorce her.[180] The twelfth-century *Sefer Hasidim*, from the Rhineland, said that a Jewish man should not shake hands with a Gentile woman, or a Jewish woman with a Gentile man, even with gloves on, presumably (although this is not stated) because of the sexual temptation.[181] Several German rabbis ruled that for a man to have sexual relations with a Gentile woman was grounds for his wife to demand that he be compelled to divorce her.[182]

Though rabbis might consider Jewish men's relationships with non-Jewish women polluting—as the Bavarian R. Joseph ben Moses (d. ca. 1490) wrote, "one who desires to guard himself from Hell should avoid impurity, as well as fornicating with impure Gentile women, for one who defiles himself with Gentile women is very difficult to save from Hell"[183]—in practice, unmarried men often had fairly casual relations with Christian women. In medieval Umbria, for example, Ariel Toaff writes that "the young Jewish man gradually became aware that his first sexual encounters would not take place in a Jewish environment, and that love and marriage ran on parallel tracks, usually with little relation between them." Such young men could expect to have their sexual initiation with a household servant, as was also common for Christians.[184]

Though Jews might not have objected too strenuously to Jewish men having sex with Christian women, Christians certainly did. In 1399, a Jewish man, Salamon son of Melutius of Foligno, was tried before the Franciscan inquisitor in Romandiola for having seduced Christian women by telling them that sex with Jews was not a sin: "Impelled by a diabolical spirit, in hatred and contempt of the Christian religion . . . he approached certain Christian women and asked that they consent to his detestable desire and fleshly lust, and when they refused to do this, the said Salomon, in order to persuade them to consent to this damnable mixing, burst forth in these quarrelsome words and heretical wisdom, against the determination of the holy Mother Church, thus, that for Christians to lie with Jews was not a sin, and that because of the said words, he seduced these women and knew them carnally."[185]

It is hard to believe that any woman would credit this claim, and there must have been more to the case than was recorded. The inquisitor did not believe the accusation: Salomon was acquitted, and this decision was ratified by the pope. But canon lawyers had trouble figuring out exactly how such men should be punished. As the Christian jurist Oldradus de Ponte (d. after 1337) wrote, in answering the question "In what way may a Jew be punished who has had carnal knowledge of a Christian woman?" a Jewish man who attempted to marry a Christian woman could be punished as an adulterer and put to death; if marriage was not involved and the woman was single and consented, canon law did not prescribe a punishment. "Nonetheless I do not say that this foul union should not receive some kind of civil punishment at the discretion of a judge." In fact, the Jew in Oldradus's case was punished with castration.[186]

But Christians did not have the same problem with a Christian man becoming involved with a Jewish woman, especially when it could lead to her conversion. The motif of the virtuous daughter of the perfidious Jew, which has its epitome in Shakespeare's Jessica, appeared frequently in medieval Christian literature, notably in the exempla of Caesarius of Heisterbach, the thirteenth-century Cistercian. Jewish women could be a threat to Christian men, particularly clerics whom they could seduce away from celibacy; on the other hand, their conversion was a positive step, especially when they could encourage the conversion of their communities.[187]

Iberia is perhaps the best place to examine the phenomenon of cross-religious unions, since it was the place where adherents of all three religions,

Christianity, Islam, and Judaism, were found in significant numbers. As David Nirenberg demonstrates, the fraught relations between Christians and Jews in the Crown of Aragon (more than relations with Muslims) led to the use of the bodies of Christian women, particularly prostitutes, as the place to draw a boundary. The acceptance by the majority culture and, to a lesser extent, the minority cultures of their men's sexual activity with the women of other religions is not unlike that found in many other places, but these "ancient and enduring sexual metaphors" were affected by "a period of rapid change in the way Christians living in the medieval Iberian Peninsula thought about religious classification." Nirenberg argues that the enduring concerns about the bodies of Christian women had to do with the personification of the church itself as a woman, the spouse of a masculine God, and all Christian women as God's daughters. The honor of the entire Christian community was at risk from the activity of Christian women, whose transgression corrupted the whole collectivity.

Nevertheless, sexual relations between Christian married women and Muslim men, though forbidden, could be treated fairly lightheartedly in the literature of the era of the Reconquest. It was prostitutes in the pre-1391 moral economy who were most often punished for intercourse that dishonored the Christian community, and they "came to play the role of specialists in the recognition (and ideally, the rejection) of religious difference." The massacres of 1391 in the Crown of Aragon and the conversions, understood as insincere, that went along with them changed the nature of the concern with the boundary between Christian and Jew: with the conversion of the Jews, distinctive Christian identity risked disappearing. Therefore the line between converts and those who remained Jews had to be emphasized. The prostitute no longer stood as the main boundary; fuller segregation was called for. The concern was not mainly with the children who might result from an interfaith union, although the Christians considered them Christian and the Jews considered them Jewish apostates. Rather, sex stood in metaphorically for a wider separation.[188] Muslim communities were equally concerned about Muslim prostitutes, though more on grounds of honor than of identity.[189] Jewish communities harshly punished Jewish women who had sex with Muslim or Christian men, and Muslim communities did the same with their women.[190] Muslim men were not prohibited under Muslim law from sex with non-Muslim women.

Christian-Muslim couples did sometimes form long-term unions that did not involve servitude; indeed, Christian men's sexual relationships with

Muslim women were more likely to be tolerated and less harshly punished than those with Jewish women.[191] Unions involving Christian women were more problematic. A 1242 charter issued by Jaume I of Aragon provided that Christian women who lived with Muslims or Jews would be denied Christian burial, and this was shortly changed to capital punishment.[192] The thirteenth-century Customs of Tortosa provided that a Christian woman who had sex with a Muslim or Jewish man was to be burned and the man drawn and quartered. There were also some laws that provided harsh punishment for Christian men having sex with Jewish women.[193] However, this capital punishment was rarely put into practice. For a Christian man and a Muslim woman, the most common penalty in the Crown of Aragon was slavery for the woman (many of them were already slaves, anyway, which reinforced the superior position of the Christian man) and a financial penalty for the man. Judges within the Muslim community, however, argued for a harsher penalty for such a woman, up to and including the death penalty, especially if she was married. The crown preferred to enslave the women, and particularly if the Christian man involved was influential, his partner could often be pardoned. Or she might choose to convert.[194]

Where Christians ruled, Jewish men were more likely to have access to Muslim women; in Muslim lands, their partners were more likely to be Christians. Although Jewish men with Jewish or non-Jewish concubines created different legal problems under Jewish law (halakha), the rabbis often tended to treat them similarly. Rabbi Moses of Coucy preached in 1236 in Spain that sexual relations with Gentile women were sinful, and sources report that many men responded to his sermon by sending away their concubines. Rashba was consulted in the case of a man who had had one child with his servant before and one after her conversion to Judaism, and urged the community to prevent such a practice. An order of excommunication (*herem*) was issued in Toledo in 1281 against those who kept Jewish or non-Jewish concubines. However, Rashba ruled that having a converted Muslim concubine (*pilegesh*) would be acceptable if it were not for that *herem* and that a formal concubinage relationship, though not generally approved, with a convert was preferable to sex with a non-Jewish woman. Rabbi Moses ben Nachman Girondi (Nachmanides, or Ramban) discouraged the keeping of all concubines because it would lead to general disregard of laws of ritual purity.[195] Rabbis disagreed about whether having sex with a non-Jewish woman was better than with a promiscuous or prostituted Jewish woman, who might not go to the ritual bath any more than would a non-Jew. Taken as a whole, the pronouncements of the Spanish rabbis indicate that the issue was a worrying one in this society of several religions.[196] There seems to have been less concern about this in Ashkenaz in the later Middle Ages. Ephraim Kanarfogel suggests that Jewish communities in Ashkenaz were relatively insular and the population more likely to follow what their rabbis said.[197]

Some conversions from Judaism to Christianity in the Crown of Aragon before the mass conversions of 1391 could have been occasioned by romantic involvement with someone of another religion. Paola Tartakoff has identified several unions in which both partners converted from Judaism to Christianity in order to marry: either they were too closely related to each other to marry under Jewish law, or the woman had been previously married and her former husband refused to give her a *get*, or bill of divorce. The Christian authorities were willing to give closely related couples dispensations to marry, in order to encourage conversion.[198] These couples, of course, are evidence for intra-religious unions, not inter-religious ones. But Tartakoff has suggested that cases involving Jews being prosecuted for circumcising Christian children may be evidence of unions between Christian men and Jewish women, the children of which both sides wanted to claim.[199] The reverse happened in an Italian case: in 1485, Innocent VIII asked the vice-treasurer of Perugia to proceed against a Jew who "knew a Christian woman carnally, and had a child by her, which he had circumcised in the Jewish manner."[200]

The church promoted marriage with converts to Christianity to encourage conversion; the rabbis tolerated or promoted marriage with converts to Judaism to avoid ritual impurity. Such conversions in order to marry were probably much more common lower on the social scale than at higher levels, where men could have a slave or other partner of low status alongside a wife of their own religion. It is with these wealthier men and their slaves or servants that the cross-religious unions overlap with those involving imbalances of power described in the earlier parts of this chapter. Nevertheless, across all the various kinds of status difference, we see commonalities. A double standard certainly applied. It was much more acceptable for an unmarried man to be sexually involved and even have children with a woman of lower status, economically, legally, or religiously, than it was for an unmarried woman, and more acceptable for a married man than a married woman to conduct a relationship on the side. Because it was more derogatory to a woman's reputation to have a partner of lower status, fewer women were likely to coerce their subordinates into a sexual union. Both partners would have experienced a complex mixture of motives, but men tended to be accorded far more freedom of action.

Chapter 3

Priests and Their Partners

When I told people that I was working on a book on couples who lived together without being married, most non-medievalists (and many medievalists) immediately said, "Oh, priests." The idea that some churchmen keep their vows of celibacy in the technical sense of being unmarried, but not in the more common sense of abstaining from sexual activity, surprises no one, whether we are talking about the Middle Ages or today, when a majority of Christians in the world belong to denominations in which the clergy may marry. The fact that "celibacy" developed to mean "chastity" as well as "the unmarried state" reflects the fact that the vast majority of Christian thinkers, across denominations and right up to the twenty-first century, have held that marriage is the only proper venue for sexual relations and therefore that anyone who is celibate in the sense of unmarried should also be celibate in the sense of abstinent.

It made a good deal of difference to medieval European attitudes toward a particular union whether the given couple had the possibility of marrying. As I have argued, the way a particular union between laypeople was regarded often depended on the woman's status and respectability. For priests' partners, this was not the case because from the twelfth century on, they could not be considered fully married under any circumstances. Some women may have been driven into such unions by economic necessity, but some women may have had other reasons to choose them, ranging from personal affection to social advantage to involvement in the church. Despite repeated and concerted campaigns to brand priests' partners as unclean, many lived undisturbed in their partnerships, unless and until either a local wave of reform or a disgruntled neighbor forced authorities to take notice. Nevertheless, the fact that these circumstances could disrupt the partnerships, the lack of legal protection for the woman and her children, and the fact that everyone knew it was not a legal marriage tended to make the woman's honor as well as her economic standing precarious. Among laypeople, a union between people of roughly similar standing had a good chance of being recognized as a marriage. In a sense, no woman could ever be of equal standing as a priest and therefore could never enter into an entirely respectable relationship with him.

But the idea that no woman—indeed, no layperson—could ever be of equal standing with a priest changed dramatically over the course of the Middle Ages. The church reformers of the eleventh and early twelfth centuries made an argument for the church's superiority over lay society on the grounds of ritual as well as moral purity. Before that time, clerical celibacy was mainly a more perfect form of an asceticism that was an unenforceable ideal for both clergy and laity.[1] In the reform era, it became part of a general effort to separate the clergy from the laity and increase the power and superiority of the church. New monastic movements emphasized asceticism as part of this separation. By the later Middle Ages, the separation, to the extent that it had ever existed in practice, had broken down. The secular clergy were not monks, and they were not very separate. The argument for celibacy became one for social order: the clergy should set a good example by not leading a disordered life. Echoes of the purity argument remained, especially in the literary treatment of priests' partners; but by the end of the Middle Ages, the church's treatment of clerical celibacy, both theoretically and in practice, was essentially about how to keep up the appearance of the greater holiness of churchmen.

The degree of acceptance of priests' partners varied, not just across different times and places within medieval western Europe but within a given community. Priests' unions were common enough that many people must have lived alongside such couples and taken them for granted; yet women who lived with priests could also be labeled "whores" by their neighbors. A partial analogy might be the way same-sex couples are regarded in the United States in the early twenty-first century. Like priests and their partners in the Middle Ages, these couples cannot legally marry in most U.S. states as of this writing (although in the United States, they can no longer be hauled into court merely for engaging in sex, whereas medieval priests could). In areas with a high concentration of such couples, their presence is routine and unremarkable. In other regions, they may encounter hostility as well as welcome. One's degree of acceptance of these unions is likely to be affected by whether one personally knows such a couple. We may imagine that things worked in much the same way for priests and their partners in the Middle Ages, although, to be sure, there were men like Peter Damian, who knew clerical couples and strongly disapproved. Today, public opinion polls can measure the extent to which same-sex relationships are accepted in society, and we can see that it is rising. But there remains a spectrum of opinion: it is both acceptable and unacceptable, tolerated and not tolerated. The same would have been true of clerical unions in the Middle Ages. A major difference, of course, is the role of gender. The two partners in a contemporary same-sex union are likely to be tolerated or objurgated equally. (An exception might be if one of the partners conforms to traditional gender appearances or roles more than the other.) Priests, however, were always men, and their partners (at least those under discussion here) were women, and they could be treated quite differently.[2]

A great deal of opprobrium was directed against the priests' partners. A simple but not very useful explanation is that in a patriarchal system, everything got blamed on women. A slightly more sophisticated one is that with new emphasis on the Eucharist in the eleventh and twelfth centuries, a corresponding emphasis was placed on the purity of the priest who consecrated it. The priest had to be ritually separated from the layman (and laywoman), and celibacy was a way of doing this. An impure priest, then, was polluted by contact with women.[3] But there is more to the condemnation of priests' partners than the abjection of women because they polluted the priests. Declaring a union not to be marriage automatically lowered the social status of the female partner. Women were in a vicious cycle: if they were not as honorable as their partners, they were not wives; if they were not wives, they were dishonored and open to an accusation of deviant sexuality (and even, in the decrees of some eleventh-century councils, to punishment by enslavement).[4] Such accusations were leveled against the male partners, too, but women often suffered more from these accusations.

This chapter begins by examining two historical moments when clerical marriage came under intense discussion: the reform era of the late eleventh to early twelfth century, and that of the sixteenth. These first two sections focus particularly on the writings of church leaders, whereas the following section considers texts with a wider audience: exempla and imaginative literature from the twelfth through the fifteenth centuries, to see what kind of picture of priests' partners medieval people would have been exposed to and could have internalized. The chapter will then turn to ways in which the church courts at the end of the Middle Ages, especially the example of Paris, policed priests' sexual activity and their involvement with women. Once again, we need to keep in mind the problems of finding evidence on questions like these. We know about behavior that was seen as transgressive because it ended up in court records or otherwise being commented on. We do not know as much about behavior that did not bother people. We have, then, to employ some version of an argument from silence to determine what would have been considered normal behavior. Although all these discourses tended to come from people who were hostile to these relationships and the men and women who participated in them, the church court records may be our best entrée into the way typical medieval people would have thought about these unions.

Jo Ann McNamara identified the reform movement at the beginning of the second millennium as a turning point in the European gender system, and other scholars following her have seen the attendant "monasticization of the clergy" as a key transformation of masculinity.[5] The Protestant Reformation, with its valorization of marriage and the patriarchal family, has been seen by many scholars as a turning point in the gender system.[6] A comparison of the discourse around clerical unions in these two historical junctures reveals that at both moments, the purity of the clergy was at issue, but the high medieval reform movement placed greater emphasis on the salvific consequences of that purity, whereas in the late Middle Ages and sixteenth century, the emphasis was more squarely on the social consequences. The sixteenth-century reform era was outside what we call the "Middle Ages," but the attitudes and arguments expressed then about marriage grow out of the centuries of medieval European experience with clerical celibacy and can demonstrate how ways of thinking about the latter changed over a period when the theory, if not the practice, was taken for granted.

Priestly Marriage in the Central Medieval Reform Era

Up until the eleventh century, clerical marriage was discouraged within the Western church—celibacy had been required, in theory, of those in major orders since the fourth century—but it was not therefore invalidated: if a priest and his partner disobeyed and married anyway, the marriage was still valid.[7] The church reform movement after the turn of the millennium placed much more emphasis on clerical celibacy than previously. In 1022, the Synod of Pavia declared that wives and children of the clergy could be subject to penal servitude. The laity were encouraged to boycott the masses performed by married priests, although the sacraments performed by such a priest were still valid. The First Lateran Council, in 1123, consolidating various legislative provisions that dated back as early as Leo IX in the mid-eleventh century, forbade clerical marriage and required separation of the spouses. Clerics who married or took concubines could be deprived of their benefices. The Second Lateran Council, in 1139, following the lead of a regional synod in Pavia in 1135, declared that such unions were invalid, in words that made clear that a line was being drawn, not between sexual activity and abstinence, but between other unions and marriage: "This type of coupling, which is contracted against the church's rule, we deem not to be marriage." Henceforth all women involved in unions with men in the holy orders of subdeacon or above were concubines and not wives; this position was reinforced in subsequent centuries by decretalists and repeated synodal decrees.[8] In the earlier Middle Ages, when we see references to a priest's concubine, it may be that the couple had deliberately chosen not to marry; after the mid-twelfth century, there was no legal alternative.[9] Extensive discussion of whether the clergy's long-term unions with women could be considered marriages, and the social and theological implications of this question, did not emerge again until the later Middle Ages and did not come to the forefront until the 1520s and 1530s.

The scholarly consensus about clerical celibacy at the time of the central medieval reform movement is that it has to do with a ritual purity that separated the clergy from the laity.[10] Politically, the church was asserting its independence from lay authority, and doing so required a morally superior clergy. (In a crasser economic sense, this independence from lay authority also required that the clergy not have dependents and heirs who would cause property to go out of the hands of the church, and clerical marriage was associated with violence and plundering for this reason.)[11] Theologically, increasing emphasis on the Eucharist elevated the priest's role and required him to be in an appropriate state to handle the body of God. The reasons for setting the clergy apart were multiple; recent scholarship has stressed the power and property element perhaps more than the theological, but both were couched in the rhetoric of purity and separation. Although abstaining from marriage was not the same thing as abstaining from all sexual activity, it was a step toward that goal in the church's eyes.

Although both Christianity and Judaism put a great deal of emphasis on abstinence from sex (at least at particular times) in understandings of ritual purity, this was not the only possible approach. In Leviticus, a priest was defiled by handling a dead body, but the reform movement did not focus on keeping the clergy away from corpses. The shedding of blood, permitted to the laity under some circumstances, did make a cleric impure, but it did not excite the same sort of concern among reformers as did sexual activity: the existence or proximity of weapons did not pose the same kind of threat as did the existence or proximity of women.[12] The selling of ecclesiastical offices did perhaps pose such a threat. Gregory VII (1073–85), the great reform pope, objected to simony (the process of buying and selling ecclesiastical offices) as much as, if not more than, he objected to clerical unchastity.[13] But this did not carry over into making the handling of money in general polluting; it was only radicals like St. Francis who opposed it. And criticism of simony was, as Conrad Leyser points out, often couched in sexual language.[14] Hugh Thomas notes that critiques of other behavior on the part of the twelfth-century clergy (particularly in England, his focus), such as avarice, gluttony, ignorance, and so forth, focused on the priest's responsibility to set a good example for his flock; with regard to sexual behavior, however, the example argument was much less important, and the focus was much more on purity.[15]

The selling of offices was a wrongful use of money and of church office; but the reformers who criticized clerical sexual activity found more to object to than just the wrongful use of the female body. That body itself was polluting. The attitude of many church reformers even toward sexual activity on the part of the married laity was ambivalent, although the central trend in high medieval theology would be toward considering reproduction a good thing.[16] When it came to the clergy, who should be "temples of God, vessels of the Lord and sanctuaries of the holy Spirit," in the words of the Second Lateran Council, not just concubinage or fornication but marriage, too, was sinful and forbidden. *All* women with a connection with priests were concubines, or whores.[17]

The best-known rant against clerical sexual activity is that by Peter Damian, who, in writing to Pope Nicholas II in 1059, said that priests with wives "make themselves one flesh with a whore." Addressing the priests, he said, "At the imposition of your hand the holy spirit descends, and with it you touch the genitals of whores."[18] In a 1064 letter to Bishop Cunibertus of Turin, he called priests' wives, specifically:

> Charmers of clerics, appetizers of the devil, expulsion from paradise, venom of minds, sword of souls, poison of drinkers, toxin of banqueters, matter of sin, occasion of ruin . . . harem of the ancient enemy, hoopoes, screech-owls, owls, wolves, leeches . . . whores, prostitutes, lovers, wallows of greasy pigs, dens of unclean spirits, nymphs, sirens, witches, Dianas . . . through you the devil is fed on such delicate banquets, he is fattened on the exuberance of your

lust . . . vessels of the anger and furor of the Lord, stored for the day
of vengeance . . . impious tigers, whose bloodstained mouths cannot
refrain from human blood . . . harpies, who fly around and seize
the lord's sacrifices and cruelly devour those who are offered to the
Lord . . . lionesses who like monsters make careless men perish in
the bloody embraces of the harpies . . . sirens and Charybdis, who
while you bring forth the sweet song of deception, contrive of the
ravenous sea an inescapable shipwreck . . . mad vipers, who because
of the impatience of the burning lust of your lovers mutilate Christ,
who is the head of the clergy.[19]

Old Testament priests, he noted, were required to abstain from their wives before performing their sacrifice (Luke 1:23); since Christian priests performed the
sacrifice of the mass daily, they needed to abstain continuously.[20] Damian was
extreme in his polemic but was widely read and influential in his day, and he
was not alone.[21] Humbert of Silva Candida, sent by the pope as an envoy to the
Greek church, wrote a tract *Contra Nicetam*, which had something of the same
tone, suggesting that a Greek who supported clerical marriage was based not in
a monastery but in a brothel and "want[ed] to make the church of God a synagogue of Satan and a whorehouse of Balaam and Jezebel."[22] The main theme of
the overwhelming cascade of imagery was transgression, pollution, and unclean-
liness, rather than greed or disorder. Pope Gregory VII himself picked up this
language.[23] It was also taken up in sermons by less prominent figures, including,
for example, the English preacher Thomas Agnellus, who attacked priests who
dared to go "from a whore's bed to the table of the lord, from a place of pollution
to a place of sanctification . . . with sordid hands and a polluted mouth," as well
as others, such as Gerald of Wales, Thomas of Chobham, and Peter of Blois.[24]

The problem with clerical marriage, then, was first and foremost a problem with sexual activity, although distracting the priest from spiritual concerns
or dissipating the goods of the church on the family of the priest also found
their way into discussions (and concerns over property may have motivated
some of the discussion of other issues). This concern for purity was not new,
but it was newly prominent.[25] If, in the words of R. I. Moore, "in drawing
a new line between the sacred and the profane celibacy became the primary
and indispensable criterion," it was the lack of sexual activity, not just the lack
of a family, that defined the clergy as separate.[26] Peter Damian notoriously
attacked sodomy as well.[27] For the most part, however, the deep suspicion
of sex translated into a deep suspicion of women, whose sexualized bodies

represented a constant temptation and threat. Conrad Leyser suggests that much of this gendered rhetoric was not about actual women, but rather used women "to think with," as a battleground for struggles among men about whether kings or churchmen should dominate, or whether bishops or monks should control the church. Similarly, Maureen Miller suggests that "[t]he real struggle in the reform movement was not men against women, but clerical men against laymen. . . . The reformers' vilification of women did harm women, but it was not directed chiefly at them." Reforming clerics wanted to claim moral superiority, and blaming women for polluting the church was a convenient way to do this. But it was still real women whose liaisons were demoted to concubinage and who were stripped of any property and inheritance rights that they may have had.[28] Indeed, popes from Benedict VIII in 1022 at Pavia to Urban II in 1089 at Melfi had called for the enslavement of priests' wives as punishment for their sacrilege.[29]

The defense of clerical marriage focused especially on the practical argument that, as the clergy could not remain chaste, it was better for them to marry than to have concubines. This was the main thrust of the eleventh-century pamphlet attributed to Ulrich of Augsburg, which circulated throughout the Middle Ages and into the Reformation, as well as other high medieval treatises.[30] The same Pauline passages (1 Cor. 7:2, "Because of fornication, let each man have his own wife and each woman her own husband," 1 Cor. 7:7, "I wish you all to be as I am; but each has a particular gift from God, some in this way and some in that," and 1 Tim. 3:2, "A bishop should be the husband of one wife") that were used in these texts would be the focus of later discussions as well. The Norman Anonymous countered the argument about the general polluting nature of women by noting that all sins are cleansed by baptism, and therefore children born in concubinage are no less worthy of ordination than those born in marriage. In so doing, he acknowledged that the relationship was indeed concubinage and not marriage.[31] Indeed, the defense of the position of priests' children, largely on the grounds of repentance and humaneness, was key in these early years of the reform, but subsequently fell out of the discussion rapidly. Serlo of Bayeux and others also attacked unmarried clergy as sodomites.[32]

Priestly Marriage in the Late Medieval/Reformation Era

A great deal of discussion about the clergy and their sexual relations—notably, a variety of synodal decrees setting out the appropriate penalties for concubinage—took place during the next three hundred years, but the discussion about whether clerical unions could include marriage did not become prominent again until the late Middle Ages, when Wycliffites in England as well as some orthodox writers denied the necessity of clerical celibacy.[33] Discussions at the Councils of Constance (1414–18) and Basel (1431–45) focused once again on suppressing concubinage rather than allowing marriage, although at Constance some leaders spoke against clerical celibacy on the grounds of its previous failure.[34] One treatise written for the Council of Constance was by the French lawyer Guillaume Saignet, although the surviving copies of his work date from the Council of Basel. Saignet suggested that nature did not permit celibacy; this did not mean that sexual license was appropriate but that marriage should be allowed to all.[35] Clerics polluted the church with fornication not because all sexual activity was sinful but because the church misguidedly prohibited a natural coupling, thus pushing the clergy into illicit unions. "They want to call themselves more than perfect and call themselves chaste but wrap themselves in the veil of hypocrisy."[36] Responding to the purity argument, Saignet said that marriage was a sacrament and therefore not impure. The theologian Jean Gerson refuted Saignet's position on marriage but argued elsewhere that under some circumstances, concubinary priests "should be tolerated like public prostitutes, lest worse things should happen."[37]

The fifteenth-century reforming tract *Reformatio Sigismundi*, drawing on a 1433–34 work by Bishop Johann Schele of Lübeck, complained that the church was not only misguided in prohibiting clerical marriage but also hypocritical in accepting other kinds of unions. Bishops brought legal cases against priests with concubines just to get money but tolerated the sin, to the damnation of their souls and those of their parishioners. Since the prohibition on priests' marriage was of human and not divine creation and did not apply to the universal church, it would be better to allow priests to marry, since under the celibacy requirement, they seduced the wives and daughters of other men, or became sodomites.[38] The Lollards also argued that lack of marriage turned priests to sodomy, as well as causing priests to seduce the wives and daughters of laymen.[39] The *Reformatio Sigismundi* was a polemic against the church hierarchy generally and an overall call for reform; clerical marriage was only a small part. It emphasized social order as a reason for clerical marriage—so that priests did not disrupt other men's patriarchal control over their households, by entering into unions with their daughters, or over their own bodies, by threatening them with sodomy. The author, like Saignet and other opponents of clerical celibacy (but unlike some of the sixteenth-century reformers), did not suggest that priests should just go ahead and marry regardless of church law. These writers proposed that the church should change the rules, not that the domestic partners with whom the clergy might already be living were in fact wives and should be treated as such. Indeed, the *Reformatio* assumed that the unions in which priests might be currently involved were not long-term partnerships.

As the discourse shifted to the social rather than the spiritual consequences of celibacy or marriage, discussions tended to treat the women involved as people existing in society rather than merely as "good to think with." But three hundred years of experience did not necessarily make the discussions less misogynistic. Women's flesh was perhaps less inherently polluting, but women were still sinful and dangerous. The earlier arguments based upon ritual purity did not, of course, disappear. Jean Raulin, who preached in late medieval Paris, left a series of sermons on marriage in which he argued that priests should not marry because they administered the sacraments to the people and should do so in purity; because they should devote themselves entirely to serving God rather than caring for a family; and because family obligations would cause them to misappropriate the goods of the church. He rehearsed the same biblical passages about Old Testament priests abstaining from sexual relations when they served in the Temple.[40] These comments, however, constituted one small section within a set of sermons that were largely concerned with the value of marriage (if properly undertaken) to society and social order.

The debate about clerical marriage framed in terms of social order continued during the sixteenth-century Reformations in both the German-speaking lands and in England.[41] In neither place was a priest's marriage simply a personal choice, either among forms of union or between sexual activity and abstinence: it was a statement about belief in church reform. A form of the "lesser evil" argument—that abstinence is good but that marriage is better than fornication for those who cannot abstain—meshed well with the Protestant idea that all humans are sinners who can be saved not by their own works but only by God's grace. Reformers generally acknowledged that chastity was a good thing for those who were called to it, but they argued that most priests were not. The choice, thus, was not between sexual activity and a precarious chastity, but between marriage and other forms of sexual activity. As Martin Luther said, if it is not possible for a man to be chaste and unmarried, it is God's wish for him to keep the commandment while relinquishing the vow: "Let him marry a wife, and the law of chastity will be easy for him. Keeping the vow not to marry leads to debauchery."[42]

But the argument was not about taking behavior that the priests were going to engage in anyway, and blessing it as marriage in order to make it less polluting. Rather, the argument that debauchery was the alternative to marriage implied that there was a distinction between two kinds of women: those who would marry and those who would enter into other kinds of unions. The Catholic priests had their partners, but those were whores, whereas the reformed clergy had married respectable women. The English Bible translator William Tyndale wrote that the clerical celibacy rule (and, indeed, the restriction on women's preaching) showed the church's hatred of women because it degraded them and that churchmen would associate only with the worst of them: "O poor women, how despise ye them! The viler the better welcome unto you. An whore had ye lever than an honest wife."[43] Luther, in his 1520 treatise "To the Christian Nobility of the German Nation," also implied that it was not just the recognition of a formal marriage that was needed to reclassify the woman from a whore to an honest wife. He placed a great emphasis on intent. When a pious and righteous priest wanted to live together with a woman "in true marital faith," it was right for them to do so, whatever the pope might say, because "the blessedness of your soul is more important than the tyrannical, arrogant, sacrilegious laws."[44] In arguing that such a union was a real marriage if the parties meant it that way, Luther implied that any permanent union could be considered a marriage but also that a different type of woman was willing to enter into marital and nonmarital relationships. This may or may not have been true in social terms. To be the wife of a reformed priest in the earlier years of the Reformation might lead to similar material disadvantages and possibly greater opprobrium than what a clerical concubine in the later Middle Ages would have experienced, but the difference is that many of the women who married Protestant clergy did so out of religious commitment. Certainly, some couples who had already been living together took the opportunity to make it a marriage, but this was far from true of all. Luther, for example, married a nun, and encouraged his followers to do so as well.

"If Priests Had Wives": Katharina Schütz Zell

The Lutheran reformer Katharina Zell, who married a priest, also spoke out in favor of clerical marriage: "If priests had wives, they would not be able to exchange one for the other, as they do with whores, toss one out and take another in."[45] Zell was one of the earliest wives of priests in Strasbourg, and her strong defense of the institution of clerical marriage gives us a clearer idea of what was at stake for women. For her, there was a clear difference between a union that was considered a marriage and one that was not.

Katharina Schütz was born around 1498 into a respectable burgher family in Strasbourg; her father was a woodworker.[46] She was literate in German. In 1518, Matthew Zell, aged forty, came from the University of Freiburg to become the priest of St. Lorenz parish. By 1521, the printing press in Strasbourg was turning out reform pamphlets, and Matthew was using Luther's German gospel in his preaching. By 1522, he was questioning purgatory and intercessory prayer from the pulpit. Katharina later described how Luther's teachings gave her the answer to her "anxiety and worry about the grace of God," though she did not say that those teachings had reached her via Matthew.[47] The bishop accused Matthew of heresy in late 1522, and the city split. By late 1523, the reformer Martin Bucer, a former Dominican who had married a nun, had come to Strasbourg with his wife and encouraged the other clergy to marry.[48] Matthew Zell preached a sermon in favor of another priest who announced that he was going to marry the woman with whom he had been living. We do not know the course of Matthew and Katharina's acquaintance; given her family status, it is not likely they lived together before their formal wedding. Bucer, who performed that wedding, wrote that Matthew Zell married "a very evangelical virgin."[49]

Matthew and five other married priests were excommunicated in 1524, but the city defended them. Katharina defended them as well, in a text that the council asked Matthew not to let her publish. Her pamphlet did appear, however, in September 1524. She also published a number of other writings, including work directed at women. She collaborated with Matthew in his pastoral efforts and corresponded with Luther and other reformers about theological and other issues; she and Matthew also traveled within Germany. Their first child, born between 1525 and 1527, died in February 1527; their second, born in the late 1520s or early 1530s, died in late 1532 or early 1533. Matthew died in 1548, and Katharina spoke at his funeral. She continued corresponding and teaching until her death in 1562.

Unlike most of the other women who appear in these portraits, Katharina Schütz Zell left a sizable footprint in the historical record. We have a number of her own writings, and contemporaries wrote about her as well. Because so much has already been written about her, I have given only a very basic sketch of her life and work here, and will not discuss her considerable contributions to Protestant theology, pastoral work, care of refugees, and the question of who holds authority in the church. Rather, the focus here is on the way Katharina Zell defended her own marriage and clerical marriage in general.

Katharina Zell presented her 1524 work, *Apologia for Master Matthew Zell*, as a defense of her husband, as well as a defense of the whole principle of clerical marriage.[50] Although a woman who was in a sexual relationship with a priest, even if she claimed to have married him, could be considered immoral, she was not directly violating canon law or a vow in the way that her husband might be, and therefore she wished to defend him, who "is now and has for a long time been maligned with such great lies."[51] She claimed that she was writing without her husband's knowledge or approval, thus exculpating him from charges of heresy, but she cleared herself from charges of disobedience by claiming that if the lies had been told about anyone other than himself, he would have challenged them. But she also referred to "very great devilish lies" told about herself.[52] She presents herself as having "helped to establish priests' marriage": "with God's help I was also the first woman in Strasbourg who opened the way for it, when I still did not wish to marry any man. But when I saw the great fear and angry resistance and the great whoredom, I married one myself, so that I could give heart and make a way for all Christians, which I hope has happened."[53] Katharina was not, in fact, the first woman in Strasbourg to marry a priest. It has been suggested that she was referring to their betrothal rather than their wedding, which fell before the other marriage in favor of which Matthew wrote, but it may also be that she meant that she was the first who had entered into marriage as a new union rather than marrying a man with whom she had previously lived.[54]

She also explained that she had married Matthew for the sake of his soul: "Having considered his life and that of others, I dared by God's grace and power to try to gain his soul and many others." Matthew had apparently not been a paragon of virtue before the marriage: "I do not want to answer about how he kept house before I became his wife. He behaved then just as pope and bishop want: those who forbid the marriage that God commanded and permit harlots whom God forbade."[55] By claiming that she was saving the souls of others as well as his own by marrying him, she implied that the clergy served as an example. Now that she had married him, she explained, she saw it as her duty to defend him, and she therefore denied rumors that he had beaten her, that he had attempted to have sex with their maid or other women, and that she had left him and returned to her parents' home. By defending him against these rumors, of course, she was also defending her own honor as a married woman. As far as Matthew's motivations for marrying, she was modest: "He began such a marriage because he wanted very much to raise up God's honor, his own salvation, and that of all his brothers. For I can perceive in him no dishonorableness, no inclination toward lust or other such thing—for I am not gifted with either overwhelming beauty or riches or other virtue that might move one to seek me in marriage."[56]

Katharina mentioned that she had sent a long letter to the bishop of Strasbourg in which she "compared marriage and harlotry [*hůrey*] with each other according to the teaching of godly scripture."[57] She suggested that there were two main reasons that the pope and bishops did not want to permit clerical marriage, despite its warrant in Paul's letters. "If a priest has a wife, he behaves like any other honorable upright citizen and gives the bishop no tax for it, because God has freely given it to them. If they have whores, they are the pope's and bishop's own people [*eigenleute*, a feudal expression]. He who wants to have one must have his permission and pay a tax."[58] Katharina was not alone in accusing the church of greed in wishing to keep clergy unmarried. Matthew Zell made a similar argument in his 1523 pro-clerical marriage work *Ein Collation*.[59] The result, Katharina said, is that "one has five, six harlots [*hůren*], another seven women in childbed at the same time and nevertheless a pretty prostitute [*metzen*] at home."[60]

The second reason that Katharina Zell gave for the church's opposition to clerical marriage was cited at the beginning of this section: the church did not wish to impose good morals on its clerics. If priests had wives, they would have to "live honorably" instead of taking up with one woman and then with another. "For in marriage the couple must have and bear many griefs with each other (on which account these priests do not wish to be bound by marriage)."[61] This was the argument from social order: priests' behavior will be better if they marry. For Katharina, the difference between marriage and other unions seems to have been its permanence. Furthermore, if a married priest sinned, he had no excuse and could legitimately be punished, rather than just claiming the weakness of the flesh. She also mentioned the position of priests' unmarried partners and how marriage would be much fairer: "Secular people cannot bear [clerical marriage], who have such whoring priests among them. When they die, the children of the marriage take the inheritance. Otherwise the relatives take it and throw out the bastards, even if the devil takes the children's souls."[62] If priests were married, their children would inherit their property, rather than the priests' lay relatives being able to dispossess them; any control of property or inheritance by the women themselves goes unmentioned, but once again, the bearing of legitimate heirs is seen as a main purpose of marriage. The laypeople who could not bear clerical marriage, she further wrote, were also those who engaged in whoredom themselves and did not want priests to behave better.

In the sermon that Katharina preached at Matthew's funeral (at least as it was printed), she was still on the defensive about clerical marriage in general and her own in particular.[63] She referred to the couple's marriage twenty-four years earlier as "without any evil motivation (God knows), acting against the wicked pope's lying and devil-spawned prohibition of marriage," and noted that during the marriage, "he and I have received much insult and infamy for the sake of the Lord Jesus."[64] She asked God's pardon if she had not served her husband as well as she might, but claimed that "I know that [Matthew] loved me and gladly forgave me everything before I asked and as much as it lay in him showed me friendly and Christian fellowship."[65] The phrase "as much as it lay in him" indicates that perhaps the union was not as entirely smooth as she would have wanted people to believe when she talked about her great sorrow at his death and her wish to be reunited with him in blessedness. She did, however, write in 1553 to Caspar Schwenckfeld: "He granted and allowed me space and time to read, hear, pray, study and be active in all good things, early and late, day and night; indeed, he took great joy in that—even when it meant less attention to or neglect in looking after his physical needs and running his household."[66]

The marriage of the clergy had social implications not only for the women they married, like Katharina, but also for their flocks. It is better to marry than to have your neighbor burn, claimed the reformers; if priests do not marry and instead fornicate, they lead others astray with bad examples. As Tyndale wrote, "It pertaineth unto the common people, and most of all unto the weakest, that their priests be endued with all virtue and honesty."[67] The Swiss reformer Ulrich Zwingli wrote that "if we marry we sin less against the little ones of Christ"[68] (Matt. 18:6); marriage prevented a priest not just from violating God's law but from harming other people. Johann Eberlin, a German Franciscan who became active in Luther's reform, put in the mouth of an unreformed priest, "Perhaps some laypeople in secret sin will be less God-fearing seeing that I have honor and wealth in public sin."[69] The argument about examples, of course, could be turned around, since a celibate clergy was supposed to set a good example of holy chastity for the laity. Both traditionalists and reformers could agree, however, that public concubinage made the church look bad. The question was how best to avoid it: by eradicating it, making it less public, or replacing it with marriage. A fundamental assumption of the reformers, articulated more by some than by others, was that chastity was not a possibility for most of the clergy, and therefore the choice was between marriage and other, sinful forms of long-term union or more casual sexual activity.

Because chastity was not possible for many, reformers argued, a concubinary clergy did not just model a disregard for the law that would lead to social disorder if it spread to the laity; they also created that disorder themselves. The fear of the clergy appropriating women under the control of other men permeated the Reformation arguments in favor of clerical marriage, although it was not unknown earlier. One of Eberlin's dialogues showed a priest having an affair with a married woman, the wife of his servant: "He threshed in my barn while I lay in his bed."[70] George Joye, an English Lutheran who also wrote under the name James Sawtry, wrote that priests "keep other men's wives, their children to sit by other men's fires, and as themselves live by other men's labors, so make they other men to cover their whores and whelpes under the only names of husband and father."[71] Laymen's control over their "wives, daughters, and servants,"[72] as Tyndale wrote, was threatened; this, to him, was more important than the moral status of the wife or the priest. The point was not saving the cleric himself, or the body of Christians for whom he should set an example, from a greater sin, but rather protecting the laity from the practical consequences of the cleric's choices. This characterization of clerics as likely to cuckold other men was hardly new to the reformers—it was a common medieval topos—but its deployment as an argument against clerical celibacy rather than just as a satire on clerics was new.

Finally, reformers argued that marriage was as positive a good for priests as for laypeople. A priest needed a wife not just because of his all-too-human sexual needs but because of the need for someone to run the household; the fact that priests' partners had done so for centuries without marriage was not mentioned. The procreation of children, too, was a positive aspect of marriage of which the clergy should not be deprived. Luther wrote in "On the Estate of Marriage" that monks and nuns who adhered to their vows were not worthy to rock or feed a baptized child, even the child of a whore.[73] Marriage could also teach a priest the patience and leadership he needed. George Joye wrote in the late 1520s to early 1530s of the benefits of marriage, citing Paul: "The governing of his house is an introduction unto a greater cure. There shall he practice . . . and learn to correct with discretion and love, now to be rough and sharp, then to be merciful and soft, all in time and in good order to keep them in subjection, fear and learning."[74]

Even the defenders of clerical celibacy in the Reformation era made their argument in terms that took much more account of the society around them than did the eleventh- and twelfth-century reformers who supported celibacy. The issue was still about separation of the clergy from the laity, but the emphasis was not mainly upon the priest's sacramental role. Rather, separation was needed because it was the basis of proper social order. A cleric who was not better than a layperson could not take his proper place in the moral hierarchy. Further, if some priests married, it would create a division and cause the laity to distrust those who did not.[75]

Early modern defenders of clerical celibacy, like their medieval counterparts, referred to women who would enter into putative marriages with the reformed clergy as whores. Helen Parish suggests that, in essence, Catholic writers took the pre-Reformation polemic against concubinary priests and applied it to married ones.[76] But the use of language was subtly different from that of the central Middle Ages. Instead of women in general posing a threat to the clergy, a sharp distinction was made between whores (including concubines) and laymen's wives. Thomas More, for example, backed away from the idea that sexuality in general is sinful, and argued that "the church both knoweth and confesseth, that wedlock and priesthood be not repugnant but compatible of their nature,"[77] except that church law required that priests take a vow. Therefore, priests' wives are whores not because all carnality is sinful but because breaking a vow defiles the priest. In fact, a German bishop argued, for a priest to marry is worse than fornication because fornication does not break the vow: "It is better that a priest through weakness sins with a poor whore than that he takes a wife, against his vow and against the custom of the church."[78]

There was, then, a distinction between a good woman who married a layperson and a corrupt one who had some kind of relationship with a priest, whether or not it was called marriage. The English Catholic writer Thomas Harding in a 1567 tract wrote: "Seeing therefore Monks, Friars and Priests that be wived, can not truly call their women wives, being indeed no wives, but strumpets; they do wisely . . . to put upon so filthy a thing the clean name of a sister, or of a yokefellow, that whereas the marriage itself is naught, yea detestable sacrilege, and therefore of right they themselves should be called sacrilegious adulterers and their women sacrilegious harlots: yet by allurement of an honest name women might be content to yoke with them, which, if they were called by their true names, would never be induced to be made instruments of so open abomination."[79] Marriage itself was honorable, not just a lesser evil. It was not (as it was in the central Middle Ages) the women who were dangerous temptations to the clergy but the clergy who were dangerous to women by convincing them that a union was marriage when it was not.

Defenders of celibacy also used the argument about priests setting a good example in the maintenance of social order—not to argue that priests should be exemplars of a chastity to which everyone should aspire, but to defend the importance of sticking to the rules. In his response to Luther in 1521, Jerome Emser wrote that allowing priests to marry would allow everyone else to slip out of their obligations as well. If priests should be allowed to marry because of human frailty, then should not wives be allowed to cheat on their husbands, and young men to steal money from their fathers to give to whores?[80] Catholic reformers also argued that toleration of nonmarital clerical unions set a bad example for the "poor laypeople" who believed that they, too, could be easily absolved for their adulteries; higher standards were necessary for this reason and also because concubinage left the church open to accusations from Protestant reformers.[81]

There were, of course, theological reasons to support or oppose celibacy. Without a belief in transubstantiation, the argument that purity was required to handle the Eucharist lost some of its force; similarly, with Luther's "priesthood of all believers," the idea that priests needed to be purer than others, or bound by a different law, made less sense.[82] But to say that changes in attitudes toward clerical celibacy were driven by theological change obscures the social context and gender implications that were undeniably present. Robert Barnes argued that the pollution of touching female flesh did not apply to wives: "For the Pope reckoneth it filthy, and not seemly, that a Priest should with his holy hands touch a woman's body, and with the same hands consecrate the holy sacrament. . . . What abominable holiness of hypocrisy is this? To reckon a priest impure, and unclean, because he has used himself in God's holy ordinance? . . . Why be not your hands defiled for handling of whores' flesh? Is whores' flesh so clean? That priests may handle it? And the flesh of an honest, and a good woman so unclean, that Priests must be burned for handling of it?"[83] Barnes, though a Lutheran, was not denying transubstantiation in this passage, but rather the relevance of celibacy to it. A good woman, subject to a husband, was not a source of impurity.

In terms of the gender system, the eleventh/twelfth-century abjection of any sexually active woman had been part of the attempt by the church to wrest political power—and, of course, control over property—from the great dynasties in which women had an important role. As such, of course, it was hotly contested, and if the views of a Peter Damian were only dubiously characteristic of the church, they can hardly be said to be characteristic of society as a whole. We can say, though, that the high medieval reformers represented part of a trend that developed more in the all-masculine spaces of the medieval monastery and university: to use women to think with in a negative way, representing all fleshly sin. As Caroline Bynum and others have shown, this negative discourse equating women with flesh was hardly universal, but the existence of an important counter-discourse of woman as positive symbol of the flesh does not mean that the negative valence was absent.[84]

In the Reformation period, marriage became much more a political symbol—whether one married was a sign of where one stood on various ecclesiological as well as theological issues. This was especially so in England, where a greater proportion of reformers seem to have married than on the Continent, although German reformers, too, wrote extensively about clerical marriage. The basic Reformation argument about a diminished sacramental and mediatory role for the clergy meant that they were not as marked off from the laity as in the Catholic view. The arguments over marriage, too, were played out largely in terms of scriptural exegesis.[85]

Despite these caveats, the overall tendency by the sixteenth century, as opposed to the central Middle Ages, was toward seeing marriage not mainly as a concession to sin, tolerable for the laity but unacceptable for the clergy, but rather as part of an ordered society. Even before the Protestants declared it not a sacrament, marriage in the later Middle Ages had become more a means of living a godly and well-regulated life than it was a symbol for the union of Christ and the church or God and the soul.[86] Ideas about nature that developed over the course of the later Middle Ages led to an emphasis on sexual activity and reproduction as part of God's ordered creation. The idea that marriage might be as great a good as perpetual virginity did not change suddenly with the Reformation but was part of a new emphasis on the family in the fifteenth century.[87]

A more positive view of marriage did not necessarily entail a more positive attitude toward women, whatever that may mean, or toward sexual partnerships in general. Both Catholics and Protestants put women into the categories of wives and whores, and agreed that women who lived with Catholic priests were the latter. It may not be better to be considered a potentially unruly force to be controlled through submission to a husband than it is to be considered a fleshly temptation. Women were dangerous in both gender systems, but in the high medieval period, they were dangerous to the soul;

in the Reformation, they were dangerous to society. The arguments about clerical celibacy were redrawn accordingly. But the changes in the attack and defense of clerical marriage were not only due to changes in attitudes about marriage more broadly; they were also due to the centuries of experience with the clergy's nonmarried partners. A look at the objurgation of these women helps show us how a celibate elite deliberately placed the blame for their own lapses on women.

Calling Names: Priests' Whores

We turn now to a period between the two eras of reform discussed above, to look at the kind of language used for priests' partners in ecclesiastical and other literary sources from the twelfth to the fifteenth centuries. In such a small space, of course, it is not possible to give a full narrative account of the development of this literature, so we will review some general trends. The institutional church fought a continuing battle of words against the presence of such women in priests' households.[88] Sometimes the women were equated with prostitutes or other promiscuous women; at other times, they were called by terms that implied a domestic relationship but were less emotionally charged.[89] *Focaria* in medieval Latin was often used for a housekeeper in a sexual relationship with her employer.[90] This word is sometimes translated as "hearth-mate" and might seem to fill a modern as well as a medieval need, as denoting a long-term domestic relationship in a somewhat less ambiguous way than "partner." However, it also carried a connotation of service: the "hearth" element derived from the woman's doing the cooking. Another euphemism, *pediseca*, originally a servant or handmaid, was also used in particular regions.[91] The fact that these terms denoting service came to mean sexual partners is an indication of the way in which it was assumed (and not just in the case of clerical households) that female servants, especially those working for men who did not have wives, would be sexually involved with their employers. The most widely used terms, however, from the twelfth century through the fifteenth, were *concubina* and, to a lesser extent, especially in nonlegal texts, *meretrix*. The use of the term *meretrix*, "whore," or its vernacular equivalents, did not necessarily denote a prostitute, although there were overtones of venality. Any woman who had sex outside of marriage could be considered the equivalent of a prostitute, and this conflation was used as a means to control women.[92] This connection was not restricted to a particular region or period.

All these terms applied only to the female partner in the relationship. A priest who was involved with such a woman could be referred to as a *concubinarius*; this was the term used by the Council of Basel in 1435 when it decreed that such priests were to lose their income for three months, and eventually to lose all their benefices.[93] It was not anywhere near as common a term as its female equivalent, however. "Whoremonger" became a common English insult in the Reformation for a priest with a partner, but was not a translation of any particular Latin term. The masculine forms *focarius* and *pedisecus* meant a kitchen boy and a footman/page, respectively, not the male partner in a male-female relationship. A priest who sinned with a woman was a sinful priest or a fornicator, but there was no insulting label to be stuck on him, as there was on the woman.

The polemics against priests' whores on the part of the institutional church did not go without response. In a series of English poems written shortly after the Fourth Lateran Council, in 1215, various priests voiced their inability to abstain from sexual relations and the risk to the wives and daughters of neighbors. Here the women with whom the priests wanted to continue relationships were referred to variously as *foemina* (woman), *uxor* (wife), *ancillula* or *famula* (servant), *meretrix* or *scorta* (whore), *coqua* (cook), or *concubina* (concubine). One poem asks, "If the creator wished priests to cease being lovers of women, for whom did the Savior die on the cross?" It concludes that, as each of the three orders has its duties, "rustics should work, knights fight, and clerics love" (the standard division was into those who work, those who fight, and those who pray). Clerics should have two concubines each, monks and canons three, and deans and bishops four or five: "Thus we shall fulfill the divine law."[94] These poems were satirical in intent, but the range of terms they used indicates that the lines among clerical marriage, concubinage, and more casual unions were not sharply drawn.

It is difficult to know which terms were used in general parlance.[95] One way of getting at what the general public would have heard, if not the words they would have spoken, is to look at how priests' partners were described in stories intended for use in sermons. These stories, *exempla*, were an international genre. From the thirteenth to the fifteenth centuries, collections circulated, first in Latin and then in the vernaculars, disseminated at first by the mendicant orders and then in forms intended for parish priests. The stories reveal the losing battle that the church was waging against priests' partners. When a text spoke of a priest being involved with a concubine, we cannot necessarily assume that this was a woman who was, for all practical purposes, a wife. The priest was not always depicted as living with her. But the fact that the language did not make careful distinctions is significant: any woman involved with a priest could be cast into the same category regardless of whether or not the union was a long-term domestic partnership. Exempla condemned these women both for their venality in attempting to acquire the goods of the church and for their lust, and they condemned them more than the priests themselves. Sometimes the tales were cautionary ones, focusing not on the sin but on its consequences for both partners or just for the woman (and, more rarely, just for the man).

A thirteenth-century English Dominican collection included a number of stories of a concubine dying suddenly, her soul being carried off by devils in view of her three children, her corpse unable to be lifted except by other concubines, and devils dragging her out of her coffin. In some of these stories, the priest was also at risk, his house consumed by fire, or he himself dying suddenly or in the arms of his partner (*fornicaria*).[96] Another collection included a story of a priest's concubine who died from being struck by lightning. She was outdoors because the priest was on his way to give an oath before the ecclesiastical court that he was not keeping a woman in his house; the traditional literary motif of the equivocal oath backfired on her.[97] The *Speculum Laicorum* (Mirror for Laypeople), compiled in England in the late thirteenth century and popular in the fourteenth and fifteenth centuries (it survives in eighteen manuscripts), included some of these same stories of priests' concubines carried away by demons in various guises. Somewhat unusually, one of these stories focused on the son of the union, a smith, who was asked to shoe a mule, which turned out to be his mother, a "priest's lover" (*sacerdotis fornicaria*) now inhabited by a demon.[98]

Jacques de Vitry, the late twelfth- to early thirteenth-century French sermon writer, was perhaps less harsh on priests' partners than the anonymous compilers of these other collections. He recounted a number of stories of clerics (not necessarily priests) and their concubines, as he called them, and put the blame on both parties. A priest and his concubine, traveling, stayed with a good woman, and she insisted that they both sleep in the latrine; the connection with filth is reminiscent of Peter Damian, but it was not the woman alone who was filthy. In another of Jacques's stories, a priest was told that he must give up either his concubine or his parish, and chose to keep the concubine, whom he referred to as a wife (*uxor*); she then left him. This story displayed her venality but also put the blame on the priest for his shortsightedness and his lust: "Unhappy are they who pay more attention to adorning the cadavers of concubines than the altars of Christ. The whore's robe is finer and more splendid than the altar-cloth, the chemise of the concubine is finer and more precious than the priest's surplice. They spend so much on the clothing of their concubines that the poor are wronged and clothed in rags."[99] An English Franciscan collection also focused more on a warning to priests than the sinfulness of their partners. It told a story of a cleric who promised to give up his concubine by a certain day; before the day arrived, he choked on his food, not having put aside his sin, "and received his judgment in infernal flame."[100]

The thirteenth-century French Dominican Étienne de Bourbon had a harsher view of priests' partners than Jacques de Vitry did. In one of Jacques's tales, a man told a whore (*meretrix*) that he must leave her because he had spent all his money on her and had nothing left but his cloak. At this, she began to weep. He attempted to comfort her, thinking that she was weeping at the thought of losing him, but she told him that she was weeping because he had managed to keep her from getting possession of the cloak as well. Jacques did not say that the man was a priest, but Étienne's and several other versions made him a priest or a university scholar.[101] Besides the cloak story, Étienne told another that was used elsewhere to illustrate the vanity of women generally, but he made it apply specifically to a priest's partners. A priest had two partners, one young and one old. Wanting him to appear young, the young one plucked out his gray hairs when delousing him, but the old one plucked out his dark hairs, until he ended up bald. Étienne added the detail, which does not appear elsewhere, that the man kept his old mistress (the *concubina* who had borne his children) even after he acquired the young one (called *focaria*, or hearth-mate), "that one for the love of their children, this one for the love of lust"; both terms implied domestic situations, but neither woman had her man's well-being at heart. Étienne went on to elaborate at length on the harm caused by *sacerdotissae*, "priestesses," who despoil the house of God.[102]

John of Bromyard, the fifteenth-century English Dominican who wrote a massive *Summa* for preachers, continued in the blame-the-woman vein. He argued that what made sacrilege so sinful as a species of lust was the violation of the vow that went with the holy orders.[103] This would suggest that the blame fell on the partner who was in orders rather than on the other. But, he noted, "The danger of the transgression of these vows rebounds not only on themselves but especially on the women with whom they sin," as he demonstrated with the same exempla that we have already seen. A priest's lover (*amasia*) died, and her corpse could not be lifted because of the weight of an unclean spirit; another's corpse was chained by demons who bridled it and rode it to hell.

Bromyard highlighted the pollution caused by the concubine, as well as her punishment. A necromancer conjured up several demons who were unable to expel a devil from a man, but when the man was placed in a bath in which a priest's concubine had bathed, the devil fled immediately.[104] The "Alphabet of Tales," an English version of a text probably by Arnoul of Liège, told several stories of priests who had lovers (*lemman*) or brief liaisons and who found the Eucharist taken from them—in one case, by a dove that swooped down and took it from his hand. The idea articulated by Peter Damian, that the hand that touches a whore should not touch the sacrament, was here given a vivid symbolic expression: "Wise men that knew him supposed that angels had taken it from him and carried it away to heaven, so that he who was a lecherous priest should not receive it to his damnation." A married priest who refused to touch his wife, or to let her touch him even as he lay on his deathbed, was also held up as a positive example.[105] This last tale presented the possibility that a married man could become a priest as long as he put away his wife—something that was theologically acceptable but not much discussed.

A Dominican collection of exempla in a mid-fourteenth-century German manuscript included another story about ritual purity. A parish priest "had a concubine as if she were a legitimate wife." When he was struck by a disease, he believed it to be a punishment from God, sent the concubine away, and was cured. However, he subsequently became very poor and the devil suggested to him that this was because he had sent away the woman who had been such a good manager (which suggests that "as if she were a legitimate wife" meant that she ran his household). He took her back and became prosperous again. The sequence of illness, expulsion, poverty, readmission, and prosperity repeated itself again. Then one day, he had a vision of demons coming to take him to torment. His sin had "become known to heaven like that of the sodomites." The devil complained mainly about the priest's failure to lead and protect his flock: "You have killed many by scandalizing them through your reprobate life." Children who had not been baptized were damned by his negligence. However, when the priest attempted to defend himself by putting on his vestments and holding a reliquary, the devil used the language of impurity: "You do not blush to put it around your neck, which was so polluted with the embraces of whores." The priest redeemed himself by joining the Cistercian order, leaving the polluted secular life altogether. The story was probably intended for clerics more than for laypeople. Yet the slippage from one woman who was almost a wife to the plural "whores" is striking.[106] The priest, before he became a monk, was not that different from a layman who could have a legitimate wife; but because he was a priest, she was automatically a whore.

The opprobrium was put on priests' partners partly because of a common medieval emphasis on women as tempters of men. The priests certainly came in for a share of blame, but the large body of didactic literature encouraging men to avoid women as temptresses placed the responsibility for men's sin on any woman who attempted to look attractive. Such tales influenced the way that people would have viewed priests' partners.[107] The *Book of the Knight of the Tower*, supposedly written by a French knight for the advice of his daughters, even said that women who had sex with priests (or married men, or monks, or servants, or worthless men) were worse than prostitutes: "They are more whores than common women at the brothel. For many women of the brothel do their sin only because of poverty, or because they were deceived by bad counsel of bawds and evil women. But all gentlewomen and others who have enough to live on, of their own or from service or otherwise, if they love this type of men, it must be because of the great ease they are in by the lust of their flesh and evil of their hearts."[108] The *Speculum Sacerdotale*, an English manual for confessors, also put the blame on women by making the penance for a priest's fornication or adultery less if it was "by sudden chance, or by the woman's steering and not of his own purpose or deliberation."[109]

The fourteenth-century English text *Handlyng Synne*, by Robert of Brunne, and the French versions on which it was based showed how individual authors could shift the emphasis subtly from the priest's partner to the priest himself; the variations in emphasis likely depended on the individual rather than the region or time period, but none of the texts blamed the priest more than they blamed his partner, even though one might think that he, as the person in authority, had more of the responsibility. The French *Manuel des Pechiez* said, "Each woman must think, when a priest wishes to kiss her, that his mouth is sacred to God." Robert of Brunne's version did not put the responsibility solely on the woman: priests should be "chaste and clean . . . of high degree in Holy Church's own retinue" and should not have dealings with women. No woman should kiss their mouths, which are hallowed to God's service, but the woman is not the only actor here: "No priest ought no woman touch, for, of foul touching, men sin much."[110] Both texts spoke of *presteresses*, or "priests' wives." The French called them she-devils who disturbed the dignity of the sacrament, and the English elaborated: it was a wonder that instead of taking any other man they would go with a priest, which is a much greater sin. The text even suggested that the sacraments, including the Eucharist at masses for the dead, were not valid if a concubinary priest performed them: "All, therefore, that now are/And that shall be, and now are gone/Shall damn that woman to be lost/And curse the time that she was born."[111] Although the idea that the sacraments were invalid because of the priest's sin was not orthodox theology, *Handlyng Synne* made this another occasion for blaming the partner. As we shall see, however, in practice, priests' partners seem in the later Middle Ages at least not to have been treated all that badly; the fulminations of the preachers had not had the desired effect.

Priests' Children

Unions that were fertile were more likely to appear in the sources than others. The birth of a child was obvious evidence of the existence of a sexual relationship, and when the father of a child or children was identified, the union was often more than casual and fleeting. The birth of a child was also likely to bring up issues of inheritance that might bring the union into the purview of the law where it had not otherwise been.[112]

Priests' sons were, in theory, denied access to holy orders, as were all those of illegitimate birth after the central Middle Ages.[113] Didactic texts as well as documents of practice, however, show that this was not always the case. *Handlyng Synne* includes a story about a priest's concubine—a woman he held "as his wife" for his entire life. When she survived him, her children "had great thought/how they were in sin forth brought/and how their mother lived in/all her life, mortal sin." They asked her to repent, but she refused, saying that she had three sons who were priests and that they would pray for her. She asked them to pray over her body for three days and she would be saved, "though I have lived a sinful life/And have been called a priest's wife." Her children's vigil, however, was disturbed by demons carrying away her body. No matter how much her children prayed for her salvation, she was damned.[114] The woman's theology was incorrect—the prayers of the devout would do no good to someone who was in hell, and she could not have been in purgatory unless she had repented.

While the idea that she had three illegitimate sons who followed the clerical vocation of their father may seem ironic, it was not far from many families' reality. It was common in the Middle Ages for sons to go into the craft or profession of their fathers, and the clergy was no exception. Already in the early Middle Ages, there were sanctions against the sons of priests entering the priesthood, and stricter rules developed after the invalidation of clerical marriage in 1139. Now that priests could not have legitimate children, the sons of priests were treated like any other bastards. Indeed, Laura Wertheimer argues, the prohibition on those born out of wedlock becoming clerics was aimed especially at the sons of clerics themselves.[115] However, for anyone prohibited from entering the priesthood because of illegitimacy (or other reasons), there was the possibility of a papal dispensation. Between 1449 and 1533, Ludwig Schmugge has discovered, 37,916 dispensations from illegitimate birth were issued, and 56 percent of these were for men whose fathers were in higher religious orders (19,558 priests or bishops, the rest monks, deacons or subdeacons, canons, or members of military or mendicant orders).[116]

Wertheimer has argued that the prohibition on the ordination of bastards, while it was directed at the sons of the clergy, was not primarily intended to create a disincentive to clerical sexual activity by removing opportunities for their children. She may be wrong about the impossibility of sophisticated medieval prelates having such a naïve intention: certainly, having a son to carry on the family business was far from the only reason for clerics to become involved in long-term relationships with women, but fatherhood was a powerful marker of masculine prestige in medieval society, and removing its privileges could have been effective. However, she makes a powerful case for the symbolic meaning of clerics' children. Particularly when they themselves served as priests before the congregation, they were the tangible manifestation of the fact that the cleric was involved in activity that violated his "cultic purity."[117] Kathryn Taglia discusses French synodal legislation from the central Middle Ages and argues similarly for the symbolic importance of priests' children as polluting the church. The evidence, however, seems to point to embarrassment rather than pollution: it is not so much that these children were out of place and "corrupt the integrity of the cultural system, because they are anomalous"[118] but rather that they constituted a public reminder that the church was not following its own rules. The priest's exemplarity was shattered by the evidence of impurity, but the church seemed more upset about the evidence than the impurity. The fact that dispensations became routine indicates that by the late Middle Ages, such priests' children were not actually all that anomalous; they merely had to be handled in a way that deemphasized the priest's transgression and emphasized the authority of the church hierarchy. Of course, if the papacy could make exceptions and allow the ordination of clerical sons, so could lay patrons. Wertheimer finds that English lay patrons were often happy for a benefice to go to the holder's son, and when illegitimately born priests were rejected, it was often because of issues about the patronage rather than about the illegitimacy.[119]

Priests' sons were not only reminders that the priest had once engaged in intercourse with a woman: they were also reminders that the priest had been involved in a union with a woman that was established enough to make paternity apparent. In other words, the acknowledged son of a priest is not likely to have been the son of a prostitute. It is, of course, not always possible to tell what kind of relationship the parents of an illegitimate child had—a long-term domestic partnership or a more casual encounter. The father himself, or a court, needed to be convinced that he was the only potential or the most likely father, but this does not mean that the relationship needed to be ongoing. However, in 3,071 of Schmugge's dispensation cases, more than one sibling in a family sought a dispensation. (Seventy-three percent of these had clerical fathers; 70 percent of those were in Spain or the German-speaking lands.)[120] These children had to have been born of long-term unions, and these cases constituted just the tip of the iceberg. There must have been many other families in which only one sibling, or none, wished to become a priest.

The preachers' attacks on clerical concubines had focused on their greed, their seeking the goods of the church for themselves. The kernel of reality behind that view is that these women needed financial support, especially for their children. They had few legal rights to it, although a priest, like any father of a child out of wedlock, might voluntarily or involuntarily pay some level of child support.[121] But if the couple had lived together as partners for a period of time, even though the woman did not legally get a widow's third upon her partner's death, instances of practice indicate that her status may have been recognized, even by the law. It is through the status of offspring and their inheritance that we are most likely to see concubines making their appearance in secular legal records. A story from a late medieval *consilia* collection (see Chapter 2 for these sources) gives us some indication of the way that jurists thought about these unions and how they reconciled the rules inherited from Roman law with the changed circumstances of a gender system constructed quite differently under Christian influence. It also gives us some idea of the difficult circumstances in which priests' partners often found themselves.

"She Can Cease Being a Concubine": Antonia

Antonia (like so many other medieval women, we have only her first name) was able to get a clever lawyer on her side and inherit property from her domestic partner, a priest, even though this went against the rule of the common law. A *consilium* by the French jurist Gui Pape (Guido Papa, ca. 1402–87), perhaps commissioned on her behalf, posed and answered a question that demonstrates how legal theories could be stretched to meet circumstances. We do not know in what region this case was being considered, but it would have been a civil court, not a church court. Antonia managed to do quite well for herself out of the case, even though she skirted the law a bit, and it seems that Gui was most concerned with making things come out right rather than sticking to the letter of the law. Either he was consulted as a neutral party and came down on her side out of a sense of fairness rather than strict legal reasoning, or someone had enough sympathy with her position to commission his opinion in her favor.

> Dom. John Comberius, a priest, left Antonia, his *ancilla* and concubine, 100 florins, and many other bequests. He left Hugh, the son of the said Antonia, his son, food and clothing until the twenty-fifth year of his age. Master Hugh Comberius, the brother and heir of the said Dom. John Comberius, claims that the said Antonia was the concubine of the said testator and thus the legacy made to her is not valid. And further, with regard to the son of the said Antonia, the said heir claims that this son is a spurious son of the said Dom. John, the testator; in response, it is said that even if the said Antonia were the concubine of the said Dom. John, the testator, still, three years before his death, he was the *compater* [fellow godparent] of the said Antonia his concubine, since he held at the sacred font the said Hugh, son of the said Antonia. Now it is asked whether the legacies made to the said Antonia and her son are valid and should be given effect.[122]

In civil and canon law, as mentioned in Chapter 2, a distinction was made between two sorts of illegitimate children: the natural and the spurious. Spurious children, those whose parents could not have been married, could not be legitimated and therefore did not have even the possibility of inheritance from the father.[123] In practice, many clerics and other fathers of *spurii* did give legacies or *inter vivos* gifts to their children; if the heirs challenged the bequests, however, the matter might be complicated. The case of Hugh Comberius, son of the concubine Antonia, depended on whether he was a spurious child. In theory, as his parents could not marry because of his father's clerical orders, it would seem that he would have been a spurious child.

The statement of the facts of the case called Antonia an *ancilla*. It is not clear exactly what Gui Pape meant by this term. In Italy, where he had studied law at Pavia and Turin, it would have meant "slave" at this time.[124] However, he more likely wrote this *consilium* when he was living in Dauphiné, from 1430 to 1487, and there it more likely meant "servant."[125] It is not clear from the *consilium* where the parties were located; no particular jurisdiction was mentioned for the legal points involved. According to some of the other jurists Gui might have cited, Antonia's status should have mattered. As we saw in Chapter 2, had she been a slave, her son could have been considered spurious for that reason alone. But Gui did not discuss Antonia's personal status at all; the opinion turned on other issues.

The *consilium* also termed Antonia a concubine. Although, as we have seen, the term was very commonly used for a priest's habitual partner, civilian jurists speaking theoretically commonly accepted the original Roman meaning: "Concubinage is correctly said to be that which exists between an unmarried man and an unmarried woman; for since concubinage takes its name by law . . . that cannot be called concubinage which is prohibited and punished by law."[126] Children of a concubine were generally considered "natural" and capable of being legitimated. Yet the jurists also used the term "concubine" in the case of couples who could not marry, referring to the concubine of a married man, or of a priest, who, though technically unmarried, was not free to marry.[127] Bartolo of Sassoferrato, after his discussion of concubines' children as natural, went on to discuss whether the children of a cleric in minor orders were considered natural. Some previous authors had denied this, on the grounds that the relationship was illicit; others had held that clerical concubinage was a crime under canon law, but not civil law, and therefore the children were natural. Bartolo agreed that the children were natural, and if the cleric were unbeneficed and later married the concubine, the children would be legitimated.[128] This required, however, that marriage be a possibility at the time that the children were conceived, so it applied only to a cleric in minor orders. A priest (or anyone else in major orders) could never marry, so he could never legitimate his children by subsequent matrimony.

There was no question in this case of Comberius marrying Antonia, to legitimate his son or for any other reason, nor did he try to legitimate him by will or institute him as heir; he only left him a legacy, as was permissible with a natural son. Strangely, however, Gui never considered in this discussion whether Hugh should be considered a natural son, nor did he mention Bartolo's discussion. Rather, he pointed out that this legacy was only alimentary, that is, sufficient to feed Hugh. This was permissible under civil law, even required under canon law, even if the child were admitted to be spurious.[129]

Gui then concluded that Hugh might receive his legacy. What about Antonia? Juridical authorities disagreed on whether a priest could leave a legacy to his concubine.[130] Such legacies were quite common in practice, at least in some places, as Roisin Cossar has shown for northern Italy, even if they were of questionable legality in theory.[131] Gui cited authorities to the effect that a priest could not make such a legacy, but instead of disagreeing with them, he argued that they did not apply in this case: "I believe, on the contrary, that the legacy made to the said Antonia is valid in the case under consideration, especially because at the time of the death of the said testator and for three years before, she had ceased being his concubine because of the said co-godparenthood. It is the situation at the time of the death and the legacy that must be investigated. For even if she was a concubine, she can cease being a concubine, as we see in the case of a concubine with whom one contracts matrimony: because as a result of matrimony the children previously born are legitimated, and the mother ceases to be a concubine."[132]

The *Decretum* made quite clear that a man who stood as godparent to his own child must cease sexual relations with the mother, even if she was his wife, because it would then be incest under canon law.[133] Gui here assumed that after the baptism of their son, John and Antonia did cease relations accordingly, and hence she was no longer a concubine. He therefore ruled that laws against leaving a legacy to a concubine did not apply. If this was the case, it could mean that they knew and respected the provisions of canon law on this subject and that the godparenthood was intentional. However, John apparently referred to her in his testament as his concubine (although the *consilium* does not contain the actual text), so it seems that he still considered her so.

But after arguing that Antonia was no longer John's concubine, and that even if Hugh was a spurious son it was still legal—even required—for John to provide for his basic support, Gui then argued that, anyway, Hugh was not John's son. This was a very strange argument for him to make. At the beginning, when he stipulated the facts of the case, Gui said that Hugh was John's son, and there was no suggestion that Antonia was unfaithful. The presumption of paternity for a married woman's child applied to a concubine as well, as Benedictus de Benedictis noted: "A child born in a man's home is presumed to be his child; thus a child born of a concubine in the home of the *concubinarius* is presumed to be his child."[134] However, Gui now said that Antonia and John had been together only for the three years preceding John's death (precisely the time since which, he had just noted, she had ceased to be his concubine!), and Hugh was ten and a half years old. A legacy to an unrelated person was licit, and since there was no claim that John was attempting to legitimize the boy, there was no advantage to treating him legally as a son.

Antonia's case indicates that the law, or those who applied it, could be flexible. The fact that "priest's concubine" was not a legally recognized or respected relationship did not stand in the way of a priest's providing for his loved ones. Given that the dissipation of the goods of the church was the reason often given for the prohibition of clerical marriage, it is worth noting that it was not the church but the testator's brother and universal heir who contested the legacies, and therefore that it was family rather than church property at issue. Gui tried out a number of twists on the facts of the case— either Antonia was not a concubine, or else her son was not John's—in order to allow the legacies. It is tempting to speculate about how a servant with a relatively small legacy was able to get an eminent jurist involved in the case on her side, or whether Gui was consulted by someone other than one of the parties.

The use of terms like "concubine" did not take place in a vacuum. In Antonia's case, whether she was a concubine had consequences for whether she could receive a legacy, and whether her son could do so. Being considered a concubine seems to have been working to Antonia's detriment, so Gui Pape argued that she was not one. In other cases, though not necessarily those involving priests, it could work in the favor of a woman and her children. If the woman were just a *meretrix* (whore), her children were spurious and could not, at least in theory, be legitimated and claim an inheritance: a son whose mother was a *meretrix* "cannot be simply said to be 'natural,' because the only one who can be such is one who is born of a single man, and a single woman kept as a concubine . . . and even if the coitus out of which he was born is not punishable [under civil law] it is still illicit and shameful [*improbatus*], since only matrimony and concubinage are seen to be licit, or at least not shameful under civil law."[135]

It is curious that Gui Pape chose the strategy of arguing that Antonia was not a concubine, since the fact that she was called one is what made it possible for him to argue in her favor in the first place. Although preachers fulminated against such women and although they had no official legal rights, nevertheless the relationship was a socially accepted one. The law could be stretched when a priest wanted to support his partner and their child because society accepted these partnerships as normal, if not desirable or entirely respectable. "Priest's whore" might be a common insult for one woman to throw at another in late medieval towns, but people nevertheless recognized that in practical terms, these partnerships and their offspring existed, and the law reacted accordingly.

Besides indicating the law's adaptation to the facts, the case also demonstrates the way that Roman law was and was not applied to medieval situations. When Gui considered the position that a man could not leave a legacy to his concubine, he cited not a ruling about a priest's concubine, but about the concubine of a *miles*, or soldier, who, in classical Roman law, could not marry. Some jurists, however, considered the Roman law on this point and concluded that the medieval knight was sufficiently different from a Roman soldier that Roman law did not apply: "Laws speaking of *milites* do not refer to the *milites* of our times. . . . [T]hey are not Roman *milites* and therefore do not accord with the name *milites* either in the privileges or the obligations, notwithstanding that they are commonly called *milites*."[136] Philip Decius (1454–1536), however, extended the provision to priests: "A fortiori this applies to a priest, who is called a knight [*miles*] of God."[137]

But the jurists did not take into account in the same manner the way in which the priest's concubine in the later Middle Ages differed from the Roman concubine. They could apply the body of law on concubinage without really considering the different functions of concubinage in the two cultures. The jurists were well aware of the technical meaning of the term in Roman law, but at the same time (in the same paragraph, if not in the same sentence) could use it in the much more general sense of any female domestic partner who was not a wife. At the same time, the choice of a concubine instead of a wife carried moral consequences in medieval culture that it did not carry in Roman; Roman soldiers' marriages were not legally recognized as *coniugium* but were perfectly respectable, not sinful and punishable like unions involving priests.

Being the concubine of a layman did not automatically confer economic benefits such as the legitimation of a woman's children and an inheritance for them. It was always the father's choice. A priest did not even have that choice (nor, indeed, did a layman under English common law). A concubine had no dowry to fall back on if she were widowed or abandoned. Nevertheless, she was not the equivalent of a prostitute. Priests' domestic partners were objurgated and terms like "whore" were often used of them, but "concubine" at least implied something more than a casual relationship.

The Quotidian for Priests' Partners

Although they might disagree on the details of how priests' concubines ought to be punished, all church authors of the Middle Ages thought of concubinage as an undesirable alternative, either to chastity or to marriage. It is a more difficult question how the communities within which these priests lived viewed them, their partners, and their children. Scholars who have studied priests' unions in different parts of Europe in the period after clerical celibacy started to be enforced have concluded that relations between partnered clerics and their parishioners were complicated, as is often the case with human relations in practice. People sometimes disapproved of their priests' liaisons, but sometimes found them preferable to more promiscuous sexual activity, or to the irresponsible behavior of abandoning dependents.

Where people objected to the family life of their clergy, the basis was often resentment rather than theology. People worried not that their priests were polluted and therefore invalidating the sacrament, but rather that they were encroaching on what laypeople saw as their own privileges. Laypeople might be less holy than the clergy, but in return for their status one step further removed from God, they had families. The visible difference of the clergy from the laity by virtue of their celibate status—not a moral difference but one of public behavior—was one thing that allowed them to maintain their superiority. If the clergy behaved no better than the laity, the laity were not likely to treat them with the respect that they thought they deserved.

Studies of clerical masculinity in various parts of the medieval period underscore this resentment. Jennifer Thibodeaux argues that the parish clergy of thirteenth-century Normandy whose behavior was found wanting were not just behaving badly but attempting to live up to secular ideals of masculinity. In fact, she argues, their sexual behavior should be seen as an expression of gender identity. "Instead of reducing priestly sexuality to an aberrant, illicit behavior we should be looking at how medieval priests, barred from legitimate sexual unions, created alternative sexualities in the form of concubinage, promiscuity, serial monogamy, and polyconcubinage.

The priest could express virility by these unions and potentially achieve a public recognition of manliness for his sexual prowess."[138] Many were sexually active, often with long-term partners, and they also visited the tavern and gambled, hunted, and brawled. Their attempt to achieve what the people among whom they lived would recognize as manhood made them more like the village men but eroded their authority as priests. Derek Neal suggests that in fourteenth- and fifteenth-century England, clergy and laymen often interacted over property as well as pastoral issues. When conflict arose around an issue like tithes, it might be couched in terms of the sexual behavior of the priest, and insults of "whoremaster" were common. Chaste sexual behavior was important to a priest's general moral worth, and therefore general hostility could be framed in sexual language.[139] But the greater concern, Neal finds, was not with priests who had their own domestic partners, but with priests who committed adultery with other men's wives (or fornication with their daughters)—a concern closely related to priests' supposed greed for laymen's property.[140]

The examples that Thibodeaux, Neal, other scholars discussed below, and I use are all drawn from hostile sources: visitation records or court records that accused priests of various offenses and that treated clerical sexual activity as something to be punished. The richness of church court records, especially, as sources of information must be balanced against the fact that penalties for this behavior maintained not only the reputation of the church but also a stream of income to local church authorities.[141] Court records do not allow us to quantify just how common clerical sexual activity was. From the people who reported on the clergy's sexual activity, who testified as witnesses, or who were accused of defaming priests, however, we can learn something about how priests and their partners were regarded by the communities in which they lived.

Church courts had jurisdiction over sexual offenses and over the clergy in general, and church court records from a variety jurisdictions in the late Middle Ages—episcopal and archidiaconal courts, plus the records of bishops' visitations, which were not judicial proceedings but which heard evidence and conducted investigations in much the same manner—are the best source of evidence on how laypeople viewed priests' partners. Many priests all over Europe were not only sexually active but had women living with them, something that the medieval gender division of labor almost demanded while at the same time criminalizing it.[142] Studies from various regions indicate a familiar pattern of day-to-day toleration, with court records representing the exceptions.

Marie Kelleher shows that in the diocese of Barcelona in the early fourteenth century, people were not all that hostile to clerical concubinage—for example, describing couples as "just like man and wife."[143] The women involved in these relationships were not fined, even though the men were, an indication that they may not have been objurgated as much as preachers and literary sources would suggest. Many of these women, however, did not live in the same household as their partners, an apparent attempt to maintain some level of discretion. A few clerical concubines were accused of other offenses by the parishioners—being a "trashy and gossipy woman," or a usurer—but the majority were not, so these accusations probably arose in relation to particular women rather than concubines as a group.[144] Michelle Armstrong-Partida moves beyond Barcelona to study the neighboring diocese of Girona. She stresses that the clerics accused of sexual offenses were largely men living in relationships that were "marriage in all but name" rather than "a lecherous, socially promiscuous clergy," and emphasizes the unusual frequency of the practice in Catalonia and elsewhere in Iberia.[145] The church's efforts were directed against those who made those relationships very public; those who did not obtrude on public attention were tolerated. In a village, the parishioners would have been familiar with the priest's living arrangements, but they presented them at episcopal visitations without any sense of outrage. Penalties were light, and, Armstrong-Partida argues, the church attempted merely to uphold the appearance of punishing concubinage. The concubines themselves were rarely fined.[146]

Daniel Bornstein's study of parish priests in Cortona shows a similar pattern of day-to-day toleration followed by crackdown when something occurred to force the authorities to take notice. Alessandro, the parish priest of Bacialla, was investigated in 1337 on a charge of having rung his church bell in the middle of the night. Witnesses from the parish explained that it was his concubine Lena di Castello who had rung the bell during a quarrel, and that she had attempted to plunder the church. They also testified that the woman living with the rector Ugolino of Sant-Andrea of Bacialla was his niece and of good character. These parishioners may have been defending and covering up the concubinary behavior of their priests. The situation was different in the town of Cortona, where people were more likely to complain about their priests' concubinage and other offenses.[147] It was probably not the sexual activity that aroused the ire of the community as much as the neglect or poor performance of priestly duties. Concubinage created the greatest problem when Simone, rector of San Giorgio, appeared to have been telling his concubine Vannuccia the secrets of the confessional.[148] On the whole, Bornstein finds, concubinage was accepted by the people of the parishes, both in the early and mid-fourteenth century, as long as the priest was otherwise popular. But it was a precarious toleration, since there was always the danger of complaints to the bishop during his visitation. Roisin Cossar, who uses documents from Bergamo and Treviso, finds that although clerical concubines were generally treated with tolerance and even affection by their communities, they were always regarded as in some ways irregular, and this irregularity could be used against them when circumstances dictated.[149]

The cases cited by Kelleher, Armstrong-Partida, and Bornstein used the term "concubine" (or vernacular equivalents). However, some jurisdictions avoided the term and phrased accusations in terms of sexual acts (fornication, carnal knowledge) rather than characterizing the nature of the relationship. Monique Vleeschouwers–Van Melkebeek calculated the number of priests accused of incontinence in the diocese of Tournai in three periods: 1446–62, 1470–81, and 1511–31. She estimates that 6 to 12 percent of all curates were accused of sexual incontinence in these time periods, the highest rate being 1470–81, but that it is impossible to tell whether these were short- or long-term liaisons.[150] Janelle Werner's study of the diocese of Hereford, based on visitation and other records, finds cases using the terminology of both concubinage and fornication, and argues that priests living in quasi-marital relationships were no less common there than elsewhere in Europe.[151] In cases from various jurisdictions in England, the priest was often accused of keeping (*tenire*) or maintaining (*manutenire*) a woman, rather than of fornication or concubinage. This implies a long-term relationship and may indicate financial support.[152] Sometimes concubinage was mentioned also—the phrasing "keeps in his house as his concubine" was common—but not always; sometimes a priest "suspiciously keeps a certain Joan living in his house," but she was not called a concubine.[153] In London, women were called "whores" whether they were professional prostitutes or living in ongoing relationships with priests; there appears to have been less recognition there of long-term unions than elsewhere in England or the rest of Europe.[154]

These offenses came to the attention of the authorities in a variety of ways, some of them more trustworthy than others. When a bishop made his visitation, the parishioners reported things that were amiss, but some of these things apparently proved not to be real concerns. The registers of Archbishop John Morton (1486–1500) contain several cases in which a priest was accused of keeping a "suspicious woman" in his house and claimed that she was his sister. In one instance, the priest was able to prove that this was the case.[155] Perhaps the parishioners simply were not aware of the sibling relationship, perhaps they were acting out of malice, or perhaps they were telling the truth and the priest was able to deceive the bishop.

This chapter has been and will be speaking mainly of priests. Lower clergy (below the level of subdeacon) were permitted to marry. But it was not always easy to identify who was a cleric in higher orders, if he did not have a parish living. In Paris in the late fourteenth century, some men had an important reason to claim that they were not married: to claim benefit of clergy. In several cases in the registers of the Châtelet (a secular court) from the early 1390s, men tried to get out of criminal accusations by claiming that they were clerics and therefore not subject to secular jurisdiction. Of course, it was easy for a man to get someone to tonsure him, the sign of clerical orders; on occasion, such suspects were imprisoned alone so that no one would have the opportunity to shave their heads for them. Raoulin du Pré had a tonsure, but there was still doubt about his clerical status. "Asked whether he is married or has affianced Jeannette de Valenciennes, his concubine, loose woman [*fille du pechié*], living in Glatigny, he says on his oath that he has long frequented and followed the said Jeannette de Valenciennes, who is his girlfriend, and that he has never married or affianced her, nor promised to take her as wife or spouse." She testified that he promised in front of witnesses "that he would keep and do good company with her as she wished" and that she would be "his girlfriend" (*s'amie par amours*). After a few days, however, according to her testimony, as she found other women were criticizing her, she refused to sleep with him again unless he promised to marry her, which he then did. On a later occasion, she said, when he was asked whether she was his wife, he said yes, "and she said that if they had not said that they were married in the various cities where they had been, the hosts where they were lodging would not have let them lodge in their houses as they did."[156] He was judged to be married because he had promised to marry her and had sexual relations afterward, which made a valid marriage under canon law. Such a man, on the edge of clerical status, had a strong interest in claiming to be unmarried; living in some other kind of union with a woman would not undermine clerical status as marriage would.

A close look at one particular body of court records from the late Middle Ages will help give us a sense of how priests and their sexual partners were treated and, to some extent, how they were viewed in a large urban community, or at least by the courts embedded within the community. These are the criminal registers of the archdeacon of Paris, which exist in an unbroken series from 1483 to 1505.[157] The archdeaconry of Paris included the portions of the city on the right bank of the Seine, and some of the suburban and rural areas between the Marne and the Oise. Besides sexual and matrimonial offenses (those not involving priests will be discussed in Chapter 4), the records include various kinds of misbehavior by priests: celebrating mass in places where they were not licensed to do so, wearing inappropriate clothing, gambling, violence, misappropriation of church funds.[158] The criminal registers contain mainly cases initiated by the archdeacon's official by virtue of his office. In some cases, an official acted at the denunciation of a named individual or an individual was named as a plaintiff, but most cases involving priests did not fall into this category. In the vast majority of the cases, the priests were simply recorded as having paid a fine for their offense (*emenda-vit*). The long depositions that are found in some of the contested matrimonial or paternity cases are, for the most part, not found in the cases involving priests. We do not know how much of a fight any given defendant put up during the investigative portion of the process, which was not recorded. Most entries noted that the defendant was cited to appear in court, but not the basis on which the citation was issued. In a few cases, the defendant was said to appear *sponte veniens*, coming forward of his or her own free will, largely because when someone brought an action under the court's civil (instance) jurisdiction, the plaintiff had to admit to his or her own failings and pay a criminal fine.[159] This did not happen very often in the cases involving priests. Some cases indicated that the accused was cited *per informacionem*, on the basis of an investigation, which may mean that rumor was circulating within the community.[160] The promoter, or court official, had the responsibility for seeking out wrongdoing, and some of them appear to have been more active than others.[161]

Of a total of 1,656 cases of sexual or matrimonial offenses in the criminal register over this twenty-two-year period, 299 of them involve priests. Table 1 lists the various charges brought against priests in these registers. The way the offenses were described can tell us a good deal about how clerical sexual behavior was understood.[162]

Table 1
Clerical Sexual Offenses in Paris Archdeacon's Registers

Accused Offense	No. of Cases
Adultery	5
Carnal knowledge	60
Concubinage	18
Defloration	4
"Frequenting"	27
"Maintaining"	37
"Frequenting" with carnal knowledge	43
"Maintaining" with carnal knowledge	30
Paternity	6
Scandal	61
Miscellaneous	8
Total	299

Some of the categories are more closely related to long-term unions than others. Several of the cases I have listed as "miscellaneous" did not directly accuse the priest of sexual activity, but rather of eating and drinking with suspicious people, or of having women in his room. One friar-priest apparently got offended when the people in the house he was visiting (owned by a woman, and possibly a brothel) suspected that he was suffering from the "Neapolitan disease." He "stripped off his clothes and, naked, showed himself front and back."[163] Other cases accused the priest of involvement in the misbehavior of others: supporting a woman who had left her husband, performing illicit marriages. In three cases, priests were accused of defaming others (two of them other priests) with sexual insults: for example, Guillaume Monson, vicar of St.-Honoré, paid a fine for saying that the priest Jacques Levanye had two children by a whore.[164]

The six cases I have called "paternity" include two in which a priest paid a fine for fathering a child, and four in which a woman paid a fine for becoming pregnant by a priest. One of the women "allowed herself to be known" by the priest for three years. In each of these cases, only one partner was fined. The cases may have arisen out of claims by the women for child support or childbirth expenses, but their claims did not appear in the civil registers of the church court for the period. Master Jean de Paris, a curate, paid a fine for having fathered a child with Jeanne la Boudisse twenty years earlier, when she had lived with him for two or three years in the parish house prior to her marriage. He had recently given in marriage the daughter of the union, which probably brought the matter to the court's attention.[165] He also paid a fine in this case for "scandal"; the public nature of his paternity, when he had taken at least part of the responsibility for his daughter's marriage, had alarmed the authorities.[166]

A case from the officiality of the cathedral chapter of Notre Dame in Paris (exempt from the archdeacon's jurisdiction) from 1488 indicates how a priest might try to stay involved with his child without formally acknowledging it. A priest named Le Barbier, a chaplain of St.-Sepulcre, paid a fine for "frequenting at intervals over a year and a half" with a certain Philipota, both in his chamber and in hers. She had borne a child, and claimed that it was his. He made a settlement with her, agreeing to take financial responsibility for the child, and entered into a contract before the notaries of the Châtelet, the secular court, to do so. He wanted to take the child from her and have it brought up in a better home; she, however, refused on the grounds that he had not paid the child support as promised. This narrative was all stated as fact in the court record: it was not just what Philipota alleged; it was what the court fined him for. However, the record also noted that he said that he did not know whether he was the father, and had agreed to the child support only "for the avoidance of scandal." It seems likely that by making a settlement with his partner, he had hoped to avoid prosecution in the church court. The prosecution may have arisen out of their later disagreement. The fine that he paid for frequenting Philipota could have been a result of a negotiated agreement with the court. There is no direct evidence of this; but under the circumstances, he could well have been fined for scandal and/or for actually fathering the child, and he was not.[167]

In fourteen of the eighteen cases in which the register labeled the union concubinage, only the man was fined; in one, only the woman; in three, both. The act of keeping a concubine was more problematic than the status of being a concubine. (This was less true for laypeople or those in lower ecclesiastical orders: in 77 concubinage cases in which the man was not a priest, 31 fined the man only, 25 the woman, and 21 both.) The longest duration of union given was twenty years, the shortest a month, with the median a year. Several of the cases were said also to have caused scandal. In the case of Georges, called Tastevyn, and his concubine Pierrette, the scandal was not just the concubinage, but the fact that they quarreled publicly: "after many words between them, she pulled out his testicles or pulled them so that blood flowed."[168]

The use of the term "concubine" in the Paris records makes a striking contrast with church court records from London in the same time period (discussed further in Chapter 4), where the term "concubine" did not appear but the term "whore" was used frequently, including cases in which the woman was not a professional prostitute. There are plenty of examples in the Paris records of defamation cases where a woman was called *putaine*, or whore, but not specifically because of her relationship with a priest, and there are no records where a woman was called a whore by the court because of such a relationship. At least in terms of the court's official language, she was no worse than her male partner.

The evidence is unclear on whether concubinage necessarily meant that the two parties were sharing living quarters. The cases in which both parties were fined included Richard Lucas and Antoinette "living with him" and Nicolas Rebacart and Jeanne, "his maid," presumably also living with him.[169] One case in which only the man was fined stated that the woman was his maid. None of the other cases gave the residence of both parties. The priest Antoine, called Le Roy, was accused of calling his pregnant concubine (whose name was left blank) his wife, which implied a serious ongoing relationship and would not make sense unless they lived together. He claimed that he had already been fined for this in the "court of Paris" (presumably, the bishop's court) and was ordered to have no further contact with her on pain of imprisonment.[170]

Richard Lucas's case, indeed, shows how a concubine may have thought of herself as entitled to certain rights, if not legally, at least morally. According to the promoter, Antoinette had been Lucas's concubine for eighteen years. However, he had been discovered by some of his parishioners in the stable of his house alone with Jeanne, wife of Simon, a local tailor. Then Antoinette burst into the stable, yelling (and these words are given in French in the record): "Hey, priest, wretched as you are, go ride your she-ass; am I not good enough for you?" Richard told the court that Antoinette was his cousin; the result of the case does not survive. Whether or not Antoinette was his concubine and the information about her reaction was true, the case indicates that a concubine might expect fidelity.

Most of the Paris cases involving priests did not mention the term "concubine" or "concubinage" but involved either "carnal knowledge," "frequenting," or "maintaining." Carnal knowledge cases used the active voice for men—Jean knew Jeanne carnally—and the passive voice for women—Jeanne permitted herself to be known by Jean. In only two of these sixty cases was a woman the sole defendant, however, and in only seven was she a codefendant: the court was concerned mainly with regulating the behavior of the priests themselves. (The numbers were much less unbalanced for laypeople: of 159 cases, there were 43 women defendants and 14 women codefendants.) Few of the carnal knowledge cases seem to have involved long-term unions: they often did not state a period of time over which the sexual intercourse took place, and when they did state it, the longest was a year. More commonly, they gave a number of occasions or said "occasionally" or "repeatedly." Only rarely was the residence of both parties given. In three of the cases, the woman was the man's maid, so presumably lived in his household. The intercourse was sometimes said to have taken place *in domo presbiterali*, in the priest's house or vicarage, sometimes in his lodging when he did not have a parish house, and only rarely in the woman's lodging. Only one case gave the domicile of a woman other than a maid who lived with a priest; in that case, he paid the fine while denying that she was living with him.[171] In seven cases, the woman was said to be married, but the term "adultery" was not used. This may have been some sort of arrangement akin to a plea bargain in which the man paid the fine for a lesser offense rather than confess an adultery charge, but there is no direct evidence of this. Two of the cases in which the fine was unusually high—three and two gold ecus, respectively—involved married women, but another with a two-ecu fine did not; in most cases, the amount of the fine was not given. The harshest punishment, a fine of three ecus plus a pilgrimage, was for a priest who had impregnated a woman whose confessor he was.[172] In this instance, she was probably not his domestic partner, but some of the married women could have been priests' partners whose previous marriages had broken down.

"Frequenting" could mean "visiting," but probably the best translation in early twenty-first-century parlance is "hanging out with." Sexual intercourse might be suspected, but the offense did not necessarily include it. The time period over which the frequenting took place, when given, was often more than a year. In one case, a woman admitted frequenting a priest but denied carnal knowledge; in another, the priest Jean Hacquard claimed that he had frequented a woman in his village "honestly," despite rumors that he had maintained her. He paid a fine for scandal as well as for the frequenting.[173] One priest paid the fine for having frequented a woman from thirty years previously up until four years previously, including having had two children by her before she was married, "and called her his sister."[174] Yet despite the long-term relationship, the case was not called maintaining or concubinage and did not mention carnal knowledge. Since more cases referred to both frequenting and carnal knowledge than frequenting alone, the court's or scribe's omission of carnal knowledge might seem deliberate. But of the twenty-seven cases that involved only "frequenting" without mentioning carnal knowledge, six involved at least alleged pregnancies. Either the court or the scribe was not very careful about the exact offense, or some defendants may have been admitting to a lesser offense.

Of the cases of "frequenting" that included accusations of carnal knowledge, the only ones that explicitly stated that the couple lived together involved a priest with his servant. In five of the cases, the intercourse was stated to have taken place in the parish house or in the priest's. In another, the couple were said to be staying in the same house, but that could just mean renting rooms from the same landlord. In every case, the priest was a defendant, and eleven of forty-three listed the woman as codefendant. The few specified fines ranged from four to twelve sous, and the time periods were mostly a year or less. One case I have included here did not actually use the phrase "carnal knowledge" but a synonym, "doing the thing" or "having an affair" (*rem habuisse*). Jean Testu, priest, paid a fine for "doing the thing with a certain Guillemette who frequented his chamber for a period of four or five years, such that the said Guillemette repeatedly slept [*dormivit*] with him in his own bed, sometimes in another bed than the bed of the said payer [of the fine], since the said Guillemette had a bed in his said chamber which belonged to her." Testu was also fined for creating a scandal in that Guillemette loudly and publicly called him a bawd and said that he maintained her in his room for two years without letting her leave.[175] This could have been a situation of imprisonment and exploitation but is more likely to have been a domestic partnership gone awry. Once again, the court was concerned with appearance and reputation as well as actual behavior.

A number of the frequenting/carnal knowledge cases seem to have come to the attention of the court through scandal: some particular misbehavior that made the liaison public. One priest brought a woman to his chamber, and a woman showed up with whom he had had a sexual relationship "now and then" (*per intervalla*) for the previous two years. The two women got into a fight, causing scandal.[176] Another case created a scandal when the woman called the priest insulting names and attacked him with a knife.[177] Jean Chevalier was fined for frequenting and having carnal knowledge of a certain Jeannette, because of which lampoons (*libelli famosi*) were posted, naming her "La Chevalière."[178] The lampoons intended to publicize and satirize the relationship, using the feminine form of the priest's name, as was sometimes done with married women and their husbands' names. The priest was fined for the sexual intercourse, not for scandal, but the court's care in noting the result of his indiscretion indicates the concern with appearance.

The most long-term, stable unions appeared in the court records as "maintaining." (I have included cases that use *tenire* and *intertenire* as well as *manutenire* in this group.) About half the cases of maintaining also mentioned carnal knowledge, and many of the rest implied it—for example, because the register mentioned the birth of children to the couple. As with frequenting, the mention of carnal knowledge in some cases and not in others may have depended on what could actually be proved; or it may have been recorded in some cases and not in others because it did not make very much difference. Not much distinguished cases of "maintaining" from cases using the term "concubinage." The range of time periods was similar—some as long as ten years, and the shortest a month and a half. The fines ranged from one sou to one ecu. Six cases listed a woman as sole accused and five as a co-accused. One priest brought a married woman with him from Burgundy to Paris, and several of the other women who were maintained by priests were married, although the term "adultery" was not used in any of the "maintaining" cases.[179]

"Maintaining" probably implied financial support, but this conclusion is based on the way the term is used in other jurisdictions, rather than textual evidence from the Paris records themselves. In two cases, the register stated that the woman lived with the man; three cases stated that she was his maid; and only one case gave different residences for the partners. One case caused scandal because the woman remained in the priest's lodging even when he was not there—an indication that they were living together, at least on a temporary basis, but also perhaps that this was not the community's expectation.[180] One of the relatively few women fined for being maintained or kept, Isabelle Desponville (called *domicella*, or demoiselle, thus likely from an elite family), "stayed and kept herself . . . and always spent the night with" (*stetisse, continue se tenuisse, semper pernoctasse*) Master Ysambard Falvart for a period of eighteen months. The use of the repetitive terms indicates a particular concern to emphasize that the couple were living together.[181] In six cases, the priest was said to maintain the woman in his house or in his chamber. One priest was accused of causing scandal by keeping a woman "as his own wife" (*tanquam propriam uxorem*); another denied that he had had carnal knowledge of the woman who lived with him or that he had called her his wife, but admitted that someone else might have thought that she was his wife.[182] These cases show that some clerical unions looked very much like the formal marriage partnerships that the laity were expected to enter.

One woman who became jealous when her priestly lover became involved with another woman gives us an indication of what "maintaining" may have meant to laypeople. Jean Perrier, a priest living near the church of St.-Eustache, paid amends for frequenting a certain Marianne, a married woman. He said that this had taken place occasionally, beginning a year earlier, and that he had not known her carnally for about forty days. The previous week, going past her house, he had stopped to greet her and she had begun to rail at him, saying that he could not maintain two women at once and that he should go take care of the child he had with another woman. She called him names and he hit her on the head so that she fell to the ground and bled.[183] Her phrasing suggests that she understood "maintaining" as an ongoing relationship that he could not have with two women at once.

The infrequency of the term "adultery" in the criminal registers is puzzling. In fact, a total absence would be less puzzling: adultery cases were supposed to be reserved to the bishop.[184] Yet this separation of jurisdiction was not consistently followed. In four of the five cases that actually used the term "adultery" (as opposed to the ones where the priest's partner was said to be a married woman but the term was not used), the priest "maintained" a woman in adultery (*manutenire, intertenire, tenire*). In other words, these priests were not accused of sleeping with a wife while the husband was out of the house; these women were no longer living with their husbands. The length of the "maintaining" was stated as one or two years. One of the cases was initiated by the woman's husband, but the others mention no aggrieved party. It is not clear whether the women were actually living with the priests in these cases, although Jean Cibart, living in the parish of St.-Paul (but not necessarily serving as priest there), paid a fine for keeping Jacqueline la Puissanne in his house "as though she were his wife, drinking, eating, and spending the night, knowing her carnally and committing adultery."[185] "As though she were his wife" and similar phrases, though relatively rare, are as clear an indication as we find of a domestic partnership.

In sixty-one of the cases, the priest was not fined for a sexual offense but for "scandal" alone. "Scandal" was a situation that gave the church a bad name: it gave rise to gossip, set a bad example, undermined authority. The archdeacon's court also prosecuted scandal involving laypeople, most often when couples who had been affianced decided not to get married. Because the promises they exchanged were in the future tense, the unions were not completely binding if they had not been consummated. However, the court clearly was concerned that they not be taken lightly. People who took it upon themselves to dissolve these unions without license were fined, but even those who obtained permission to dissolve the betrothal were fined for "scandal" because they set a bad example.

Priests fined for scandal, too, were setting a bad example or bringing public disrepute on the church.[186] The priest Nicolas le Maigre was fined for creating a scandal because Tassine la Clergesse, an "old woman," frequented his house. He claimed that he did not know her carnally but admitted to the scandal: he had to confess that her visits looked suspicious.[187] This pattern, in which a priest paid the fine for scandal but denied actual sexual wrongdoing, was not unusual. We do not have the original accusation, but only the offense for which the defendant was fined; when he is said to have denied the sexual behavior, we may assume that he had been accused of it. Philippe Chesnart paid a fine for scandal when he admitted frequenting two sisters, both named Marguerite, in the house where he was staying, but he denied having carnal knowledge of them.[188] Jean le Vilain, a curate, paid the fine for a scandal in which an unnamed woman "many times, over a long period, frequented his house, even though he does not admit maintaining her, but she came to him because he is old and sick."[189] In some cases, the record specifically stated that the fine for scandal was a punishment for creating rumor. Denis Bernard, chaplain of Neuilly-sur-Marne, paid a fine for scandal because it was "common fame" in the village that he was maintaining the wife of Étienne de Neuilly. The register did not indicate whether the common fame was true.[190] Friar Guillaume Pahet was fined for scandal because it was rumored in the village of Villemomble that he maintained a married woman named Alison, "although he did not confess it." (The scribe originally wrote "maintained in concubinage," then crossed out "concubinage" and wrote "adultery," indicating an effort to maintain the distinction.)[191] It is possible that the priests confessed to "scandal" as a lesser offense, but the amount of the fine was given so rarely that it is not possible to discern patterns. In cases where the priest did not deny the sexual contact—"Jean made amends for the scandal in that he frequented Jeanne for a period of two years and knew her carnally"—it seems that the fact of scandal made the offense worse, especially since so many other priests were fined simply for the sexual offense, without a scandal connected with it.[192]

Other priestly acts besides sexual intercourse were also considered scandalous: bringing women into the parish house (*domo presbiteralis*), eating with prostitutes, being found with a woman of ill fame, committing defamation and violence, "frequenting," spending the night (without reference to "carnal knowledge"), being alone with a woman, being deloused by a "young girl" in the public square, or renting property to a woman of irregular sexual behavior.[193] Eating and drinking with women was a recurrent issue: it was not a sexual offense per se, but looked bad to the neighbors. Pierre du Clos, a priest living in the parish of St.-Eustache, paid a fine for scandal because he ate and drank with a certain Olive.[194] Being alone with a woman, especially in a bedchamber, looked very suspicious, too. Some of these cases of scandal where the record did not mention sexual intercourse certainly implied a long-term relationship: in two cases, the woman was said to have a set of keys to the man's lodging.[195]

In Brie, another archdeaconry within the same diocese, Jean Morin and Robine the widow of Guillaume Cousin were prohibited from sleeping in the same bed or further "frequenting in suspect places" because of the scandal they had created: he had maintained her in concubinage in his house, and the people of the village called her "the priest's wife" when she baked communion bread. He claimed that he was an invalid and she was hired for four francs a year to look after him; both denied carnal knowledge of each other. If the judge believed that they were indeed in a concubinary relationship, they would undoubtedly have had a more serious punishment than a warning, particularly since it was not clear that her husband was dead (she said that she did not know, but that she had not seen him in nineteen years). But the rumor, even if the official did not think it was true, was enough to merit the warning.[196]

We may infer that it was the people of the community who were scandalized, that the archdeacon's court was concerned not just with priests' reputation among the clergy but among the laity, and that indeed the laity sometimes took it upon themselves to police the behavior of their clergy. Nicolas Paoul, vicar of Espiais, was fined for scandal because "certain companions went to his vicarage and placed a ladder against the wall, and through the window they saw a certain woman of ill fame, which created a scandal, whom he immediately escorted out of the house through the back door."[197] Nicolas was not exactly misbehaving publicly, although the neighbors must have had suspicions that prompted them to bring the ladder to his house in the first place. Once they confirmed the woman's presence, it became a scandal, although the couple was apparently not caught in the act or fined for carnal knowledge or frequenting. Five years later, Nicolas Paoul was again fined for scandal in that a certain Catherine came repeatedly to his room, although he swore that he did not know her carnally.[198] The chaplain of Le Plessis-Gassot was fined because six years earlier, a scandal had occurred when he had gotten a woman pregnant and she had brought the child to his door, proclaiming that it was his. He did not deny paternity, but it was for the scandal—the public nature of his misdeed—and not for the paternity that he was fined.[199] Someone must have remembered and reported it.

Some scandals were forced on the public's attention rather than the community suspecting and seeking them out. Gervaise Cayet, vicar of Montsoult, went to the home of Pierre Prevost, a stonemason. When Gervaise removed his tunic to sleep with (*dormire cum*) Pierre's wife, some servants who were in the house beat him. In this case, Gervaise was not cited to appear in court but did so of his own accord, meaning that he probably brought a claim against Prevost for the beating and had therefore to confess the circumstances. He was fined eight sous, a fairly large amount.[200] A woman named Marguerite came to the priest Jean le Pelle's house and pounded on the door, crying (the words are given in French), "Open up, wimp, I want my gown," to which he responded, "I will not open up. Here, have a gown," and tossed one out the window.[201] Publicity was also at issue with Guillaume de la Croix, who brought Jeanne la Boursiere to his house "with many people seeing."[202]

In some cases in which the priest was not fined specifically for scandal, but the term was mentioned, it may have been used in a less technical and more general sense. One vicar in the archdeaconry of Brie was fined for carnal knowledge of one of the parishioners. She had given birth to a child she claimed was his, and he had baptized it despite the fact that it might have been his, "to avoid scandal among the people."[203]

But the court failed to label, or decided not to label, as scandalous numerous cases of clerical sexual activity, many of them related to long-term unions. There was a good deal of resentment at priestly sexual activity, particularly when it involved married women. I have suggested elsewhere that the prosecution of priestly sexual activity in London secular courts, which did not actually have jurisdiction over priests, was a reflection of anticlericalism more than strict morality.[204] Similar resentment may have led to the activity being reported, whether it was considered scandalous or not. But in a number of instances, the activity went on for a good long time, apparently without being fined. People must have known about it and simply let it go. Where the priest was a well-liked member of the community and did not quarrel over other issues, people might not be eager to go out of their way to get him prosecuted for his sex life, especially if he conducted it in a stable partnership. On the other hand, it took only one resentful parishioner to get him into trouble. Clerical sexual activity in late fifteenth-century Paris, as elsewhere in medieval Europe, was at the same time tolerated and not tolerated.[205]

What of the women with whom these priests were living? In some cases, the priests were ordered to "throw them out" or to have no further contact with them. In most cases, however, no such order was recorded. The priests involved were prosecuted more than were their female partners, and the latter were not called "whores" in the records, as were their counterparts in London. Being a priest's partner may have been no worse in late medieval Paris than being anyone else's unmarried partner. But the records contain no evidence that being a priest's partner gave the woman special status more than any other unmarried woman; these women and their children had no protections.

Chapter 2 argued that although theoretically any single man and any single woman could marry, in practice unions between people of different social levels would not be considered marriage. Status, rather than the religious ceremony, legal contract, or property settlement, could be the deciding factor. A priest, of course, was never single in the sense of being available for marriage. And to a certain extent, any woman was of a different social status than a priest, who, by virtue of being a member of the clergy, was in a separate group. This disparity, as much as or more than the disparity between a nobleman and a non-noble woman (but perhaps not so much as that between a Christian and a Jew), placed the woman in a devalued position, despite the everyday normality of their life together.

The sources from Paris confirm those from various parts of Europe in that many people regarded priests' long-term unions as akin to marriage. But more than the absence of legal protections made these unions insecure for the women. A priest's partner risked being repudiated at any time, if the man were in legal jeopardy for any reason, or if he simply tired of her. She might have the support of her family, but she might not. Her neighbors might be quite tolerant of the partnership and the community might treat them as a recognized couple, as long as the priest was on good terms with his parish. If not, the union would be another tool to use against him. The Paris records show that the church did not focus on punishing women as a way of maintaining the reputation of the clergy, but the women could end up as collateral damage if the court determined that the union existed, or even that rumors of it created a scandal.

Chapter 4

On the Margins of Marriage

Priests and their partners did not have the choice of formalizing their union; neither did slaves or servants pressured or forced into relations by their employers. This chapter examines some couples who had a choice of types of union, and chose not to make a formal marriage. Either they preferred a temporary union, thought marriage was uneconomical, faced family pressures or widely discrepant social standing, or chose deliberately to leave the situation vague. We look here at a microcosm: Paris at the end of the fifteenth and beginning of the sixteenth century. Many, though not all, of these cases appeared in the records because the two parties disagreed on the nature of the partnership. This chapter attempts to tease out some of the reasons for people's choices, and the ways in which the community around them regarded their unions. Did couples see no social or legal need to marry? Did one partner settle for a non-sanctioned relationship in the hope of later marrying? Did one or both parties interpret the law in such a way as to believe that they were actually married? Did couples who lived together without marriage offend the standards of the community? How well did the kinds of unions that people understood themselves as forming map onto the legal categories through which we learn about them?

In this particular medieval moment, marriage was no longer in question as it had been in previous centuries. It was accepted for the most part as a bulwark of the social order rather than a necessary evil. By the sixteenth century, as we have seen, reformers were making this claim even for clerical marriages, a reflection of how thoroughly the idea had permeated society. Conduct literature, aimed especially at a bourgeoisie and lower aristocracy, valued marriage highly for both men and women. Yet the records tell us that marriage was not the only means that people, especially working people, used to create stable bonds.

Much recent scholarship on marriage emphasizes it as a multistage process, in which questions arose when one of the stages stalled. In this view, nonmarital unions were generally on the way to becoming marriage but never got there.[1] Many cases examined in this chapter do reflect failed marriage formation. It is also useful, however, to understand medieval pair bonds as a set of statuses to choose from rather than a set of stages through which a given couple passed. Not everyone passed through the same stages, and not everyone intended to marry. Concubinage, in the case of laypeople as well as priests, had some recognition as a legal status in Paris as well as in some other parts of Europe. In between it and marriage was a gray area that could be treated as marriage or not as marriage under the law, and, I argue, also within the social community, depending on circumstances.[2] Some people deliberately chose that gray area. Many were women who thought it was the best they could get and would have chosen marriage had they had the opportunity; but many chose to enter a semipermanent union, anyway, knowing that they were not on the road to marriage. We know about these people mainly from hostile sources, the records of institutions set up to punish them.

Canon Law and Its Enforcement

By the end of the fifteenth century, the rules on formation of marriage had been settled canon law for three hundred years. The rules that Pope Alexander III had articulated in the latter half of the twelfth century would remain in place until the Council of Trent in the sixteenth century and indeed, in some respects, after. Research into church court records from across Europe indicates that the courts generally enforced Alexander's rules quite consistently. There were differences in practice from one part of Europe to another, which reflected local customs of marrying by words of present or future consent.[3] Whether cases were brought by one of the parties (*ab instantia*, instance, or civil cases) or by church officials (*ex officio*, office, or criminal cases), they were decided on the same general principles, although the means of putting those principles into practice could vary from region to region or even in different dioceses within a region.[4]

The rule that consent between the parties alone could make a marriage inevitably led to a great deal of confusion. Publicity, as we saw in Chapter 1, had been key to marriage during the early Middle Ages and was still required for a marriage to take place fully in accordance with the law. In Paris in the late fifteenth century, it was customary for the parties to make their promises of marriage at the church door. Whether or not they followed that custom, the parties were required to have the banns proclaimed in their parish church on three Sundays, so that anyone who knew of an impediment to the marriage had a chance to come forward. They then were to solemnize the marriage, followed by a nuptial mass. The customary nature of these practices may have been relatively new in the late fifteenth century.[5] Although these elements of publicity were required, and the parties could be punished for not performing them, their absence did not invalidate the marriage. But clandestine marriages (the term generally used, at least in France, for any marriage performed without banns, even if the marriage was not secret) could be very hard to prove, and the line between such a marriage and a nonmarital union could be blurry.[6]

Today in North America and Europe, most matrimonial litigation is about the dissolution of marriages; disputes over the existence and validity of opposite-sex marriages in the first place are relatively rare.[7] Licensing and recording by the relevant authorities is part and parcel of marriage formation. In the Middle Ages, although quite a lot of documentation was created in the process of forming marriages among the property-holding members of society, it was usually documentation not of the marriages themselves but of the financial arrangements that took place on the occasion. Parish registers of marriages did not come into widespread use until the sixteenth century or later; even if a marriage was carried out with all the proper public forms, it might create no footprint in the written sources. The sources that do tell us about the formation (or not) of marriage are the records of the church courts.[8] The English church court records, which are especially rich, have been extensively used to write the history of marriage—both legal and demographic—and of sexuality.[9] This chapter, like Chapter 3, draws extensively on a set of French records, from the court of the archdeacon's official of Paris, and focuses on the history of unions that were not marriage or that were on the borderline of marriage.[10]

Paris is important because of its size and the kind of information that its records present. The largest city in Europe, it had a population of about 200,000 before the Black Death and possibly near that number at the end of the fifteenth century. More than 1,600 cases in the twenty-two-year period from 1483 to 1505, even within the area of the archdeaconry where the population would have been somewhat smaller, must be the tip of the iceberg in terms of the amount of illicit sexual behavior going on. Nevertheless, it is only by looking at what was prosecuted that we can find evidence for everyday behavior. We cannot take it as typical of European or even of northern

French regulation of sexual relations between women and men, nor of the entire Middle Ages, but it provides a snapshot of the ways in which people in a particular medieval society formed their unions, formal and less formal.[11]

As a large city, Paris provided more opportunities for anonymity than a village. Yet, as in all medieval cities, people lived in fairly cramped quarters. Servants and other residents in large households shared bedrooms and even beds. Vendors and laundresses came and went from wealthy homes. Single people often shared rented rooms in someone else's home. Parishes paid attention to the lives of their priests. There were plenty of chances to observe other people's behavior. It may be, as is often the case, that the city population was more tolerant and less censorious than that of villages, but the archdeaconry included rural as well as more urbanized areas.[12] Paris also appears to have been more tolerant than London in the same time period, in terms of the number of fines per capita for sexual offenses.[13] This chapter will consider the range of sexual offenses for which laypeople were prosecuted, as well as matrimonial cases, in order to look at how nonmarital sexual behavior related to the formation of long-term unions, whether marriage or not.

We look here at the same criminal registers from the Paris archdeaconry that were examined in Chapter 3. In cases involving laypeople, the distinction between the criminal and civil records was not always sharp. The terms "civil" and "criminal" appear on the front pages of the registers themselves; this terminology is far from universal in church court records, which used a variety of terms for cases brought by one of the parties and cases brought by an official, but the distinction that theologians made between a sin and a crime was evidently not upheld here. The court apparently heard the cases in the same sessions. Some cases recorded in the civil registers were brought at the instance of the promoter, the court official who was responsible for investigating and bringing cases,[14] and some of those recorded in the criminal register were brought at the denunciation of a co-participant or a victim of the activity being prosecuted.[15] One case in the criminal register in which a woman was seeking permission to marry because her husband had disappeared has a marginal note: "Should be placed in the other register."[16] A civil suit for the enforcement of marital promises (a promise to marry, which could be considered future consent) could also end up in the criminal register. These suits often were accompanied by, or occasioned, the prosecution of the parties for clandestine marriage; for carnal knowledge after marital promises, which amounted to a presumed marriage that was valid if proven; or the prosecution of the man for deflowering the woman. Cases from other courts from the same period in the same region (the archdeaconry of Brie and the exempt jurisdiction of the cathedral chapter of Notre Dame) are also used here as examples but are not included in the statistical analysis; they can show to what extent the practices of the Paris archdeacon's court were typical.

The majority of the sexual and matrimonial cases (1,153 of 1,620) that appeared in the Paris records stated that the defendant paid a fine (*emendavit*). In some cases, the accused made amends for only some of the alleged offenses.[17] In other cases, the accusation was contested and further procedural events were recorded, including questioning of the defendant or witnesses. Unfortunately, however, these contested cases in which interrogatories or depositions were recorded, which provide the most information, often did not record the result of the case. And even when we do have a result, we do not have the back story: the information presented in court did not give the whole picture. Further complicating the relation between records and lived reality was the fact that many people's lives and relationships never reached the court; these are, after all, records of criminal prosecutions. There were undoubtedly additional cases, not noted, in which there were accusations but initial investigation did not provide enough evidence to proceed.[18] And there would have been even more instances of illicit behavior that never came to the attention of the authorities. The vast majority of people did not end up in court, and probably most of these were people who followed the rules by marrying and remaining faithful; but an unquantifiable but sizable group of people chose other paths.

Even though the church courts across Europe enforced the same basic rules, there were different patterns in litigation and different terminology in different regions that may or may not represent different social practice. Charles Donahue has stressed the law enforcement function of the French courts' treatment of clandestine marriage, which was prosecuted by the church officials as a criminal offense, in contrast with the English church courts, in which marriages not conducted in church came to the court's attention because of a suit brought by one of the parties. Yet many of the cases in the Paris criminal register did come to the attention of the court through the bringing of a private lawsuit.[19] For example, Pierrette Alispere was fined for "allowing herself to be deflowered and repeatedly carnally known" by Hugues Valengelier. The fine did not result from her being cited by the court. Rather, her voluntary (*sponte*) confession was recorded in the criminal register on the same day that the civil register recorded her acknowledgment of having received two hundred francs in gold from Hugues's brother and her renunciation of any claims of marital promises.[20] In order to claim enforcement of the marriage, she had to admit to the sexual offense, and when she dropped that claim because of the settlement, her confession still stood. In a more typical fact pattern, Jeanne la Fayne appeared in the criminal register making amends for "clandestine marriage, in that after spousals she allowed herself to be known carnally by Pierre Mesnard." "Spousals" (*sponsalia*) was a slightly unusual term in this court; in other jurisdictions, it usually referred to the betrothal stage, although occasionally it could mean marriage by words of present consent.[21] Jeanne was said to have been cited, rather than coming forward *sponte*, and we may wonder why only she was cited and not Pierre. The answer is that she brought a suit that appeared in the civil register on the same day, alleging marital promises at the church door followed by carnal knowledge (in other words, future consent followed by consummation) and asking that Pierre be compelled to solemnize the marriage. Pierre admitted the promises but denied the carnal knowledge.[22] Given that he was not cited in the criminal register, it seems clear that her "citation" resulted from her confessing to the offense as part of her civil case. The court here was not enforcing the law on its own but rather reacting to private action.[23] This was one of the possible patterns of clandestine marriage: the couple had made their promises publicly, but there was no mention of banns, and the marriage had not been solemnized. This was what canonists sometimes called *matrimonium presumptum*, presumed marriage, in that the sexual intercourse after the promises presumed marital consent. It is not clear, however, that both parties continued to intend that the couple be formally married.

The two parties might be fined for different offenses—for example, the woman for clandestine marriage and the man for carnal knowledge, even though the court did not hold the two to be married. Why would the court fine one party for a clandestine marriage when it did not determine that such a marriage existed? It was probably going by the parties' consciences—in essence, fining them for what each had confessed, even if the court did not accept the confession in making its decision on the status of the union.[24] Even if the party claiming marriage won her case, however, the court did not always fine both. For example, Marianne Durande, a former maid of the abbess of Malnoue in the archdeaconry of Brie, was fined for being carnally known by Pierre Riche, a shepherd of the abbey, and for clandestine marriage with him. He was not fined. Her original claim does not appear in the register, but she must have brought a claim for breach of promise; when she was interrogated, she claimed that he broke off their engagement because he was having an affair with the abbess. He denied that he had promised her marriage but said that he was prepared to marry her if she could prove that her previous husband was dead. She claimed that she had seen him die but offered no other evidence.[25] In this case, the court judged the parties to be married, and no follow-up was recorded in this register against Pierre and the abbess for a sexual relationship or for Marianne for defaming the abbess.

Not all cases found in the criminal register came to the court because of a disagreement between the parties. Gilbert Pichet, a barber, came into court *sponte*, or voluntarily, and confessed that he had maintained Pierrette Burguete for several years (the number is left blank). They had several children together, and now, he said, he wanted to marry her.[26] He may have known that calling the banns would make it obvious that the woman with whom he was living and had children was not already his wife, and wished to come forward now to clear the record. In many other cases in which people were said to have come before the court voluntarily, a story like this may lie behind it. Gilbert obviously knew that despite his long-standing union with Pierrette, something was lacking. Did he know that if they promised marriage and then had intercourse, the union would be a marriage, although still not entirely licit? He did not confess to clandestine marriage but only to maintaining Pierrette. It is hard to believe that in a city like Paris, three and a half centuries after Alexander III, people did not know that promises followed by sexual intercourse created a marriage.[27] Certainly, preachers made clear what was expected for a valid marriage and what impediments might prevent it.[28] For example, Jean Raulin, preaching in Paris in the late fifteenth century, attacked clandestine marriage.[29] But some cases were quite complicated, and a few give us clues as to how well people knew the details of marriage law.

In using the Paris archdeaconry records to study the formation of unions and the kind of relationships that people saw themselves as entering, we ought to take into account how the cases reached the court. However, unless one of the parties instigated the case, we do not know whether the initiative came from a neighbor, from the promoter picking up on general rumor, or from someone intimately concerned in the case. Paris may have been a sophisticated urban community, but not everything was tolerated, and some people must have informed on their neighbors, perhaps out of moral disapproval but perhaps also when the neighbor had offended in some other way.

Although the Paris records reveal differences in procedure and in the terminology used even with other jurisdictions in northern France, let alone elsewhere, the larger social patterns may not be all that different. The evidence from Paris is fairly consistent with that from English towns as to the involvement (or lack of involvement) of families in the formation of unions by young people who were living away from home.[30] Silvana Seidel Menchi and Diego Quaglioni led a series of studies on material from Italian ecclesiastical archives that show great variation and complexity across Italy.[31] It would be wrong to take patterns of behavior in Paris as typical of "medieval Europe" or even "late fifteenth-century Europe," but they can provide a case study of the possibilities for the regulation of marriage under the aegis of the medieval church.

"In Ignorance of the Law": Marianne la Pierresse, Jeanne the Widow of Jean le Roy, and Guillemette Dorange

Women who had transgressed the boundaries that limited sexual activity to marriage might plead ignorance of the law, but they were not necessarily always that ignorant. A few examples leave open the possibility that they could navigate the complex rules and manipulate them to suit their goals. In 1505, Marianne, daughter of the late Jean Pierre, brought a civil case for breach of promise of marriage and also claimed dowry because of defloration (*causa matrimonialis et dotis*) in the court of the archdeacon of Paris against Simon de Grain.[32] As a result of this case, Simon was interrogated on criminal charges, and the record survives.[33] Somewhat unusual is the fact that Simon had been married to someone else at the time of the claimed promises and defloration. He had frequented Marianne la Pierresse for eighteen or nineteen years of his twenty-year marriage; a year earlier, he had married off the daughter she bore him. As he testified, his wife had died four weeks previously, and this was likely what prompted Marianne's claim: she knew that she could not sue for enforcement of marital promises while her partner was married to another woman. Simon did not deny his relationship with Marianne, and the case stands as evidence for the kinds of long-term unions outside of marriage that could develop in a culture without divorce. It is not clear whether Simon lived with his wife throughout the period, but he and Marianne certainly retained a bond over the years, and his giving of their daughter in marriage supports the seriousness of that bond.

Marianne la Pierresse may have brought the civil (instance) suit now because she saw the opportunity finally to have the legal status of a wife, or because she saw the opportunity for a cash settlement (which she eventually got). If what she wanted was marriage, however, she went about her action in the wrong way. The valid and unbreakable marriage automatically created by a promise followed by sexual intercourse would not have applied to the promise that she claimed Simon had made to her during the lifetime of his wife. Indeed, not only did that promise not create marriage; it prevented it. A promise of marriage between adulterers created the impediment of crime, a diriment impediment that invalidated any subsequent marriage between them.[34] Had Marianne been manipulating the law in an effort to construct the most favorable story, she would have had to claim that they had not exchanged promises until after the death of his wife. She, however, apparently thought that the long-standing nature of the relationship gave it some status. She may not have been familiar enough with the arcana of canonical impediments.

But perhaps Marianne knew that promises during Simon's first wife's lifetime invalidated any possible marriage between them, and her claim was nourished by a grudge. Daniel Smail suggests that this was the case with many civil (not ecclesiastical) actions in Marseille, where people brought cases not to achieve the result that they were nominally claiming, but rather out of hatred or a desire for revenge.[35] Marianne may have felt herself entitled to marriage and been bitterly disappointed that it was not forthcoming after the wife's death. Her claim of a promise during the lifetime of Simon's wife could have been malicious rather than naïve, intended to get him into trouble rather than snare him as a husband. Simon was asked to respond to a claim that she had made during the investigation (which did not appear in the record) that he had made a pilgrimage to Santiago de Compostela to pray for his wife's death so that he could marry his lover. Had the impediment of crime not already existed, attempting to bring about the death of his wife would have created it. It is not likely that Marianne could have believed that this claim would have strengthened her case; it may have been a result of anger at Simon for not marrying her. Simon denied seeking his wife's death but did not deny going to Compostela. The court fined him five ecus, the largest amount for any of the more than 1,600 sexual or matrimonial cases in the Paris criminal registers, and he also paid Marianne an unspecified amount in settlement. Ultimately, we cannot know whether she brought the whole case simply to get back at Simon. Since she was at the same time incriminating herself, it was likely that she thought that she could get something worthwhile out of it, as indeed she did.[36]

The size of the fine probably means that the court thought that there was something to Marianne's story; it was much higher than fines for other married men keeping women on the side. (Few of these cases were labeled adultery; as discussed in Chapter 3, crimes of adultery were reserved to the bishop, although a few were prosecuted in the archdeacon's court, as well as in the court of the cathedral chapter of Notre Dame.) Her legal claim to be married to Simon was clearly erroneous. She may not have been represented by counsel, as not everyone in this court was. But although we may guess that her claim arose out of bitterness, or a sense of moral rather than legal entitlement, the court found him culpable enough to fine him heavily. While Marianne may not have known that marital promises between adulterers created an impediment, she did know that marital promises followed by sexual intercourse usually created an enforceable marriage; while she did not get what she was formally asking for, she did get some satisfaction from the case. We may suspect that she knew what she was doing.

Unlike Marianne, Jeanne the widow of Jean le Roy was labeled "simple" by the court, but that does not mean that they did not hold her responsible for her mistakes. Jeanne was accused of leaving Jean le Masson after they had been affianced (*affidati*). She had broken the engagement before two notaries of the Châtelet. The involvement of notaries of the Châtelet, the secular court, was not unusual in cases of the formation or rupture of marital promises and, in this instance, likely represents the abrogation of a property settlement. According to the register, Jeanne stated that "she did not think she was doing wrong, because she had been advised to do this by a certain priest, whom she named, and weeping asked mercy of the official, and the official said that he would have regard for her poverty." The fact that the priest's name was not recorded, that the official said that he would take account of her poverty but not her simplicity, and that she was fined anyway indicates that the official did not believe her about not knowing any better. It may be that she thought her weeping and plea of ignorance would get her off the hook. Meanwhile, her erstwhile fiancé apparently thought that he was released from the promises of marriage as well, because he paid a fine for contracting marriage with another woman, despite the fact that he was affianced to Jeanne and acquitted of that marriage at the Châtelet.[37]

Guillemette, daughter of the late Robin Dorange, also pleaded ignorance. She was fined for allowing herself to be carnally known by her sister's fiancé Gilet Soulas. She claimed that he had raped her, then the next day promised to marry her, and she, "in ignorance of the law," accepted. They had sex several more times, and she had a child as a result.[38] It is an interesting question just what law she was claiming ignorance of here. If he and the sister had exchanged promises but not had sex, and he then exchanged promises and had sex with

Guillemette, it was the second union that would have been valid (although he could have been fined for breaking the first). The only way the first union would invalidate the second was if it had been by words of future consent followed by intercourse, or words of present consent. The word used of Gilet's engagement to Guillemette's sister, *desponsare*, is often used in sources to mean "betroth," but Carole Avignon notes that it can also be used for a present-tense agreement of marriage, not yet consummated, but more than a betrothal because present consent made a valid marriage.[39] Of course, if he had previously had sex with her sister, with or without marital promises, that would have created an impediment of consanguinity to Guillemette and Gilet's marriage. It is likely that this case reflects not a mistaken understanding of a specific law but a more generalized wishful thinking; the plea of ignorance was meant to garner sympathy. She may very well have been in need of that sympathy, if Gilet had raped her and she maintained a relationship with him afterward because she did not see any alternative. Or the rape story could have been another attempt to deflect responsibility from herself; we have no way of knowing.

It was not only women who claimed, or were attributed, an ignorance of the law that might or might not excuse their actions. The claim of ignorance might be easier for women than men because of general assumptions about them, but some men were clearly less knowledgeable than others. Gilles Renard, a thresher of the grange of Sarcelles (Seine-et-Oise, now a northern banlieu), who was called *valde simplex* (extremely simple), seems to have been easily manipulated by the local vicar, Jean Auber. On 21 June 1493, Gilles was led into court by his local curate. This is unusual phrasing, and implies that he would not have been able to come on his own. The events for which he made amends were not labeled as a particular offense, but merely recounted. The vicar Jean Auber had persuaded Gilles to come to a certain house and there had affianced him to a *iuvencula* (girl), Jeanne la Gavinelle, "asserting that she was a good girl [*filia*]." This is an example of priests' involvement in marriage even when the betrothal did not take place at the church door or was not accompanied by the banns; priests were involved in clandestine marriages, too. Jeanne may have been the same *iuvencula* mentioned in another case earlier that month. On 9 June 1493, the chaplain of Sarcelles, Jean Obier (possibly the same person as the vicar Jean Auber, despite the different title and different spelling), made amends for having caused a *maximum scandalum* by having a girl delouse him in the public square of the village several months previously.[40] Delousing, even in the case of head lice, was a very intimate act, one that family members often performed for one another. It could be that Auber was trying to find a husband for the young woman with whom he had created this scandal. After the betrothal, however, Gilles saw that Jeanne was alone, *solus cum sola*, with the vicar "in places apt for carnal coupling," and found out that she had given birth to a priest's child. He therefore told the vicar that he did not wish to solemnize marriage with her. The vicar then called the couple together again, had them clasp hands, and spoke the words *je vous deffiance*, "I un-betroth you,"[41] a parody of what the priest would have done in a normal ceremony. The following day, Jeanne was fined for having allowed herself to be deflowered by a certain Jean de Fresnay, by whom she had borne a child but who was not referred to here as a priest.[42] And on 15 July, Auber paid a fine of four sous (the amounts of the other fines were not given) for the same events for which Gilles had made amends.[43]

Poor Gilles had been duped and was foolish enough to think that some words from a priest could break his *affidationes*, which amounted to a promise of marriage. In fact, such promises were quite frequently dissolved for similar reasons by the court on the petition of one of the parties, but Gilles was apparently not knowledgeable enough to bring such a petition. Yet even this simple man knew the stages of matrimony—*affidationes* followed by solemnization—as they were commonly practiced in the Paris region and elsewhere in France. This is not surprising: the two-stage process would have been fairly ingrained. In the thirteenth century, synodal statutes were concerned that people would be confused about the differences between present and future promises, and there may indeed have still been some confusion, but it is likely that most people would have understood normal practice.[44] It is possible, as Carole Avignon suggests, that increased clerical involvement at the earlier stage of *affidationes* led people to think that that was all that was necessary for marriage, yet surely this involvement would also have given the priest the opportunity for reminding the couple of the deadline for solemnizing.[45]

One would think that the words that created a marriage would also have been fairly common knowledge. Just as in contemporary culture, everyone knows that marriage happens when you say, "I do," and the officiant says, "I pronounce you man [or husband] and wife," medieval people would have known that the words "I take you in marriage" or "I will take you in marriage" were the correct form. In a 1487 case to which we shall return, Tassine la Martine claimed breach of promise against Mathieu Coquillen.[46] A neighbor testified that she had heard Mathieu speak the words *je te prends en mariage* ("I take you in marriage") after Tassine refused to have sex with him otherwise.

This was a present-tense vow, which would have created binding matrimony even without intercourse. The fact that the witness reported this simple and legal form of words perhaps indicates that she knew what the law required. The proper form was not always used, however: in another case, a woman testified that the man who promised her marriage said, "the Devil take my body and soul if I don't marry you."[47] Marguerite la Massiere alleged (and Jean le Page admitted) that she refused to have sex with him unless he promised to marry her: she told him *ne viens pour reans se se nest en tout bien et pour mavoir en mariage* ("don't bother coming here unless it's in good faith and to have me in marriage"), and asked "if he wanted to promise the faith of his body to take her in marriage," and he said yes.[48] In none of these instances was a formal ceremony alleged. Some people seem to have known enough about the traditional form of words either to use them in a clandestine marriage or to claim that they had used them, but others did not even make the claim. Not using the traditional wording did not in itself invalidate the marriage, but using it removed one possible ambiguity.

Disputed Marriages or Post Facto Claims?

Sometimes ambiguity was just what was wanted, by one or both parties. In many court cases, the point at issue was whether a particular union was marriage or not, and the canon law provided a set of rules to apply to determine this. However, for unions that did not (or were not expected to) end up in court, the line was not necessarily clearly drawn, and there was little occasion to apply formal rules. The form of words indicating consent was the key in the canon law. In many times and places in medieval Europe, as we have seen, dowry or other financial arrangements helped determine whether people would regard the union as a marriage, even if they were not canonically required. The statements of the participants and witnesses in the Paris cases indicated other parts of the ritual that they thought made a marriage, or at least a promise of marriage: a handclasp, a kiss, a gift, a meal.[49] The circumstances under which these were claimed to have taken place could be informal in the extreme, but claimants still alleged the existence of these elements as part of their claim that a marriage had been intended. We have no statements from the court indicating that these exchanges weighed heavily as evidence, but the fact that they were so frequently mentioned indicates that they were part of what made a marriage in the eyes of the public.

When people did explain in court what went on in the informal ceremonies that they had witnessed, it is not at all clear whether they saw them as part of a process and expected a dowry or a solemnization in church to follow at some point. They may have thought of a marriage contract as a moment rather than a process, and understood that these other elements were not legally required. Or it may be that the court was not particularly interested in the other elements, and found the words, gifts, and meal the best evidence of consent. People who had gone through such an informal ceremony could be seen, as Cordelia Beattie suggests, as on the margins of singleness, not quite married but not entirely unmarried, either.[50] It was marriage, however, that was the marked category, the one that required some action, and therefore it makes sense to think of promises of future marriage as being on the margins of marriage rather than of singleness, or as moving toward the category of marriage. But not all couples necessarily wanted to move; they may have been happy where they were. The margin of marriage was a gray and ambiguous area, not only because there might be some confusion as to which legal category people fit, but also because that confusion might be deliberate. People could make use of it as circumstances dictated; to the extent that the union was less formally created, it could be less formally ended, and many couples may have been happy with that. We only see the occasions on which problems arose from it.

Marriage as practiced in Paris had the same stages required by canon law, with some specific additions. The parties might exchange promises privately (*promissiones*); if the promises were exchanged publicly, especially at the church door (*in facie ecclesie*), as they were supposed to be, they were called *affidationes*.[51] Some couples performed both the private and then the public promises. A ring or belt often accompanied the promises. For example, Michel Cosnel denied in court that he had ever seen the ring he was alleged to have given Pierrette Fanoise.[52] Gifts could be convincing evidence of the existence of a marriage contract. Guillemette, widow of Jean Galeren, made amends (paid a fine) for herself and Jean Regier for the scandal they had created. They had been publicly betrothed (*affidati*), with banns proclaimed. Afterward, however, the court allowed them to withdraw the promises because of her bad faith in that she had previously accepted the gift of a silver ring from Denis Brule in the name of marriage.[53] If she had previously promised to marry Denis, that would indeed be an impediment and make the second promises invalid; but the register did not phrase her interaction with Denis as a previous promise but rather as the acceptance of gifts in name of marriage. The case of Denise Vallette and Jean Faucq further illustrates what "in the name of marriage" meant. Jean made amends for not solemnizing their union and also for fathering her child "in the name of marriage." Denise made amends for giving birth "by his deed, which the said Faucq did to her in the name of matrimony," as well as for being maintained by him, permitting herself to be carnally known after matrimonial promises, and causing scandal thereby.[54] The use of "in the name of matrimony" here clearly alludes to her claim of matrimonial promises, and the gifts and acts that were said to be done "in the name of matrimony" make the same allusion. The acceptance of gifts was the functional or evidentiary equivalent of the exchange of promises.[55]

After the *affidationes*, the banns were supposed to be called three times. This did not always happen and things did not always run smoothly to solemnization, as with Guillaume Carret, who betrothed two different women both *in facie ecclesie*.[56] A property settlement, if there was to be one, would be finalized before solemnization, which was supposed to take place within forty days.[57] This settlement usually took the form of sums promised by the bride's father. These were recorded in contracts before notaries of the Châtelet. These property arrangements were mentioned in the church court records only in passing; they were incidents of marriage but not proof of it. The cordwainer Guillaume Paillard, who was fined for clandestine marriage with Catherine Vaillante, provided an example of the role that these contracts played. He confessed the *affidationes* but said that the marriage was never solemnized because she did not bring him the promised dowry, and there was a lawsuit in the Châtelet about it.[58] He was not claiming that the marriage was not valid because there was no dowry, but that he had declined to proceed to the next legal step because the dowry had not been paid.

A marriage that missed the step of public betrothal and banns or the step of solemnization was clandestine. A marriage in which the couple exchanged vows of present consent privately was also clandestine, but more common was one in which they exchanged promises or vows of future consent and then had sexual intercourse. A clandestine marriage created by future vows and sexual intercourse, or *matrimonium presumptum*, could also be called a de facto marriage, but as Carole Avignon suggests, based on evidence from Rouen, this term seems to have been reserved for cases in which the marriage was not valid because of an impediment.[59] Indeed, in one case, Charles du Molly and Marguerite Toussains were accused of having a "clandestine marriage de facto" by exchanging promises followed by carnal knowledge, even though she had previously been determined by the court to be married to someone else and thus it was no marriage at all. They denied any sexual intercourse and paid the fine for the scandal of frequenting each other.[60] Rarely in these de facto marriages did the register specify the tense in which the vows were made, but if they were in the present tense, they would, if there were no diriment impediment, have been binding without the intercourse.[61]

Depositions or interrogatories provide us with the most detailed evidence of how people behaved (or said they behaved), the clearest sense of the circumstances under which marriages were formed (or under which one of the parties claimed that they had been formed), but survive from only a small subset of cases. They are especially common in defloration cases (100 cases out of 1,620), in which a man was prosecuted for having taken a woman's virginity. Some of these cases had their origin in civil actions brought by the women; others did not; in yet others, the civil register does not survive from the corresponding period, so we do not know. Even when there was no civil suit, the woman was involved in the prosecution of the case, bringing a complaint before the official, who then prosecuted the man (and sometimes also the woman, for allowing herself to be deflowered). A defloration case was often part of a *causa matrimonialis*, a breach-of-promise claim. This type of claim was more than just a broken future promise: the allegation was that the man had promised future marriage, and then sexual intercourse had transformed the future promise into a binding marriage. But in some defloration cases, the woman was not able to claim matrimonial promises because the man was a priest or was already married. In this case, she could bring a *causa defloracionis et dotis*, a claim for her deflowerer to pay a dowry so that she could marry someone else. Often this type of claim resulted when she became pregnant. There are some cases in which only the defloration was alleged and no promises, even though the man was single and free to marry.

When someone described in court the circumstances in which a marriage was initiated, we do not know that she or he was telling the truth. The stakes for women, especially, were very high in terms of reputation, and this has led some scholars to believe that women largely claimed marriage after the fact. As a leading canon law scholar wrote in 1973, the fact that future promises followed by intercourse created a binding marriage created "first of all a windfall for girls in search of husbands," and court cases were brought by families "finding that negotiations were dragging or the boy was escaping."[62] There is little basis for the assumption that all such cases were trumped up. Most cases in the archdeacon's court registers do not indicate that family members were present when consent was exchanged (see below). We do see the usual "he said, she said," where one party's testimony directly contradicted the other's and there is no way of knowing whom to believe. But we also see occasions on which people showed a respect for oaths and a reluctance to commit perjury—to place their hand on the Gospels and imperil their salvation—that indicates that they were not constructing their story purely in pursuit of their own interests. I work from the assumptions that many people believed themselves to be telling the truth as they saw it, and that claims had to be plausible. Unfortunately, we do not have the results in many of the cases, so we do not know how plausible the court actually found them. In only about 20 percent of cases did the court determine that a marriage did exist;[63] in others, no result survives and the parties may have reached an accord.

Informal, spur-of-the-moment agreements may not have been the modal way of forming a marriage but appear to have been common enough to make a plausible story. Such cases often involved servants (see Tables 2 and 3 later in this chapter); it is not surprising that family would be less involved in marriage formation at a social level where property transactions were less important. Sometimes there was no plausible story and the claim of marriage was probably an afterthought. Marianne de Rambures was fined in February 1488 for "repeatedly being with" Denis le Bref and becoming pregnant by him. A month later, she appeared bringing a case against him, saying that they had lived together for two months. She sought payment of her expenses in childbirth, and to be adjudged his wife. He denied knowing her carnally, but after two witnesses testified under oath that he had told them he had done so, he confessed it.[64] He was ordered to pay the expenses, but the record says nothing about her being his wife; he was apparently not even questioned about marital promises. It is possible that Denis did make or imply some promise, but it seems more likely that Marianne's claim of marriage was flimsy; it may have been a fairly routine claim for women to make whether it was warranted or not. In some cases, no one claimed promises, although one party hoped for them. Jeanne Merande paid a fine for allowing Nicolas, whose surname was left blank, to have carnal knowledge of her six or seven times, "hoping that he would marry her, although there were no marital promises between them."[65] These relationships may not have been long-term domestic partnerships, but they do indicate a common pattern of sexual activity without marriage, although perhaps looking forward to marriage.

All marriage agreements were subject to some level of ambiguity, since there was no written record of the promises or solemnization. Eyewitness testimony, even if not deliberately mendacious, could be tinged by wishful thinking or eroding memory. But when the promises were not public—when they were made only between the parties or before witnesses who happened quite randomly to be present at the time—the level of ambiguity rose significantly.

The case of Tassine la Martine mentioned above is a good example of alleged informal formation of marriages. The court asked Tassine why she had caused Mathieu Coquillen to be imprisoned. (Imprisonment of the defendant—indeed, also of the complainant—pending trial was fairly common in this court.) She replied that it was because he had promised her marriage. Informed that this was not a sufficient accusation to warrant his imprisonment pending trial, she then claimed that he had deflowered her after the promise of matrimony. It may be that Tassine was a quick learner who changed her story, but she would have told the story previously, when he was first put into prison, and would have had to allege more than promises; probably, the official was just reminding her to tell the whole story. The result of Tassine's case was not recorded in the register—the last we see of the case, Mathieu had been out on bail and was back in jail—but another man paid a fine three and a half months later for slandering Tassine by saying that he had known her carnally.[66] He may have been recruited by Mathieu as a defense to the defloration claim.

Tassine was not suggesting that she and Mathieu had lived together as domestic partners; she claimed that he had come to her master's house at night to see her. Although her witness claimed words of marriage in the present tense, Tassine's claim was for promises. The court, and hence the woman in this situation, tended to describe promises followed by sexual intercourse as incomplete or unfulfilled marriages. Although such unions were complete enough to be binding in the eyes of the law, there were further legal steps that had not been taken. Nor were the marriages complete socially until the couple were living together. It may be, as Carole Avignon has suggested, that such clandestine marriages were considered by those involved in them, especially the women, as a sort of pregnancy insurance. The exchange of vows gave the woman a legal claim to fall back on if she did become pregnant.[67]

Colin Maillard, who testified that the (unnamed) woman he was with told him that she would have sex with him only in the name of matrimony, provides another example of informal marriage formation. Colin said that he would not marry her, but they had intercourse anyway. She also claimed that he gave her marriage gifts; he admitted giving her gifts, but not in the name of marriage. He may, of course, have been lying outright, but it is also possible that both parties believed that they were telling the truth or deliberately leaving things ambiguous. She could have sincerely believed, or hoped, that his having intercourse with her meant that he had changed his mind about the conditions, or he could have believed or hoped that she had changed hers.[68] One partner's consent to sex in the hope of marriage had a power in the

Middle Ages that it lacks today because the sexual intercourse made promises binding; but while the other partner (usually the man) could not legally take the promises back, he could certainly deny that he had made them in the first place, or word them ambiguously.

The case of Jean Sarrasin and Denise Esperlant is, in some ways, the ultimate he-said-she-said case, again indicating the informal nature of the entry into marriage.[69] Jean Sarrasin was a cart driver for Simon de Neufville, receiver of Paris (a royal official).[70] Denise Esperlant also worked for Neufville and reported that Sarrasin first knew her carnally in the stables of Neufville's residence, where he slept. Many such incidents seem to have taken place in the stables, where male servants often slept.[71] One man, defending himself against a charge of defloration, claimed that the woman was no virgin, but a vagrant public woman, "running from stable to stable."[72] In Denise's case, only one stable was involved. She swore that she was a virgin when she first had sex with Sarrasin. Jean's first interrogation was equivocal: he claimed that he did not know her carnally but that he did not remember whether he had ever kissed her. He declined to rely on her oath on these issues because she had previously committed perjury against him, although when he explained, he said that he meant that she had falsely told their master and mistress that he had had sex with another one of the servants, which was not technically perjury, as it was not under oath.[73] The two were confronted with each other, and she repeated to his face that he had both kissed and deflowered her, and that he gave her a belt (which she displayed) in the name of marriage. He said that he did not know whether he had seen the belt before, but that he did not give it to her.

The next day, Jean was interrogated "after a solemn oath, touching the holy Gospels" (a phrase found in few interrogations). He said that he was never alone in the stable with Denise, and never kissed her when they were alone, but may have done so when he was with several of the maids of the house and they were fooling around (the record noted the French term he used; *riblerent*). Asked whether he had ever put his hand on her breast or her genitals, he said no. Asked whether he was ever alone with her in her room, he said that he was there many times, but never alone. They agreed on some of the details—the date on which he was in her bedroom—but not why he was there. He said that he did not know whether she was pregnant, and "that some say that she is not pregnant, and she did this in order to entrap him by this means" (and here the record again slipped into French). Jean Sarrasin's claims ring false; for him not to remember whether he had kissed her, but to be certain that he had not done so in private, sounds self-serving. He was released from jail pending trial, based on a letter from his employer, who said that he needed him. A month later, the judge declared that there were too many conflicting statements and the matter needed to be investigated further. Eventually, the judge ordered Jean to pay the expenses of childbirth, although Denise had to post bond that she would repay the money if he were eventually judged not to be the father. No further record exists, although the result may have been in the civil register that does not survive for this year.

That sexual intercourse took place in such a situation of proximity—two servants in the same house—is hardly surprising. That it would be thought plausible or likely that marital promises were exchanged in this situation, spontaneously, is perhaps slightly more surprising. If there were promises, they were made in a very casual manner. The belt Denise claimed that Jean gave her as a marital gift was not a particularly special one—presumably, just what he was wearing at the time. If Denise's story were true, it may be that she hoped informal promises would be followed later by solemnized marriage, but certainly not anytime soon, and it may have been much more a hope than a concrete expectation. Not all marriages were this informal, of course; many did show family involvement. But many did not, as indicated by the testimony of Pierre Godart, who admitted betrothing a woman "whose surname he does not know, and does not know who her parents are or what village she is from."[74] Neither Jean Sarrasin nor any other defendant asserted lack of familial involvement as a factor that would make the claims of marital promises any less plausible. The fact that such spontaneous and informal promises of marriage were so commonly claimed indicates that marriage was seen as an important goal by many women and men, but also that the line between it and other kinds of relationship was not sharp.

The cases involving Tassine la Martine and Mathieu Coquillen, Colin Maillard and his unnamed partner, and Denise Esperlant and Jean Sarrasin were all cases of promises followed by sexual intercourse. Over the twenty-two-year period, the criminal registers included seventy-two cases of parties prosecuted for clandestine marriage and sixty-seven for "carnal knowledge after promises," which legally amounted to clandestine marriage but was not always labeled as such.[75] Sometimes the two were said to be the same thing: "clandestine marriage, in that after matrimonial promises between them he maintained her and knew her carnally."[76] "Carnal knowledge after promises" is the same offense as what is called "future spousals followed by *copula carnalis*" in the fourteenth-century Paris episcopal court.[77] In few of the cases recorded as "carnal knowledge after promises" were the parties ordered to solemnize the marriage: in 15 cases, both were fined; in 15, the man; in 23, the woman; and in 14, neither. The fact that many of these cases were not labeled clandestine marriage is probably not just sloppy record-keeping. In one case, the couple were fined and the scribe interlineated "clandestine marriage, in that" before "he knew her carnally after matrimonial promises," suggesting that the register was proofread.[78] Each partner's offense was listed separately, and "clandestine marriage" was interlineated in both. Its insertion here and not in other cases was likely not random. In some cases, it could be that the court treated carnal knowledge after promises as a lesser offense: perhaps the parties agreed not to contest the case if the court did not label it a marriage.[79]

Seventeen of the fifty-four "carnal knowledge after promises" cases from years with surviving civil registers originated in civil claims; these claims were brought despite stiff penalties for having engaged in clandestine marriage.[80] The only case in which people were fined for "carnal knowledge after promises" after they were adjudged to be married is that of Jeanne, daughter of Gracian Texier, who sued Pierre le Rohe. They were ordered to solemnize and also fined for carnal knowledge after promises.[81] In several of the cases, the court found that the parties were not married, but still fined one of them for carnal knowledge after promises (in one case, also fining the other for carnal knowledge only). Even when the complaint was not upheld, the person who brought it was fined for the behavior to which she or he confessed by bringing the claim. Rather than being considered perjured, the claimant was assumed to have been telling the truth according to conscience, and fined accordingly.[82] The marriage of Jean Aboclart and Matilde the widow of Pierre le Coci is an example, or at least so she claimed: she brought a suit for breach of promise, he confessed only to frequenting her, and she was fined for allowing herself to be known by him following marital promises.[83]

These cases of carnal knowledge after promises, as opposed to those labeled clandestine marriages, to the extent that they were not false claims, may represent unions initiated by couples themselves rather than betrothals arranged by the families. The couples seem to have had no intention of solemnizing anytime soon. Although marriage was supposed to follow *affidationes* within forty days, these relationships sometimes went on for years. Denis Petit and Jeanne Maillarde both paid a fine for clandestine marriage; they had been together for five years and had a child, but had not solemnized.[84] In this case, neither of them was claiming anything against the other, and they may have chosen together not to solemnize the union. Behavior like theirs created the gray area in which there was room for different views on whether the parties were legally married. The partners often did not move in together (especially if one or both were in service), so it is difficult to label the unions as domestic partnerships.

The common result in a case labeled clandestine marriage was a fine and an order to solemnize the marriage. Whether these cases, when not instigated by one of the parties, were based on rumor (common fame) or a specific accusation from a third party, we do not know. We also do not know whether the couple had not solemnized the marriage because one or both of them changed their minds, whether they planned to solemnize at some future date, or whether they deliberately wished to keep their relationship more informal.[85] The fact that these clandestine unions are occasionally called concubinage or cohabitation points to the latter possibility.[86] The same possibilities held for couples who exchanged their marital promises not clandestinely but at the church, and were later fined for not solemnizing the marriage.

In a case from Brie, a couple recognized the difference between formal marriage and the union in which they lived, but still chose the latter. Guillaume Baudry of Sucy-en-Brie, aged forty, a tanner, admitted that he had maintained Cecilia la Bernadete, aged thirty, for ten or eleven years, and described the various places where the couple had lived. She remembered the length of time as ten or twelve years, and said that she was able to remember the date by when the late king had married.[87] They both said that in several places where they had lived, they had called each other husband and wife and that they had promised to marry. He said that they had no children, and if they had, he would have married her by now. The court made each of them swear that they had never contracted marriage with anyone else, and when they did so, the official betrothed them to each other and ordered them to solemnize. They were fined two ecus of gold for the ten to twelve years during which he maintained her.[88] If their testimony is to be believed, they agreed that they were not formally married and were both happy with the situation, living together as long-term partners.

Not all couples agreed, as we saw with such cases as that of Tassine la Martine. Because marriage formation in Paris typically (although technically not necessarily) included several stages, with promises and then solemnization, there was room for actual misunderstandings in which one partner thought that there was a marriage and the other did not; these could have been caused by bad faith on one person's part, or by actual confusion about the rules. People must have been generally aware that future promises followed by sexual intercourse amounted to a complete and valid marriage—plaintiffs commonly alleged this sequence of events in court to claim a marriage—and yet the emphasis that the Paris archdeacon's court put on solemnizing marriages may have led people to think that the latter was an essential step to complete the marriage.[89] Odine, the widow of Gautier Gresine, was fined for clandestine marriage with Colin Gourle, for whom she worked as a maid. They had supposedly been married clandestinely for three years and were ordered to solemnize the marriage within forty days, on pain of ten livres. Interestingly, however, the register first listed the offense as "frequenting," which was then crossed out and replaced with "clandestine marriage."[90] This could be just a scribal error, but it could also be symptomatic of some confusion. The register often records only the bare result of a case, but if there had been substantial discussion of whether the master and servant's relationship amounted to marriage, this could explain the recording error. It may be that Odine and Colin, and other couples, deliberately left their status ambiguous because they had tacitly agreed to disagree as to whether they were married.

Usually, it was women who sought to be declared married. Marriage provided women with financial support for themselves and their children that they would not otherwise have if the male partner died or abandoned them. It could also bolster their community reputation. At the same time, it took away their freedom to leave the union. Men had a similar set of advantages and disadvantages to balance, but as they tended to be the larger earners or the controllers of wealth, the balance was different. We might attempt to find out something about women's motives by examining whether widows—who were likely, on average, to be better off than never-married women—were trying to have their unions declared marriages. There were in all, as shown in Table 3, 178 cases of carnal knowledge, frequenting, and defloration in which we have some knowledge about the woman's marital status (assuming that servants and women living in the home of an apparently unrelated person are not married). Twenty-four of those were widows. Of the seventeen cases of "carnal knowledge after promises," which we know to have been initiated by a suit of one of the parties, four were brought by widows. Because there is a much larger group of women for whom we have no marital status information, the data are not sufficient to tell us whether widows were more content to remain unmarried than never-married women, or to tell us how much of a role economic need played, but the numbers do tell us that some widows sought remarriage.

Some people may not have solemnized their marriage to avoid paying the priest for the benediction, although this may not have been a wise financial decision, given the fines that they risked. What there is little evidence for in

Paris, or elsewhere in northern France, is that partners formed clandestine marriages deliberately to present their parents with a fait accompli.[91] People who were independent of their families entered into such marriages, but it does not seem that they usually did so to avoid their parents' scrutiny.

Independent Children and Parental Involvement

The cases of servants like Tassine la Martine or Denise Esperlant were at one end of a spectrum of familial involvement in their children's marital choices, or at least recorded familial involvement. The level of parental involvement is highly relevant to our understanding of what kind of unions people chose. We assume that the more the family was involved, the less sexual freedom their children had and the less likely individuals were to enter into informal unions; this would be particularly true of young women, whose families wished them to be respectable. Jeanne la Rongour and Robert le Bys were somewhere in the middle of the spectrum, since he was living in his father's house, although she was living on her own. She claimed that he had given her a job making caps, and came to her chamber and knew her carnally two or three days in a row. Then they promised each other marriage and drank together in the name of matrimony. He continued to spend the night with her nearly every night, "treating her like his wife," and they exchanged rods (another common sign of marriage).[92] He also took her, she said, as though she were his wife to Ste.-Geneviève de Nanterre, where his sister lived, and slept with her in his sister's house. He admitted that he had had carnal knowledge of her and had taken her to his sister's, but claimed that he had slept with her as a whore (*meretrix*) in the front chamber, which was a public place, and denied that he had given her anything at the time they were sleeping together. She was fined for the clandestine marriage that she claimed, but he was fined only for concubinage with her.[93] She lost the civil case that she had brought, and they were not ordered to solemnize, but she was still fined for what she had admitted. In this case, unlike some of those discussed above, the couple agreed as to the occasions on which they had had sexual intercourse, but differed on whether he had treated her as a wife. Again, either claim was plausible. No testimony was recorded but only her allegations and his response, so it is hard to know for sure, but no members of her family were said to have been involved. The question that is raised in the case is whether his family recognized the union as a marriage, but her family does not seem to have been a part of the process.

The existence of cases without the involvement of the woman's parents does not mean that this involvement was not the frequent expectation. Colette, daughter of Jean Gerouse, brought a civil claim against Nicolas Michelet for marital promises; the promoter also associated himself with her in a criminal action. Nicolas confessed carnal knowledge of Colette but said that he did not promise her anything because her father refused to give her a dowry. He offered to marry her for twenty francs. The court ordered them to solemnize the marriage immediately.[94] The official apparently believed that Nicolas had made a conditional promise, the condition disappearing after sexual intercourse. Colette did not invent her claim; although Nicolas denied the promises, he admitted that dowry negotiations were going on. The case reflected the way that parents' wishes could interact with those of their children and the way that the parties' choices were made. The case of Bertrand Paillard and Jeanne Dauffremont may go further to reflect parent-initiated and not just parent-approved marriage. Bertrand had known Jeanne since childhood and knew her parents. He said that they had spoken of marriage and of her father giving them some goods in marriage, but that the father had not done so; however, after both sets of parents had discussed the possibility, the couple kissed and clasped hands and drank together in the name of matrimony. Bertrand denied carnal knowledge of Jeanne, however, although they were alone together on several occasions, including in the stables. They ended up both being fined for clandestine marriage, although the record does not say that they were ordered to solemnize.[95]

It is difficult to know how common any of these patterns were and how many women acted independently of their families. (Men's families are mentioned less frequently, and it is even more difficult to determine; this discussion will focus on women because received scholarly opinion holds that it was especially women whose families made the arrangements for them.) The average age at which women either were married or claimed to have been deflowered seems to have been in the late teens or early twenties, but there are too few data points to say for sure.[96]

Table 2 includes all cases in which depositions provided information about the domestic situation of women who entered into contested marriages or nonmarital unions. Most of these were defloration, breach of promise, or paternity cases. For the male partners, I have given their occupation if the text gave it, and noted if they were said to live with their employer. I have omitted cases for which we have no information on the woman other than her name.

Table 2
Employment and Domicile Status of Sex Partners

Woman's Name	Source (all AN, Z/1o)	Age	Woman's Employment/Domicile	Partner's Status
Jeanne Houssaye	18/42v	20	Lives with her master/mistress	General merchant (*omnia mercatoria*); lives in another's house
Jeanne la Rousselle	18/43r	20	Recently arrived from Normandy	
Jeanne la Sagiette	18/194v	18	Lives in house of aristocrat	
Marianne Patin	18/199v	17	Orphan, stepmother placed her as servant	Tenterer (*tensor pannorum*)
Matheline la Petite	18/213v	25	He claims that she was a public woman	Merchant, married 13–14 years
Tassine la Martine	18/237v	22	Lives with her master/mistress	Servant of the king
Colette Poitevine	19/42r	16–17	Servant, lives with master/mistress	Works for his father as fruit seller
Pacquette Hennelle	19/72r	20–21	Lives with her father	Merchant
Jeanne la Souflette	19/76r	22	Lives with her father	Lives with his mother and stepfather
Pierrette Fanoise	19/113v	19	Lives with her stepfather	Merchant
Jeanne Garnier	18/7v		Lives with a guardian	Cart driver
Pierrette la Ceque	18/25r		Servant	Her guardian, a chaplain
Marguerite le Boucher	18/39v		Servant (her father appears for her)	Her master
Jeanne Rebourse	18/40v		Lives in house of a laborer	Her master
Jeanne Fordyr	18/45r		Servant	Her master
[unnamed]	18/53v		Servant	Parishioner of her master
Pierrette Alispere	18/55v		Father dead, brother pays her fine	
Arnolette Cortenue	18/144v		Servant, lives with a perfumer	Barber, lives in same house
Alison Fautinet	18/152v		Father named	Laborer, married, her relative
Jeanne de Noes	18/185v		Father named; living with a scribe	Illuminator, living in same house
Pierrette Moisie	18/213v		In home of nonrelative; gives birth there	Lives in same house
Marguerite la Meresse	19/7r		In home of nonrelative	Lives in same house
Jeanne de Servain	19/7t		Servant of lord; father appears for her	Manual worker (*manoperarius*)
Agnes Poivret	19/7t		Wool worker, biretta maker; father named	Biretta maker
Daughter of Denis Hudes	19/40v		Her own name not given	Cart driver, her relative
Denise Esperlant	19/6ov		In household of receiver of Paris; father named	In household of receiver of Paris, cart driver
Jeanne Maire	19/95v		Servant, lives with employer (a saddler)	Servant of same employer
Guillone Gavin	19/99v		Servant, lives with master	Son of previous master

Woman's Name	Source (all AN, Z/1o)	Age	Woman's Employment/Domicile	Partner's Status
Katherina	19*143r		Servant	Her master
Jeanne Martine	19*170r		Servant	Her master
Jeanne de la Roche	19*205v		Servant	Her master (married man, laborer)
Marguerite Danniet	19*202v		In home of nonrelative	In same house
Marguerite la Massonne	19*252v		In home of nonrelative	Son of woman she is living with
Colette Josart	19*274r		Lives with her father	Married man, cleric
Marguerite Manguet	19*275r		In home of nonrelative	Brother of man she is living with
Marianne daughter of Jean Housel	2C/37r		Lives with her father	Married man
Jeanne la Couronne	2C/101r		Lives with her master	Priest
Jeanne Fourmere	21*147r		Servant, father appears for her	Her master, cloth merchant, husband of her godmother
Jacqueline Laupes	21*341r		In home of nonrelative	Living in same house
Marianne la Lavandiere	18*8v		Widow	Living in same house
Denise Le Grand	18*15v		Widow; servant	Priest
Marianne	18*32r		In home of a woman she is caring for during and after childbirth	Husband of the woman she is caring for
Jeanne la Valce	18*87r		In home of nonrelative	Fisherman, servant of house she is living in
Gilette la Brebie	18*120v		Seamstress, in home of nonrelative	Man living in same house
Jeanne Tumel	18*125r		Servant; lives with master; father named	Son of her master's neighbors
Denise la Doynelle	18*164r		Servant; widow	Laborer, in house of same master
Marguerite la Mastiere	18*170v		Her own home, in village	
Marianne de Rombute	19*44r		In home of nonrelative	Living in same house
[unnamed]	2C/11r		Lives with her parents	Fiancé she knew from childhood
Colette	2C/42v		Servant	Her master
Marianne Tanelle	2C/52r		In home of nonrelative	Son of man she is staying with
Agathe de Vonges	2C/66r		In home of nonrelative; her stepmother testifies	Blacksmith
Jeanne Danneau	2V*29v		Living with her parents	Priest
Jeanne la Rongour	2V*35v		Weaver, living on her own	Master cap maker
[unnamed]	2V*157r		Servant of a draper	Priest
Jeanne Petite	2V*310r		Servant of a widow	
Colette Grouse	2V*349r		Father involved in dowry negotiations	
Alison Bouchere	2V*380v		Parents involved in her marriage	Cart driver for same household

Not counting widows, the list includes thirty-four women living independently of their natal families, either as servants or in some other capacity in someone's home, or on their own.[97] A variety of words for servant—*ancilla, famula, servitrix*—appeared, as well as more specific occupational terms, but sometimes the register said only that the woman was living in that house and did not mention her work. Some of these may have been servants, some may have been lodgers, and some may have been poor relations.[98] When the householders were called *magister/magistra*, I have assumed that the woman was a servant. Besides the thirty-four instances in which no family members were mentioned, an additional eight women were not living with their families, although relatives (father, stepmother, brother) were mentioned in the case or the woman was listed as "daughter of" her father. In contrast with these forty-two women who were not living with their parents, six were stated to be living with them, and in five cases, a parent was named but place of residence was not mentioned.

We cannot say that all the women who did not live with their parents were making independent decisions about their sexual liaisons and marriages. Some of the women in service obviously kept in close contact with their families, since their parents or brothers appeared or paid their fines, and some whose families went unmentioned may have kept in touch as well. Jeanne Maire is a good example of a servant not living with her parents but still closely involved with them. She claimed she was deflowered by Tassino Jovelle, a fellow servant, after promises of marriage. Tassino agreed that he had indeed promised her marriage, but only on condition that she governed herself well, and that she had violated that condition by having sex with their master, Geoffroi Geroult. Tassino's testimony was unclear as to whether intercourse with Geoffroi intervened between the promises and the intercourse with Tassino; if it did, it would have violated the condition he placed on the promise, but if it came later, the condition would have been null and the promise binding. The court fined Tassino for the defloration; the result of the breach of promise case does not survive. Relevant for our purposes is that Jeanne explained that her parents had settled with Tassino for three ecus of gold for the defloration, and she would be satisfied on that count when they were paid. (The court ordered him to pay her, in addition to another ecu of gold as his fine.)[99] Thus, although she was in service and living apart from her family, her parents were clearly involved with her life decisions.

The women about whom we have details are not, of course, representative of the female population of Paris as a whole. Women serving in someone else's household had more opportunity to become sexually involved with a man—whether or not under color of a matrimonial promise—than women living with their parents. The women in cases where detailed information survived may not be typical of all the cases in the criminal registers. Table 3 gives what information there is about the residence status of the 572 women named (some as defendants, some as named partners of male defendants) in the 609 cases of carnal knowledge (with or without promises), "frequenting," or defloration.[100]

In more than half the cases (those where no name, only a name, or a name and residence were given), there is no way of determining whether the woman was living in her parents' household, in that of someone else, or on her own. We know from the cases with surviving testimony that not every woman identified by her father's name was living in the latter's household; but even if they all were, and leaving out widows, married women, and nuns, we would have fifty-six women who could be identified as living with their families, and sixty-three who could be identified as living elsewhere. The significance of these numbers is undercut by the large number for which there is no evidence and on which we can only speculate. It may be that most of these lived with their fathers, and this was not thought worth mentioning. Nevertheless, it is clear that it was far from universal for women to live under direct parental control until marriage. Those who lived away from their parents' control were freer to make sexual choices. Of

Table 3
Residence/Personal Status of Women in Cases of Carnal Knowledge, Frequenting, and Defloration

Labeled as servants	
Accused with employer	27
Accused with fellow servant	5
Accused with someone else	5
Not labeled as servants	
Married	34
Widowed	24
Living with parent(s)	6
Religious	1
Living in someone else's house	
Accused with householder	11
Accused with other household member	5
Accused with someone else	10
Residence but not householder's name given	127
Woman identified by father's name	50
Woman identified by name only	267

course, the same could be true of men, but that is often the case even in societies in which parents exercise relatively strict control over their daughters.

A few couples who made choices of partner on their own were not entirely independent but rather went behind their parents' backs. There are several cases of people marrying in the exempt jurisdiction of St.-Germain-en-Laye (which did not require banns and which was illegal but not invalid) "out of fear of their parents."[101] Such marriages, which were clandestine because of the lack of banns and publicity in the appropriate parish, were common despite efforts to combat them by punishing clergy who participated in them.[102] But some couples preferred to enter into their unions even more secretly. Catherine, the daughter of Guillaume Larchier, despite being identified as her father's daughter, clearly was not entirely under his control. She paid a fine for exchanging marital promises with Jean Gueneau even though she had previously exchanged them with Guillaume Joliveau, "saying that she did not dare to tell her father," presumably about the previous promises.[103] Lack of parental consent put some people in the gray area of what may or may not have been marriage—for example, André Vyart and Pierrette Pauli, who were fined for not solemnizing their marriage because his parents did not approve.[104]

A number of scholars have argued that lower levels of parental involvement and more independence of the marriage partners, especially women, were associated with a later age at marriage and found particularly in England.[105] This has been recently questioned by scholars like Dana Wessell Lightfoot, who finds women in fifteenth-century Valencia entering domestic service, saving for their own dowries and making their own spousal choices.[106] Even the data from the Florentine *catasto* of 1427, which is most often cited for an early age at marriage in the Mediterranean region, show that the age was a bit older for women in lower social groups.[107] It is at least possible that the very young age at marriage for girls attributed to dowry inflation in late medieval Italian towns is the exception, and women making independent marital choices were to be found throughout Europe in the later Middle Ages.

Living Together

Many cases discussed in the previous sections involve couples in which at least one partner claimed, whether at the outset of the relationship or after the fact, to be married, but many couples lived in long-term unions and never made marital claims at all. We know about them because they were fined, whether for clandestine marriage or other sexual offenses. The court records in the carnal knowledge, maintaining, and frequenting cases provide a good deal less information than those in which one party alleged marriage or defloration, but still tell us something about how and why some people entered these unions. The first step is to identify instances in which people were actually living together. In cases where the man was accused of keeping a concubine, or the woman of being kept as a concubine, it is fairly clear. The cases in which the man was said to maintain the woman, or the woman to be kept or maintained, are a good deal more difficult.[108] Men were accused of maintaining or keeping (*manutenire* or *tenire*) their partners over periods of time from several months to many years. The couple were sometimes said to live in different places, as with Jean de Grusi living in Rue St.-Paul, who maintained a certain Marianne living in Rue Jean Beausier, although that does not mean that financial support was not involved.[109] *Intertenire* was sometimes used instead of *manutenire*, and sometimes simple *tenire* seems to have meant something other than financial maintenance, with the couple said to "keep each other" or the woman to "keep herself with" the man.[110] Occasionally, a man was said to maintain the woman "as a wife."[111]

Maintaining sometimes did mean living together. Master Jean Masnier was accused of maintaining a certain (unnamed) woman for six years or longer; according to the promoter, she had a child by him two years earlier and was now pregnant again. Jean defended himself by saying that he was seventy years old and had a hernia, presumably implying that he could not have fathered the child; then he confessed that the woman did live with him and they occasionally had sexual intercourse, although he said that he doubted he was the father of her children.[112] The initial denial could have been an outright lie on his part, or she could have been a housekeeper living with him whom he did not think of as a domestic partner, whether or not they had sex. In the case of Jacques du Tiers and Jeanne du Bois, what was at issue was whether a couple living under the same roof were sexual and domestic partners. Asked whether he "maintained and maintains" Jeanne, Jacques denied it and said that he "wished she would go to all the devils." Asked "what is the name of the woman who keeps [*tenet*] herself with you," he replied "Jeanne du Bois, but that she did not keep herself with him but he lodged with her for money for the last three years." He said that her "chamber" (*camera*) was rented from Nicolas Fromagier and that he paid the landlord four francs for it. Asked why he paid the landlord since the landlord didn't rent anything to him, he replied that both of them paid the landlord.[113] Here, it seems, "maintaining" the woman meant paying her rent, which he denied doing. Jean le Bourguignon was accused of carnal knowledge of his servant Colette and admitted that for three years, he had "maintained her as his wife." This probably meant that they lived together, although when asked if they always slept (*cubere*) together, he said, "sometimes yes, sometimes no." He was also accused of keeping a brothel "since he keeps four or five women of ill fame, in French *paillardes*."[114] Presumably, this was the same house in which she was living with him.

Not all people who were charged with "maintaining" had set up their own households; some were in domestic service and lived together within the household of an employer. For example, André Halle confessed having maintained a certain Jeanne for four months in the home of his master, Jacques Norquet.[115] They lived under the same roof for ten to twelve months, so the shorter period when he admitted that he maintained her may have been the period when they were sexually active together. He denied being the father of her child, although he admitted that he had thought at first that he was. Alison la Boulangere was interrogated in a case that clearly indicated domestic partnership, although the beginning was not recorded, so we do not know exactly what the accusation was. Asked how long she had stayed with the carter Olivier le Gras, she responded that "she kept herself with him for five or six years, and it is now six years since he maintained her or knew her carnally, and she paid amends in the court of Paris a year ago." She had no children with Olivier but was apparently living with a son of his who married her daughter by her late husband. Asked whether Olivier was staying with her, she replied no, but he stayed in one room and she in another right next to it.[116] It is not clear whether this living arrangement was any different from what it had been when he was "maintaining" her. To remain living under the same roof years after their relationship had ended, if indeed this was true, was evidence either of continuing friendly relations or severe economic need.

Aimery Girard, a vineyard worker, and Laurence (no surname given) had clearly been domestic partners, but both seem to have been determined not to marry. They were living together in Montmartre at the time of their court case. Asked how long he had maintained her, Aimery said eight years: first, for two months in the village of Champigny-sur-Marne, and then in Deuil-la-Barre. They had five children, and when they were in Deuil, he had called Laurence his wife. When the judge suggested that it would be good for Aimery to take her as his wife, however, he said that he did not want to. Under repeated questioning, Aimery still claimed not to be married. Laurence did not testify, or her testimony was not recorded, and no result survives.[117] Even though the two were in a continuing relationship and apparently single, and therefore could have married, Laurence did not seem to have claimed marital promises, nor was the union called concubinage. In this type of case, the court could have declared the parties married and ordered them to solemnize the union, but this would have been unusual when both parties denied that they had ever exchanged vows. This court did not use the procedure of abjuration *sub pena nubendi*, as practiced in some English church courts, in which the couple would be made to exchange marriage vows in the future tense, which would become binding if they ever had sexual intercourse in the future.[118] If a couple did not wish to marry, as Aimery and Laurence clearly did not, the court would not force them, although it might prohibit further relations.

Unlike Aimery and Laurence, however, some people who were accused of maintaining took steps toward marriage. Thomas du Buc and Catherine, his fiancée, paid a fine for his having maintained her for seven or eight years. The matter came to the attention of the court because they had been affianced in front of the church, for the sake of their children.[119] Under canon law, marriage legitimated previous children of the union, and this may have been their reason. Nevertheless, the betrothal brought to the court's attention that their quite durable relationship had never been formalized. Raoul Bautier paid a fine for maintaining Cardine, his maid, for two years, during which time she had his child. At the time he was fined, they had been affianced at the church door and the banns had been proclaimed. Raoul agreed to solemnize the marriage and was fined forty-three sous *favore matrimonii*—"in favor of marriage"—presumably meaning that because of the plan to marry, he was being fined less.[120] In both these instances, the parties had been together for a good while, and neither claimed that there had been a marriage. We have no way of knowing whether the neighbors believed that Thomas and Catherine, or Raoul and Cardine, were married before they took steps to formalize the union, whether they knew they were not, or whether they simply turned a blind eye for years and did not ask.

Not all cases of maintaining had a marital outcome or intention, of course. When Henriette Goyne and Pierre Gosse each paid a fine for not solemnizing their marriage, he was also fined for maintaining Jeanne de la Salle for fifteen years and having carnal knowledge of her, as well as for carnal knowledge of Henriette.[121] Far from planning to marry Jeanne, the woman with whom he had a long-term partnership, he had taken steps to enter a marriage with someone else. Similarly, the concubinage between Jeanne Quinperte and the barber Alain Henry, for which she was fined (he was fined for frequenting and carnal knowledge), apparently came to light when he affianced someone else. She came forward when the banns were proclaimed and claimed an impediment. Henry, however, was allowed to marry the other woman.[122] The existence of a previous union, if no steps had been taken to formalize it as a marriage, did not impede a later marriage.

The difference between maintaining and concubinage is hard to discern. Concubinage accounted for a total of ninety-three and maintaining accounted for one hundred of the cases.[123] The lengths of time during which people were said to have participated in the relationship fell into the same range, from a week or two to years (the longest period was thirty years for "maintaining" and fourteen for concubinage).[124] With both offenses, sometimes it was specified that they lived in the same house and sometimes different residences were specified; in most cases, however, the woman's residence was not given. A few cases equated the two offenses. Marianne daughter of Jean le Page was accused of allowing herself to be deflowered by Jean de la Croix and afterward remaining in concubinage with him. She denied that he had deflowered her and refused to say who did: "adding that she was not required to say who deflowered her, upon which the official asked the opinion of the canon lawyer Robert La Longue whether he should compel her to declare or name the one who deflowered her, which opinion said no." She admitted, however, that Jean de la Croix had maintained her for a month, and she paid a fine for concubinage with him for a month, the terms here appearing interchangeable.[125] Maintaining and concubinage were also equated in the case of Jeanne Bourdeselle and her employer Jacques Feron; she lived with him for a period of four years and had two children. She was fined for concubinage and he for maintaining her.[126] Another couple who were living together (at least, their residences were given as the same) both paid fines, he for maintaining her and for carnal knowledge, and she for concubinage.[127] Raoul le Merchaunt was accused of concubinage with a woman named Charlotte, who bore his child; according to the promoter, he had previously been cited on a charge of maintaining her, which he denied, but continued to maintain her.[128]

Sometimes the court observed a distinction between concubinage and maintaining. When Jean Garnet was fined for maintaining a woman named Barbara "as though she were his spouse" and spending the night with her regularly (although their residences were different), the scribe carefully interlineated the words "in concubinage" after "maintained." She was also fined for concubinage. The fact that the term had to be added here and in two other cases suggests that "maintained in concubinage" meant something more than "maintained" alone, but that there was some overlap between the two.[129] In the archdeaconry of Brie, Guillaume Noerte paid a fine for maintaining Jeanne Delahaye for four years and having a child with her before their betrothal. At the time in December 1500 when the case was recorded, they had been betrothed for six weeks. There was no indication that the archdeacon's official had anything do with prodding them to marry, although he may have done. The scribe, after entering the case, went back and added "in concubinage" after "maintaining."[130] It is not clear whether this was originally part of the fined offense and he just forgot to write it, or whether it was information added later; in either circumstance, this was one of the few cases in which a couple married (or at least planned to marry) after their living arrangements were called concubinage, as well as one of the ones that indicate a distinction between concubinage and maintaining. For the most part, concubinage seems to have been an alternative to marriage rather than a prelude to it.

One of the most common situations of unmarried couples living together, whether called maintaining or concubinage, was between master and servant. Relatively few of these partnerships involved allegations of matrimonial promises, possibly because these allegations would be less credible coming from a woman of lower social standing. Jeanne Martine, however, claimed that her employer, the widowed Miletus Jovan, had deflowered her and promised to marry her. He denied the promises but confessed that while she was in childbed, he had notaries from the Châtelet come to the house and promised in front of them to give her ten francs if she accepted it as settlement. It is not clear whether this money was for child support or expenses of childbirth, or whether it was so that she would not bring a claim of marriage; it may have been ambiguous at the time.[131] Because of the defloration charge, we have more detail on this than on many other cases, but it is probably not atypical of what occurred between single male householders and their servants. There are no cases in which a master and servant were adjudged to be married.

The fact that the Paris records used the terms "concubine" and "concubinage" when those from England, for example, rarely did so, indicates a level of recognition for this type of union, even though it was a negative recognition, recognized in order to be punished. Concubinage was not respectable, but it was not the same thing as simple fornication or carnal knowledge. The use of the term may be an indication of the influence of Roman law categories in France, not on the level of jurists and commentators, but on the level of public recognition—a diffuse and general influence, perhaps a linguistic remnant, not the invocation of a specific provision. Its use did not likely derive from inheritance law: customary law in the Paris region prevented all bastards from inheriting, although a natural child could be legitimated by the parents' later marriage or left a substantial legacy.[132] Fewer than a quarter of concubinage cases mentioned pregnancy or children (though offspring, when they existed, were commonly mentioned in all varieties of cases), and some involved priests or married people, so the parents were not, in any case, capable of marrying.[133] But we may still wonder whether the use of the term was more than just linguistic habit, especially since there were plenty of clandestine marriage cases in the book of sentences of the officiality of Brussels, another jurisdiction that followed what Donahue calls the "Franco-Belgian" marriage pattern; yet the word "concubine" only appeared once, in a case involving a priest who had several of them.[134]

Although the use of "concubinage" may not have been intended to confer legal rights, it did denote an ongoing and serious relationship. When Jean de Bussonoye was accused of frequenting a woman named Madeleine in concubinage five or six years earlier, his defense was that she was "public," that is, a whore.[135] He clearly expected the penalty to be lighter if the relationship had been fleeting rather than ongoing. The use of the term "concubinage" may have been an attempt to distinguish between situations that were temporary, albeit long-term—"maintaining" or repeated carnal knowledge—and those that were quasi-permanent. Yet the "concubine" of canon law as applied in the Paris archdeacon's court was not simply a wife whose marriage had not been finalized.[136] Concubinage was largely an offense of the unmarried, as indicated by an entry in which the term "concubinage" was crossed out and replaced by "adultery," but there were also cases of married people confessing to concubinage.[137] Pierre Hedin and Annette, his wife (as she is called in the register), were accused of concubinage, and the clear implication was that the promoter thought that Pierre had kept Annette as a concubine during her first husband's lifetime. They claimed that they were married, not living in concubinage, and that the child she had was fathered by her late husband—in other words, not evidence of a union during the latter's lifetime.[138] Jacques Petit and Jeanne Aumer were fined for concubinage, and she was also fined for previous concubinage with Martin de Faye. Jeanne confessed that Martin had said that if she governed herself well, he would marry her; since sexual intercourse followed, the court deemed the condition on the promise to be invalidated and the union a marriage.[139] Of course, such previous marriages were sometimes invented to avoid a current marriage.[140] Jeanne, however, was not fined for living apart from her legal husband, Martin, nor for adultery, but for concubinage, indicating that even a married woman could be a concubine and that the court did not consider her concubinage with Jacques a prelude to marriage, since she was still legally married to Martin.

The fine line between concubinage and clandestine marriage is indicated by the case of Gérard Garnier and Jeanne Bretier.[141] In May 1500, after Jeanne claimed carnal knowledge after promises, they were ordered to solemnize their marriage. That register entry noted that they had been fined for concubinage six months previously. However, the register entry from December 1499 shows that he was actually fined for carnal knowledge of her and she was fined for carnal knowledge after marital promises, with no mention of concubinage, and they were also declared not to be married and given license to marry elsewhere.[142] The court seems to have inadvertently slipped from carnal knowledge after promises to concubinage. The fact that someone's memory failed in this particular way indicates that couples' living together, with marital promises alleged by one of them but not upheld, was not all that different from concubinage. Eloi Martin and Robine, who "lived together and often spent the night" (an indication that "spending the night" was a euphemism for sexual intercourse, not just staying over), were fined for concubinage, but both insisted that no marital promises had been made. They clearly did not want to be bound to each other, but the fact that this insistence was necessary indicates that the line between types of union could be hard to find.[143]

The gray area caused by the frequency of clandestine marriage in the form of *matrimonium presumptum*—promises followed by intercourse—made room for concubinage as a category. Although many accusations of clandestine marriage arose when one party brought a civil claim, the majority of clandestine marriage entries in the criminal register have no corresponding entries in the civil register because neither party brought a case of breach of promise and they were content simply to go along as they were. Couples who proceeded to consummation after promises, whether made at the church door or more privately, may have understood themselves as being less than completely married, or at least have understood the relationship as containing some ambiguity, and have preferred to continue in an unsolemnized union.

Failed Marriages

As the examples of married people living in concubinage with others show, for many long-term couples, marriage was not a possibility because one of them was already married to someone else. In an era without divorce as we know it, a failed marriage left people with a number of far-from-ideal alternatives.[144] They could bring a suit for separation. In Paris, the court not infrequently granted couples a separation of goods and permission to live apart, but they might still retain the right to sexual intercourse with each other—the payment of the "marriage debt" that either partner could demand—sometimes even if the ground for the separation was cruelty or leprosy.[145] They could separate by mutual agreement without the sanction of the court; this would potentially subject both of them to a fine, as happened in eight cases in the criminal registers. If there was no mutual agreement, one party might simply leave the other and take another partner. In none of these cases, however, was remarriage permitted.

The size of Paris made it a good place for dissatisfied spouses, whether local or from the provinces, to make a new life. In several cases, an accused bigamist was alleged to have been married elsewhere before coming to Paris. Sara McDougall, in her work on bigamy in fifteenth-century Troyes, suggests that the number of cases of remarriage that turn up in the court indicates that people took formal Christian marriage quite seriously indeed.[146] Elsewhere—for example, in Regensburg, as Christina Deutsch has found—the bishop's court was willing to recognize the marriages of couples who were living together even though one of them had been previously married and the spouse was not known to be dead.[147] In France, though, this was not the custom; in Paris, many people left failed marriages but remained in less formal unions.[148]

An example of a couple who lived as married but knew that they could not have their union legally recognized, Marguerite Toussains and Charles du Molly, were accused of clandestine marriage. According to the accusation, the court had previously judged her to be the wife of a certain Jacques, a barber; but afterward, Marguerite and Charles had promised marriage "and afterward contracted clandestine marriage de facto and lived together for a long while in the same house and joined together carnally." The promoter asked that they be fined and ordered not to have contact (*ne in simul conversarent*) any more. Under oath, they admitted "frequenting" in the same house but claimed that they had separate rooms and denied both the sexual intercourse and the promises, "except that the said Marguerite admitted having said to Charles that she would be glad to have him as her husband if she could." They both paid a fine for the scandal occasioned by the frequenting and were ordered "not to have further conversation except honestly."[149] It seems unlikely that if they lived in the same house and admitted wishing that they could marry, they were not actually sexually involved; but they knew that they could not get away with claiming to be married. Similar cases could be brought at the instigation of the woman's legal husband. A man whose name was left blank in the record complained to the official that Michel Guilbert had maintained the former's wife for two years, frequenting her in his (Guilbert's) house and eating and drinking together, creating a very great scandal. Yves Goujan complained that Master Pierre Poully had "suborned and lured away" his wife, Michelle, taking her in and maintaining her.[150]

Marguerite and Charles got away with a lesser offense, but when people formally contracted two marriages, they had committed a serious crime that often required disentangling which of the marriages, if any, was valid.[151] I use the term "bigamy" somewhat loosely here because the sources did not always use it when it was a matter of two exchanges of promises rather than two formal marriages.[152] Sometimes the bigamy took the form of a first marriage and a second marital promise, not actually living in domestic partnership with the new partner, as with Roland Geoffroy, who was accused of exchanging promises with Marianne la Vallette even though he was previously married in Brittany and had several children with his wife there.[153] Similarly, Jean Basset confessed only to promises with his second fiancée. He was married to a certain Jeanne and then affianced another (also named Jeanne), knowing that his wife was alive. He confessed doing so "in foolishness" and because he was upset with his wife's leaving him for a priest. He acknowledged that his second union was invalid: asked what the name of his first wife was, he answered that he had only one wife and that he had only betrothed (*affidavit*) the second Jeanne at the church, not married her, a year after his wife had left him. When the second Jeanne found out that he was married and his wife was alive, she left him, too; he claimed that he had never known her carnally, although if she had not left him, he would have completed the marriage. Asked whether he had previously confessed in the "Court of Paris" (presumably the bishop's court) to having two wives, he said that he had, because he felt harassed and had said in anger, "Yes, by the devil, I have two or three," but in fact he had not married any but the first. However, two weeks after his first questioning, he also confessed that he had betrothed another woman (yet another Jeanne) at St.-Germain-en-Laye. He confessed having carnal knowledge of the third Jeanne, but she was previously married. This is one of the few cases for which the register recorded an actual sentence: Jean Basset was condemned to stand with a placard on the scaffold at the parvis of Notre Dame during mass, and then to two years' imprisonment on bread and water.[154] Until the third union came to light, Basset had insisted that he did not actually marry the second

woman, only promised to do so, without the promise being followed by intercourse. The court, in the sentence, called this marriage by future words, which
it was, according to canon law, and Basset clearly knew that if not consummated, it was a lesser offense.

Cardinus Marqueau of Champs-sur-Marne in the archdeaconry of Brie
was condemned to a year in prison commuted to two ecus of gold, an unusually large amount, for betrothing or marrying (*desponsare*) two women. At
the time of his interrogation, he was about thirty years old, he said. Asked
if Simone Conveline, who lived with him, was his wife, he said that they
had never been married but that he had maintained her for seven years and
had called her his wife to preserve her honor. He admitted having previously
affianced another woman named Jacquette in the church of Presles-en-Brie
ten or twelve years previously, but claimed that the marriage had never been
completed (at least, this is what we must here conclude is meant by *desponsare*,
since it is used to mean a stage beyond the *affidationes*) and that he had never
known her carnally.[155] He persisted in the latter denial under oath. It is not
clear whether the judge simply did not believe him or whether the penalty was
for betrothing one woman and then living with another even without the first
marriage being completed or the second union claimed to be a marriage. It
seems likely that this was not a matter of Cardinus being unsure about the status of his marriage: his denials that the first union had moved beyond future
consent and that the second union had been a marriage at all indicated that
he, or someone who was advising him, knew the canon law reasonably well.

Accused bigamists commonly claimed that they heard that their first
spouse had died. Mariannette la Gelet, for example, confessed that she had
allowed herself to be known carnally by her fiancé; then, when she heard that
he had died (clearly, they were not still living together), she became affianced
to Pierre Barbier.[156] She did not say that she was previously married—only
affianced—but the court clearly recognized that promises followed by sexual
intercourse were binding, since she was prohibited from proceeding any further with Barbier. She might or might not have been telling the truth about
her knowledge of the whereabouts of her husband. Jeanne la Porteboise was
fined for becoming affianced to another man without knowing her husband
was dead, although he did die before she appeared in court.[157] Jeanne, wife
of Michel du Moustier, who was affianced to Guillaume de la Roux at the
church of St.-Gervais, claimed that she thought that her husband was dead.[158]
Olivière la Thomasse paid a large fine for marrying Jean du Pont; she claimed
that she thought Pierre Furet, whom she had married twenty-six years earlier,

had died in the five years since she had left him.[159] Nicolas Geffroy claimed that he had been married in Brittany but had not seen his wife for six years and did not know whether she was alive when he became engaged to another woman.[160] Cardina or Marianne, daughter of Ursin Pichon (she claimed to have changed her name at confirmation, although the court seems to have been dubious about the circumstances), had been married to a man named Jean for nine years (according to him) or fourteen to fifteen years (according to her). She claimed that he left her just before Lent and she waited until after Easter, then came to Paris and worked for Jean du Pont for seven years. When, she said, she did not hear from her husband, she married Yves Gigot, with whom she stayed for eight years and had two daughters. She claimed that she would never have married Yves if she had known that Jean was living. A year earlier, she had heard that he was still alive but did not see him until the previous Thursday. In an apparent attempt to invalidate the marriage to Jean, she also claimed that Jean had been contracted to someone else before they first married. She apparently lost the case, though, because she later appeared as Jean's wife, suing for child support from Yves.[161]

Maurice Chauveau, a weaver from Tours living in Paris, was a particularly brazen bigamist. He was accused of marrying first Jacqueline Tasse, thirteen years earlier, and then Marianne Valle, five years earlier. He claimed that certain of his acquaintances had told him that his first wife had died in the Maison-Dieu in Paris. When asked why he had not gone there to confirm that she had died there, he said that he did not know. Maurice then claimed that he had gone there about two years earlier and inquired about his first wife and was told that she had died the day before; he then married another wife, Gillette la Chevrette. He had children by all three women. Asked why he had married a third wife when the second was still living, he said that a priest had told him that the second marriage was null because the first wife had been living at the time (which was correct, in terms of canon law). When the archdeacon's official told him that this was ill done, he responded that he agreed and begged mercy of God. He admitted that he had returned to the first wife (probably meaning the second) after marrying the third and that he did not tell the second wife that he had married the third but she suspected. He was ordered imprisoned for four months and to pay maintenance to the second wife.

For some bigamists, there was no recorded claim that they thought that their spouse was dead. Jean Lengles left his wife because of a condition of which she later died, and was fined for keeping Jeannette du Paul in concubinage and for carnal knowledge after marital promises.[162] Jean Noirey admitted having maintained Alison Raymonde during the lifetime of her husband, Jean le Forestier, who was *impotens* (not necessarily sexually impotent; possibly disabled). He said that he had had one child by her during her husband's lifetime and one after his death. He had promised Alison marriage before and after the death of her husband and then had affianced her at St.-Sauveur after his death.[163] These may have been situations where the marriage was already moribund and a dissatisfied spouse jumped the gun on the spouse's death.[164] Aimery de Beauvais confessed that he had left his wife fourteen years earlier and had maintained Pierrette Flatret for twelve of those years, during which they had had five living children, and during which time he had promised to marry Pierrette. They had apparently not been living together for all that time because he said that "for the past year, he had stayed overnight with her nearly every night."[165] Pierrette, for her part, confessed that Aimery's deposition was the truth. Apparently, she had been using foul language to or about him, because she was asked, "Why did you speak indecently [*inhoneste*]?" Her answer is recorded in French rather than Latin, so despite being in the third person, it may be close to her actual words: "that no man would be the master of her cunt and that she would do what she wanted with it."

In many instances of failed marriage, though, bigamy was not an issue, and the register reveals no claim of a second marriage; the abandoned or abandoning spouse was involved in a union of some other sort. Robin le Vasseur tried to make the case that because his marriage to Guillemine was clandestine, without banns and without solemnization, he should not have to live with her even though the ecclesiastical court in Rouen had previously determined that the two were married. After leaving the woman adjudged to be his wife, he had "maintained" another woman also named Guillemine, for six or seven years.[166] Fines for concubinage and clandestine marriage as well as for maintaining sometimes reflected failed marriages. Couples seem to have intended a permanent domestic partnership but could not risk having the banns called because there was an impediment to the marriage.[167] Jean Mannillain paid a fine for keeping Blanche la Cossine in concubinage for fourteen years. Part of his interrogation appeared in the register—unusual for a case in which amends were made.[168] He admitted that he had been cited in "the court of Paris" (probably the bishop's court) five years earlier about the matter, and his wife had withdrawn to St.-Gervais (he lived in St.-Paul, about half a kilometer farther east). He was also asked under oath whether he had thought his wife was dead, and responded that two witnesses had told him that she was very

ill and was more likely to die than to live. At this point, he had obtained a
dispensation from the archdeacon to marry Blanche, since he was from a different diocese. He and Blanche had a child, after which he left her and went
back to his wife. No one in this case was upholding the legality of the union
with Blanche (the civil register from this time does not survive, so we cannot
be sure that there was no civil case, but nothing in the criminal entry indicates
that there was). There is no claim that he actually attempted to marry Blanche
after receiving the dispensation. It is not clear why this case gives so much detail about the circumstances of the concubinage. The amount of the fine is not
given, so we do not know whether this was considered a particularly egregious
case. But this fact pattern could explain a number of cases of concubinage in
which the couple had been treating each other as permanent partners but had
not attempted to formalize the union. Gilette, wife of Jean Daussey, was fined
for carnal knowledge with Philippe Chassin: the scribe first wrote "clandestine
marriage" and then, presumably realizing that she was already married, wrote
"affiancing Philippe Chassin in front of the church and allowing herself to be
carnally known by him, even though she was already married."[169] These elements would have added up to a valid marriage if she were single. Again, the
amount of the fine is not given, so we cannot see how seriously this behavior
was taken. It is clear, though, that a failed first marriage ranked high among
the reasons for forming nonmarital unions.

These cases in which the partners in failed marriages tried again with
someone else—either in a second (invalid) marriage or a less formal union—
were undoubtedly the tip of the iceberg. Many other cases of clandestine marriage, maintaining, and concubinage in the registers may also (unknown to
the court) have been people who did not want to marry publicly because one
of them was already married. Divorce in the modern sense, allowing remarriage, was not a possibility for these people, but this did not stop them from
forming new lives. Both men and women sought out new opportunities in
this way, and the gray areas of marriage practice in late medieval Paris made it
possible for them to do so.

By the late fifteenth century, marriage was clearly the expectation of the
church courts. These courts were hardly divorced from the community: people from a wide range of social status brought cases to them, reported to them
on their neighbors, or testified. The centrality of marriage as a model for the
courts reflects its centrality in the society, and even people who did not enter
it or chose not to sometimes pretended to be married for the sake of appearances, or used "like marriage" as a way to describe the way they lived together

or treated each other. Yet although the court records give us only a small subset of all couples, they show us that far from everyone who could have married did, or even attempted to, and that marriage was not the only way of living in a long-term relationship. The records of hostile authorities attempting to punish people cannot tell us what we would like to know about those people's intimate lives, and the need to categorize each union within a system of punishable offenses may distort the way people actually behaved or felt. But it can certainly tell us that late medieval society as a whole did not subscribe wholesale to the church's ideal of what a union should be. There is little evidence that this was a matter of outright rejection of the sacrament of marriage on theological grounds; more likely, it was a question of not taking the sacrament of marriage as seriously as the church would have liked, particularly since this sacrament did not require the participation of a priest.[170]

For many of the couples who appeared in the Paris registers, we do not have enough information to determine the disparities in social status between the parties. The cases of women servants' sexual involvement with their masters, however, indicates that even here, where slavery was unknown and servants were often not deracinated, a power differential continued to operate; in these situations of masters and servants, the women rarely claimed expectations of marriage. In unions between two people of roughly the same social level, it was usually the woman who sought to make the union a marriage, but many women living in such unions never brought legal action to change the situation, and many couples likely preferred it to marriage or at least were content with it.

Conclusion

This work has looked at the range and variety of pair bonds in which people engaged across the space of western Europe over a thousand-year period. It has attempted to bring to the fore alternatives to what medieval people considered marriage, or what we now consider marriage. Yet all these varieties of unions existed within a world in which marriage was considered the standard pattern of pair bond. The centrality of marriage can be seen in the fact that people who rejected sexual activity for religious reasons, or who wrote about people who rejected it, described this choice in terms of the rejection of marriage. That is, most late antique and medieval discussions of the advantages and disadvantages of marriage implied that the point of comparison was chastity, whether performed through the rejection of pair bonds or by keeping those bonds sexless. It is important to keep in mind, however, that this vision of chastity as the only valid alternative to marriage was pushed by a particular group of literate elite and did not necessarily reflect the views of all medieval people. The example of Heloise, who explicitly argued in favor of sexual unions other than marriage, shows what we might find if we had access to a wider range of voices.

A variety of unions other than marriage existed at various points in the Middle Ages because they were of some benefit to one or both parties. Though marriage was taught universally by the church, and it provided a set of enduring metaphors for various other social and cultural institutions,[1] an institution can be culturally dominant and still not be universally accepted or practiced. We cannot assume that people who formed informal unions therefore did not have respect for Christ's union with the church, nor can we assume that they, like Heloise, were deliberately critiquing or rejecting marriage. People entered into other relationships not just as an alternative to formal, sacramental marriage, but also with no thought to marriage as a model or a possibility. Even without discussing abandonment, bigamy, and abuse, it is hard to look at the medieval period as a golden age for marriage or a tradition that we should try to recover. The church did come to privilege it but not for reasons that necessarily made sense to or benefited the entire population.

The portraits of individual women presented in this book have allowed us to see how the various systems of pair bonding might have affected individual lives, but also show us how little we know. Heloise, Ingeborg of Denmark, and Katharina Zell left us some indication of how they felt about the unions in which they were involved. Heloise's suggestion that some other form of union would be preferable to marriage was meant to emphasize the unique nature of her and Abelard's love, and their intellectual life, which was not to be bound by traditional family structures. Ingeborg preferred her union to be classified as a marriage not because of love for her partner but because of her pride in her status and perhaps a sincere belief in the binding nature of vows. Katharina was very concerned that her partnership with Matthias Zell receive the label of marriage not only for social reasons—so that she would not be considered a "whore"—but also in order to make a theological statement about the nature of the priesthood.

Other women left few clues as to how they felt about their participation in long-term unions with the fathers of their children. Did the mother of Adeodatus attempt to get Augustine to say no to the marriage proposed by Monnica, or did she take for granted that their relationship had a natural end point? Did Waldrada want to help out her family by playing the role of queen to Lothar, or would she have been just as happy living on the lands he gave her and raising her children? Did Katharine Swynford feel that she would be socially or emotionally vindicated by formal marriage to John of Gaunt after many years of partnership, or was it a largely pragmatic move intended to secure rights for their children? Did Melkorka continue for the rest of her life to resent Hoskuld, whose sexual coercion she responded to with years of silence, or did their shared bed and parenting lead to an accommodation? We can tell a variety of stories about each of these women: although there are some attitudes that it is hard to imagine a woman in their position having taken, there are a variety of plausible possibilities.

When we know about the woman's situation mainly from legal documents, it has often been adjusted, not to say twisted, to meet the legal requirements. We may think that we can read behind the sources to find out what was really going on. Antonia ended up getting what she presumably wanted—a legacy and support for her son—but her relationship with John Comberius had to be redefined by a clever lawyer in order to achieve it. Beneventa may have taken matters into her own hands to acquire the dowry promised her by her partner, but for all we know, she was a thief seeking an excuse. Marianne la Pieresse may have wanted to convert her years-long union into a marriage, but she may also have wanted to get back at her partner. We can say that the unions described in legal sources represent the tip of the iceberg, in terms of the cases that did not appear in court and in terms of the unknown details of the cases that did appear.

Within the great variation by region and period we have seen, a few generalizations can be made, or at least general questions raised. Where one party in a union was of higher status than the other, it was more often the man. It is possible that there were asymmetric unions in which the woman was of higher status that did not make their way into the record because such women would have less property to pass to their offspring or because they took measures not to conceive. Such a woman might not want to marry because it would give her husband control over her property (a greater or lesser degree of control depending on where she lived). She would have had to deal with the social opprobrium that a fornicating woman incurred, always more serious than that of a man in a similar position. It is not likely that a large number of these unions slipped in under the radar. Women with access to wealth, at least until they were widowed, were more likely to be monitored by family members than were poorer women, and "resource polyandry" is not a common phenomenon across societies.

If a union was recognized as marriage, or if one party tried to make it so, it had a place within the legal system; otherwise, it did not. This is both the explanation for the dearth of information on other forms of unions and the reason that the legal system can be seen as centering on marriage. In other forms of union, the partners had no right to each other's property or to financial support from each other; for the most part, their children had no such right, either, although the father could give it to them, and in some cases a persistent mother might be able to acquire it through the courts. Women might have benefited from the lack of a legal bond because husbands commonly had great, if not entire, control over their wives' property. Yet, because men controlled and disposed of so much more wealth than did women, freedom from a partner's claims could be important to them, too. In any opposite-sex union, women typically gained more in terms of material goods than men did, whereas men gained more in terms of the provision of household labor. Either might suffer materially from abandonment by the other, but men of any given social group generally had more economic alternatives to fall back on than women of the same group. For this reason, the church's push toward turning as many heterosexual unions as possible into marriages may be seen as benefiting women, although it also subjected both women and men to surveillance and regulation of their sexual behavior.

Freedom to leave a union may seem a huge advantage to twenty-first-century North Americans and Europeans who, even though many of us deplore divorce, all know people for whom it was the only way out of a miserable situation. Given the emphasis on the indissolubility of marriage in the earlier Middle Ages but increasingly from the twelfth century, and the inability to remarry even if a couple received permission to cease living together, a less formal type of union may have seemed seem much less onerous. Yet the ability to leave also brought with it the possibility of being left—and for a variety of reasons, not just cruelty or misery. Even today, with increased economic opportunities for women, men generally become better off economically after a divorce and women worse off.[2] Men tend to have higher incomes than women; after divorce, women lose access to that income. This would have been all the more the case for unions other than marriage in the Middle Ages. If both partners worked for wages, the man's was likely to be higher; if they worked together in a household-based enterprise, the man was likely to own the tools, equipment, or land involved. Either party might want out of a union for emotional reasons, or find someone preferable to live with, but the woman was more likely to suffer economically; marriage and the consequent difficulty of dissolving the union were more likely to be a protection for her. Of course, if the woman was a slave, she could simply be sold or assigned to other work at her owner's wish.

These issues only came into play if one of the partners wished to separate. As many of the examples here have shown, some couples were quite content together for years, and despite the fulminations of preachers against fornication, medieval society was often content to let them remain so. In a time when marriage was often determined by property arrangements or connections between families, other forms of unions—particularly between people who did not have much property to speak of, or were in a position to make their decisions about life partnerships independently of their families—allowed people to form bonds of their choice. Some of these relationships, between people of different social groups and religions, people who had left unhappy marriages, clergymen and their partners, could easily be marriages today but could not because of the medieval legal system.

Although it is widely recognized that there were people who lived together in the Middle Ages who could not legally marry, there was also a group
of unknown size who could legally have been married and were not. Since the
1970s, it has become increasingly common in North America and Europe for
heterosexual couples to live together without marriage. Some people lament
this as a decline of morals and the social fabric, a result of a welfare state that
takes away incentives for stable unions by making state support available. Others would argue that the availability of these choices, coupled with easier access to divorce, creates a more humane society in which people are not trapped
in abusive and unbearable situations. The provision of legal recognition in
terms of property and child-support obligations has meant that marriage is no
longer the only way for people to claim certain rights, as it once was.

But those who would look back to the Middle Ages as an era of a more
organic society where people behaved in a socially responsible, rather than an
individualistic, manner are refusing to recognize that marriage was (and is) not
the only way of creating a permanent pair bond, and was not as universal or
as satisfying to the partners and to the society at large as we might think. Medieval marriage was a legal contract sanctioned by the church; but for many
people, rejecting it in favor of another form of union meant rejecting a partner
chosen for them and negotiating their own relationships. Christian and Jewish marriage liturgies resemble and are based on those practiced in the Middle
Ages, but we should not let ritual similarity obscure the multiple alternatives
available to medieval people and their difference from those available today.

Notes

AN   Paris, Archives Nationales
BL   London, British Library
EETS   Early English Text Society
MGH   *Monumenta Germaniae Historica*
PL   *Patrologia Latina*
SSRG *Scriptores rerum germanicarum*

INTRODUCTION

1. Stephanie Coontz, *Marriage, a History: From Obedience to Intimacy or How Love Conquered Marriage* (New York: Viking, 2005).

2. E.g., Charles J. Reid, Jr., *Power over the Body, Equality in the Family: Rights and Domestic Relations in Medieval Canon Law* (Grand Rapids, Mich.: Wm. B. Eerdmans, 2004); see my review in the *Journal of the History of Sexuality* 14 (2005): 474–79.

3. Cordelia Beattie, "Living as a Single Person."

4. E. Kathleen Gough, "The Nayars and the Definition of Marriage," *Journal of the Royal Anthropological Institute of Great Britain and Ireland* 89 (1959): 33–34.

5. Dyan Elliott, *Spiritual Marriage.*

6. John Boswell, *Same-Sex Unions in Premodern Europe* (New York: Vintage, 1995); for an example of critique, see Elizabeth A. R. Brown, "Introduction" and "Ritual Brotherhood in Western Medieval Europe," Brent Shaw, "Ritual Brotherhood in Roman and Post-Roman Societies," and Claudia Rapp, "Ritual Brotherhood in Byzantium," all in *Traditio* 52 (1997): 261–382. See Dyan Elliott, *The Bride of Christ Goes to Hell.*

7. James Brundage, *Sex, Law, and Marriage in the Middle Ages*; Elliott, *Spiritual Marriage*; Christopher Brooke, *The Medieval Idea of Marriage* (Oxford: Oxford University Press, 1989), and Georges Duby, *The Knight, the Lady, and the Priest.*

8. Ginger Frost, *Living in Sin: Cohabiting as Husband and Wife in Nineteenth-Century England* (Manchester: Manchester University Press, 2008), provides a similar study of another time period. She recognizes three groups: those who could not marry, did not marry,

or would not marry because they were opposed to the institution. Heloise is the only medieval example I can adduce of a woman in the last category. Many of the couples Frost describes cohabited because of factors that made their ceremony invalid, and a ceremony was crucial in the creation of a bond in that context. The group who could not marry, because of previous marriages or consanguinity, was by far the largest.

9. See James A. Schultz, "Heterosexuality as a Threat to Medieval Studies," *Journal of the History of Sexuality* 15 (2006): 14–29, and Karma Lochrie, *Heterosyncrasies*, xix–xxii.

10. D. Catherine Brown, *Pastor and Laity in the Theology of Jean Gerson* (Cambridge: Cambridge University Press, 1987), 217. Gerson cited Hugh of St. Victor; Bonaventure said much the same thing. I am grateful to Sara McDougall for this point.

11. See Elliott, *The Bride of Christ Goes to Hell*; Megan McLaughlin, *Sex, Gender, and Episcopal Authority in an Age of Reform*, 51–91.

12. Nor does marriage seem to have been a religious institution elsewhere in the ancient Near East. Karel van der Toorn, *From Her Cradle to Her Grave: The Role of Religion in the Life of the Israelite and the Babylonian Woman*, trans. Sara J. Denning-Bolle (Sheffield: Sheffield Academic Press, 1994), 59–76, argues that it was, in fact, a religious institution; although he does point out some religious aspects, the argument is not convincing overall.

13. Simon B. Parker, "The Marriage Blessing in Israelite and Ugaritic Literature," *Journal of Biblical Literature* 95 (1976): 23–30.

14. Riffat Hassan, "Islamic Hagar and Her Family," in *Hagar, Sarah, and Their Children: Jewish, Christian, and Muslim Perspectives*, ed. Phyllis Trible and Letty M. Russell (Louisville, Ky.: Westminster John Knox, 2006), 149–67, and Rudi Paret, "'Ismāʿil," *Encyclopedia of Islam*, 2nd ed., ed. P. Berman et al. (Leiden: Brill, 2009).

15. "The Laws of Hammurabi," trans. Martha Roth, 144–46, 170–71, in *The Context of Scripture*, vol. 2, *Monumental Inscriptions from the Biblical World*, ed. William W. Hallo et al. (Leiden: Brill, 2000), 344–46; Raymond Westbrook, "Old Babylonian Period," 381.

16. *Glossa Ordinaria* to Gen. 16:1, in *PL* 113:121d. The gloss is attributed to Hrabanus Maurus. See also Marcia Colish, *Peter Lombard*, 2:663–64, on the development of this question among other theologians.

17. Augustine, *De doctrina Christiana*, 3:12:20, Select Library of Nicene and Post-Nicene Fathers, 1st series, vol. 2, ed. Philip Schaff, http://www9.georgetown.edu/faculty/jod/augustine/ddc3.html.

18. Elizabeth Clark, "Interpretive Fate and the Church Fathers," in *Hagar, Sarah, and Their Children*, ed. Trible and Russell, 127–47, here 128.

19. *Glossa Ordinaria*, 122b. See McLaughlin, *Sex, Gender, and Episcopal Authority*, 127–28.

20. Corinna Friedl, *Polygynie in Mesopotamien und Israel*, 140.

21. Louis Epstein, *Marriage Laws*, 54, suggests that the sons of Bilhah and Zilpah were of secondary status because in Gen. 33:2, Jacob arranges them first in the line of danger. However, he also puts Leah and her sons in front of Rachel and hers, indicating a preference for Rachel but not necessarily a higher social or legal status. It is entirely plausible that the sons of the slaves were of lower social status and more expendable yet still considered full sons with the same rights as any of the brothers other than the eldest.

22. Ibid., 50. Epstein draws the idea that a slave is freed on her owner's death from the Hammurabi's law rather than the Bible itself, which nowhere states this.

23. The *Glossa Ordinaria*, *PL* 113:163, does not comment on the choice of words, noting only that a concubine represents the Old Testament as a wife represents the New. *Genesis Rabbah*, the major Jewish biblical commentary, does not comment, either. *Midrash Rabbah*, vol. 2, trans. H. Freedman (London: Soncino, 1983).

24. Avraham Grossman, "The Historical Background to the Ordinances on Family Affairs Attributed to Rabbenu Gershom Me'or ha-Golah."

25. L. Epstein, 62–63, and Michael L. Satlow, *Jewish Marriage in Antiquity*, 193.

26. Satlow, 75.

27. Friedl, 151. Deut. 22:29, which is sometimes also taken as evidence of *mohar*, also deals with sexual intercourse with a woman without her father's permission, and does not use the term. Millar Burrows, *The Basis of Israelite Marriage* (New Haven, Conn.: American Oriental Society, 1938), suggested that *mohar* was a Canaanite institution and mainly functioned to establish the prestige of the husband and his family.

28. "Laws of Hammurabi," 128–84, pp. 344–47. Current scholarly consensus is that the Babylonian *terhatum* denoted bridewealth, but earlier scholars stressed that it should be understood as a purchase price. Paul Koschaker, *Rechtsvergleichende Studien zur Gesetzgebung Hammurapis, Königs von Babylon* (Leipzig: Veit, 1917), argued that *tirhatum* (as he transliterated it) came from a more archaic *Kaufehe*. The use of Germanic patterns to interpret Near Eastern patterns by analogy, in view of what the last part of this Introduction demonstrates about the unreliability of theories about Germanic culture, created a circular argument. M. Stol, "Women in Mesopotamia," *Journal of the Economic and Social History of the Orient* 38 (1995): 126–27, accepts Koschaker's view that marriage was basically a sale. See Martha T. Roth, "Marriage and Matrimonial Prestations in First Millennium B.C. Babylonia," in *Women's Earliest Records*, ed. Barbara S. Lesko (Atlanta: Scholars Press, 1989), 245–48, on the problems of translating a variety of social practices with the same terms. Whether bridewealth was required for a valid marriage is a complex question. The Hammurabi Code, as well as the earlier Code of Eshnunna, does say that "if a man take a woman to wife, but have no marriage contract, this woman is no wife to him," but the term for "contract" here is not *terhatum*, "bridewealth": as Westbrook, "Old Babylonian Period," 386, notes, the latter was not required by the law. See Samuel Greengus, "The Old Babylonian Marriage Contract," 75–77.

29. Bezalel Porten, "Elephantine," in *A History of Ancient Near Eastern Law*, ed. Raymond Westbrook, vol. 2, Handbook of Oriental Studies, section one, The Near and Middle East, 72:2 (Leiden: Brill, 2003), 875.

30. Dowry paid by the woman's family also appears in the Bible, and it has been suggested that the purpose was to support the woman in her old age and that if the family could not afford such a dowry, they would sell her as a slave. However, the Bible does not explicitly state this or make dowry a requirement for marriage. Allen Guenther, "A Typology of Israelite Marriage: Kinship, Socio-Economic, and Religious Factors," *Journal for the Study of the Old Testament* 29 (2005): 387–407, here 389.

31. In Greece, at least at the higher levels of society for which there is evidence, a property transaction and a public ritual were important to the creation of formal marriage. Athenian law, however, like that of the Bible, was not concerned to set out specifically what did and did not constitute a valid marriage, and the marriage contract was not a necessary step in public law. It is clear that the children of concubines had fewer rights than the children of the wife, and their mothers lacked rights as well; Athenian citizen women did not become concubines. Cynthia B. Patterson, "Marriage and the Married Woman in Athenian Law," in *Women's History and Ancient History*, ed. Sarah B. Pomeroy (Chapel Hill: University of North Carolina Press, 1991), 48–72, argues that marriage could not be defined by a legal criterion but is "something that occurs over time and is demonstrated to the community by appropriate behavior" (59).

32. An ancient form of marriage, *confarreatio*, involved a sacrifice to the gods, but this had fallen out of use by the time of the empire.

33. Susan Treggiari, *Roman Marriage: Iusti Coniuges from the Time of Cicero to the Time of Ulpian* (Oxford: Oxford University Press, 1991), 13.

34. Reynolds, *Marriage in the Western Church*, 21.

35. On the Roman law of concubinage and its reception in western Europe, see Andrea Esmyol, *Geliebte oder Ehefrau?*, 37–43.

36. Brent Shaw, "The Family in Late Antiquity," 16, and Adolar Zumkeller, "Die geplante Eheschließung Augustins und die Entlassung seiner Konkubine," 34.

37. Judith Evans-Grubbs, "Marrying and Its Documentation in Later Roman Law," 92–94.

38. Judith Evans-Grubbs, *Law and Family in Late Antiquity: The Emperor Constantine's Marriage Legislation* (Oxford: Oxford University Press, 1995), 302–3.

39. Evans-Grubbs, "Marrying and Its Documentation," 79.

40. Shaw, "The Family in Late Antiquity," 33.

41. I have discussed this in detail in "The History of Marriage and the Myth of *Friedelehe*." At the time I wrote that article, I had not yet read Esmyol, *Geliebte oder Ehefrau?*, 1–36, which discusses the historiography of *Friedelehe* in detail. In the rest of the book, Esmyol attempts a fresh look at the status of the concubine, unencumbered by the construct of *Friedelehe*.

42. Suzanne Wemple, *Women in Frankish Society*, 34.

43. Le Jan, for example, accepts the reality of a *Friedelehe*, although after the church's declaration in the eighth century that a *dos* was required for marriage, the *Friedelfrau*'s situation approached that of a concubine. Prior to this development, she suggests, citing Paul Mikat, *Dotierte Ehe—Rechte Ehe*, the *Friedelfrau* had received a *Morgengabe* and had been a true wife, although one of second rank. Régine Le Jan, *Famille et pouvoir dans le monde franc*, 271. Le Jan's account of what happened in the Carolingian period with the distinction between legitimate, dowered wife and concubine is thorough and well argued, but the idea that there was a sharp distinction previously between *Friedelehe* and *Muntehe*, with the *Friedelfrau* being recast as a concubine, is based on the work of previous scholars and not on a fresh examination of the sources.

44. Rainer Schulze, "Eherecht," in *Reallexikon der Germanischen Altertumskunde*, ed. Johannes Hoops (Berlin, 1986), 491. See W. Ogris, "Friedelehe," in *Handwörterbuch zur deutschen Rechtsgeschichte*, ed. Adalbert Erler and Ekkehard Kaufmann (Berlin: Erich Schmidt, 1971), 1:1293–96, for the more traditional view, treating *Friedelehe* as an existing institution rather than a term of convenience.

45. Herbert Meyer, author of the seminal article "Friedelehe und Mutterrecht," was not a Nazi, but his ideas about the ancient Germans were in line with National Socialist ideology and supported the view of a praiseworthy common German past. On his politics, see Hans Hattenhauer, *Rechtswissenschaft im NS-Staat: Der Fall Eugen Wohlhaupter* (Heidelberg: C. F. Müller, 1987), 16, and Friedrich Ebel, *Rechtsgeschichte: Ein Lehrbuch* (Heidelberg: C. F. Müller, 1993), 2:222. Meyer's account of prehistoric Germanic marriage relies a great deal on the existence of the *Sippe* or clan, another construct that has been called into question. See Alexander Callendar Murray, *Germanic Kinship Structure: Studies in Law and Society in Antiquity and the Early Middle Ages* (Toronto: Pontifical Institute of Medieval Studies, 1983). Meyer's student Karl August Eckhardt was more circumspect with his use of sources. His standard textbook on Germanic law did not discuss *Friedelehe* at all, noting "relationships similar to marriage," which he assumes substitute for what he calls "marriage" in a basically monogamous system. Karl August Eckhardt, ed., *Germanisches Recht, von Karl von Amira*, 4th ed., 2 vols., Grundriss der germanischen Philologie 5 (Berlin, 1967), 2:75.

46. As Régine Le Jan puts it, "the constitutive element of the Germanic *Vollehe* was the transfer of the *mundium*, acquired initially by the payment of the *pretium nuptiale* to the holder of the *mundium*, without the production of a written act" (268). See Emmanuelle Santinelli, "Ni 'Morgengabe' ni *tertia* mais *dos* et dispositions en faveur du dernier vivant: Les échanges patrimoniaux entre époux dans la Loire moyenne (VIIe–XIe siècle)," in *Dots et douaires dans le haut moyen âge*, ed. François Bougard, Laurent Feller, and Régine Le Jan (Rome: École française de Rome, 2002), 246–53, and Régine Le Jan, "Aux origines du douaire médievale," in Le Jan, *Femmes, pouvoir et société dans le haut Moyen Age* (Paris: Picard, 2001), 53–67, on the transition from bride price to *dos*. For a good summary of the medieval "economics of dotation," see Reynolds, "Marrying and Its Documentation in Pre-Modern Europe," 30–37.

47. Many scholars claim that any marriage with a *dos* also included the transfer of the *Munt*: e.g., Le Jan, "Aux origines du douaire médievale," 56. Not one, however, cites any evidence other than the Lombard laws for a bride price that purchased guardianship over the bride, let alone a *dos* paid to the bride that did so.

48. Hans-Werner Goetz, "La *dos* en Alémanie (du milieu du VIIIe au début du Xe siècle)," in *Dots et douaires*, ed. Bougard, Feller, and Le Jan, 308. Benedictus Levita, *Capitula*, 2:133, ed. Georg Heinrich Pertz (Hannover: Hahn, 1837), *Capitularia Spuria*, *MGH*, *Legum* 2:2, p. 80. Many other scholars take "legitimate marriage required a *dos*" to mean "only *Muntehe* was legitimate marriage," i.e., the existence of a *dos* is seen as indicating *Muntehe* even in the absence of any discussion of a *Munt*. E.g., Stefan Chr. Saar, *Ehe–Scheidung–Wiederheirat*, 176. On this dictum, see Philip L. Reynolds, "Dotal Charters in the Frankish Tradition," in *Marriage and its Documentation*, ed. by Reynolds and Witte,

125. The Visigothic law in the recension of King Ervig's recension is headed "Ne sine dote coniugium fiat," and goes on to say that where there is no written evidence of *dos*, there is no evidence of the marriage but not that it is invalid. *Lex Visigothorum*, 3:1.9, in *Leges Visigothorum*, ed. Karl Zeumer, *MGH, Leges Nationum Germanicarum* (Hannover: Hahn, 1902), 1:131–32. It thus requires the dowry but does not make marriage without it invalid. Reynolds, *Marriage in the Western Church*, 90, 113, 405.

49. *Pace* Schmidt-Wiegand, who argues that although all the evidence for the *mundium* comes from the Lombard laws, "it would nevertheless be wrong to conclude from this fact, as has actually been done, that the Franks, for example, lacked marital or gender-based guardianship. Ruth Schmidt-Wiegand, "Der Lebenskreis der Frau im Spiegel der volkssprachigen Bezeichnungen der Leges barbarorum," in *Frauen in Spätantike und Frühmittelalter: Lebensbedingungen—Lebensnormen—Lebensformen*, ed. Werner Affeldt (Sigmaringen: Jan Thorbecke, 1990), 202–3. I am particularly grateful to Felice Lifshitz for calling to my attention Schmidt-Wiegand's argument.

50. Reynolds, *Marriage in the Western Church*, also finds the institution "remarkably similar to that of the old Roman *manus*-marriage" (93).

51. Gaius, *Institutiones*, 1:108–15, ed. Johannes Baviera, in *Fontes iuris Romani antejustiniani*, ed. S. Riccobono et al. (Florence: G. Barbera, 1940), 2:29–31.

52. *Lex Romana Visigothorum*, ed. Gustav Haenel (Leipzig: B. G. Teubner, 1849), 314–37.

53. Francis de Zulueta, ed., *The Institutes of Gaius* (Oxford: Clarendon, 1946), 2:3–5, and Tomasz Giaro, "Gaius," in *Der neue Pauly*, ed. Hubert Cancik and Helmuth Schneider (Stuttgart: J. B. Metzler, 1998), 4:738.

54. See Ian N. Wood, "The Code in Merovingian Gaul," in *The Theodosian Code*, ed. Jill Harries and Ian Wood (Ithaca, N.Y.: Cornell University Press, 1993), 161–77.

55. On this point, see, e.g., Steven Fanning, "Tacitus, *Beowulf*, and the *Comitatus*," *Haskins Society Journal* 9 (1997): 17–38, esp. 33–35.

56. Tacitus, *Germania*, 18, in *Opera Minora*, ed. M. Winterbottom and R. M. Ogilvie (Oxford: Clarendon, 1975), 46.

57. Hughes's claim that "Tacitus' failure to mention brideprice may indicate that even by the end of the first century it had fallen from prominence among those tribes that lived on the fringes of the Empire" and that "by the time these West German tribes issued their codes, brideprice had generally disappeared" begs the question of what evidence there is for bride price predating the written sources. She finds vestiges of it in the eastern Germanic laws. Diane Owen Hughes, "From Brideprice to Dowry in Mediterranean Europe," *Journal of Family History* 3 (1978): 262–96, quotations at 266–67.

CHAPTER 1

1. See Philip Lyndon Reynolds, *Marriage in the Western Church*, 213–26, on the development of this doctrine.

2. On the Stoics, see Peter Brown, *The Body and Society: Men, Women, and Sexual Renunciation in Early Christianity* (New York: Columbia University Press, 1988), 21.

3. See David G. Hunter, "Marrying and the *Tabulae Nuptiales* in Roman North Africa," for the differential spread of the nuptial blessing in different parts of the late empire, and Reynolds, *Marriage in the Western Church*, xix. Reynolds later notes that the earliest surviving marriage liturgy dates from the seventh century (323).

4. Judith Evans-Grubbs, "Marrying and Its Documentation in Later Roman Law," 85–88.

5. See Matthew Kuefler, *The Manly Eunuch: Masculinity, Gender Ambiguity, and Christian Ideology in Late Antiquity* (Chicago: University of Chicago Press, 2001), 70–102, on changes in the Roman household, and Hunter, 113.

6. Cited in James J. O'Donnell, *Augustine, Confessions: Commentary* (Oxford: Clarendon, 1992), 2:384. This pattern of condemning married men for keeping concubines continued in Gaul; see examples in Andrea Esmyol, *Geliebte oder Ehefrau?*, 78–79.

7. *PL*, 54:1204–5. See Reynolds, *Marriage in the Western Church*, 163–69, on this letter. Reynolds says that "Leo does not affirm, as early medieval churchmen and some modern scholars have assumed, that *no* marriage is legitimate without dotation and public nuptials" (165). In the case of a woman of unfree or freed status, however, these procedures were required as evidence of marital intent. See also discussion in Esmyol, 82–83.

8. Evans-Grubbs, "Marrying and Its Documentation," 90.

9. Most scholars date this relationship from the time Augustine was eighteen; this is the latest that it can have begun, given that the couple's son was about fifteen in the spring of 387. Danuta Shanzer, "*Avulsa a latere meo*," 168, suggests that it may have begun earlier, and O'Donnell (2:207) dates it to 371 or perhaps even 370, before he began his studies. The account here draws heavily on Shanzer's important article. For less scholarly approaches, see Louis Bertrand, *Celle qui fut aimée d'Augustin*, who, after sprinkling his historical account with concepts like "the African temperament" (25), attaches a piece of short fiction about a later meeting between the two, and Pierre Villemain, *Confessions de Numida: L'innommée de Saint Augustin*, a novel told in the first person by the woman. He presents her as expecting to marry Augustine (41), and takes a very negative view of the latter, who treats Numida as simply an outlet for his carnal lust even at the beginning of their relationship, and a symbol of his sin later.

10. *Confessions*, 4.2.2, ed. O'Donnell, 1:33.

11. Ibid., 6.15.25, 1:71.

12. Ibid., 6.15.25.

13. Adolar Zumkeller, "Die geplante Eheschließung Augustins und die Entlassung seiner Konkubine," 27.

14. Reynolds, *Marriage in the Western Church*, 257.

15. *Confessions*, 4.2.2.

16. Zumkeller, 23.

17. *Confessions*, 6.15.25.

18. Shanzer, 160–64.

19. Augustine, *De bono coniugali*, 5, ed. and trans. P. G. Walsh (Oxford: Clarendon, 2001), 11–13. I am grateful to Dyan Elliott for calling my attention to this passage.

20. Shanzer, 169.

21. Bertrand, 114, and Villemain, 62, make Monnica's religious principles the main reason, though Villemain puts more emphasis on class difference than does Bertrand.

22. O'Donnell, 384 n. 10; see also Brent Shaw, "The Family in Late Antiquity," 45.

23. Stefan Chr. Saar, *Ehe—Scheidung—Wiederheirat*, 165; see also Paul Mikat, *Dotierte Ehe—Rechte Ehe*, 34–47, who connects dotation with the Roman *honestae nuptiae* rather than explicitly with a distinction from concubinage.

24. "Ad Rusticum Narbonensum episcopum," *Sancti Leonis magni Romani pontificis epistolae*, 167:4, *PL*, 54:1204a–b. Reynolds, *Marriage in the Western Church*, 163–65, points out that although Leo was espousing traditional Roman doctrine, he did it by citing biblical as well as Roman legal authorities.

25. *Pactus Legis Salicae*, 44, 100, ed. Karl A. Eckhardt, *MGH*, *Leges Nationum Germanicarum*, 4:1 (Hannover: Hahn, 1962), 168–73, 256–57.

26. *Lex Ribuaria*, in H. F. W. D. Fischer, ed., *Leges Barbarorum in usum studiosorum*, Textus minores 3 (Leiden: Brill, 1948), 37:2, 15.

27. Régine Le Jan, *Famille et pouvoir dans le monde franc*, 268–74, argues that unions without *dos* were reduced to concubinage; but note that even if she is right, it does not mean that this was the case in the pre-Christian period. See Yitzhak Hen, *Culture and Religion in Merovingian Gaul, A.D. 471–751* (Brill: Leiden, 1995), 35–38, on *formulae* as a genre.

28. *Lex Saxonum*, 40, in Fischer, *Leges Barbarorum*, 39.

29. For discussion of the other "barbarian" *leges*, see Ruth Mazo Karras, "The History of Marriage and the Myth of *Friedelehe*."

30. On polygyny in the royal family, see Suzanne Wemple, *Women in Frankish Society*, 38–41.

31. On the slipperiness of terminology, see Reynolds, *Marriage in the Western Church*, 109.

32. For recent scholarship on Gregory, see Kathleen Mitchell and Ian Wood, eds., *The World of Gregory of Tours* (Leiden: Brill, 2002), and Martin Heinzelmann, *Gregory of Tours: History and Society in the Sixth Century*, trans. Christopher Carroll (Cambridge: Cambridge University Press, 2001).

33. Gregory of Tours, *Historiarum Libri Decem*, 2:12, 2:28, pp. 1:94, 1:114; cf. Fredegar, *Die vier Bücher der Chroniken des sogennanten Fredegar*, 3:20, ed. Herwig Wolfram and Andreas Kusternig, Ausgewählte Quellen zur deutschen Geschichte des Mittelalters (Darmstadt: Wissenschaftliche Buchgesellschaft, 1982), 106.

34. Gregory of Tours, 3:7, p. 1:154.

35. Ibid., 3:23, 3:27, p. 1:178.

36. Fredegar, 3:39, p. 118. On this case, see Esmyol, 48.

37. Gregory of Tours, 4:28, p. 1:232.

38. Ibid., 4:9, 4:26, pp. 1:128, 1:204; cf. Fredegar, 3:49, 3:57, pp. 122, 128–30.

39. Gregory of Tours, 4:27, p. 1:230.

40. Fredegar, 4:35, pp. 188–90. Wemple, 56–57, calls these unions *Friedelehen*, or quasi-marriages, but, as she recognizes, the sources treat them as marriages. Mikat, 61, suggests that it is not possible to tell, except in the case of foreign princesses, whether the marriages of Merovingian kings and their sons were *Muntehen* or *Friedelehen*. It is not clear why he thinks that the determination can be made in the case of foreign princesses, except that wealth was clearly transferred; however, as discussed above, there is no indication that among the Franks, the transfer of bridewealth brought the husband particular rights over the wife. I suggest that there was no line between the two; the distinction is a modern creation.

41. *Polyptyque de l'abbé Irminon*, ed. M. B. Guérard (Paris: Imprimerie Royale, 1836–44), and Emily R. Coleman, "Medieval Marriage Characteristics: A Neglected Factor in the History of Medieval Serfdom," *Journal of Interdisciplinary History* 2 (1971): 205–19.

42. On Merovingian councils, see Gregory Halfond, *The Archaeology of Frankish Church Councils*.

43. Council of Orleans (541), 22, in *Concilia Galliae*, ed. Charles de Clerc, Corpus Christianorum Series Latina 148A (Turnhout: Brepols, 1963), 137–38, and Council of Tours, 20 (21), p. 187. On Carolingian church law, see Karl Heidecker, *The Divorce of Lothar II*, 20.

44. Concilium Baiuwaricum, 12, *MGH, Legum sectio 2, Concilia*, vol. 2, *Concilia aevi Karolini*, ed. Albert Werminghoff (Hannover: Hahn, 1906), 1:1:53.

45. Concilium Vernense, in *MGH, Legum sectio 2, Capitularia Regum Francorum*, ed. Alfred Boretius (Hannover: Hahn, 1883), 1:36.

46. Concilium Moguntium, 12, ed. Alfred Boretius and Victor Krause, *Capitularia Regum Francorum*, vol. 2, *MGH, Leges* (Hannover: Hahn, 1890), 2:189. See Heidecker, 26. This council said that any woman without such a betrothal is a concubine, though it went on to quote Pope Leo requiring the *mysterium nuptiale* for a valid marriage. Reynolds, *Marriage in the Western Church*, 171, notes that Leo's point about the formal betrothal being necessary for marital intent in cases of unequal partners has gotten lost.

47. "Decreta Evaristi Papae," in *Isidori Mercatoris Decretalium Collectio, PL*, 130:81b–81c. See Heidecker, 31.

48. J. M. Wallace-Hadrill, *The Frankish Church*, 407.

49. Benedictus Levita, 2:130, p. 80, and *Lex Visigothorum*, 12:3:8, p. 436. See Heidecker, 30.

50. Jonas of Orleans, *De institutione laicali*, 2:2, *PL*, 106:171a.

51. Ibid., 2:4, 106:174c–177c. See Esmyol, 197–200.

52. Halitgar, *De vitiis et virtutibus et de ordine poenitentium*, 4:12, *PL*, 105:683b.

53. Reynolds, *Marriage in the Western Church*, 409–10, discusses whether it was, in fact, "the church" that took the position that publicity and formality were necessary, or whether the Frankish and Roman churches differed on this.

54. Nicholas I, *Epistolae*, 99, in *MGH*, Epistolae 6, Epistolae Karolini Aevi 4, ed. Ernst Perels (Berlin: Weidmann, 1925), 570. See Wallace-Hadrill, 407.

55. Glenn W. Olsen, "Marriage in Barbarian Kingdom and Christian Court," in idem, *Christian Marriage: A Historical Study* (New York: Crossroad, 2001), 146–212, here 163–64,

distinguishes between Roman concubinage, which involved women of lower status than their partners, and Germanic concubinage, which was polygynous. But this is a modern distinction and assumes "concubinage" as a modern category—as discussed in the Introduction, nonecclesiastical Germanic sources (whether in Latin or another language) do not use this or any equivalent term until quite late.

56. Silvia Konecny, *Die Frauen des karolingischen Königshauses*, 24–26.

57. Ibid., 43, 65, and Esmyol, 146–52. Le Jan, 244, does not consider her a concubine but a *Friedelfrau*.

58. Einhard, *Vita Karoli*, 19, ed. Georg Heinrich Perta, *MGH*, Scriptores 2 (Hannover: Hahn, 1889), 454. Wemple, 79, calls the relationships they had with men *Friedelehen* and their lovers *Friedelmänner*.

59. Nithard, *Historiarum libri IIII*, 1:2, ed. Ernst Müller, *MGH*, *SSRG* (Hannover: Hahn, 1856), 2; Astronomus, *Vita Hludowici Imperatoris*, 23, ed. and trans. (into German) Ernst Tremp, *MGH*, *SSRG* 64 (Hannover: Hahn, 1995), 352.

60. Wemple, 79, and Konecny, 74–77.

61. Karl Schmid, "Ein karolingische Königseintrag im Gedenkbuch von Remiremont," *Frühmittelalterliche Studien* 2 (1968): 96–134, here 128–34, argues that based on the evidence of people with whom Waldrada was listed in monastic memorial books, she was of the nobility but not of the highest aristocracy, as was Theutberga.

62. Rachel Stone, pers. comm., 1 March 2011, suggests that the evidence for families being involved in this kind of union is fairly limited, citing several examples of noblemen entering into unions without their parents' approval.

63. See Heidecker, 125.

64. Esmyol, 161, points out that according to the records of the 862 Council of Aachen, Lothar admitted that Waldrada was a concubine and not a wife; but how voluntary this statement was remains a question.

65. Schmid, 114.

66. Konecny, 104–5.

67. Hincmar of Reims, *De Divortio Lotharii regis et Theutbergae reginae*, is the key text here. The modern editor calls Waldrada a *Friedelfrau* (4). A partial English translation is now available online: http://hincmar.blogspot.com. The most recent and thorough study of this case is that of Heidecker, *The Divorce of Lothar II*, whose work was published after this section was initially drafted but has added greatly to my understanding; see, esp., 77–84 on Hincmar.

68. Le Jan, 276–77; see also Stuart Airlie, "Private Bodies and the Body Politic in the Divorce Case of Lothar II," *Past & Present* 161 (1998): 14 n. 33; Konecny, 113, and Esmyol, 70, rejecting the *épouse de jeunesse* category.

69. Wemple, 90–94; see also Le Jan, 273.

70. Heidecker, 64, 110–19, 125.

71. Esmyol, 165.

72. Janet L. Nelson, *Charles the Bald*, 199–200, 215–17, and Eleanor Searle, *Predatory Kinship and the Creation of Norman Power*, 20–21. Heidecker does not go quite this far but

notes that Hincmar was reluctant to get involved; in other cases where the political situation was different, he "trimmed the Church's rules to fit the case in question" (99).

73. For another churchman's view, see Regino, *Chronicon*, ed.Friedrich Kurze, *MGH, SSRG in usum scholarum separatim editi* (Hannover, 1890), s.a. 864 (actually 857), p. 80. See Heidecker, 123–28.

74. Konecny, 111–14.

75. Nelson, 198.

76. Heidecker, 45, cites an 863 charter referring to Waldrada in this way.

77. Adventius of Metz, "Epistolae ad Divortium Lotharii II Regis Pertinentes," 5, in *Epistolae Karolini Aevi*, ed. Ernst Dümmler, *MGH*, Epistolae 6 (Hannover: Hahn, 1902), 215–17.

78. Mikat, 46; Esmyol, 155–56; *Annales Bertiniani*, s.a. 869, ed. Georg Waitz, *MGH, in usum scholarum separatim editi* (Hannover: Hahn, 1883), 107: "Richildem . . . in concubinam accepit"; s.a. 870, p. 108: *predictam concubinam suam Richildem desponsatam atque dotam in coniugem sumpsit.*

79. Airlie, 14–17, and Heidecker, 110–19.

80. Airlie, 15, 26.

81. Rachel Stone, pers. comm., 1 March 2011.

82. Catherine Rider, *Magic and Impotence in the Middle Ages* (Oxford: Oxford University Press, 2006), 31–36; Hincmar, 15–17, pp. 205–17, and *Annales Bertiniani*, s.a. 862, 60.

83. *Vita sancti Deicoli*, 13, ed. Georg Waitz, *MGH*, Scriptores 15 (Hannover: MGH, 1888), 678.

84. Heidecker, 132, 154, 169, 174–76.

85. Genevra Kornbluth, "The Susanna Crystal of Lothar II"; see also Rider, 35.

86. See Searle, 95; 141 on marriage *more Danico*. Searle relies on Elizabeth Eames, "Mariage et concubinage légal en Norvège à l'époque des Vikings," *Annales de Normandie* 2 (1952): 195–208, for a statement of what marriage customs were like in Norway, on which she bases her account of marriage *more Danico*; Eames relies a bit too much on the extant laws as direct evidence for the situation in pre-Christian times. See also Jean-Marie Maillefer, "Le mariage en Scandinavie médiévale," in *Mariage et sexualité au Moyen Age: Accord ou crise?*, ed. Michel Rouche (Paris: Presses de l'Université de Paris-Sorbonne, 2000), 91–106, here 105, who equates marriage *more Danico* with Roman marriage *sine manu*, or concubinage; however, Roman marriage *sine manu* was definitely not concubinage (see below). The *Gesta Normannorum Ducum*, 7(4), of William of Jumièges, Orderic Vitalis and Robert of Torigni, ed. and trans. Elisabeth C. M. van Houts (Oxford: Oxford University Press, 1995), 2:96 (a section by Orderic), is the first to mention Herleve by name, and calls her "concubina . . . Fulberti cubicularii ducis filia."

87. *Gesta*, 4:18, pp. 1:128–29; 8:36, pp. 2:266–68.

88. See Reynolds, *Marriage in the Western Church*, 112, on Richard and Gunnor's marriage.

89. Bernadette Filotas, *Pagan Survivals, Superstitions, and Popular Cultures in Early Medieval Pastoral Literature* (Toronto: Pontifical Institute of Mediaeval Studies, 2005), 297.

90. Arbeo of Freising, *Vita vel passio Haimhramni spiscopi et martyris Ratisbonensis*, ed. Bruno Krusch, *MGH, SSRG in usum scholarum separatim editi*, 13, 89.

91. Carl Hammer, "A Slave Marriage Ceremony from Early Medieval Germany: A Note and a Document in Translation," *Slavery and Abolition* 16 (1995): 243–49.

92. Georges Duby, *The Knight, The Lady, and the Priest*, 19.

93. Christof Rolker, *Canon Law and the Letters of Ivo of Chartres*, 213–17.

94. Ibid., 230–43.

95. M. T. Clanchy, *Abelard*, 173–74, for Heloise's age; most previous scholars had assumed she was a teenager when she and Abelard began their relationship. Peter the Venerable mentions in a letter that he knew of her as a learned woman when he was still young, and since he was born in 1092 or 1094, Clanchy and others consider that she must have been slightly older.

96. Constant J. Mews, *Abelard and Heloise*, 59, and Guy Lobrichon, *Heloïse*, 119–21.

97. Peter Abelard, *Historia Calamitatum*, 63, and *The Letters and Other Writings*, trans. William Levitan, 2.

98. Abelard, 71; trans. Levitan, 11.

99. Abelard, 72; trans. Levitan, 11.

100. Abelard, 72–73; trans. Levitan, 12.

101. The attribution of these letters to Abelard and Heloise is highly contested, although Heloise, in her later, soundly attributed correspondence, mentions that they did at one time exchange love letters. Making the case for the attribution is Constant J. Mews, *The Lost Love Letters of Heloise and Abelard: Perceptions of Dialogue in Twelfth-Century France* (New York: St. Martin's Press, 1999); against, Jan Ziolkowski, "Lost and Not Yet Found: Heloise, Abelard, and the *Epistolae duorum amantium*," *Journal of Medieval Latin* 14 (2004): 171–202, and Peter von Moos, "Die *Epistolae duorum amantium* und die 'säkulare Religion der Liebe': Methodenkritische Vorüberlegungen zu einem einmaligen Werk mittellateinischer Briefliteratur," *Studi Medievali* 44 (2003): 1–115. See also C. Stephen Jaeger, "*Epistolae duorum amantium* and the Ascription to Heloise and Abelard"; Giles Constable, "The Authorship of the *Epistolae duorum amantium*: A Reconsideration," and C. Stephen Jaeger, "A Reply to Giles Constable," in *Voices in Dialogue*, ed. Linda Olson and Kathryn Kerby-Fulton, 125–86. Lobrichon, 43–48, is agnostic on the attribution of these letters.

102. Abelard, 75; trans. Levitan, 13–14.

103. Abelard, 75; trans. Levitan, 14.

104. Abelard, 78; trans. Levitan, 17.

105. Mews, *Lost Love Letters*, 35.

106. Heloise, first letter, ed. J. T. Muckle, "The Personal Letters Between Abelard and Heloise," 71; trans. Levitan, 55, except that Levitan has "lover" for *amica* and I have substituted "friend." Bracketed Latin terms inserted by me.

107. Abelard, 76; trans. Levitan, 15.

108. Étienne Gilson, *Abelard and Heloise*, trans. L. K. Shook (Ann Arbor: University of Michigan Press, 1960), 9–14, discusses this point. See also Clanchy, 188, and Lobrichon, 188–92.

109. Abelard, 79; trans. Levitan, 18.

110. Heloise, third letter, ed. Muckle, 79; trans. Levitan, 76. Lobrichon, 121–22, questions how Abelard's castration and humiliation could be seen as raising the status of Heloise's family; I read the passage as saying that he had already made amends by marrying her, thus raising the status of her family (she uses the pluperfect tense here), and yet he was additionally punished with the castration.

111. Lobrichon, 124–25.

112. Clanchy, 186.

113. Abelard, 81; trans. Levitan, 20.

114. Heloise, first letter, ed. Muckle, 72; trans. Levitan, 59.

115. Heloise, third letter, ed. Muckle, 79; trans. Levitan, 75. Bracketed Latin terms inserted by me.

116. On Heloise's use of misogynist topoi and the way scholars have ignored same-sex desire, especially in Heloise's third letter, see Karma Lochrie, *Heterosyncrasies*, 26–46. Lochrie suggests that Heloise's rejection of marriage was in part a rejection of heterosexual desire. Neither Heloise's nor Abelard's description of their feelings at the time of their sexual relationship seems to me to point this way, although certainly they are not incompatible with her experience of same-sex desire within the convent.

117. Heloise, third letter, ed. Muckle, 80; trans. Levitan, 78.

118. Heloise, first letter, ed. Muckle, 70; trans. Levitan, 54. Bracketed Latin terms inserted by me.

119. See Mews, *Lost Love Letters*, 48–50, and John Marenbon, "Authenticity Revisited," in *Listening to Heloise: The Voice of a Twelfth-Century Woman*, ed. Bonnie Wheeler (New York: St. Martin's Press, 2000), 19–34, on the discussions of authenticity of these later letters (this discussion refers to the monastic letters edited by Muckle, not the "Lost Love Letters").

120. Jack Goody, *The Development of the Family and Marriage in Europe* (Cambridge: Cambridge University Press, 1983), 221. This is a summary of a complex argument.

121. This can be seen in Marcia Colish, *Peter Lombard*, 2:693–94.

122. Joan Cadden, *Meanings of Sex Difference in the Middle Ages: Medicine, Science, and Culture* (Cambridge: Cambridge University Press, 1993), 241–58, quotation at 249.

123. Megan McLaughlin, *Sex, Gender, and Episcopal Authority in an Age of Reform*, 24–25.

124. Anders Winroth, *The Making of Gratian's Decretum* (Cambridge: Cambridge University Press, 2000), gives the details about the creation of this work, significantly revising the previous historiography. Winroth's analysis shows that the sections on marriage in the earlier recension were expanded in the second.

125. Gratian, *Decretum*, pars 2 c. 27 q. 2 dictum ad 34, in Emil Friedberg, ed., *Corpus Juris Canonici*, 1:1073.

126. Colish, *Peter Lombard*, is the standard work, with an excellent discussion of theologians and canonists on marriage at 2:628–98.

127. On disputation as a genre, see Alex Novikoff, *The Culture of Disputation* (Philadelphia: University of Pennsylvania Press, forthcoming).

128. Peter Lombard, *Sententiae in IV libris distinctae*, bk. 4, dist. 27, chaps. 2–3, ed. Ignatius Brady, 2:422. Although this is the efficient cause, the final cause is the procreation of children.

129. Ibid., bk. 4, dist. 27, chap. 3, vol. 2:435: "We say therefore that consent to cohabit or to carnal coupling does not make a marriage, but consent to conjugal society, expressed in words of the present tense, as when a man says 'I take you as my' not lady, not maid, but wife."

130. Ibid., bk. 4, dist. 26, vol. 2:416–17, quotation at chap. 6, pp. 419–20.

131. The best summary of this synthesis is in Charles Donahue, Jr., *Law, Marriage, and Society in the Later Middle Ages*, 14–45. Decretals of Alexander III are incorporated along with those of other popes on marriage in the *Liber Extra*, compiled by Raymond of Penafort for Gregory IX, bk. 4, Friedberg 2:661–732.

132. Charles Donahue, Jr., "The Canon Law on the Formation of Marriage and Social Practice in the Later Middle Ages," *Journal of Family History* 8 (1983): 44–58, here 45.

133. Christiane Klapisch-Zuber, *Women, Family, and Ritual in Renaissance Italy*, 179–80.

134. Margaret Paston to Sir John Paston, 1469, in *The Paston Letters*, ed. James Gairdner, 6 vols. (London: Chatto & Windus, 1904), 5:38–39. See Colin Richmond, *The Paston Family in the Fifteenth Century*, 94–95.

135. C. 30, q. 5, c. 6, quoting the Council of Orleans. His dictum here notes that the point is that nuptials that are not public are prohibited, but he does not conclude that they are invalid.

136. For practice in London, see Shannon McSheffrey, *Marriage, Sex, and Civic Culture in Late Medieval London*, esp. 27–32 and 121–34; for Florence, see Klapisch-Zuber, 178–96.

137. Clandestine marriage will be further discussed in Chapter 4. The term, as we will see, could be used in a variety of ways; in London, e.g., it was used for marriages contracted at church but not properly solemnized. McSheffrey, *Marriage, Sex, and Civic Culture*, 31.

138. John W. Baldwin, *Masters, Princes and Merchants*, 1:335, quoted in Latin on 2:225 n. 179.

139. Donahue, *Law, Marriage, and Society*, presents a number of cases in which complicated negotiations were likely going on behind the scenes and people were, if not lying, twisting their stories to conform them to what the courts needed to hear. See, e.g., 52–57.

140. Jim Bradbury, *Philip Augustus*, 58.

141. John W. Baldwin, *The Government of Philip Augustus: Foundations of French Royal Power in the Middle Ages* (Berkeley: University of California Press, 1986), 82–83.

142. Rigord, *Gesta Philippi Augusti*, 92, 1:125.

143. James M. Powell, trans., *The Deeds of Pope Innocent III by an Anonymous Author*, 48 (Washington, D.C.: Catholic University of America Press, 2004), 64.

144. John W. Baldwin, "The Many Loves of Philip Augustus," 68.

145. Powell, *Deeds of Pope Innocent III*, 48, p. 64.

146. Rigord, 92, 124–25.

147. Bradbury, 178–79.

148. On bad breath and the possibility that he found her not to be a virgin, see William of Newburgh, *Historia Rerum Anglicarum Willelmi Parvi*, 4:26, ed. Hans Claude Hamilton, 2 vols. (London: English Historical Society, 1856), 2:78.

149. Bradbury, 180, makes the suggestion that Ingeborg may have been too pure.

150. Jane Sayers, *Innocent III: Leader of Europe 1198–1216* (London: Longman, 1994), 116.

151. Powell, *Deeds of Pope Innocent III*, 49, p. 65. I have modified Powell's translation here based on the original.

152. Celestine III letters, *PL*, 206:1095c, 1098b.

153. *Epistolae sancti Guillelmi abbatis s. Thomae de Paracleto*, 7, in *Recueil des historiens des Gaules et de la France* 19, ed. Michel-Jean-Joseph Brial (Paris: Imprimerie Royale, 1833), 314. Ingeborg's letters to and from her Danish advisers are also included in this collection.

154. Innocent's activity in this regard is summarized in John C. Moore, *Pope Innocent III (1160/61–1216): To Root Up and to Plant* (Leiden: Brill, 2003), 58–63.

155. *Die Register Innocenz III*, vol. 1, ed. Othmar Hageneder and Anton Haidacher (Graz: Böhlau, 1964), letter 171, 243–46, quotation at 246.

156. As pointed out by Raymonde Foreville, *Le Pape Innocent III et la France*, 301.

157. Rigord, 136, 1:150–51.

158. William of Newburgh, 4:32, vol. 2:94, and Robert Davidsohn, *Philip II: August von Frankreich und Ingeborg* (Stuttgart: J. G. Cotta, 1888), 51.

159. William of Newburgh, 5:16, vol. 2:167.

160. Ibid., 5:16, 2:167.

161. Powell, *Deeds of Innocent III*, 53, p. 68.

162. Ibid., 54, p. 70.

163. Davidsohn, 172–73.

164. See Foreville, 300–305, on this process.

165. Baldwin, "The Many Loves of Philip Augustus," 73; Colish, 2:673–85, and Adhémar Esmein, *Le marriage en droit canonique*, 1:232–67, esp. 256–57, for more detailed discussion of the development of law on this point.

166. Ingeborg to Celestine I, 1196, *Epistolae sancti Guillelmi*, 17, p. 320.

167. Jean Gaudemet, "Le dossier canonique du mariage."

168. *Die Register Innocenz III*, letter 4, 1:11, and Baldwin, "The Many Loves of Philip Augustus," 75. This is the phrasing from 1198

169. Davidsohn, 254–70.

170. Innocent III to Philip II, *Die Register Innocenz III*, 6:180, p. 300. See Gaudemet, 19–20. On the meaning of the metaphor, see Torben K. Nielsen and Kurt Villads Jensen, "Pope Innocent III and Denmark," in *Innocenzo III: Urbs et orbis*, ed. Andrea Sommerlechner, Istituto storico italiano per il medio evo, Nuovi studi storici 55 (Rome: Società Romana di storia patria, 2003), 1133–68, here 1145.

171. Ingeborg to Innocent III, *Die Register Innocenz III*, vol. 6, no. 85, ed. Othmar Hageneder, John C. Moore, and Andrea Sommerlechner, Publikationen der Abteilung für

historische Studien des Österreichishen Kulturinstituts in Rom, Abt. 1, Reihe 1, vol. 6 (Vienna: Österreichishen Akademie der Wissenschaften, 1995), 133.

172. Étienne de Tournai, *Epistolae*, 262; *PL*, 211:525.

173. Ingeborg to Celestine, 1196, *Epistolae sancti Guillielmi*, 17, p. 320.

174. Bradbury, 181.

175. Davidsohn, 228.

176. Ingeborg to Innocent, 6:85, p. 134.

177. See Gratian, C. 15, q. 6, c. 1.

178. Gaudemet, 24.

179. Donahue, *Law, Marriage, and Society*, 16–17.

180. That marriage was dissolved by a council of French bishops and did not occasion a struggle between the French and Roman churches as did Philip and Ingeborg's; this is perhaps less of an indication of the relative power of the institutions and more due to the fact that the two parties were in agreement.

181. See Brian Tierney, "*Tria quippe distinguit iudicia . . .* : A Note on Innocent III's Decretal *Per Venerabilem*," *Speculum* 37 (1962): 48–59.

CHAPTER 2

1. On the origins of Christian law on "disparity of cult," see Hagith Sivan, "Why Not Marry a Jew? Jewish-Christian Marital Frontiers in Late Antiquity," in *Law, Society, and Authority in Late Antiquity*, ed. Ralph W. Mathisen (Oxford: Oxford University Press, 2001), 208–19, and "Rabbinics and Roman Law: Jewish-Christian Marriage in Late Antiquity," *Revue des études juives* 156 (1997): 59–100.

2. Megan McLaughlin, *Sex, Gender, and Episcopal Authority*, 27, notes that Ivo of Chartres declared unions between serfs and free people invalid as marriages, but I read Ivo as being somewhat equivocal on this issue if the free person knew the unfree status of the partner before the marriage. Ivo of Chartres, *Epistolae*, 242, *PL*, 162:249–50.

3. See Jenny Jochens, "The Politics of Reproduction: Medieval Norwegian Kingship," *American Historical Review* 92 (1987): 327–49, for a medieval example of this process.

4. See Jack Goody, *The Development of the Family and Marriage in Europe*.

5. This argument is forcefully made by Debra Blumenthal, *Enemies and Familiars*.

6. This simplifies a complicated issue, on which my views are still similar to those I set out in my *Slavery and Society in Medieval Scandinavia*, esp. chap. 1, "Slavery and Servitude in Medieval European Society," 5–39.

7. James Brundage, *Law, Sex, and Christian Society in Medieval Europe* (Chicago: University of Chicago Press, 1981), 196, and Anders Winroth, "Neither Slave nor Free," 97–109. The laws about "unfree persons," or *servi*, applied to what we call serfs as well as slaves.

8. See Michael L. Satlow, *Jewish Marriage in Antiquity*, 158, on the talmudic view on this.

9. In the section on different religions, especially, I rely on the works of other scholars who have linguistic expertise that I lack.

10. Judith M. Bennett and Amy M. Froide, eds., *Singlewomen in the European Past 1250–1800* (Philadelphia: University of Pennsylvania Press, 1999), and Cordelia Beattie, *Medieval Single Women*.

11. A single woman known to be in a sexual relationship with a man to whom she was not married would have had a hard time making charges of rape or battery stick, but the law would not compel her to remain in the union.

12. Georges Duby, *Medieval Marriage: Two Models from Twelfth-Century France* (Baltimore: Johns Hopkins University Press, 1978), 93.

13. Cameron Bradley and Ruth Mazo Karras, "Masculine Sexuality and a Double Standard in Early Thirteenth-Century Flanders?" *Leidschrift* 25 (2010): 63–77.

14. There is now a detailed biography by Alison Weir: *Mistress of the Monarchy*. Weir's research is thorough; she makes a lot of conjectures but is always careful to label them as such. See also discussion in Anthony Goodman, *John of Gaunt*, esp. 362–64. As to her family status, Weir discusses and dismisses the idea that Katherine's family was closely related to the ruling family of Hainault (8).

15. Weir dates the marriage to no later than 1365 and possibly as early as 1362.

16. Jean Froissart, *Oeuvres de Froissart*, ed. Kervyn de Lettenhove, 4:73, mentions that it was during the lifetime of Blanche of Lancaster, but other sources make it unlikely that this was the case. The date of Hugh Swynford's death is unclear (Weir, 110, says that it was 13 November 1371), as is the exact date of the birth of Katherine and John of Gaunt's first son, John de Beaufort, between 1371 and 1373. Richard III, in contesting Henry Tudor's claim to the throne, claimed that Henry's ancestor John de Beaufort was conceived "in double adultery," i.e., while both Katherine and John had living spouses. See references in G. E. Cokayne, *The Complete Peerage*, rev. Geoffrey H. White (London: St. Catherine Press, 1953), 12:40 n. a, and Simon Walker, "Katherine, Duchess of Lancaster (1350?–1403)," *Oxford Dictionary of National Biography* (Oxford: Oxford University Press online ed., 2008), http://www.oxforddnb.com/view/article/26858. There is also dispute over the date of birth of Thomas Swynford, Hugh and Katherine's son; see Weir, 89–90. Sydney Armitage-Smith, *John of Gaunt, King of Castile and Leon, Duke of Aquitaine and Lancaster, Earl of Derby, Lincoln, and Leicester, Seneschal of England* (1904; reprint, New York: Barnes and Noble, 1964), appendix 8, 462–63, lists Gaunt's gifts to Katherine and argues that they become significant starting in 1372; Walker believes that the union did not begin until after Hugh Swynford's death, as does Weir, 116, who suggests that the papal dispensation of 1398, which said that Katherine had been unmarried at the time of the adultery, is to be believed.

17. The gifts from Gaunt to Katherine may be found throughout *John of Gaunt's Register, 1372–1376*, ed. S. Armitage-Smith, 2 vols., Camden 3rd series, 20–21 (London: Camden Society, 1911), and *John of Gaunt's Register, 1379–1383*, ed. E. C. Lodge and R. Somerville, 2 vols., Camden 3rd series, 56–57 (London: Camden Society, 1937). Weir, passim, also recounts them in detail.

18. *Records of the Borough of Leicester*, ed. Mary Bateson (London: C. J. Clay and Sons, 1899), 155, 171.

19. Anya Seton, *Katherine* (Boston: Houghton Mifflin, 1954).

20. *Rotuli parliamentorum; ut et petitiones, et placita in parliamento*, John Strachey, ed., 3:343.

21. *Calendar of Entries in the Papal Registers Relating to Great Britain and Ireland*, vol. 4, *1362–1404* (London: HMSO, 1902), 545.

22. Froissart, 15:239–40.

23. Thomas Gascoigne, *Loci e Libro veritatum: Passages Selected from Gascoigne's Theological Dictionary Illustrating the Condition of Church and State, 1403–1458*, ed. J. E. Thorold Rogers (Oxford: Clarendon, 1881), 137.

24. *Chronicon Angliae*, s.a. 1378, ed. E. M. Thompson, Rolls Series, 64 (London, 1874), 196.

25. *Anonimalle Chronicle 1333–1381*, ed. V. H. Galbraith (Manchester: Manchester University Press, 1927), 153.

26. Henry Knighton, *Chronicon*, ed. J. R. Lumby, Rolls Series, 92 (London, 1895), 147–48.

27. Thomas Walsingham, *Historia Anglicana*, s.a. 1381, ed. H. T. Riley, Rolls Series, 28:1 (London, 1863–64), 2:43.

28. Weir, 201–2.

29. Testament of John of Gaunt, duke of Lancaster, in Armitage-Smith, *John of Gaunt*, appendix 1, 420–36.

30. John of Trokelowe, *Chronica et Annales*, ed. H. T. Riley, Rolls Series, 28 (London, 1866), 3:314.

31. Armitage-Smith, *John of Gaunt*, appendix 5, 451. The decoration of Katherine's own tomb in Lincoln cathedral did not survive the Civil War, but in 1641, the antiquary William Dugdale included her tomb brass and that of her daughter in his *Book of Monuments*: BL, Add MS 71474, fol. 107. I thank Gabriel Hill for checking this citation for me.

32. Quoted in Carol Lansing, "Concubines, Lovers, Prostitutes," 93–94. Under canon law, if Zannos had promised to marry her after they had had children and subsequently had sexual intercourse with her, the condition would have become null and the marriage binding; however, the Bologna court was not applying canon law here.

33. Emlyn Eisenach, *Husbands, Wives, and Concubines: Marriage, Family, and Social Order in Sixteenth-Century Verona* (Kirksville, Mo.: Truman State University Press, 2004), 135.

34. Ibid., 144.

35. Lansing, 95–96.

36. See Eisenach, 148.

37. Alan Watson, *Roman Slave Law* (Baltimore: Johns Hopkins University Press, 1987), 10.

38. Judith Evans-Grubbs, "'Marriage More Shameful than Adultery,'" and Watson, 14–15.

39. Stefan Chr. Saar, *Ehe–Scheidung–Wiederheirat*, 128–29.

40. Evans-Grubbs, "'Marriage More Shameful than Adultery,'" 141–44.

41. Saar, 238–546, and Andrea Esmyol, *Geliebte oder Ehefrau?*, 132–33.

42. By this time, some scholars think that the term *servus* is well on its way to meaning "serf" rather than "slave," but the Latin term remained the same, and the distinction that is usually made in English between these two groups is a social/economic and not a legal one: the Roman law of slavery was still applied, depending on the region. For canon law, see John Gilchrist, "The Medieval Canon Law on Unfree Persons: Gratian and the Decretist Doctrines, c. 1141–1234," *Studia Gratiana* 19 (1976): 271–301, at 274–75; for English common law, see Paul Vinogradoff, *Villainage in England* (Oxford: Oxford University Press, 1892), 48, 127–28, although this is based on a dictum of the legal text known as *Bracton* and not actually applied in practice.

43. Decretum Vermeriense, 6–8, in *MGH, Legum sectio 2, Capitula regum Francorum*, ed. Alfred Boretius (Hannover: Hahn, 1883), 1:40. The council is dated to 756 by Gregory I. Halfond, *The Archaeology of Frankish Church Councils*, 243–44.

44. Concilium Triburense, c. 38, Additamenta ad capitularia regum Franciae orientalis, no. 252, in *MGH, Legum sectio 2, Capitularia regum Francorum*, ed. Alfred Boretius and Victor Krause (Hannover: Hahn, 1897), 2:235. The editor places "ingenua" in scare quotes.

45. Concilium Cabillonense, 30, *MGH, Concilia* 2:1, *Concilia Aevi Karolini* (Hannover: Hahn, 1906), 279.

46. Youval Rotman, *Byzantine Slavery and the Mediterranean World*, trans. Jane Marie Todd (Cambridge, Mass.: Harvard University Press, 2009), 142–43.

47. Winroth, 106.

48. Ibid., 108–9.

49. Gratian, *Decretum*, c. 29, 1:1091–95, and Winroth. Not all errors allow the defrauded party to invalidate the marriage: e.g., if the man thought the woman was chaste and she is a prostitute, he is still married to her. Gratian, c. 29, q. 1, 1:1091.

50. On this alleged custom, see Alain Boureau, *The Lord's First Night: The Myth of the Droit de Cuissage*, trans. Lydia G. Cochrane (Chicago: University of Chicago Press, 1998).

51. See David Herlihy, *Opera Muliebria: Women and Work in Medieval Europe* (Philadelphia: Temple University Press, 1990), 77–91.

52. For Venice, see Dennis Romano, *Housecraft and Statecraft*, 129–35.

53. Debra Blumenthal, *Enemies and Familiars*, 85–86.

54. David Herlihy and Christiane Klapisch-Zuber, *Tuscans and Their Families*, 112 n. 41, and Sally McKee, "Domestic Slavery in Renaissance Italy," 320. Susan Mosher Stuard argues that in Ragusa, there was a shift from female domestic slavery to contract labor by the early fourteenth century, although it did not result in an improvement in the status of these workers: "To Town to Serve," 48–51.

55. Jacques Heers, *Esclaves et domestiques au moyen-âge dans le monde méditerranéen*, 145–51, 154, discusses the situation of *anime*, who were technically free but sold into service and not paid.

56. Karras, *Slavery and Society in Medieval Scandinavia*, 134–40.

57. See Sven Ekdahl, "The Treatment of Prisoners of War during the Fighting between the Teutonic Order and Lithuania," in Malcolm Barber, ed., *The Military Orders* (Aldershot: Variorum, 1994), 1:263–69.

58. Olivia Remie Constable, *Trade and Traders in Muslim Spain* (Cambridge: Cambridge University Press, 1994); for sources of Muslim slaves in fifteenth-century Valencia, see Blumenthal, 10–20.

59. Heers, 129–30, and McKee, "Domestic Slavery," 319.

60. Susan Mosher Stuard, "Urban Domestic Slavery in Medieval Ragusa," *Journal of Medieval History* 9 (1983): 155–71, here 164.

61. Stephen Bensch, *Barcelona and Its Rulers, 1096–1291* (Cambridge: Cambridge University Press, 1994), 85. Bensch also notes that raiding and combat would have brought in more men than women and suggests that the preponderance of women on the market is due to demand rather than supply (79).

62. Mark Meyerson, "Prostitution of Muslim Women in the Kingdom of Valencia: Religious and Sexual Discrimination in a Medieval Plural Society," 87–95.

63. Susan M. Stuard, "Ancillary Evidence for the Decline of Medieval Slavery," *Past & Present* 149 (November 1995): 3–28, esp. 17–28.

64. Sally McKee, "The Implications of Slave Women's Sexual Service in Late Medieval Italy," 106.

65. Mark D. Meyerson, "Slavery and Solidarity: Mudejars and Foreign Muslim Captives in the Kingdom of Valencia," *Medieval Encounters* 2 (1996): 286–343, here 302.

66. Iris Origo, "The Domestic Enemy," 340, 345.

67. Stuard, "To Town to Serve," 165.

68. Charles Verlinden, *L'esclavage dans l'Europe*, 2:140–237.

69. William D. Phillips, Jr., *Slavery from Roman Times to the Early Transatlantic Trade*, 103–6.

70. Verlinden, 2:320.

71. Heers, 126.

72. Bensch, 82.

73. Verlinden, 2:263.

74. Blumenthal, 18, 40.

75. McKee, "Domestic Slavery," 307; see also Christoph Cluse, "Frauen in Sklaverei: Beobachtungen aus genuesischen Notariatsregistern des 14. und 15. Jahrhunderts," in *Campana pulsante convocati: Festschrift anläßlich der Emeritierung von Prof. Dr. Alfred Haverkamp*, ed. Frank G. Hirschmann and Gerd Mengten (Trier: Kliomedia, 2005), 85–123, here 91.

76. Verlinden, 2:616.

77. McKee, "The Implications of Slave Women's Sexual Service," 103.

78. Idem, "Domestic Slavery," 320; Cluse, 96–104, esp. 103–4, and Thomas Kuehn, *Illegitimacy in Renaissance Florence*, 111.

79. Heers, 228.

80. Steven Epstein, *Speaking of Slavery*, 132.

81. Kuehn, 143.

82. Alfonso Franco Silva, "Los negros libertos en las sociedades andaluzas entre los siglos XV al XVI," in *De l'esclavitud a la llibertat: Esclaus i lliberts a l'edat mitjana—Acts*

de Colloqui Internacional celebrat a Barcelona del 27 al 29 de maig de 1999, ed. Maria Teresa Ferrer i Mallol and Josefina Mutgé i Vivés (Barcelona: CSIC, 2000), 578.

83. McKee, "Domestic Slavery," 308–14; S. Epstein, 79–81, and Blumenthal, 272–77.

84. Guy Romestan, "Femmes esclaves à Perpignan aux XIVe et XVe siècles," 189.

85. Blumenthal, 56.

86. McKee, "Implications of Sexual Service," 104.

87. S. Epstein, 99–100, on the penalty for rape of slaves belonging to another owner.

88. Cited and translated in Blumenthal, 88, 131–32.

89. Meyerson, 302.

90. Blumenthal, 215–16.

91. Meyerson, 302.

92. Blumenthal, 87–88, 92–93.

93. Origo, 321–66.

94. Blumenthal, 174–89.

95. Ibid., 192.

96. Trevor Burnard, *Mastery, Tyranny, and Desire: Thomas Thistlewood and His Slaves in the Anglo-Jamaican World* (Chapel Hill: University of North Carolina Press, 2004), 211. See 228–40 for the story of Phibbah, mistress of Thomas Thistlewood, who was able to accumulate property and improve her family's status.

97. Heers, 198.

98. See, e.g., for some cases from Chios: Laura Balletto, "Schiavi e manomessi nella chio del genovesi nel secolo XV," in *De l'esclavitud a la llibertat,* 659–94.

99. Heers, 216.

100. Verlinden, 2:380.

101. Maria Serena Mazzi, *Prostitute e lenoni nella Firenze del Quattrocento* (Milan: Il Saggiatore, 1991), 119.

102. Blumenthal, 169–72.

103. Sally McKee, "Greek Women in Latin Households of Fourteenth-Century Venetian Crete," 240–41.

104. Verlinden, 2:248.

105. S. Epstein, 130.

106. For Florentine examples, see Kuehn, 193.

107. G. Pistarino, "Fra liberti e schiave a Genova nel Quattrocento," *Anuario de Estudios Medievales* 1 (1964): 343–74, here 365.

108. Pistarino, 373, and Luigi Tria, *La Schiavitù in Liguria,* 86.

109. McKee, "Greek Women," 230, 241.

110. McKee, "Inherited Status and Slavery in Late Medieval Italy and Venetian Crete," 47–48.

111. McKee, "Greek Women," 240, and "Inherited Status and Slavery," 37.

112. Cited and translated in Blumenthal, 261.

113. Heers, 229. See Blumenthal, 260–65, on the status of slave children in Valencia.

114. Sally McKee, "Households in Fourteenth-Century Venetian Crete," 54–55.

115. Sally McKee, ed., *Wills from Late Medieval Venetian Crete (1312–1420)*, 3 vols. (Washington, D.C.: Dumbarton Oaks, 1997), 1:343, 361.

116. McKee, "Greek Women," 245–46.

117. Origo, 345.

118. Silva, 578.

119. Heers, 272; for Ragusa, see Stuard, "To Town to Serve," 170.

120. *Regesten der Lübecker Bürgertestamente des Mittelalters*, ed. Ahasver von Brandt, Veröffentlichungen zur Geschichte der Hansestadt Lübeck, Bd. 24 (Lübeck: M. Schmidt-Römhild, 1964), 1:172.

121. S. Epstein, 36.

122. Kuehn, 41; see also David Nicholas, *The Domestic Life of a Medieval City: Women, Children, and the Family in Fourteenth-Century Ghent* (Lincoln: University of Nebraska Press, 1985), 104.

123. Franciscus Accoltus, *Consilia domini Francisci de Aretio*, 48 (Lyon: Vincentius de Portonariis, 1536), fol. 39r–v.

124. Ingrid Baumgärtner, "Consilia: Quellen zur Familie in Krise und Kontinuität," in *Die Familie als sozialer und historischer Verband: Untersuchungen zum Spätmittelalter und zur frühen Neuzeit*, ed. Peter-Johannes Schuler (Sigmaringen: Thorbecke, 1987), 43–66, here 45.

125. On the relation of *ius proprium* and *ius comune*, see Manlio Bellomo, *The Common Legal Past of Europe*, trans. Lydia G. Cochrane (Washington, D.C.: Catholic University of America Press, 1995), 78–111, 149–202.

126. Kuehn, 36.

127. See S. Epstein, 130.

128. Ludovicus Pontanus, *Consilia D. Ludovici de Ponte Romani*, 194 (Frankfurt: Sigmund Feyerabendt , 1577), fols. 97v–98r. He is careful to note that this conclusion assumes that the father did not have legitimate or natural children already and that the mother had not married another man (in which case, it would not have been possible for the parents to marry, and therefore the child would be considered spurious). He does not discuss the father's marital status.

129. Trans. in Kuehn, 92.

130. Trans. in ibid., 254.

131. Benedictus de Benedictis, *Consilia Benedicti Caprae Perusini ac Ludovici Bolognini Bononiensis*, 127, fols. 163v–164r.

132. S. Epstein, 24. Epstein suggests that the objection was that the woman was of a different race; the passage he quotes does not say this explicitly, but this is his sense of it.

133. Franciscus Curtius, *Reportorium de novo excusum* 136 (Lyon: Vincentius de Portonariis and Jacques de Giuntes, 1584), fol. 64v.

134. Blumenthal, 170–74.

135. Kuehn, 131.

136. Guido Ruggiero, *The Boundaries of Eros: Sex Crime and Sexuality in Renaissance Venice* (New York: Oxford University Press, 1985), 45–69.

137. Angelus de Gambilionibus, *Consiliorum siue responsorum Angeli de Gambilionibus* 74 (Venice: Apud Marcum Amadorum, 1576), 283.

138. Curtius, fol. 64r.

139. The painter Parmigianino, born in 1503, was also named Francesco de Mazolis; as names were often passed on in the same family, this could have been a relative.

140. Bartolomeo Cipolla, *Consilia Criminalis Celeberrimi D. Bartholomei Caepollae Veronensis* 26, fols. 59v–60.

141. For Venice (whose currency the ducat was), the dowries of servants ranged from thirty to two hundred ducats; in the latter case, it is not clear that that was all wages. Romano, 155–64.

142. This caused some controversy during the late 1990s and early 2000s as a for-profit company, deCODE, received legal access to the medical records of all Icelanders. It has also become a plot point in some contemporary Icelandic detective fiction.

143. This simplifies a complex scientific discussion. See Agnar Helgason et al., "Estimating Scandinavian and Gaelic Ancestry in the Male Settlers of Iceland," *American Journal of Human Genetics* 67 (2000): 697–717; Agnar Helgason et al., "mtDNA and the Origin of the Icelanders," *American Journal of Human Genetics* 66 (2000): 999–1016.

144. *Laxdæla saga*, 12, in *Íslendinga sögur*, ed. Bragi Halldórsson et al., 3:1546, trans. in *The Complete Sagas of Icelanders*, ed. Viðar Hreinsson et al. (Reykjavík: Leifur Eiríksson, 1997), 5:11.

145. *Laxdæla saga*, 13, trans. p. 12.

146. *The Book of Settlements, Landnámabók*, 105, trans. Hermann Pálsson and Paul Edwards, University of Manitoba Icelandic Studies 1 (Winnipeg: University of Manitoba Press, 1972), 54, says that Hoskuld had two sons with the slave, so even if Olaf had been conceived before Hoskuld's return to Iceland, they must have resumed sexual relations at some point. The saga only names one son from the union; it also disagrees with *Landnámabók* on other points, such as the name of Hoskuld's wife.

147. *Laxdæla saga*, 13; trans. p. 13.

148. Ibid., 20; trans. p. 24.

149. Ibid., 23; trans. p. 32.

150. This appears only in a seventeenth-century manuscript of the work, but modern editors think that it may go back to a very early exemplar. Pálsson and Edwards, 6.

151. Else Ebel, *Der Konkubinat nach altwestnordischen Quellen: Philologische Studien zur sogenannten "Friedelehe"* (Berlin: Walter de Gruyter, 1993), 105.

152. Agnes S. Arnórsdóttir, "Two Models of Marriage? Canon Law and Icelandic Marriage Practice in the Late Middle Ages," in *Nordic Perspectives on Medieval Canon Law*, ed. Mia Korpiola (Helsinki: Matthias Calonius Society, 1999), 79–92, here 82.

153. The similar story of the *frilla* Nereiður in *Vatnsdæla saga*, whose son successfully claims kinship with the earl of Orkney through his mother, is likely derived from the *Laxdæla saga* story. *Vatnsdæla saga*, 37, 42, in *Íslendinga sögur*, 3:1888, 1896–97, and E. Ebel, 52.

154. *Brennu-Njáls saga*, 25, in *Íslendinga sögur*, 1:154.

155. Richard Cleasby and Gudbrand Vigfusson, *An Icelandic-English Dictionary*, 2d

ed., William A. Craigie (Oxford: Clarendon, 1957), s.v. "elja" defines it as "concubine" and says that it is "wrongly" used in *Njál's saga*, where it is used by Hrodny about Bergthora. None of the examples cited in the definition clearly refers to concubines, however; the term was used to translate "wife" in biblical passages that refer to plural marriage, e.g., Lev. 18:18, 1 Sam. 1:6. It seems a bit presumptuous for a modern scholar to assert that the only time the word appears in the Icelandic sagas, the saga writer has used it erroneously.

156. *Brennu-Njáls saga*, 116, 1:262; 124, 1:275.

157. *Vopnfirðinga saga*, 6, in *Íslendinga sögur*, 3:1992–93.

158. *Egils saga Skallagrímssonar*, 57, in *Íslendinga sögur*, 1:444.

159. Karras, *Slavery and Society in Medieval Scandinavia*, 135–36.

160. Snorri Sturluson, *Haralds saga ins harfagra*, 37, ed. Bjarni Aðalbjarnarson, Íslensk fornrit 26 (Reykjavík: Hið Íslenzka fornritafélag, 1951), 143, and *Olafs saga Helga*, 122, ibid., 27:209. See E. Ebel, 63–71.

161. *Grágás: Islændernes lovbog i fristatens tid*, 118, ed. Vilhjálmur Finsen (Copenhagen: Berling, 1852), 219.

162. Ibid., 113, p. 201.

163. Gulathing law, 104, in *Norges gamle love indtil 1387* [*NGL*], ed. R. Keyser and P. A. Munch, 1:48. Cf. Frostathing law, 10:47, *NGL*, 1:228.

164. The Frostathing law refers to the situation when the man "lies with her at home in the house," as opposed to the type of relationship in which the intercourse takes place in the woods, implying that the publicity is the important factor. See Ruth Mazo Karras, "The History of Marriage and the Myth of *Friedelehe*," *Early Medieval Europe* 14 (2006): 134–35.

165. "Kong Sverres Christenret," 69, *NGL*, 1:428, and Arne Boe, "Kristenretter," *Kulturhistoriskt Lexikon för Nordisk Medeltid* (Malmö: Allhems forlag, 1964), 9:301.

166. Gulathing law 125, *NGL*, 1:54; cf. "Ældre Borgarthings-Christenret," 2:10, *NGL*, 1:357.

167. "Kong Haakon Magnussöns förste Rettebod for Island," 4, *NGL*, 4:347–48. The Swedish and Danish law codes are later and more clearly influenced by canon law; I have discussed them in my "History of Marriage," 135–36.

168. Ruth Mazo Karras, "Concubinage and Slavery in the Viking Age," *Scandinavian Studies* 62 (1990): 141-62.

169. McKee, "Domestic Slavery," 313–14.

170. It is especially in Iberia where all three groups were present that this was the case. See Brian Catlos, *The Victors and the Vanquished*, 305–7, and David Nirenberg, *Communities of Violence*, 127–65, for a full account of attitudes toward "miscegenation" among all three communities.

171. Elisheva Baumgarten, *Mothers and Children: Jewish Family Life in Medieval Europe* (Princeton, N.J.: Princeton University Press, 2004), 8, 136.

172. Avraham Grossman, *Pious and Rebellious: Jewish Women in Medieval Europe* (Waltham, Mass.: Brandeis University Press, 2004), 137, and S. D. Goitein, *A Mediterranean Society: The Jewish Communities of the Arab World as Portrayed in the Documents of the Cairo Geniza*, vol. 3, *The Family* (Berkeley: University of California Press; reprint, 2000), 48. Such provisions were not found in Ashkenaz, where polygyny was much less common.

173. Elliott Horowitz, "The Worlds of Jewish Youth in Europe," in *Ancient and Medieval Rites of Passage*, vol. 1 of *A History of Young People in the West*, ed. Giovanni Levi and Jean-Claude Schmitt, trans. Camille Naish (Cambridge, Mass.: Harvard University Press, 1997), 83–119, here 110, and Isidore Epstein, *Responsa of Solomon ibn Adreth of Barcelona (1235–1310) as a Source of the History of Spain: Studies in the Communal Life of the Jews in Spain as Reflected in the "Responsa"* (London: K. Paul, Trench, Trübner, 1925; reprint, 1982), 1:610, 4:314.

174. Avraham Grossman, "The Historical Background to the Ordinances on Family Affairs Attributed to Rabbenu Gershom Me'or ha-Golah," and Ze'ev W. Falk, *Jewish Matrimonial Law in the Middle Ages* (Oxford: Oxford University Press, 1966), 1–16.

175. Grossman, *Pious and Rebellious*, 137.

176. Chaim ben Isaac Or Zarua, *Sefer she'elot u-teshuvot Maharach Or Zarua*, 50, ed. Yehuda Romberg (Leipzig: Vollrath, 1860), 14.

177. Asher ben Yehiel, *She'elot u-teshuvot*, 32:1 (Vilna: L. L. Maza, 1881), 62.

178. Horowitz, 111, and Nissim ben Reuben Gerondi, *She'elot u-teshuvot*, 68, ed. Aryeh L. Feldman (Jerusalem: Mekhon Shalom, 1968), 305.

179. Concilium Lateranense IV, 68, *Concilium Oecumenicorum Decreta*, ed. Joseph Alberigo et al. (Basel: Herder, 1962), 242.

180. Jacob b. Judah Weil, *She'elot u-teshuvot*, 8 (Jerusalem, 1959; reprint, Bar-Ilan University, http://www.responsa.co.il), and Asher b. Yehiel, *She'elot u-teshuvot le-Rabenu Asher ben Yehiel* (Jerusalem: Makhon or hamizrah, 1993), 32:7.

181. *Sefer Hasidim*, portions translated into German in Susanne Borchers, *Jüdisches Frauenleben im Mittelalter* (Frankfurt am Main: Lang, 1998), 240.

182. Grossman, *Pious and Rebellious*, 144.

183. Joseph ben Moses, *Sefer leket yosher*, 1:121:1, ed. Yaakov Freimann (Berlin, 1903; reprint, Jerusalem: n.p., 1964), trans. David Shyovitz. The context is not a legal case involving such behavior but a discussion of the etymology of the word for "barley," which is derived from the word for "hell."

184. Ariel Toaff, *Love, Work, and Death: Jewish Life in Medieval Umbria*, trans. Judith Landry (London: Littman Library of Jewish Civilization, 1996), 6, 12.

185. Shlomo Simonsohn, *The Apostolic See and the Jews*, 1:527. I thank Susan Einbinder for this reference.

186. *Consilium* 333, trans. in Norman Zacour, *Jews and Saracens in the Consilia of Oldradus de Ponte* (Toronto: PIMS, 1990), 68, and Nirenberg, 131.

187. Caesarius of Heisterbach, *Dialogus Miraculorum*, 2:23, vol. 1:102, and Ivan G. Marcus, "Jews and Christians Imagining the Other in Medieval Europe," *Prooftexts* 15 (1995): 209–26, esp. 218–22.

188. Nirenberg, 144–48; see also idem, "Conversion, Sex, and Segregation: Jews and Christians in Medieval Spain," *American Historical Review* 107 (2002): 1065–93 (quotations at 1066, 1075). The reproductive logic that was concerned with purity of blood did not begin until the 1430s or 1440s and was a different process.

189. Meyerson, 87–95.

190. Nirenberg, 136–38.

191. Ibid., 140.

192. Catlos, 307.

193. Nirenberg, 132.

194. Maria Teresa Ferrer i Mallol, *Els Sarraïns de la Corona Catalano-Aragonesa en el segle XIV: Segregació i Discriminació* (Barcelona: CSIC, 1987), 17–39.

195. On the *herem*, see Nirenberg, 130. For the views of the rabbis, see I. Epstein, 88; Ephraim Kanarfogel, "Rabbinic Attitudes toward Nonobservance in the Medieval Period," in *Jewish Tradition and the Nontraditional Jew*, ed. Jacob J. Schachter (Northvale, N.J.: Jason Aronson, 1992), 3–36, here 17–23.

196. See Yom Tov Assis, "Sexual Behavior in Mediaeval Hispano-Jewish Society," in Ada Rapoport-Albert and Steven J. Zipperstein, *Jewish History* (London: P. Halban, 1988), 25–59, at 36–37, in which he notes that Jewish men were more likely to have Muslim concubines in Christian Spain and Christian concubines in Muslim Spain. Even poor men had concubines, who could be less expensive to maintain than wives.

197. Kanarfogel, 31.

198. Paola Tartakoff, *Between Christian and Jew: Conversion and Inquisition in the Medieval Crown of Aragon* (Philadelphia: University of Pennsylvania Press, forthcoming 2012). The papacy consistently ruled that Jews or others who converted to Christianity and were married within the degrees of relationship forbidden by Christianity, including levirate marriage, could remain married. Simonsohn, *The Apostolic See and the Jews*, 1:65 (Clement II, 1187–91); 1:72 (Innocent III, 11:98); 1:79 (Innocent III, 1201); 2:586 (Benedict XIII, 1415; in this case, in Toledo, it was a couple who had been betrothed but not married while Jews); 2:592 (Benedict XIII, 1415); 2:684 (Martin V, 1419).

199. Tartakoff.

200. Simonsohn, 2:1337.

CHAPTER 3

1. On clerical marriage in the early church, which I do not attempt to cover here, Helen Parish, *Clerical Celibacy in the West*, 15–86, provides an excellent summary.

2. Of course, there were priests who had sexual relations with other men. I know of no examples, however, where they lived in long-term domestic partnerships that were also sexual. I do not doubt that some such unions existed, but I will not talk about them without evidence. There is evidence for relationships between monks or between nuns, but because of the communal context, I would not call these "quasi-marital."

3. On pollution, see Dyan Elliott, *Fallen Bodies: Pollution, Sexuality, and Demonology in the Middle Ages* (Philadelphia: University of Pennsylvania Press, 1999), esp. 82ff.

4. Megan McLaughlin, "The Case Against Clerical Wives," unpublished article.

5. Jo Ann McNamara, "The *Herrenfrage*: The Restructuring of the Gender System, 1050–1150," in *Medieval Masculinities: Regarding Men in the Middle Ages*, ed. Clare A. Lees

and Thelma Fenster (Minneapolis: University of Minnesota Press, 1994), 3–30, and Jacqueline Murray, "One Flesh, Two Sexes, Three Genders?," in *Gender and Christianity in Medieval Europe: New Perspectives*, ed. Lisa M. Bitel and Felice Lifshitz (Philadelphia: University of Pennsylvania Press, 2008), 52–75.

6. Lyndal Roper, *The Holy Household: Women and Morals in Reformation Augsburg* (Oxford: Clarendon, 1991), and Stephen Ozment, *When Fathers Ruled*.

7. On the history of clerical marriage, see Parish, *Clerical Celibacy*, and Ann Llewellyn Barstow, *Married Priests and the Reforming Papacy*. Most of this chapter was written before Parish's book came into my hands, so in many cases for which we use the same sources, I have not relied on her work; I cite her work below on points for which I have.

8. First Lateran Council 7 and 21, Second Lateran Council 6 and 7, in Joseph Alberigo et al., eds., *Conciliorum oecumenicorum decreta*, 2nd ed. (Basel: Herder, 1967), 2:167, 170, 174; see Martin Boelens, "Die Klerikerehe in der kirchlichen Gesetzgebung vom II. Lateranzonzil bis zum Konzil von Basel." For general accounts of the establishment of clerical celibacy, see Jean Gaudemet, "Le célibat ecclésiastique: Le droit et la pratique du XIe au XIIIe siècles," *Zeitschrift der Savigny-Stiftung für Rechtsgeschicht: Kanonistische Abteilung* 68 (1982): 1–31, and Charles Frazee, "The Origins of Clerical Celibacy in the Western Church," *Church History* 57, supp. (1988): 108–26. See also Brundage, *Law, Sex, and Christian Society*, 220.

9. Gaudemet, "Le célibat ecclésiastique," 3.

10. The articles in Michael Frassetto, ed., *Medieval Purity and Piety*, comprise a good statement of this consensus; see also Megan McLaughlin, *Sex, Gender, and Episcopal Authority*, 31–32.

11. Amy Remensnyder, "Pollution, Purity, and Peace: An Aspect of Social Reform Between the Late Tenth Century and 1076," in *The Peace of God: Social Violence and Religious Response in France Around the Year 1000*, ed. Thomas Head and Richard Landes (Ithaca, N.Y.: Cornell University Press, 1992), 280–307, here 294, and McLaughlin, *Sex, Gender, and Episcopal Authority*, 32.

12. Although, as Remensnyder argues, clerical as well as lay violence was a concern of the eleventh-century peace movement.

13. H. E. J. Cowdrey, *Pope Gregory VII 1073–1085* (Oxford: Clarendon, 1998), 543–46, 550–54. On the interconnectedness of clerical sexual activity, use of weapons, and simony in "one complex of pollution fears," see Remensnyder, 280–307; see also McLaughlin, *Sex, Gender, and Episcopal Authority*, 68–77.

14. Conrad Leyser, "Custom, Truth, and Gender in Eleventh-Century Reform," 77, and Cowdrey, 545.

15. Hugh M. Thomas will address this in his work in progress, tentatively titled *The English Secular Clergy in the Twelfth-Century Renaissance*.

16. See Peter Biller, *The Measure of Multitude: Population in Medieval Thought* (Oxford: Oxford University Press, 2000), 19–59, 111–32.

17. James A. Brundage, "Concubinage and Marriage in Medieval Canon Law," *Journal of Medieval History* 1 (1975): 1–17; McLaughlin, *Sex, Gender, and Episcopal Authority*, 34–35, and Second Lateran Council 6, in Alberigo, 174.

18. Peter Damian, letter 61, *Die Briefe des Petrus Damiani*, 4 vols., ed. K. Reindel, *MGH*: Die Briefe der deutschen Kaiserzeit 4.1–4 (Munich, 1983–93), 2:214–16. For more on Damian, see Elliott, *Fallen Bodies*, 95–106.

19. Damian, letter 112, ed. Reindel, 3:278–79. See McLaughlin, "The Bishop as Bridegroom: Marital Imagery and Clerical Celibacy in the Eleventh and Early Twelfth Centuries," in Frassetto, 223–24, and Elliott, *Fallen Bodies*, 101.

20. Damian, Letter 112, ed. Reindel, 3:270.

21. For Damian's influence in the eleventh and twelfth centuries, esp. on Manegold of Lautenbach, see Barstow, 77–79.

22. Humbert of Silva Candida, "Responsio sive contradictio adversus Nicetai pectorati libellum," 21 and 26, in Cornelius Will, ed., *Acta et scripta quae de controversiis ecclesiae Graecae et Latinae saeculo undecimo composita extant* (Lippe: G. Elmert, 1861), 137, 147. On Gregory VII's views on purity (albeit in more restrained language), see James A. Brundage, "Sexuality, Marriage, and the Reform of Christian Society in the Thought of Gregory VII," *Studi Gregoriani* 15 (1991): 68–73.

23. Parish, *Clerical Celibacy*, 111.

24. I thank Hugh Thomas for the permission to quote the Agnellus sermon from his unpublished *English Secular Clergy.*

25. See Phyllis Jestice, "Why Celibacy? Odo of Cluny and the Development of a New Sexual Morality," in Frassetto, 81–115, here 93ff., for earlier expressions.

26. R. I. Moore, "Property, Marriage, and the Eleventh-Century Revolution: A Context for Early Medieval Communism," in Frassetto, 179–208, here 190; see also Moore, *The First European Revolution, c. 970–1215* (Oxford: Blackwell, 2000), 87–88, on the lack of reproduction, which in the Middle Ages was an inextricable part of sexual activity.

27. Mark D. Jordan, *The Invention of Sodomy in Christian Theology* (Chicago: University of Chicago Press, 1998), 29–66.

28. Leyser, 86–87, and Maureen Miller, "Masculinity, Reform, and Clerical Culture: Narratives of Episcopal Holiness in the Gregorian Era," *Church History* 72 (2003): 28–52, here 49.

29. McLaughlin, "The Case Against Clerical Wives."

30. Erwin Frauenknecht, *Die Verteidigung der Priesterehe in der Reformzeit* (Hannover: Hahn, 1997). Pseudo-Ulrich also mentions other issues, such as that those who oppose clerical marriage do not shrink from other and far worse sexual sins (Frauenknecht, 96). Other pro-marriage arguments included that the sacrament was unaffected by the moral status of the celebrant (e.g., Sigibert of Gembloux); Barstow, 149, points out that the papacy did not go quite so far as to make this Donatist argument. See Parish, *Clerical Celibacy*, 109.

31. Norman Anonymous, "De Coniugio legitimo et non legitimo atque de sacerdocio (Apologia pro filiis sacerdotum)," J22 and J26, in *Die Texte des normannischen Anonymous*, ed. Karl Pellens (Wiesbaden: Franz Steiner, 1966), 116–25. See also J25, 204–9, on marriage as a better alternative for priests than burning, and Karl Pellens, *Das Kirchendenken des normannischen Anonymous* (Wiesbaden: Franz Steiner, 1973), 207–14.

32. Barstow, 135–36.

33. Henry Hargreaves, "Sir John Oldcastle and Wycliffite Views on Clerical Marriage," *Medium Aevum* 6 (1973): 141–45. I have not been able to find references to Hussite support of clerical marriage except in Parish, 136, unreferenced. The fact that clerical marriage became an issue in the fifteenth century does not mean that the idea was not debated before this. See, e.g., John W. Baldwin, *Masters, Princes and Merchants*, 1:337–40. Parish, 130–32, provides further examples.

34. Philip H. Stump, *The Reforms of the Council of Constance (1414–18)* (Leiden: Brill, 1994), 140–41 and 364–65; Basel decree in Alberigo, 485–87; Johannes Helmroth, *Das Basler Konzil*, 336, and Boelens, 613.

35. On the use of the argument from nature already in the twelfth century, see Thomas, chap. 7.

36. Guillaume Saignet, "Lamentacio humane nature adversis nicenam constitucionem," in Nicole Grevy-Pons, *Celibat et nature: Une controverse medievale—à propos d'un traité du début du XVe siècle* (Paris: CNRS, 1975), 146; see Grevy-Pons, passim, for the entire discussion. On sexual intercourse as "natural," see also Hugh White, *Nature, Sex, and Goodness in a Medieval Literary Tradition* (Oxford: Oxford University Press, 2000), 21–32, 56–64, and passim.

37. Jean Gerson, "Rememoratio agendam durante subtractione," in *Oeuvres complètes*, ed. Palémon Glorieux (Paris: Desclee, 1965), 6:108–14, at 112. See Brian Patrick McGuire, *Jean Gerson and the Last Medieval Reformation* (University Park: Pennsylvania State University Press, 1975), 193.

38. *Reformation Kaiser Siegmunds*, ed. Heinrich Köller, *MGH*, Staatsschriften des späteren Mittelalters 6 (Stuttgart: Anton Hiersemann, 1964), 148–52; Lothar Graf zu Dohna, *Reformatio Sigismundi: Beiträge zum Verständnis einer Reformschrift des fünfzehnten Jahrhunderts* (Göttingen: Vandenhoeck and Ruprecht, 1960), 127, and Hermann Heimpel, "Reformatio Sigismundi, Priesterehe und Bernhard von Chartres," *Deutsches Archiv für Erforschung des Mittelalters* 17 (1961): 527–37.

39. Heimpel, 528, and Dyan Elliott, "Lollardy and the Integrity of Marriage and the Family," in *The Medieval Marriage Scene: Prudence, Passion, Policy*, ed. Sherry Roush and Cristelle Baskins (Tempe: Arizona State University Press, 2005), 37–54.

40. "Le *De Matrimonio* de Jean Raulin," ed. in Carole Avignon, "L'église et les infractions au lien matrimonial," 943–1097, sermon 2, 951–52.

41. For England, see Helen L. Parish, *Clerical Marriage and the English Reformation: Precedent Policy and Practice*, and Eric J. Carlson, *Marriage and the English Reformation* (Oxford: Blackwell, 1994).

42. Martin Luther, "De votis monasticis iudicium," in *D. Martin Luthers Werke* (Weimar: Böhlau, 1853), 8:632.

43. William Tyndale, *An Answer to Sir Thomas More's Dialogue*, ed. Henry Walter, 18, and Mary Prior, "Reviled and Crucified Marriages: The Position of Tudor Bishops' Wives," in *Women in English Society 1500–1800*, ed. idem (London: Methuen, 1985), 118–48, at 120.

44. Luther, "An den christlichen Adel deutscher Nation," in *Luthers Werke*, 6:442.

45. Katharina Schütz Zell, "Entschuldigung Katharina Schützinn für M. Matthes

Zellen jren Eegemahel de rein Pfarrher und dyener ist im wort Gottes zů Straßburg: Von wegen grosser lügen uff jn erdiecht," ed. Elsie Anne McKee, *Katharina Schütz Zell*, vol. 2, *The Writings: A Critical Edition*, 36.

46. Biographical details from Elsie Anne McKee, *Katharina Schütz Zell*, vol. 1, *The Life and Thought of a Sixteenth-Century Reformer*.

47. Zell, "Ein Brieff an die gantze Burgerschafft der statt Straßburg von Katherina Zellin . . . Betreffend Herr Ludwigen Rabus," in *The Writings*, 171; trans. Elsie McKee, *Church Mother*, 226.

48. Roland Bainton, "Katherine Zell," in *Medievalia et Humanistica*, n.s., 1 (1970): 3–28, at 3–4.

49. Martin Bucer to Hector Poemer, 28 November 1523, in *Correspondance de Martin Bucer*, ed. Jean Rott (Leiden: Brill, 1979), 1:211. He was apparently talking about the betrothal, as he mentioned that the parents had consented and the wedding (*nuptiae*) was to be celebrated soon.

50. On the latter point, see Thomas Kaufmann, "Pfarrfrau und Publizistin," 181–89.

51. Zell, "Entschuldigung," 22; trans. McKee, *Church Mother*, 63.

52. Ibid., 24; trans. McKee, *Church Mother*, 64. McKee understands this as speaking theoretically, saying that one should defend oneself and thus all the more she should defend her husband. I read this passage, however, as indicating that she explicitly intended the pamphlet to be taken as a defense of herself as well.

53. Ibid., 39–40; my translation.

54. McKee, *The Writings*, 39 n. 83, and Kaufmann, 181–82 n. 33.

55. Zell, "Entschuldigung," 43; trans. McKee, *Church Mother*, 79.

56. Ibid., 40; trans McKee, *Church Mother*, 77–78. Cf. letter to Caspar Schwenckfeld, *The Writings*, 124.

57. Zell, "Entschuldigung," 35; trans. McKee, *Church Mother*, 73.

58. Zell, "Erlaubnis," *Writings*, 35; my translation, as McKee's is not sufficiently literal here.

59. McKee, ed., *The Writings*, 35 n. 62.

60. Zell, "Entschuldigung," 36; trans. McKee, *Church Mother*, 75.

61. Zell, "Entschuldigung," 37; trans. McKee, *Church Mother*, 75.

62. Zell, "Entschuldigung," 37; my translation. Some priests' whores, she says, manage to provide for themselves well and live like nobility, and this is not wrong of them to do.

63. On accounts of her speaking at the funeral, see McKee, ed., *The Writings*, 66.

64. Zell, "Klag red und ermahnung Catharina Zellen zum volk by dem grab m: Matheus Zellen pfarer zum münster zu Straßburg," in McKee, *The Writings*, 73–74; trans. McKee, *Church Mother*, 106.

65. Zell, "Klag," 80; trans. McKee, *Church Mother*, 111.

66. Katharina Schütz Zell to Caspar Schwenckfeld, 19 October 1553, in *The Writings*, ed. McKee, 124; trans. McKee, *Church Mother*, 188, except that I have translated "wil" as "time" instead of "will" in this context.

67. Tyndale, 158.

68. Ulrich Zwingli. *Suplicatio quorundam apud Helvetios euangelistarum ad R. D. Hugonem episcopum Constantiensem ne se induci patiatur, ut quicquam in preiudicium euangelii promulget neve scortiationis scandalum ultra ferat, sed presbyteris uxores ducere permittat aut saltem ad eorum nuptias conniveat*, in *Huldreich Zwinglis sämtliche Werke*. Corpus Reformatorum, vol. 88 (Berlin, C. A. Schwetschke und Sohn, 1905), 1:206.

69. Johann Eberlin von Günzberg, *Syben frumm aber trostloss pfaffen flagen ire not einer dem anderen und ist niemant der sye troste Gott erbarme sich ire*, in *Flugschriften des frühen 16. Jahrhunderts*, ed. Hans-Joachim Köhler (Zug, Switzerland: Inter Documentation Co., 1978–87), fiche 17, nr. 71, A4v.

70. Ibid., A3r.

71. James Sawtry [George Joye], *The defence of the Mariage of Priestes: Agenst Steuen Gardiner bishop of Wynchester, Wylliam Repse bishop of Norwiche, and agenst all the bishops and preistes of that false popissh secte, with a confutacion of their vnaduysed vowes vnadvysedly diffined: whereby they haue so wykedly separated them whom God coupled in lawfull mariage* (Antwerp: Jan Troost, 1541), STC2 21084, 31.

72. Tyndale, 164. See also Robert Barnes, "That by God's Word it is Lawfull for Priestes that hath not the gift of chastitie, to marry Wives," STC2 19046, 2:312.

73. Martin Luther, "Vom ehelichen Leben," in *Luthers Werke*, 10.2:297.

74. George Joye, *The letters which Iohan Ashwel priour of Newnham Abbey besids Bedforde, sente secretely to the Bishope of Lyncolne in the yeare of our lord M.D.xxvii. Where in the sayde priour accuseth George Ioye that tyme being felawe of Peter college in Cambridge, of fower opinios: with the answer of the sayed George vn to the same opinions* (N.p: n.d., probably Antwerp: M. de Keyser, 1531). I have modernized the spelling in the quotation.

75. *Handlung des Bischofs von Merseburg mit den zwei Pfarren von Schönbach und Buch* (1523), reprinted in *Flugschriften aus den ersten Jahren der Reformation*, ed. Otto Clemen (Leipzig: R. Haupt, 1907), 1:87. This argument was articulated by the bishop of Merseburg, according to two pastors of Lutheran leanings with whom he disputed.

76. Parish, *Clerical Marriage*, 168.

77. Thomas More, *The Co[n]futacyon of Tyndales answere made by syr Thomas More knyght lorde chau[n]cellour of Englonde*, STC2 18079, 147.

78. *Handlung des Bischofs von Merseburg mit den zwei Pfarren* (1523), 87.

79. Thomas Harding, *A Reioindre to M. Iewels replie against the sacrifice of the Masse. In which the doctrine of the answere to the .xvij. article of his Chalenge is defended, and further proued, and al that his replie conteineth against the sacrifice, is clearely confuted, and disproued* (Louvain: Apud Joannem Foulerum, 1567), 168. I have modernized the spelling of the quotation.

80. Hieronymus Emser, *Wider das vnchristenliche buch Martini Luters Augustiners, an den twetschen adel*, in *Luther und Emser: Ihre Streitschriften aus dem Jahre 1521*, ed. Ernst Ludwig Enders (Halle an der Saale: M. Niemeyer, 1890–92), Neudrucke deutscher Literaturwerke des XVI. und XVII. Jahrhunderts 83–84, 1:85.

81. Johannes Eck, cited in August Franzen, *Zölibat und Priesterehe in der Auseinandersetzung der Reformationszeit und der katholischen Reform des 16. Jahrhunderts* (Münster:

Aschendorff, 1969), 70; see also 77ff for other authors. Quotation from anonymous tract in Ozment, 5.

82. When Thomas More suggested that "priests should live chaste for reverence of the sacraments," Tyndale responded that "the priest toucheth not Christ's natural body with his hands," and therefore there was no reason why someone who said mass should live chastely more than one who heard it. Many Catholics might have agreed chastity was the best for everyone, but that the distinction between the clergy and the laity should be between those who were able to keep to it and those who were not. Such a distinction, for Tyndale, was not only theologically incorrect but also undercut social order. Tyndale, *Answer*, 162.

83. Barnes, 317.

84. Caroline Bynum, *Holy Feast, Holy Fast: The Religious Significance of Food to Medieval Women* (Berkeley: University of California Press, 1987).

85. This had been true in the period of the medieval reform movement, but much more so for the Protestant reformers; the arguments I have cited here are dwarfed by the deployment of Biblical citation, and the differences in emphasis are in part a result of Protestant exegetical style.

86. On the earlier symbolic importance of marriage see David d'Avray, *Medieval Marriage: Symbolism and Society* (Oxford: Oxford University Press, 2004).

87. Clarissa Atkinson, *The Oldest Vocation: Christian Motherhood in the Middle Ages* (Cornell: Cornell University Press, 1991), 144–93.

88. See Thomas, Chapter 7, for discussion of the course of these efforts in England in the central Middle Ages.

89. On the language used see Roisin Cossar, "Clerical 'Concubines' in Northern Italy in the Fourteenth Century," *Journal of Women's History* 23 (2011): 110–31, here 112.

90. See *Dictionary of Medieval Latin from British Sources*, ed. D. R. Howlett (Oxford: Oxford University Press, 1989) s.v. "focarius": the feminine form is "woman who shares one's house and home, concubine," with examples from the twelfth to the sixteenth centuries; Charles DuFresne Du Cange, *Glossarium mediae et infimae latinitatis*, 10 vols. (Niort: L. Favre, 1883–87), s.v. "focaria." The term is generally used interchangeably with "concubine" except without the residual juridical meaning of the latter.

91. Sara McDougall, pers. comm., 9 August 2011, points out that it is used fairly frequently in late medieval church court registers from Troyes, although not in ones from Paris.

92. Karras, *Common Women*, 131–42.

93. Boelens, "Die Klerikerehe in der kirchlichen Gesetzgebung zwischen den Konzilien von Basel und Trient," 62–3.

94. Thomas, Chapter 7, forthcoming; "De concubinis sacerdotum," "Consultatio sacerdotum," and "De convocatione sacerdotum," in *The Latin Poems Commonly Attributed to Walter Mapes*, ed. Thomas Wright, Camden Society vol. 16 (London: Camden Society, 1841), 171–83, quotations from "Consultatio sacerdotum," 178–79.

95. Records of church court suits for defamation show the use of sexually loaded terms like *hore* in England or *putaine* in France, of course, less defamatory terms might not occasion a lawsuit.

96. BL, Royal 7.D.i, 132r–135v; H. L. D. Ward and J. A. Herbert, *Catalogue of Romances in the Department of Manuscripts in the British Museum*, 3 vols. (London: British Museum, 1883–1910), 3:501–2.

97. BL, Add 33956, 82v, a Franciscan collection in which many of the tales originate in the south of France. She is called a *meretrix* (whore) as well as concubine; this text also uses *fornicaria*.

98. J. Th. Welter, *La "Tabula exemplorum secundum ordinem alphabeti": Recueil d'"exempla" compilé en France à la fin du XIIIe siecle*, no. 117 (Paris: E.-H. Guitard, 1926), 45, using the term *concubina* as well as *fornicaria*. See also [Étienne de Besançon], *Alphabet of Tales*, no. 456, 1:310, in which a knight sees a priest's concubine chased by demons; Caesarius of Heisterbach, *Dialogus Miraculorum*, 6:35, p. 1:387; 12:20, p. 2:330, for more stories of the eternal punishment of priests' concubines.

99. Jacques de Vitry, *The Exempla or Illustrative Stories from the Sermones Vulgares of Jacques de Vitry*, 240–42, ed. T. F. Crane (London: Folklore Society, 1890), 100–101. The story of the latrine also appears in another text, the *Tabula exemplorum secundum ordinem alphabeti*, a late thirteenth-century French collection: Welter, *La "Tabula exemplorum,"* no. 191, 52.

100. A. G. Little, ed., *Liber exemplorum ad usum praedicantium*, no. 110 (Aberdeen: Typis Academicis, 1908), 63.

101. Jacques de Vitry, no. 81; Étienne de Bourbon, *Anecdotes historiques*, 406; see also F. Tubach, *Index Exemplorum: A Handbook of Medieval Religious Tales*, Folklore Fellows Communications, 204 (Helsinki: Suomalainen Tiedeakatemia, 1969), no. 2440; BL, Add MS 33956, fol. 125r.

102. Étienne de Bourbon, nos. 451–52, 390–91.

103. John of Bromyard, *Summa Praedicantium*, s.v. "Luxuria," L.7.14–15 (Venice: Nicolino, 1586), 495r–v ff.

104. Bromyard, L.7.17, 460r. Bromyard also uses the term *focaria*.

105. *Alphabet of Tales*, 689, p. 462; 691, pp. 462–63; 742, pp. 494–95.

106. Joseph Klapper, ed., *Erzählungen des Mittelalters*, 81 (Breslau: M. and H. Marcus, 1914), 299–300.

107. This is fairly ubiquitous; for Bromyard, see Karras, "Gendered Sin and Misogyny in John of Bromyard's *Summa predicantium,*" *Traditio* 47 (1992): 233–57, at 250.

108. *Le livre du chevalier de la Tour Landry*, ed. Anatole de Montaiglon (Paris: Jauret, 1854), 124, p. 255.

109. *Speculum Sacerdotale*, ed. E. H. Weatherly, EETS, original ser., 200 (London: Oxford University Press, 1936), 89.

110. Robert of Brunne, *Handlyng Synne*, ed. Frederick J. Furnivall, EETS, original ser., 119 (London: Kegan Paul, Trench, Trübner, 1901), 244–45.

111. Ibid., 253.

112. On the inheritance of churches in England in the Central Middle Ages, see Thomas, chap. 5.

113. Gratian, *Decretum*, pars. 1, dist. 16, cols. 719–23, adduces authorities saying that

the sons of priests can be priests, but he explains that these were sons born of legitimate marriages of priests before they were prohibited.

114. Robert of Brunne, 255–56. This story was well known, found as far away as Iceland: Hugo Gering, *Islendzk Æventyri: Isländische Legenden, Novellen und Märchen*, 36 (Halle an der Saale: Buchhandlung des Waisenhauses, 1883–82), 1:124, a fairly direct prose translation, from AM 624, 40, fols. 61–64. For other collections in which it appears, see Tubach, no. 2461.

115. Laura Wertheimer, "Children of Disorder," 383; see also Bernhard Schimmelpfennig, "*Ex fornicatione nati*: Studies on the Position of Priests' Sons from the Twelfth to the Fourteenth Century," *Studies in Medieval and Renaissance History*, n.s., 2 (1979): 1–50, here 12–20, 29.

116. Ludwig Schmugge, *Kirche, Kinder, Karrieren*, 33, 183. Wertheimer, however, suggests that although a high percentage of those seeking papal dispensations were the sons of the higher clergy, there were also a large number of sons of unmarried lay parents, who could be granted dispensations by authorities lower than the level of the pope (406).

117. Wertheimer; quotation at 394.

118. Kathryn Ann Taglia, "On Account of Scandal," *Florilegium* 14 (1995–96): 57–79, at 61.

119. Wertheimer, 404.

120. Schmugge, 192–93.

121. See Wertheimer, 385–86, on the Roman law background to the law about inheritance by illegitimate children.

122. *Consilia domini Guidonis Pape*, 115, fol. 90r.

123. The definitive canon law treatment is X.4.17, 2:709–17. See also Hostiensis (Henry of Segusio), *Summa Aurea* (Venice: Bottega d'Erasmo, 1574; reprint, Turin, 1963), cols. 1379–84, and Thomas Kuehn, *Illegitimacy in Renaissance Florence*, 44.

124. See Steven Epstein, *Speaking of Slavery*, on the prevalence of slavery in Italy. Professor Epstein has kindly confirmed to me that that is the likely meaning of the term in an Italian context at this period. Pers. comm., 18 March 2005.

125. G. Letonnellier, "Gui Pape," in *Dictionnaire de droit canonique*, ed. R. Naz (Paris: Letouzey, 1953), 5:1009–11.

126. Baldus de Ubaldis, *Baldi Ubaldi pervsini . . . consiliorvm, sive responsorvm* 267, vol. 1, fol. 79v.

127. See, e.g., Franciscus Curtius, *Consiliorum sive responsorum d. Franchischini Curtii Iunioris . . . liber tertius* 328 (Venice: Ioannes and Baptista Somaschi, 1574), fols. 283r–284v, and Philippus Decius, *Consiliorum sive responsorum . . . tomus primus* 132, fols. 142v–143.

128. Bartolo de Sassoferrato, *Opera* (Venice: Giuntas, 1580), 3:38v. See Anna T. Sheedy, *Bartolus on Social Conditions in the Fourteenth Century* (New York: Columbia University Press, 1942), 58. Decius, 133, fol. 143v, follows Bartolo on this issue "even though concubinage is completely prohibited to the clergy."

129. See Kuehn, 35.

130. I am grateful to James Brundage for his information on this point. Decius, 132,

fols. 142v–143, argued that a priest could not make gifts to his concubine. In classical Roman law, a man was allowed to make an *inter vivos* gift to his concubine but not to his wife: see Judith Evans-Grubbs, "Marrying and Its Documentation in Later Roman Law," 51. However, the question of priests did not arise there.

131. Cossar, 117–24.

132. *Consilia domini Guidonis Pape*, 115, 90r.

133. Gratian, pars. 2, c. 30, q. 1, c. 1, 1:1095–96.

134. Benedictus de Benedictis, *Consilia Benedicti Caprae Perusini ac Ludovici Bolognini Bononiensis*, 2, fol. 4r.

135. Paulus de Castro, *Consilia Pauli de Castro* (Frankfurt: S. Feyerabendt, 1582), 19, 3:14–16.

136. Baldus, 248, vol. 1, fols. 71r–71v; 262, fol. 77v; 267:2, fols. 79v–80r.

137. Decius, 132, fol. 143r.

138. Jennifer Thibodeaux, "Man of the Church or Man of the Village? Gender and the Parish Clergy in Medieval Normandy," *Gender & History* 18 (2006): 380–99, and "The Sexual Lives of Medieval Norman Clerics: A New Perspective on Sexuality," in *Sexuality in the Middle Ages and in Early Modern Times: New Approaches to a Fundamental Cultural-Historical and Literary-Anthropological Theme*, ed. Albrecht Classen (Berlin: Walter de Gruyter, 2008), 471–83, quotation at 477.

139. Derek G. Neal, *The Masculine Self in Late Medieval England* (Chicago: University of Chicago Press, 2008), 93–96, 106–12.

140. Ibid., 108–10. This ties in to Neal's larger argument that the clergy's celibacy was not as central to their masculinity or lack thereof as other scholars have argued, and that their honesty was much more important.

141. On the practice of church courts with regard to clerical concubines, see Oskar Vasella, "Über das Konkubinat des Klerus im Spätmittelalter," in *Mélanges d'histoire et de littérature offerts à monsieur Charles Gilliard* (Lausanne: F. Rouse, 1944), 269–83.

142. E. J. G. Lips, "De Brabantse geestelijkheid en de andere sekse," *Tijdschrift voor Geschiedenis* 102 (1989): 1–29, here 11.

143. Marie A. Kelleher, "'Like Man and Wife': Clerics' Concubines in the Diocese of Barcelona," *Journal of Medieval History* 28 (2002): 349–60 at 349–50.

144. Ibid., 355.

145. Michelle Armstrong-Partida, "Priestly Marriage: The Tradition of Clerical Concubinage in the Spanish Church," *Viator* 40 (2009): 221–253, here 221.

146. Ibid., 232, 239–42.

147. Daniel Bornstein, "Parish Priests in Late Medieval Cortona: The Urban and Rural Clergy," in *Preti nel medioevo*, ed. Mauricio Zangarini (Verona: Cierre, 1997), 165–93.

148. Ibid., 175.

149. Cossar, 117.

150. Monique Vleeschouwers–Van Melkebeek, "Mandatory Celibacy and Priestly Ministry in the Diocese of Tournai at the End of the Middle Ages," in *Peasants and Townsmen in Medieval Europe: Studia in Honorem Adriaan Verhulst*, ed. Jean-Marie Duvosquel

and Erik Thoen (Ghent: Snoeck-Ducaju and Zoon, 1995), 681–92. Lips, 19, suggests that in Brabant in the late fifteenth and early sixteenth centuries, 45–60 percent of the clergy would be fined for sexual offenses at some point in their careers.

151. Janelle Werner, "Promiscuous Priests and Vicarage Children: Clerical Sexuality and Masculinity in Late Medieval England," in *Negotiating Clerical Identities: Priests, Monks and Masculinity in the Middle Ages*, ed. Jennifer D. Thibodeaux (London: Palgrave, 2010), 159–81.

152. Ruth Mazo Karras, "The Latin Vocabulary of Illicit Sex in English Ecclesiastical Court Records," *Journal of Medieval Latin* 2 (1992): 1–17, and Werner, 169.

153. E.g., *The Register of John Morton, Archbishop of Canterbury 1486–1500*, Worcester sede vacante, no. 485, ed. Christopher Harper-Bill, Canterbury and York Society 75, 78, 79 (Woodbridge: Boydell, 1987–2000), 2:146; ibid., vol. 3, Norwich sede vacante, no. 257, p. 152. This sort of relationship was especially serious if the woman was the spiritual daughter of the priest; it could be considered a form of incest. Ibid., vol. 3, Norwich sede vacante, no. 284, p. 159.

154. Karras, *Common Women*, 138.

155. *Register of John Morton*, Norwich sede vacante, no. 373, p. 175.

156. *Registre criminal du Châtelet de Paris du 6 septembre 1389 au 18 mai 1392*, ed. H. Duplès-Agier (Paris: C. Lahure, 1861), 1:149–52.

157. AN, Z/10/18, 19, 20, and 21.

158. Léon Pommeray, *L'officialité archidiaconale de Paris*, 235–76.

159. Registers of the civil or instance jurisdiction of the same court survive as Paris, AN, Z/10/6 through Z/10/9. These registers cover some of the same period as the criminal registers but are not in unbroken sequence. See further discussion in Chapter 4. "Civil" here does not mean "nonecclesiastical"; it refers to church court cases that were brought by one of the parties. It is called "civil" because that is the label used in the registers themselves.

160. Pommeray, 129–30.

161. See Donahue, *Law, Marriage, and Society*, 395, 409ff., 425ff., 614 for differences in prosecution patterns among different promoters in Cambrai and Brussels.

162. The categories are not formal headings or names of offenses but simply the statement of what the priest paid the fine for. In some cases, like "paternity," I have lumped together several descriptions; where not noted, I have not done so. By tabulating offenses like this, I have, to some extent, reified them beyond what the source does.

163. AN, Z/10/21, fol. 105v.

164. AN, Z/10/19, fol. 113r.

165. AN, Z/10/21, fol. 306r.

166. Scandal is discussed further below. The scandal cases listed in the table are those for which the fine was only for scandal and not one of the listed sexual offenses.

167. AN, Z/10/27, fol. 34v.

168. AN, Z/10/21, fol. 319r.

169. AN, Z/10/20, fol. 173r; Z/10/18, fol. 192r.

170. AN, Z/10/18, fol. 14r.

171. AN, Z/10/20, fol. 85r.

172. AN, Z/10/19, fol. 118r, and Pommeray, 244.

173. AN, Z/10/20, fol. 51v.

174. AN, Z/10/21, fol. 116r.

175. AN, Z/10/21, fol. 58r–58v.

176. AN, Z/10/19, fol. 15r.

177. AN, Z/10/20, fol. 186v.

178. AN, Z/10/21, fol. 150v.

179. AN, Z/10/21, fol. 102r, for the former. See also Chapter 4.

180. AN, Z/10/20, fol. 213r.

181. AN, Z/10/21, fol. 336r.

182. AN, Z/10/21, fols. 181r and 197v.

183. AN, Z/10/20, fol. 191r.

184. Pommeray, 206, and Anne Lefebvre-Teillard, *Les officialités à la veille du concile de Trente*, 45.

185. AN, Z/10/19, fol. 282v.

186. For increasing accusations of scandal against the Norman clergy in the 1530s, see Avignon, 338; on the theology of scandal, 687–711.

187. AN, Z/10/18, fol. 240v. The name "La Clergesse" probably just means that her father's surname was "Le Clerc" and need not imply anything about her relationship with a priest.

188. AN, Z/10/21, fol. 9v.

189. AN, Z/10/21, fol. 121r.

190. AN, Z/10/20, fol. 28v.

191. AN, Z/10/18, fol. 62r. Cf. a case from the court of the cathedral chapter of Notre Dame, in which a priest was accused of "concubinage or adultery," causing scandal, and the promoter was ordered to undertake further investigation: AN, Z/10/27, 71r. The priest denied having intercourse with her, and it is not clear whether the further investigation was on that question, on the question of whether she was married, or both.

192. I have listed such cases as "scandal" because that was what the fine was stated to be for; the intercourse was merely an explanation.

193. For the last two: AN, Z/10/20, fol. 191r, and Z/10/27, fol. 82v.

194. AN, Z/10/19, fol. 266v.

195. AN, Z/10/21, fol. 109v, and Z/10/20, 104v.

196. AN, LL/29, 6v. Jean was later found to be a "vagabond" who did not reside in his parish: AN, LL/29, 12r.

197. AN, Z/10/19, fol. 237v.

198. AN, Z/10/20, fol. 168v.

199. AN, Z/10/18, fol. 226r.

200. AN, Z/10/20, fol. 74v.

201. AN, Z/10/19, fol. 135v.

202. AN, Z/10/18, fol. 161r.

203. AN, LL/29, fol. 101v.

204. Karras, *Common Women*, 17.

205. This combination of toleration and intolerance is different from what Anna Clark, *Desire: A History of European Sexuality* (London: Routledge, 2008), 6–7, terms "twilight moments," in which people committed acts or felt desires but "returned to their everyday life, and evaded a stigmatized identity as deviant." The priests' behavior was open and most of the time met with the "grudging acceptance" that Clark terms "toleration."

CHAPTER 4

1. Philip L. Reynolds and John Witte, Jr., eds., *To Have and to Hold*, generally takes this view; see Reynolds, "Marrying and Its Documentation in Pre-Modern Europe," 5.

2. Cordelia Beattie uses the phrase "gray area" in "'Living as a Single Person.'" Since we arrived at the term independently (I first used it publicly in a paper presented in January 2007), I continue to use it. We are describing a similar phenomenon, although our arguments are different, as discussed below.

3. This is the main theme of Charles Donahue, Jr., *Law, Marriage, and Society*; see Carole Avignon, "L'église et les infractions au lien matrimonial," 417.

4. See, e.g., the cases from Rouen and Chartres analyzed by Avignon.

5. Avignon, 378, suggests for Normandy a "clericalization" of betrothal in the late fifteenth century.

6. The term "clandestine" was sometimes used more narrowly. E.g., in Bavaria, the term was used for a marriage in which there was an impediment, whereas one that met canonical requirements was not so labeled even if it had been conducted secretly. However, Deutsch found that for the diocese of Regensburg in the late fifteenth century, none of the seven cases that she found termed "clandestine" involved an impediment. Christina Deutsch, *Ehegerichtsbarkeit im Bistum Regensburg*, 270–73. For the understanding of forbidden clandestine marriage in France, see *Le synodal de l'ouest*, 65, in *Les statuts synodaux français du XIIIe siècle, precedes de l'historique du synode diocésain depuis ses origines*, vol. 1, *Les statuts de Paris et le synodal de l'ouest (XIIIe siècle)*, ed. and trans. Odette Pontal, Collection de document inédits sur l'histoire de la France, section de philologie et d'histoire jusqu'a 1610, Série in 8°, 9 (Paris: Bibliothèque Nationale, 1971), 180, and Deutsch, 277–80, on Regensburg. In London, McSheffrey found, contrary to the meaning of "clandestine" in ecclesiastical statutes, the term was used for marriages improperly solemnized in a church rather than contracted outside of a church: Shannon McSheffrey, *Marriage, Sex, and Civic Culture*, 28–32.

7. Far fewer U.S. states recognize "common-law marriage" now than was once the case. By contrast, litigation involving economic obligations of the parties in other unions (including "palimony" cases), where all parties agree there was no marriage, is a more recent development.

8. Charles Donahue, Jr., ed., *The Records of the Medieval Ecclesiastical Courts*, 2 vols. (Berlin: Duncker and Humblot, 1989), lists most of those extant.

9. Ibid.; P. J. P. Goldberg, *Women, Work, and Life Cycle in a Medieval Economy*; Frederik Pedersen, *Marriage Disputes in Medieval England* (London: Hambledon, 2000); McSheffrey; Richard M. Wunderli, *London Church Courts and Society on the Eve of the Reformation* (Cambridge, Mass.: Medieval Academy of America, 1981), 7–23; Richard H. Helmholz, *Marriage Litigation in Medieval England*, and Ruth Mazo Karras, *Common Women*.

10. The scholarship on marriage in church courts in medieval France is mostly more recent than that on England. Two recent dissertations, Sara McDougall, "Bigamy in Late Medieval France" (Yale University, 2009), focusing on Troyes, and Avignon, "L'église et les infractions au lien matrimonial," focusing on Rouen and Chartres, represent a new wave of excellent work on the topic.

11. See Avignon, 310, for the difficulty of comparing across jurisdictions even in northern France.

12. A register survives from Brie, another archdeaconry in the same diocese, from 1499 to 1505 (AN, LL/29). However, because there are far fewer cases (about thirty folios a year for both civil and criminal business, as opposed to nearly two hundred a year in Paris for criminal alone) and they are mainly civil, it is not possible to compare patterns of sexual cases with the Paris registers. Cases from the archdeaconry of Brie have not been included in the quantitative analyses in this chapter, but are used as examples. The same procedure has been followed with cases from the officiality of the cathedral chapter of Notre Dame of Paris, where one register survives from the period 1486–98 (AN, Z/10/27). Four parishes that depended on the chapter were exempt from the jurisdiction of the archdeacon. There were other exempt jurisdictions as well, and people within the archdeaconry sometimes went to them to marry, but this is the only one for which a register survives from the period.

13. Ruth Mazo Karras, "The Regulation of Sexuality in the Late Middle Ages: Paris and London," *Speculum* 86 (2011): 1010–39.

14. Léon Pommeray, *L'officialité archidiaconale de Paris aux 15.–16. siècles*, 125–38.

15. The practice of keeping separate registers began sometime in the middle of the second half of the fifteenth century. AN, Z/10/1 through 3 are mixed registers from the 1460s. Z/10/4 through 10 are civil registers covering, with some gaps, 1477 to 1508 (and continuing after a break, from 1513 on). The criminal registers from 1506 to 1515 are missing, but Z/10/22 covers 1515–18 and Z/10/23 covers 1521–26.

16. AN, Z/10/21, fol. 118v.

17. I.e., the defendant may admit to a lesser part of the accusation, such as carnal knowledge, while denying another part, such as deflowering. E.g., AN, Z/10/21, fol. 229v, 31 January 1502 [1501]. She had brought a civil case claiming that he deflowered her: AN, Z/10/8, fol. 163r, 26 January 1502 [1501].

18. The register of the chapter of Notre Dame reports cases at a stage when an accusation has been brought and an investigation is necessary before proceeding further: e.g., AN, Z/10/27, 46r, 71r, 115r.

19. Cf. Donahue's discussion of promoters in other courts being "helped" by one of the parties (*Law, Marriage, and Society*, 615).

20. AN, Z/10/18, fol. 55v and Z/10/6, fol. 103, both 20 March 1484 [1483].

21. Avignon, 271, 321–22.

22. AN, Z/10/20, fol. 46v and Z/107, fol. 206v, both on 14 April 1494. He is called Petrus Bernard in the criminal register and Petrus Mesnard in the civil. The civil case was adjourned, and the outcome does not appear. His admission of the promises but denial of carnal knowledge was unusual; more often, it went the other way around.

23. Donahue, *Law, Marriage, and Society*, 599, wrote that "in the Paris archdeacon's court . . . the great bulk, indeed perhaps all, of the marriage cases, other than separation cases, are office cases." This is true of the majority—slightly more than two-thirds—but by no means all. Some of these clandestine marriage cases (or cases involving "carnal knowledge after promises of marriage," which legally amounted to clandestine marriage but were not labeled as such) came to the court's attention as the result of instance claims. A total of 54 of the 67 clandestine marriage cases are from the years where civil registers survive, and 17 of the 54 cases originated there.

24. E.g., AN, Z/10/19, fols. 260r, 264r.

25. AN, LL/29, fols. 43r–46.

26. AN, Z/10/20, fol. 205r. Several items in this entry—the period of time, the place where she came from—are left blank, indicating that the scribe did not have the full information.

27. See Avignon, 633, for Norman examples of people aware of the law.

28. Ibid., 630, 720–40.

29. Jean Raulin, sermon 2, edited in Avignon, 950, trans. into French, 1018.

30. Karras, "The Regulation of Sexuality," 1036–37.

31. See Silvana Seidel Menchi and Diego Quaglioni, eds., *Matrimonio in dubbio: Unioni controverse e nozze clandestine initalia del XIV al XVIII secolo: I processi matrioniali degli archive ecclesiastici italiani* 2 (Bologna: Il Mulino, 2001). *I tribunali del matrimonio (secoli XV–XVIII)* (Bologna: Il Mulino, 2006).

32. On defloration cases, see Donahue, *Law, Marriage, and Society*, 351ff.

33. AN, Z/10/9, fol. 224v; Z/10/21, fol. 394r–v.

34. Donahue, *Law, Marriage, and Society*, 26. Donahue also cites (350) a somewhat parallel case in which a woman claims *sponsalia* during the lifetime of her first husband and the man admits intercourse but denies the contract; they pay a fine for concubinage (not adultery). Donahue suggests that this is a "strike suit" to declare that there were not promises and thus no impediment to their later marriage.

35. Daniel Lord Smail, *The Consumption of Justice: Emotions, Publicity, and Legal Culture in Marseille, 1264–1423* (Ithaca, N.Y.: Cornell University Press, 2003), 16 and passim.

36. Even if the civil claim ended in a settlement, the criminal case could still be pursued. On the canon law on this issue in the twelfth and thirteenth centuries, see Daniel Klerman, "Settlement and the Decline of Private Prosecution in Thirteenth-Century England," *Law and History Review* 19 (2001): 1–65, here 47–49.

37. AN, Z/10/18, fol. 27v. Cf. Avignon, 631.

38. AN, Z/10/18, fol. 31v.

39. Avignon, 31, 90.

40. AN, Z/10/20, fol. 191r. The difference of spelling between "Obier" and "Auber" is no greater than that between different renditions of the same name elsewhere in this register; however, since the position given is also different, chaplain or vicar, they may not have been the same person.

41. AN, Z/10/20, fol. 193r.

42. AN, Z/10/20, fol. 193v.

43. AN, Z/10/20, fol. 197v.

44. See Avignon, 260.

45. Ibid., 399.

46. AN, Z/10/18, fols. 237–39r. The civil register does not survive for the period of this case; the record in the criminal register begins with Tassine's interrogation and does not indicate how the case came to the court's attention. Although Coquillen denied the claim, witnesses testified to the matrimonial promises.

47. AN, Z/10/18, fol. 125r.

48. AN, Z/10/18, fol. 170v. Her account then says that "saying the words of affidation they clasped each other's hands in the name of marriage." It is not clear whether these are additional words, since her response to the question of what words were used was the exchange just quoted.

49. On the ring, see Avignon, 555.

50. Beattie, 328.

51. Cf. Avignon, 318 and 617, where she notes that *affidationes* involved a priest but not necessarily at a church. She says that vows *in facie ecclesie* were present tense, but that is not so in many of the Paris cases.

52. AN, Z/10/19, fol. 114r.

53. AN, Z/10/18, fol. 70v.

54. AN, Z/10/21, fol. 352r.

55. For the importance of the marriage gifts elsewhere, see Deutsch, 207.

56. AN, Z/10/21, fol. 212r.

57. Pommeray, 315.

58. AN, Z/10/21, fol. 112r.

59. AN, Z/10/20, fol. 8r; Avignon, 346. Carole Avignon, "Marché matrimonial clandestine et officines de clandestinité à la fin du Moyen Âge: L'exemple du diocèse de Rouen," *Revue historique* 302 (2010): 515–49, outlines the canon law on clandestine marriage and the specifics of practice in the Rouen region, demonstrating that many clandestine marriages were performed in the presence of clerics.

60. AN, Z/10/21, fol. 8r.

61. See AN, Z/10/20, fol. 162r, and Z/10/21, 132r, for examples where it is specifically stated that the vows were *de futuro*.

62. Anne Lefebvre-Teillard, *Les officialités à la veille du concile de Trente*, 174, 149.

63. Ibid., 149. Lefebvre-Teillard suggests that many of these cases were brought by families and points out that even when property was not an issue, rivalries between groups within a village also made marriages part of a family strategy.

64. AN, Z/10/19, 40r and 44r.

65. AN, Z/10/21, fol. 104v.

66. AN, Z/10/19, fol. 11v.

67. Avignon, 684.

68. AN, Z/10/18, fol. 198bis; Z/10/19, fol. 285r. The first reference is to a separate slip of parchment, undated, which has been bound into the book; the second is an identical, dated entry. This suggests how the register may have been compiled: each case noted on a separate slip and then copied into the register.

69. AN, Z/10/19, fols. 60v, 61v. Denise is called the daughter of Roland Esperlant, which Donahue (*Law, Marriage, and Society*, 319) suggests should indicate that she was under her father's control, but she was in service and the circumstances under which she claimed the marriage occurred did not include any family. In general, fewer women were described as "daughters" in these records than in those Donahue used, which may reflect different record-keeping practice a century later or the fact that more of the women in these cases were independent of their parents. E.g., AN, Z/10/18, fol. 185v, where a woman called "Johanna filia Johannis de Noes" is living in the home of someone else. On the other hand, the eighteen-year-old Jeanne la Sagiete, not given a patronymic, who was living in someone else's house, was released into the custody of her father. AN, Z/10/18, fol. 194v.

70. He was also a clerk in minor orders, who would have been permitted to marry.

71. Cf. Avignon, 585, for the locations of clandestine marriages.

72. AN, Z/10/18, fol. 213v. For another case in a stable, AN, Z/10/19, fol. 72r (Pacquette Hennelle and Clement de Rennes); Z/10/19, fol. 100v (Guillone Gavin and Pierre Prevost), in which not the defloration but kissing was alleged to have taken place in the stable.

73. For the procedure of relying on someone else's oath, see Ruth Mazo Karras, "Telling the Truth."

74. AN, Z/10/19, fol. 104v.

75. Deutsch, 281–82, presents similar examples from Regensburg of cases involving marriage by future consent and carnal copula that were also not labeled as clandestine.

76. AN, Z/10/21, fol. 349r.

77. Donahue, *Law, Marriage, and Society*, 345–62.

78. AN, Z/10/21, fol. 257v; similarly, fol. 303r.

79. The amounts of fines for the two types of cases are not given often enough to draw a statistically significant conclusion about whether one is more serious than the other; those for carnal knowledge after promises range from ten sous to three ecus of gold, and for clandestine marriage, from four sous to three ecus of gold, but the fines depended not only on the seriousness of the offense but also the wealth of the parties. See Avignon, 341–43, on the relatively infrequent (although increasing) use of the term "clandestine" in the church court records from Rouen.

80. Avignon, 401ff., for the variation across jurisdictions in whether clandestine marriage cases were brought civilly or criminally.

81. AN, Z/10/7, fol. 29r, and Z/10/19, fol. 237v.

82. Colette la Platriere, fined for carnal knowledge after promises, Jean Cleret only for carnal knowledge: AN, Z/10/7, fol. 62r and Z/10/19, fol. 264r; similarly, Z/10/8, fol. 29r and Z/10/21. 142r; Z/10/9, fol. 36r and Z/10/21, fol. 311r; Z/10/9, fol. 180v–181r and Z/10/21, fol. 380r. In some cases, the party who brought the claim was denied license to marry elsewhere, as well as fined for carnal knowledge after promises, even if the couple were judged not to be married. AN, Z/10/8, fol. 203r and Z/10/21, fol. 250v. For fourteenth-century examples in which only the defendant was given license to marry elsewhere, see Donahue, *Law, Marriage, and Society*, 348. In one unusual case, Marianne, widow of Guillaume le Gru, sued François le Gendre, alleging matrimony; although they were declared not married and both given license to marry elsewhere, the defendant was fined for carnal knowledge after promises and the plaintiff was not. AN, Z/10/8, fols. 140r, 140v, 141r, 142v, and Z/10/21, fol. 214r. For fourteenth-century fines (amends) for intercourse in cases determined not to be marriage, see Donahue, 349.

83. AN, Z/10/18, fol. 45v; civil case at Z/10/6, fols. 89r and 90v.

84. AN, Z/10/18, fol. 32r.

85. Cf. Avignon, 388.

86. For concubinage, AN, Z/10/18, fols. 105v, 76r, 91v; Z/10/19, fol. 223r; Z/10/20, fol. 26r. For cohabitation, AN, Z/10/18, fol. 38r. Cf. Avignon, 383.

87. Charles VIII married Anne of Brittany in 1489, twelve years before the case in question.

88. AN, LL/29, fols. 42r–42v.

89. If a couple exchanged vows in the present tense without going through a betrothal stage, the marriage would be clandestine but not invalid.

90. AN, Z/10/18, fol. 234v.

91. Avignon, 624.

92. Jean Raulin, sermon 7, edited in Avignon, 975, trans. into French, 1053.

93. AN, Z/10/21, fols. 35v–36r.

94. AN, Z/10/21, fols. 349r, 350r.

95. AN, Z/10/20, fols. 11r and 13v.

96. For the data on ages, see Karras, "The Regulation of Sexuality." There is slightly more information on the ages of men at marriage, and they seem to be slightly older.

97. Where no relationship, either of kinship or of employment, is stated, I have assumed that the person with whom the woman lives is not a relative. There are no instances of a woman living with someone with whom she shares a name unless the relationship is described. Where stepparents and godparents are mentioned, I have noted this. However, while it is a fair assumption that if the relationship is not named, the householder is not a parent, uncle/aunt, or sibling, it is entirely possible that he (or she) is a more distant relative or had a close tie other than kinship to the servant's family.

98. For an Italian example of the custom of large households taking in related or unrelated orphans, see David Herlihy and Christiane Klapisch-Zuber, *Tuscans and Their Families*, 245.

99. AN, Z/10/19, fols. 95v and 96r.

100. I have omitted "maintaining" and concubinage cases because here we are interested in the beginning of the liaison, not in partnerships that have been going on for a while.

101. AN, Z/10/18, fol. 41v.

102. Avignon, 479ff.

103. AN, Z/10/18, fol. 160v.

104. AN, Z/10/18, 63v.

105. Maryanne Kowaleski, "Singlewomen in Medieval and Early Modern Europe: The Demographic Perspective," in *Singlewomen in the European Past 1250–1800*, ed. Judith M. Bennett and Amy M. Froide (Philadelphia: University of Pennsylvania Press, 1999), 38–81, summarizes the demographic evidence. Alan Macfarlane has made the most outspoken case for English exceptionalism in family structures and marriage practices: *Marriage and Love in England*. The case is more carefully stated by Richard M. Smith, "Marriage Processes in the English Past: Some Continuities," in *The World We Have Gained: Histories of Population and Social Structure*, ed. Lloyd Bonfield, Richard M. Smith, and Keith Wrightson (Oxford: Blackwell, 1986), 43–99. Goldberg follows in Smith's tradition with new and better data: *Women, Work, and Life Cycle in a Medieval Economy*.

106. Dana Wessell Lightfoot, "The Projects of Marriage."

107. Tovah Bender, "Negotiating Marriage: Artisan Women in Fifteenth-Century Florentine Society" (Ph.D. diss., University of Minnesota, 2009).

108. Cf. Avignon, 395.

109. AN, Z/10/21, fol. 47v. Most of the time, the woman's residence is simply not given, so it is not possible to know whether they were living together.

110. AN, Z/10/21, fol. 336r; Z/10/19, fol. 237v. Sometimes *intertenire* was used along with *manutenire*, implying that it had a different meaning, but not often; Z/10/21, fols. 308v, 325r, 393v. This could be an example of legal repetitiveness, like *pregnans et gravida* (Z/10/21, fol. 310r).

111. AN, Z/10/19, fol. 63v.

112. AN, Z/10/21, fol. 101r.

113. AN, Z/10/19, fol. 131r.

114. AN, Z/10/20, fol. 42v.

115. AN, Z/10/18, fol. 42v. André did not call himself a servant, saying that he lived with Jacques; but later in his deposition, he refers to Jacques and his wife as his master and mistress, pointing to the possibility that many people who are simply stated to be living in the house of someone else are servants.

116. AN, Z/10/20, fol. 158r.

117. Ibid., fol. 165v.

118. Michael Sheehan, "The Formation and Stability of Marriage in Fourteenth-Century England: Evidence of an Ely Register," *Mediaeval Studies* 33 (1971): 238–76, here 254–55. Cf. Avignon, 455–56.

119. AN, Z/10/19, fol. 218v.

120. AN, Z/10/21, fol. 170r.

121. Ibid., fols. 172r and 173v.

122. Ibid., fols. 326r and 326v. Pommeray, 314, explains that the word "nihil" in the margin of the entry about the banns indicates that it did not belong here but rather in the civil register. This might indicate that other cases from the period where the civil register does not survive had similar origins. However, the civil register does survive from this period (July 1504), and this case does not appear in it.

123. The choice to use the term "concubinage" in some cases and not in others seems not to have to do with whether the man is a priest: 27 percent of the maintenance cases involve priests, compared with 15 percent of the concubinage cases. See Chapter 3 for more detail about cases involving priests.

124. AN, Z/10/21, fols. 182v, 37v.

125. AN, Z/10/19, fol. 114r. See Pommeray, 94, 572. Pierre du Clos was also fined for maintaining her: Z/10/19, fol. 113r.

126. AN, Z/10/20, fols. 11v–12r.

127. AN, Z/10/21, fol. 175v.

128. AN, Z/10/18, fol. 28v.

129. AN, Z/10/21, fol. 206r. Similarly, fol. 297v; Z/10/20, fol. 18v.

130. AN, LL/29, fol. 21v.

131. AN, Z/10/19, fols. 170r, 170v, 172r. The result is not given.

132. François Olivier Martin, *Histoire de la coutume de la prévôté et vicomté de Paris* (Paris: Ernest Leroux, 1930), 2:427; Philippe Godding, *Le droit privé dans les Pays-Bas méridionaux du 12e au 18e siècle*, Académie Royale de Belgique, Mémoires de la Classe des Lettres, 40, 2nd series, 14 (Brussels: Palais des Académies, 1987), 115–17, notes for the customary law not only of the southern Low Countries but of northern France that it did not distinguish between natural children and other bastards as far as inheritance was concerned. Roman law, Godding explains, entered the legal system in these regions primarily through canon law.

133. For a married woman as a concubine, see AN, Z/10/18, fol. 192v.

134. *Liber Sententciarum van de Officialiteit van Brussel 1448–1459*, ed. Cyriel Vleeschhouwers and Monique Van Melkebeek, 2 vols. (Brussels: Ministerie van Justitie, 1982), no. 1036, 2:668.

135. AN, Z/10/18, fol. 7r.

136. But see above, p. 186 and n. 86.

137. AN, Z/10/18, fol. 62r (the male partner was a priest, the female a married woman); also ibid., fol. 67v; Z/10/20, fol. 210v for a married man with a concubine.

138. AN, Z/10/21, fol. 333v.

139. AN, Z/10/18, 83v. Jacques was fined a week later for spending the night with Jeanne after being prohibited from further contact (her name is given as Daumraye, but it is probably the same person).

140. See Donahue, *Law, Marriage, and Society*, 109, for a possibly false claim of precontract from York. This was an instance case: a woman claiming marriage and a man raising the defense of precontract with another woman. This situation could also arise in multiparty actions; Donahue, 128. Helmholz, 65 and 162–63, presents a similar case.

141. See Avignon, 384, on women reduced to *concubina*, when they should have been *uxor*, or wife.

142. AN, Z/10/21, fols. 128r and 149r, and Z/10/8, fol. 9r.

143. AN, Z/10/21, fol. 251r.

144. Sara M. Butler, "Runaway Wives: Husband Desertion in Medieval England," *Journal of Social History* 40 (2006): 337–59, discusses wives' motivations for leaving their husbands in late medieval England.

145. For leprosy, Joseph Petit, ed., *Registre des causes civiles de l'officialité épiscopale de Paris, 1384–1387* (Paris, 1919), 310. There are many cases of separation for violence in the same register; see James A. Brundage, "Domestic Violence in Classical Canon Law," in *Violence in Medieval Society*, ed. Richard Kaeuper (Bury St. Edmunds: Boydell, 2000), 183–97. Similar examples involving violence or cruelty are found in the civil registers used in this project, and in mixed civil/criminal registers from the middle of the fifteenth century that have not been used here (AN, Z/10/4–6).

146. Sara McDougall, *Bigamy and Christian Identity in Late Medieval Champagne*.

147. These are what Deutsch refers to as *tolleramus* cases: Deutsch, 296–98.

148. Philippa C. Maddern, "Moving Households," suggests the same thing for late medieval England.

149. AN, Z/10/21, fol. 8r.

150. AN, Z/10/18, fols. 42r, 128r.

151. See Sara McDougall, "Bigamy: A Male Crime in Medieval Europe?" *Gender & History* 22 (2010): 430–46.

152. Cf. Avignon, 340, 369.

153. AN, Z/10/18, fol. 78v, and another case at Z/10/18, fol. 80v.

154. AN, Z/10/18, fols. 243v, 246r, and 247r; Z/10/19, fol. 28v. Sentence transcribed in Pommeray, 562. McDougall, "Bigamy: A Male Crime," finds that the punishment of standing on the scaffold was common for bigamy in Troyes; this is the only time that it is mentioned in the Paris records, but as the sentences are rarely recorded, it could have been common here, too.

155. See Avignon, 91, 262, on the continuing confusion as to the meaning of this term.

156. AN, Z/10/18, fol. 173v, and a similar case at Z/10/18, fol. 177r, in which a woman claims that she thought her husband was dead.

157. AN, Z/10/18, fol. 197r.

158. AN, Z/10/20, fol. 45r.

159. AN, Z/10/19, fol. 291v.

160. Ibid., fol. 189r.

161. Ibid., fols. 151v, 153v, 156r. Her husband Jean's name is given differently (and not very legibly) in the three different places.

162. AN, Z/10/20, fol. 26r.

163. AN, Z/10/21, fol. 138v.

164. The term "bigamy" is not used in most of these cases. See McDougall, "Bigamy: A Male Crime."

165. AN, Z/10/19, fol. 213r. For another case in which the man was married and the woman perhaps not, see Z/10/18, fol. 73r.

166. AN, Z/10/21, fol. 108r. The frequency of cases in which a man is involved with several women by the same name is likely due to the small corpus of women's first names.

167. Cf. Avignon, 612.

168. AN, Z/10/21, fol. 37v.

169. AN, Z/10/20, fol. 15r.

170. See, by contrast, a case from England identified by Judith Bennett for a statement attacking marriage as a sacrament: Kew, National Archives, KB9/435 m. 78. I thank Judith Bennett for calling it to my attention and providing a digital photograph.

CONCLUSION

1. For examples of marital metaphors that were central to medieval culture, see Dyan Elliott, *The Bride of Christ Goes to Hell*, and David d'Avray, *Medieval Marriage*.

2. In Britain, a man's available income increases on average by a third when he divorces; a woman's falls by 20 percent. Amelia Hill, "Men Become Richer after Divorce," *The Observer*, 25 January 2009, http://www.guardian.co.uk/lifeandstyle/2009/jan/25/divorce-women-research. The pattern for the United States is similar.

Bibliography

This bibliography is intended to enable the reader to locate items that appear in short-form notes. Items that appear in only one note—or in several consecutive notes—so that full information is available in the notes are not included.

MANUSCRIPTS

BL, Add MS 33956.
BL, Royal 7.D.1, 132r–135v.
Civil Registers of the Archdeaconry of Paris, 1483–1505. AN, Z/10/6 through Z/10/9.
Criminal Registers of the Archdeaconry of Paris, 1483–1505. AN, Z/10/18 through Z/10/21.
Register of Civil and Criminal Cases of the Archdeaconry of Brie, 1499–1505. AN, LL/29.
Register of the Officiality of the Cathedral of Notre Dame, 1486–98. AN, Z/10/27.

PRINTED PRIMARY SOURCES

Abelard, Peter. *Historia Calamitatum.* Edited by J. Monfrin. Paris: Librairie Philosophique J. Vrin, 1978.
———, and Heloise. *The Letters and Other Writings.* Translated by William Levitan. Indianapolis: Hackett, 2007.
Augustine. *Confessions.* Edited by James J. O'Donnell. Oxford: Clarendon, 1992.
———. *De bono coniugali.* Edited and translated by P. G. Walsh. Oxford: Clarendon, 2001.
Baldus de Ubaldis. *Baldi Ubaldi Perusini . . . consiliorum, sive responsorum.* 5 vols. Venice: Hieronymus Polus, 1575.
Barnes, Robert. "That by God's Word it is Lawfull for Priestes that hath not the gift of chastitie, to marry Wives." In *The Whole Works of W. Tindall, Iohn Frith, and Doct. Barnes three worthy martyrs, and principall teachers of this Churche of England collected and compiled in one tome together, being before scattered, now in print here exhibited to the Church.* London: John Daye, 1573.
Bartolomeo Cipolla. *Consilia Criminalis Celeberrimi D. Bartholomei Caepollae Veronensis* 26. Venice: n.p., 1555.

Benedictus de Benedictis. *Consilia Benedicti Caprae Perusini ac Ludovici Bolognini Bononiensis*. Venice: Candentis Salamandrae Insigne, 1576.

Benedictus Levita. *Capitularia Spuria*. Edited by Georg Heinrich Pertz. *MGH, Legum* 2. Hannover: Hahn, 1837.

Brennu-Njáls saga. In *Íslendinga sögur*, vol. 1. Edited by Bragi Halldórsson, Jón Torfason, Sverrir Tómasson, and Örnólfur Thorsson. Reykjavík: Svart á Hvítu, 1987.

Caesarius of Heisterbach. *Dialogus Miraculorum*. 2 vols. Edited by Joseph Strange. Cologne: Heberle, 1951.

The Complete Sagas of Icelanders. 5 vols. Translated by Viðar Hreinsson, Robert Cook, Terry Gunnell, Keneva Kunz, and Bernar Scudder. Reykjavík: Leifur Eiríksson, 1997.

Conciliorum oecumenicorum decreta. 2nd ed. Edited by Joseph Alberigo, Perikle P. Joannou, Claudio Leonardi, and Paulo Prodi. Basel: Herder, 1967.

Decius, Philippus. *Consiliorum sive responsorum . . . tomus primus*. Venice: Nicolo Antonio Gravati, 1575.

[Étienne de Besançon]. *Alphabet of Tales: An English 15th Century Translation of the Alphabetum Narrationum of Étienne de Besançon, from additional MS. Add. 25719 of the British Museum*. Edited by Mary MacLeod Banks. London: Kegan Paul, Trench, Trübner, 1904.

Étienne de Bourbon. *Anecdotes historiques, légendes et apologues, tirés du recueil inédit d'Étienne de Bourbon dominicain du 13e siècle*. Edited by A. Lecoy de la Marche. Paris: Librairie Renouard, 1877.

Fredegar. *Die vier Bücher der Chroniken des sogennanten Fredegar*. Edited by Herwig Wolfram and Andreas Kusternig. Ausgewählte Quellen zur deutschen Geschichte des Mittelalters. Darmstadt: Wissenschaftliche Buchgesellschaft, 1982.

Friedberg, Emil, ed. *Corpus Juris Canonici*. Graz: Akademische Druck- u. Verlagsanstalt, 1959.

Froissart, Jean. *Oeuvres de Froissart*. Edited by Kervyn de Lettenhove. Brussels: Victor Devaux, 1872.

Gratian. *Decretum*. In *Corpus Juris Canonici*. Edited by Emil Friedberg. Graz: Akademische Druck- u. Verlagsanstalt, 1959, vol. 1.

Gregory of Tours. *Historiarum Libri Decem*. Edited by Rudolf Buchner. Berlin: Rütten and Loenig, 1967.

Heloise. First letter. In "The Personal Letters Between Abelard and Heloise." Edited by J. T. Muckle. *Mediaeval Studies* 15 (1953): 47–94.

Hincmar of Reims. *De Divortio Lotharii regis et Theutbergae reginae*. Edited by Letha Böhringer. *MGH, Concilia* 4, supp. 1. Hannover: Hahn, 1992.

Íslendinga sögur. 3 vols. Edited by Bragi Halldórsson, Jón Torfason, Sverrir Tómasson, and Örnólfur Thorsson. Reykjavík: Svart á Hvítu, 1987.

Lex Visigothorum. MGH, Leges Nationum Germanicarum. Hannover: Hahn, 1902.

Lombard, Peter. *Sententiae in IV libris distinctae*. 2 vols. Edited by Ignatius Brady. 3rd ed. Grottaferrata: College of S. Bonaventure, 1981.

More, Thomas. *The Co[n]futacyon of Tyndales answere made by syr Thomas More knyght lorde chau[n]cellour of Englonde*. London: William Rastell, 1532.

Norges gamle love indtil 1387. 5 vols. Edited by R. Keyser and P. A. Munch. Christiania: Chr. Gröndahl, 1846.

Pape, Guido. *Consilia domini Guidonis Pape.* Lyon: Mareschall, 1519.

Petit, Joseph, ed. *Registre des causes civiles de l'officialité épiscopale de Paris, 1384–1387.* Paris: Imprimerie Nationale, 1919.

Powell, James M., trans. *The Deeds of Pope Innocent III by an Anonymous Author.* Washington, D.C.: Catholic University of America Press, 2004.

Rigord. *Gesta Philippi Augusti.* 2 vols. In *Oeuvres de Rigord et de Guillaume le Breton.* Edited by H. François Delaborde. Paris: Renouard, 1882.

Rotuli parliamentorum; ut et petitiones, et placita in parliament. Edited by John Strachey. Londmon, 1767–77.

Tyndale, William. *An Answer to Sir Thomas More's Dialogue.* Edited by Henry Walter. Cambridge: Cambridge University Press, 1850.

William of Newburgh. *Historia Rerum Anglicarum.* 2 vols. Edited by Hans Claude Hamilton. London: English Historical Society, 1856.

Zell, Katharina Schütz. *Katharina Schütz Zell,* vol. 2, *The Writings: A Critical Edition.* Edited by Elsie Anne McKee. Leiden: Brill, 1999.

———. *Church Mother: The Writings of a Protestant Reformer in Sixteenth-Century Germany.* Translated by Elsie Anne McKee. Chicago: University of Chicago Press, 2006.

SECONDARY WORKS

Avignon, Carole. "L'église et les infractions au lien matrimonial: Mariages clandestins et clandestinité. Théories, pratiques et discours, France du nord-ouest du XIIe siècle au milieu du XVIe siècle." Ph.D. thesis, Université de Paris-Est, 2008.

Baldwin, John W. "The Many Loves of Philip Augustus." In *The Medieval Marriage Scene: Prudence, Passion, Policy,* edited by Sherry Roush and Cristelle L. Baskins, 67–80. Tempe, Ariz.: ACMRS, 2005.

———. *Masters, Princes and Merchants: The Social Views of Peter the Chanter and His Circle.* 2 vols. Princeton, N.J.: Princeton University Press, 1970.

Barstow, Ann Llewellyn. *Married Priests and the Reforming Papacy: The Eleventh-Century Debates.* New York: Edwin Mellen, 1982.

Beattie, Cordelia. "'Living as a Single Person': Marital Status, Performance and the Law in Late Medieval England." *Women's History Review* 17 (2008): 327–40.

———. *Medieval Single Women: The Politics of Social Classification in Late Medieval England.* Oxford: Oxford University Press, 2007.

Bertrand, Louis. *Celle qui fut aimée d'Augustin.* Les Grandes repenties. Paris: Albin Michel, 1935.

Blumenthal, Debra. *Enemies and Familiars: Slavery and Mastery in Fifteenth-Century Valencia.* Ithaca, N.Y.: Cornell University Press, 2009.

Boelens, Martin. "Die Klerikerehe in der kirchlichen Gesetzgebung vom II. Laterankonzil bis zum Konzil von Basel." In *Ius Sacrum*, edited by Audomar Scheuermann and Georg May, 593–614. Munich: Ferdinand Schöningh, 1969.

Bradbury, Jim. *Philip Augustus: King of France 1180–1223*. London: Longman, 1998.

Brundage, James. *Sex, Law, and Marriage in the Middle Ages*. Brookfield, Vt.: Variorum, 1993.

Catlos, Brian. *The Victors and the Vanquished: Christians and Muslims of Catalonia and Aragon, 1050–1300*. Cambridge: Cambridge University Press, 2004.

Clanchy, M. T. *Abelard: A Medieval Life*. Oxford: Blackwell, 1997.

Colish, Marcia. *Peter Lombard*. 2 vols. Leiden: Brill, 1994.

Cossar, Roisin. "Clerical 'Concubines' in Northern Italy in the Fourteenth Century." *Journal of Women's History* 23 (2011): 110–31.

d'Avray, David. *Medieval Marriage: Symbolism and Society*. Oxford: Oxford University Press, 2004.

Deutsch, Christina. *Ehegerichtsbarkeit im Bistum Regensburg (1480–1538)*. Forschungen zur kirchlichen Rechtsgeschichte und zum Kirchenrecht 29. Cologne: Böhlau, 2005.

Donahue, Charles, Jr. *Law, Marriage, and Society in the Later Middle Ages: Arguments about Marriage in Five Courts*. Cambridge: Cambridge University Press, 2007.

Duby, Georges. *The Knight, the Lady, and the Priest: The Making of Modern Marriage in Medieval France*. Translated by Barbara Bray. New York: Pantheon, 1983.

Elliott, Dyan. *The Bride of Christ Goes to Hell: Metaphor and Embodiment in the Lives of Pious Women, 200–1500*. Philadelphia: University of Pennsylvania Press, 2011.

———. *Spiritual Marriage: Sexual Abstinence in Medieval Wedlock*. Princeton, N.J.: Princeton University Press, 1993.

Epstein, Louis. *Marriage Laws in the Bible and Talmud*. Cambridge, Mass.: Harvard University Press, 1942.

Epstein, Steven. *Speaking of Slavery: Color, Ethnicity, and Human Bondage in Italy*. Ithaca, N.Y.: Cornell University Press, 2001.

Esmein, Adhémar. *Le mariage en droit canonique*. 2 vols. Paris: Larose et Forcel, 1891.

Esmyol, Andrea. *Geliebte oder Ehefrau? Konkubinen im frühen Mittelalter*. Cologne: Böhlau, 2002.

Evans-Grubbs, Judith. "'Marriage More Shameful than Adultery': Slave-Mistress Relationships, 'Mixed Marriages,' and Late Roman Law." *Phoenix* 47 (1993): 125–54.

———. "Marrying and Its Documentation in Later Roman Law." In Reynolds and Witte, *To Have and to Hold*, 43–94.

Foreville, Raymonde. *Le Pape Innocent III et la France*. Päpste und Papsttum 26. Stuttgart: Anton Hirsemann, 1992.

Frassetto, Michael, ed. *Medieval Purity and Piety: Essays on Medieval Clerical Celibacy and Religious Reform*. New York: Garland, 1998.

Friedl, Corinna. *Polygynie in Mesopotamien und Israel: Sozialgeschichtliche Analyse polygamer Beziehungen anhand rechtlicher Texte aus dem 2. und 1. Jahrtausend v. Chr.* Alten Orient und Altes Testament 277. Münster: Ugarit, 2000.

Gaudemet, Jean. "Le dossier canonique du mariage de Philippe Auguste et d'Ingeburge de Danemark (1193–1213)." *Revue historique de droit français et étranger* 67 (1984): 15–26.

Goetz, Hans-Werner. "La *dos* en Alémanie (du milieu du VIIIe au début du Xe siècle)." In

Dots et douaires dans le haut moyen âge, edited by François Bougard, Laurent Feller, and Régine Le Jan, 305–27. Rome: École française de Rome, 2002.

Goldberg, P. J. P. *Women, Work, and Life Cycle in a Medieval Economy: Women in York and Yorkshire c. 1300–1520*. Oxford: Clarendon, 1992.

Goodman, Anthony. *John of Gaunt: The Exercise of Princely Power in Fourteenth-Century Europe*. London: Longman, 1992.

Goody, Jack. *The Development of the Family and Marriage in Europe*. Cambridge: Cambridge University Press, 1983.

Greengus, Samuel. "The Old Babylonian Marriage Contract." *Journal of the American Oriental Society* 89 (1969): 505–32.

Grossman, Avraham. "The Historical Background to the Ordinances on Family Affairs Attributed to Rabbenu Gershom Me'or ha-Golah ('The Light of the Exile')." In *Jewish History*, edited by Ada Rapoport-Albert and Steven J. Zipperstein, 3–23. London: P. Halban, 1988.

Halfond, Gregory I. *The Archaeology of Frankish Church Councils, AD 511–768*. Leiden: Brill, 2009.

Heers, Jacques. *Esclaves et domestiques au moyen-âge dans le monde méditerranéen*. Paris: Fayard, 1981.

Heidecker, Karl. *The Divorce of Lothar II: Christian Marriage and Political Power in the Carolingian World*. Translated by Tanis M. Guest. Ithaca, N.Y.: Cornell University Press, 2010.

Helmholz, Richard H. *Marriage Litigation in Medieval England*. Cambridge: Cambridge University Press, 1974.

Helmroth, Johannes. *Das Basler Konzil 1431–1449: Forschungsstand und Probleme*. Cologne: Böhlau, 1987.

Herlihy, David, and Christiane Klapisch-Zuber. *Tuscans and Their Families: A Study of the Florentine Catasto of 1427*. New Haven, Conn.: Yale University Press, 1985.

Hunter, David G. "Marrying and the *Tabulae Nuptiales* in Roman North Africa." In Reynolds and Witte, *To Have and to Hold*. 95–113.

Karras, Ruth Mazo. *Common Women: Prostitution and Sexuality in Medieval England*. New York: Oxford University Press, 1996.

———. "The History of Marriage and the Myth of *Friedelehe*." *Early Medieval Europe* 14 (2006): 119–51.

———. *Slavery and Society in Medieval Scandinavia*. New Haven, Conn.: Yale University Press, 1988.

———. "Telling the Truth about Sex in Late Medieval Paris." Forthcoming.

Kaufmann, Thomas. "Pfarrfrau und Publizistin: Das Reformatorische 'Amt' der Katharina Zell." *Zeitschrift für historische Forschung* 23 (1996): 169–218.

Klapisch-Zuber, Christiane. *Women, Family, and Ritual in Renaissance Italy*. Translated by Lydia Cochrane. Chicago: University of Chicago Press, 1985.

Konecny, Silvia. *Die Frauen des karolingischen Königshauses: Die politische Bedeutung der Ehe und die Stellung der Frau in der fränkischen Herrscherfamilie vom 7. bis zum 10. Jahrhundert*. Vienna: Verband der Wissenschaftlichen Gesellschaften Österreichs, 1976.

Kornbluth, Genevra. "The Susanna Crystal of Lothar II: Chastity, the Church, and Royal Justice." *Gesta* 21 (1992): 25–39.

Kuehn, Thomas. *Illegitimacy in Renaissance Florence.* Ann Arbor: University of Michigan Press, 2002.

Lansing, Carol. "Concubines, Lovers, Prostitutes: Infamy and Female Identity in Medieval Bologna." In *Beyond Florence: The Contours of Medieval and Early Modern Italy,* edited by Paula Findlen, Michelle Fontaine, and Duane J. Osheim, 85–100. Stanford, Calif.: Stanford University Press, 2003.

Lefebvre-Teillard, Anne. *Les officialités à la veille du concile de Trente.* Paris: Pichon and Durand-Auzias, 1973.

Le Jan, Régine. *Famille et pouvoir dans le monde franc (viie–xe siècle): Essai d'anthropologie sociale.* Paris: Publications de la Sorbonne, 1995.

Leyser, Conrad. "Custom, Truth, and Gender in Eleventh-Century Reform." In *Gender and Christian Religion,* edited by R. N. Swanson, 75–91. Studies in Church History 34. Woodbridge, U.K.: Boydell, 1998.

Lightfoot, Dana Wessell. "The Projects of Marriage: Spousal Choice, Dowries, and Domestic Service in Early Fifteenth-Century Valencia." *Viator* 40 (2009): 333–53.

Lips, E. J. G. "De Brabantse geestelijkheid en de andere sekse." *Tijdschrift voor Geschiedenis* 102 (1989): 1–30.

Lobrichon, Guy. *Heloïse: L'amour et le savoir.* Paris: Gallimard, 2005.

Lochrie, Karma. *Heterosyncrasies: Female Sexuality When Normal Wasn't.* Minneapolis: University of Minnesota Press, 2005.

Macfarlane, Alan. *Marriage and Love in England: Modes of Reproduction 1300–1840.* Oxford: Blackwell, 1986.

Maddern, Philippa C. "Moving Households: Geographical Mobility and Serial Monogamy in England, 1350–1500." *Parergon* 24 (2007): 69–92.

McDougall, Sara. *Bigamy and Christian Identity in Late Medieval Champagne.* Philadelphia: University of Pennsylvania Press, 2012.

McKee, Elsie Anne. *Katharina Schütz Zell,* vol. 1, *The Life and Thought of a Sixteenth-Century Reformer.* Leiden: Brill, 1999.

McKee, Sally. "Domestic Slavery in Renaissance Italy." *Slavery and Abolition* 29 (2008): 305–26.

———. "Greek Women in Latin Households of Fourteenth-Century Venetian Crete." *Journal of Medieval History* 19 (1993): 229–49.

———. "Households in Fourteenth-Century Venetian Crete." *Speculum* 70 (1995): 26–67.

———. "Inherited Status and Slavery in Late Medieval Italy and Venetian Crete." *Past & Present* 182 (2004): 31–53.

———. "The Implications of Slave Women's Sexual Service in Late Medieval Italy." In *Unfreie Arbeit: Ökonomische und Kulturgeschichtliche Perspektiven,* edited by M. Erdem Kabadayi and Tobias Reichardt, 101–14. Hildesheim: Georg Olms, 2007.

McLaughlin, Megan. *Sex, Gender, and Episcopal Authority in an Age of Reform, 1000–1122.* Cambridge: Cambridge University Press, 2010.

McSheffrey, Shannon. *Marriage, Sex, and Civic Culture in Late Medieval London*. Philadelphia: University of Pennsylvania Press, 2006.

Mews, Constant J. *Abelard and Heloise*. Oxford: Oxford University Press, 2005.

Meyer, Herbert. "Friedelehe und Mutterrecht." *Zeitschrift der Savigny-Stiftung für Rechtsgeschichte: Kanonistische Abteilung* 47 (1927): 198–286.

Meyerson, Mark. "Prostitution of Muslim Women in the Kingdom of Valencia: Religious and Sexual Discrimination in a Medieval Plural Society." In *The Medieval Mediterranean: Cross-Cultural Contacts*, edited by M. J. Chiat and Kathryn L. Reyerson, 87–95. St. Cloud, Minn.: North Star, 1988.

Mikat, Paul. *Dotierte Ehe—Rechte Ehe*. Rheinisch-Westfälische Akademie der Wissenschaften. Opladen: Westdeutscher, 1978.

Nelson, Janet L. *Charles the Bald*. London: Longman, 1992.

Nirenberg, David. *Communities of Violence: Persecution of Minorities in the Middle Ages*. Princeton, N.J.: Princeton University Press, 1996.

Olson, Linda, and Kathryn Kerby-Fulton, eds. *Voices in Dialogue: Reading Women in the Middle Ages*. Notre Dame, Ind.: University of Notre Dame Press, 2005.

Origo, Iris. "The Domestic Enemy: The Eastern Slaves in Tuscany in the Fourteenth and Fifteenth Centuries." *Speculum* 30 (1955): 321–66.

Ozment, Stephen. *When Fathers Ruled: Family Life in Reformation Europe*. Cambridge, Mass.: Harvard University Press, 1983.

Parish, Helen. *Clerical Marriage and the English Reformation: Precedent Policy and Practice*. Aldershot, Hampshire: Ashgate, 2000.

———. *Clerical Celibacy in the West: c. 1100–1700*. Farnham, Surrey: Ashgate, 2010.

Phillips, William D., Jr. *Slavery from Roman Times to the Early Transatlantic Trade*. Minneapolis: University of Minnesota Press, 1985.

Pommeray, Léon. *L'officialité archidiaconale de Paris aux 15.–16. siècles: Sa composition et sa compétence criminelle*. Paris: Sirey, 1933.

Reynolds, Philip Lyndon. *Marriage in the Western Church: The Christianization of Marriage During the Patristic and Early Medieval Periods*. Leiden: Brill, 1994.

———. "Marrying and Its Documentation in Pre-Modern Europe: Consent, Celebration and Property." In Reynolds and Witte, *To Have and to Hold*, 1–42.

———, and John Witte, Jr., eds. *To Have and to Hold: Marrying and Its Documentation in Western Christendom, 400–1600*. Cambridge: Cambridge University Press, 2007.

Richmond, Colin. *The Paston Family in the Fifteenth Century: Fndings*. Manchester: Manchester University Press, 2000.

Rolker, Christof. *Canon Law and the Letters of Ivo of Chartres*. Cambridge: Cambridge University Press, 2010.

Romano, Dennis. *Housecraft and Statecraft: Domestic Service in Renaissance Venice, 1400–1600*. Baltimore: Johns Hopkins University Press, 1996.

Romestan, Guy. "Femmes esclaves à Perpignan aux XIVe et XVe siècles." In *La femme dans l'histoire et la société méridionales (IXe–XIXe S.), Actes du 66e CFHMLR*, 187–218. Montpellier: Fédération historique du Languedoc méditerranéen et du Rousillon, 1995.

Saar, Stefan Chr. *Ehe–Scheidung–Wiederheirat: Zur Geschichte des Ehe- und des Ehescheidungsrechts im Frühmittelalter (6.–10. Jahrhundert)*. Ius Vivens, Abteilung B: Rechtsgeschichtliche Abhandlungen 6. Münster: LIT, 2002.

Satlow, Michael L. *Jewish Marriage in Antiquity*. Princeton, N.J.: Princeton University Press, 2001.

Schmugge, Ludwig. *Kirche, Kinder, Karrieren: Päpstliche Dispense von der unehelichen Geburt im Spätmittelalter*. Zürich: Artemis and Winkler, 1995.

Searle, Eleanor. *Predatory Kinship and the Creation of Norman Power, 840–1066*. Berkeley: University of California Press, 1988.

Shanzer, Danuta. "*Avulsa a latere meo:* Augustine's Spare Rib—*Confessions 6.15.25*." *Journal of Roman Studies* 92 (2002): 157–76.

Shaw, Brent. "The Family in Late Antiquity: The Experience of Augustine." *Past & Present* 115 (May 1987): 3–51.

Simonsohn, Shlomo. *The Apostolic See and the Jews*. 8 vols. Toronto: PIMS, 1988–91.

Stuard, Susan Mosher. "To Town to Serve: Urban Domestic Slavery in Medieval Ragusa." In *Women and Work in Preindustrial Europe*, edited by Barbara A. Hanawalt, 39–53. Bloomington: Indiana University Press, 1986.

Tria, Luigi. *La Schiavitù in Liguria (recherchi e documenti)*. Genoa: Società ligure di storia patria, 1947.

Vasella, Oskar. "Das Konkubinat des Klerus im Spätmittelalter." In *Mélanges d'histoire et de littérature offerts à monsieur Charles Gilliard*, 269–83. Lausanne: F. Rouse, 1944.

Verlinden, Charles. *L'esclavage dans l'Europe médiévale*. 2 vols. Bruges: De Tempel, 1955–77.

Villemain, Pierre. *Confessions de Numida: L'innommée de Saint Augustin*. Paris: Editions de Paris, 1957.

Wallace-Hadrill, J. M. *The Frankish Church*. Oxford: Clarendon, 1983.

Weir, Alison. *Mistress of the Monarchy: The Life of Katherine Swynford, Duchess of Lancaster*. New York: Ballantine, 2009.

Wemple, Suzanne. *Women in Frankish Society*. Philadelphia: University of Pennsylvania Press, 1981.

Wertheimer, Laura. "Children of Disorder: Clerical Parentage, Illegitimacy, and Reform in the Middle Ages." *Journal of the History of Sexuality* 15 (2006): 382–407.

Westbrook, Raymond. "Old Babylonian Period." In *A History of Ancient Near Eastern Law*, edited by Raymond Westbrook, vol. 2, Handbook of Oriental Studies, section one, 72:1, 372–430. Leiden: Brill, 2003.

Winroth, Anders. "Neither Slave nor Free: Theology and Law in Gratian's Thoughts on the Definition of Marriage and Unfree Persons." In *Medieval Law and the Origins of the Western Legal Tradition: A Tribute to Kenneth Pennington*, edited by Wolfgang P. Müller and Mary E. Sommar, 187–218. Washington, D.C.: Catholic University of America Press, 2006.

Zumkeller, Adolar. "Die geplante Eheschließung Augustins und die Entlassung seiner Konkubine." In *Signum Pietatis*, edited by Adolar Zumkeller, 21–35. Würzburg: Augustins, 1989.

Index

Acknowledgments

I am very grateful for the support of research and writing provided by a sabbatical fellowship from the American Philosophical Society in 2004–5 and an American Council of Learned Societies fellowship in 2010–11. Both were supplemented by the College of Liberal Arts, University of Minnesota. Travel was also supported by the Provost's Imagine Fund for the Arts and Humanities and by the Department of History, University of Minnesota.

The generous support for research offered by the College of Liberal Arts also allowed me to employ a series of excellent research assistants, most of whom were then students at Minnesota but have since completed their PhDs and, in some cases, published their own books. Tovah Bender, David Perry, Marianne Samayoa, and David Shyovitz (at the time an undergraduate at the University of Pennsylvania) assisted with sources in languages that I read only with difficulty, as did Michael Ryan, as a colleague rather than an assistant. Ellen Arnold, Thomas Farmer, Jonathan Good, Philip Grace, Jeff Hartman, and Michael Sizer also helped me conduct research that went into the book, and Jeff Hartman helped with the final preparation of the manuscript as well.

A portion of the research for this book was carried out at the CARAN (Centre d'acceuil et recherche des Archives Nationales) in Paris, which was most accommodating with access to manuscripts and permission to take photographs for later reference. The British Library in London is always a home away from home, providing not only access to manuscripts but an unparalleled collection of published materials and an accommodating work space. The rare-book libraries at the University of Pennsylvania, Princeton University, the University of Notre Dame, and Union Theological Seminary were also very welcoming. Michael Sizer conducted research for me in the rare-book collection at the Library of Congress.

All my colleagues at the University of Minnesota have been supportive of this project; I would like to thank particularly M. J. Maynes, Eric Weitz, and Gary Cohen, successive chairs of the Department of History, who made it possible for me to complete the work while meeting my other responsibilities. Kay Reyerson, Bernard Bachrach, and John Watkins have been wonderful sounding boards and founts of bibliographical information.

Although none of the chapters of this book has appeared in its current form, portions of some of the chapters come from my previously published work. Permission is gratefully acknowledged for the use of parts of "The History of Marriage and the Myth of *Friedelehe*," *Early Medieval Europe* 14 (2006): 119–51, in the Introduction and Chapter 1; "Marriage, Concubinage, and the Law," in *Law and the Illicit in Medieval Europe*, ed. Ruth Mazo Karras, Joel Kaye, and E. Ann Matter (Philadelphia: University of Pennsylvania Press, 2008), 117–29, in Chapters 2 and 3; and "The Regulation of Sexuality in the Late Middle Ages: England and France," *Speculum* (2011): 1010–39, in Chapter 4.

Over the years I worked on this book, I presented portions of it at many venues. I would especially like to thank the conveners who invited me and the audiences who commented on my presentations at the following institutions: Mellon Seminar on Medieval Subjectivity, Northwestern University; Medieval Club of New York; Marriage Seminar, CUNY; Delaware Valley Medieval Association; Furniss Lectureship, Department of History, Colorado State University; Goliard Society, Western Michigan University; Henry Charles Lea Lectureship, University of Pennsylvania; Program in Medieval Studies, Northwestern University; Program in Medieval Studies, University of Wisconsin, Madison; Medieval Studies Program and Gender Studies Program, University of Nottingham; Center for British and Irish Studies, University of Southern California; Institute for Humanities, John Carroll University; Center for Medieval Studies, Fordham University; and the Medieval Institute, University of Notre Dame.

I have relied on the work of many scholars for this book, including some work that has not yet appeared in print. I thank Hugh Thomas, Paola Tartakoff, and Megan McLaughlin for allowing me to cite their as yet unpublished work, and Michelle Armstrong-Partida, Dyan Elliott, Sara McDougall, Jennifer Thibodeaux, and Janelle Werner for advance peeks at work which has now appeared.

Jerry Singerman of the University of Pennsylvania Press supported this project from the beginning. Among other major contributions, he persuaded Sally McKee and Shannon McSheffrey to read the manuscript for the Press. Their suggestions have greatly helped to shape it, and I am very glad that they both revealed their identities so that I could thank them publicly. Dyan Elliott and Chris Karras also read the entire manuscript and made very helpful comments. Sara McDougall, Talya Fishman, and Eva Von Dassow read sections of it and saved me from many errors. Judith Bennett and John Van Engen have been sources of critical questions as well as constant support.

I hope that people will take away from the book that marriage is not a transhistorical given, but that it and other forms of unions are what societies and individuals make of them. I thank Chris Karras for making things work during the logistically complicated period during which the book was written: what a long, strange trip it's been! This book is dedicated to the newest long-term couple in my family. I look forward to the day when everyone has the option to choose marriage as they have done, but also to choose other forms of partnership or singleness without incurring legal or social disadvantages.